D1237644

Volume One

Women in the Biblical World

A Study Guide

Women in the World of Hebrew Scripture

by
Mayer I. Gruber

ATLA Bibliography Series, No. 38

**The American Theological
Library Association
and
The Scarecrow Press, Inc.
Lanham, Md., & London**

SCARECROW PRESS, INC.

Published in the United States of America
by Scarecrow Press, Inc.
4720 Boston Way
Lanham, Maryland 20706

4 Pleydell Gardens, Folkestone
Kent CT20 2DN, England

Copyright © 1995 by Mayer I. Gruber

British Cataloguing-in-Publication Information Available

Library of Congress Cataloging-in-Publication Data

Gruber, Mayer I. (Mayer Irwin)
Women in the biblical world : a study guide / by Mayer I. Gruber.
p.   cm. — (ATLA bibliography series, no. 38)
Includes bibliographical references and indexes.
Contents: v. 1. Women in the world of Hebrew scripture.
1. Women in the Bible—Bibliography. 2. Bible—Bibliography.
3. Women—Middle East—Bibliography. I. Title. II. Series.
Z7770.G77 1995   [BS680.W7] 016.2209'082–dc20 95-35831 CIP

ISBN 0-8108-3069-8 (v. 1) (cloth : alk. paper)

In Memory of Judith

זכרתי לך חסד נעוריך אהבת כלולותיך
לכתך אחרי במדבר בארץ לא זרועה

I recall your youthly devotion, your love as a bride,
your following me in the desert, in an unsown land
(Jeremiah 2:2).

CONTENTS

	page	item #
Editor's Foreword	vi	
Preface	vii	
Introduction	xv	
Abbreviations	xxi	
1. General Works on Women in Antiquity	1	1
2. Women in Ancient Near East: Books, Articles, and Dissertations	6	53
3. Women in the Art and Archaeology of the Ancient Near East: Books, Articles, and Dissertations:	12	122
4. Women and Womanhood in Hebrew Scripture: Books	19	209
5. Women and Womanhood in Hebrew Scripture: Articles	50	626
6. Women and Womanhood in Hebrew Scripture: Theses and Dissertations	153	1972
7. Women and Womanhood in Ancient Egypt: Books and Dissertations	156	1998
8. Women and Womanhood in Ancient Egypt: Articles	162	2072
9. Women and Womanhood in Elephantine	179	2299
10. Women and Womanhood in Ancient Mesopotamia: Books and Dissertations	180	2311
11. Women and Womanhood in Ancient Mesopotamia Articles	186	2376
12. Women and Womanhood at Mari	206	2632
13. Women and Womanhood among the Hittites	208	2654
14. Women and Womanhood among the Hurrians	212	2697
15. Woman and Womanhood at Ugarit	216	2739
16. Women and Womanhood in Elam and Persia	224	2843
17. Women and Womanhood among the Phoenicians	225	2857
18. Asherah: Books, Articles, and Dissertations	227	2883
Author Index	233	
Subject Index	253	
Index of Biblical References	263	
Index of Hebrew and Akkadian Terms	269	
About the Author	271	

EDITOR'S FOREWORD

Since 1974 the American Theological Library Association has been publishing this bibliography series with the Scarecrow Press. Guidelines for projects and selections for publication are made by the ATLA Publications Section in consultation with the editor. Our goal is to stimulate and encourage the preparation and publication of reliable bibliographies and guides to the literature of religious studies in all of its scope and variety. Compilers are free to define their fields, to make their own selections, and to work out internal organization as the unique demands of the subject indicate.

We are pleased to publish Mayer Gruber's *Women in the Biblical World: A Study Guide*, Volume I: *Women in the World of Hebrew Scripture* in the ATLA Bibliography Series.

Mayer I. Gruber completed an undergraduate program in history at Duke University, studied theology at the Jewish Theological Seminary of America, and took the M.A., M. Phil., and Ph.D. degrees in Middle East Languages and Cultures at Columbia University. His 1977 doctoral dissertation was titled "Aspects of Nonverbal Communication in the Ancient Near East." Dr. Gruber began his teaching career at Spertus College of Judaica in Chicago. Since 1980 he has taught in the Department of Bible and Ancient Near East at Ben-Gurion University of the Negev in Beersheva, Israel, where since 1984 he has held the rank of Senior Lecturer. He has also taught at the Hebrew University of Jerusalem, Levinksy College of Education, Tel Aviv, and Eilat College. He has twice been honored with Visiting Scholar appointments in the Department of Near Eastern Languages and Literatures at the University of Chicago. He is the author of four books and a large number of scholarly papers.

Kenneth E. Rowe
Series Editor

Drew University Library
Madison, NJ 07940
USA

PREFACE

This *Guide* is meant to provide scholars, clergy, seminarians, college students, and all other interested people access to books and articles—both technical and semi-popular—which shed light on women in antiquity in Israel and Judah and the surrounding countries, which play a role in the entire corpus of sacred literature commonly called "The Bible." The first volume is meant to provide access to books and articles, which shed light on women in the world of Hebrew Scripture, which is commonly called "The Old Testament." The second volume is meant to provide access to books and articles, which shed light on women in the world of the Apocrypha and the New Testament.

From the end of the eighteenth century the world regained direct knowledge of the history, language, literature, religion, and day-to-day life of ancient Egypt,[1] which borders Israel on the southwest and which is mentioned explicitly in Hebrew Scripture 680 times. Egypt was the birthplace of the first of the Hebrew prophetesses, Miriam, and the place where according to Ex. 12:1–2 Israel received the first of its divine commandments. It was also the place where, according to Gen. 12:10–20, Sarai, the first of the matriarchs, risked committing adultery with Pharaoh in order to save her husband Abram from possible murder. It was in Egypt also that in 586 B.C.E. the prophet Jeremiah castigated the exiled Jewish women for worshipping the Sumerian goddess of love, Inanna (Jer. 44).

From the middle of the nineteenth century the world regained direct knowledge of the history, language, literature, religion, and day-to-day life of ancient Iraq (Sumer, Assyria, and Babylonia),[2] which was the probable location of the Garden of Eden referred to in the second and third chapters of the first book of Hebrew Scripture. It is generally accepted that the birthplace of Abram and his wife and half-sister Sarai was none other than the Sumerian city of Ur.[3] Moreover, Mesopotamia was the place to which both Israelites and Jews were carried away captive by Sargon II in 722 B.C.E. and by Nebuchadnezzar in 597 and 586 B.C.E. Moreover, Assyria[4] and Babylonia,[5] often personified as women, feature prominently in the biblical books of Kings, Isaiah, Jeremiah, Ezekiel, and Nahum.

Almost all knowledge of the history, language, literature, religion, and day-to-day life of the aboriginal peoples of ancient Syria-Palestine, whom Hebrew Scripture generally refers to most frequently as Amorites and Canaanites derives from the abundant archaeological finds including manifold written records from 1) the eighteenth century B.C.E. Amorite kingdom of Mari on the Tigris;[6] 2) the Syrian site of Ras Shamra or Ugarit;[7] 3) the Syrian sites of Alalakh[8] and Emar;[9] and 4) Phoenician inscriptions. [10]

Knowledge concerning the Hittites[11] and Hurrians[12] has been provided by documents from all over the ancient Near East but especially by texts recovered from Boghazköy (ancient Hattusas) in Anatolia and Yoghlan Tepe (ancient Nuz) in southern Kurdistan, respectively.

To persons with some knowledge of both the origins of Western civilization in the ancient Near East and the drama of their rediscovery it should come as no surprise either that all kinds of interesting and useful facts, ideas, outlooks, and artificacts can disappear for millenia at a time or that some of these facts, opinions, and things can be recovered.

The new discipline called "Women's history" grew, inter alia, out of 1) the realization that by and large women had been written out of the history of western civilization; 2) the intuition that women like other outsiders such as the Jews[13] can be restored to their rightful place in the documentation of the history of humankind; and 3) the realization that groups who can claim a past have a greater claim to recognition in the present. [14]

I believe, therefore, that it was my training in the history, languages, and cultures of the ancient Semites, which were dramatically recovered from archaeological sites during the last century and a half, that made me believe that the history and culture of women in the biblical world could also be recovered. It is probably no accident that a majority of the outstanding feminist biblical scholars received their initial graduate academic training in the study of the languages and cultures of the ancient Near East.

Nevertheless, it cannot be an accident that most of the scholarly books and articles on women in ancient Israel were published after the mid-1970s nor that the other period during which a significant number of studies on the subject appeared was 1890-1930.

My generation of biblical philologists began our graduate studies believing that our task was to investigate the original meaning of every obscure word in Hebrew Scripture and to establish its meaning on the basis of comparative Semitic linguistics. We believed that proper utilization of parallels from the literatures of the ancient Near East would enable us to establish beyond a shadow of doubt the objective meaning of all of Hebrew Scripture for the benefit of all persons regardless of denominational origin or affiliation.

I even believed that my interest in the study of women and womanhood in Hebrew Scripture grew out of my attempt to engage in an objective philological analysis of the Hebrew prophets. Preparing this *Guide* has demonstrated to me, however, that it is no coincidence that since the 1970s numerous scholarly articles have been devoted to such previously neglected subjects as Huldah the prophetess, feminine similes applied to God in Isaiah 40–66, and women in ancient Israelite worship. The sudden interest in such topics must be understood against the background of the movement for women's liberation, which placed the subject of women on the public agenda. The study of women has become recognized in the academy.[15]

I suggest, therefore, that objective biblical exegesis, which cannot possibly deal with much less solve every enigma presented in and by Scripture, is and should be influenced by the larger world to notice issues, which may not have been raised in the larger world in which some previous generations of exegetes did their work. This is to say that just as the reconstruction of the history of women in the biblical world depends on the work of archaeologists and linguists so can the work of these specialists be enriched by feminist movements and ideologies.[16]

It should not be forgotten that almost all that survives of the literary and cultural legacy of ancient Israel is Hebrew Scripture, whose history and narrative seldom deal deliberately with the everyday life of ordinary people. It is nevertheless quite amazing how much feminist biblical scholars have been able to reveal in the last decades simply by asking questions that had not generally been asked in the immediately preceding generations. It should be recognized, however, that archaeologists have recovered from ancient Israel's neighbors abundant information about the day-to-day lives of all classes of people—including letters and contracts written by, on behalf of or about women. Hence, it should not be surprising that the publication and analysis of ancient Near Eastern texts and artifacts pertaining to women has proceeded steadily ever since the modern study of the ancient Near East[17] began while in biblical studies the study of women was all but suspended between the 1930s and the 1970s.[18] Nevertheless, it should not be surprising that the study of the civilizations of the ancient Near East has lately been influenced by the women's movement and women's history to ask new and important questions.[19]

A significant factor in the increased attention on the part of scholars to the subject of women in the Bible is the increased tendency to treat biblical narrative as literature rather than simply as the raw materials for the reconstruction of the history of ancient Israel. When biblical narrative is treated seriously as literature the treatment and behavior of characters—both male and female—cannot be ignored. During the previous generation, exemplified by the commentary on Genesis by E. A. Speiser, the narrative of Dinah (Gen. 34) is declared to be "history novelistically interpreted."[20] Not surprisingly, Dinah herself is mentioned only once in the more than two full pages

Speiser devotes to the narrative in question. In the more recent treatments of biblical narrative as literature no such escape from confronting Dinah's humanity is afforded.[21] Unfortunately, the realization that Speiser's philology has so little to contribute to the understanding of matriarchal narratives has led some scholars to a total disparagement of Semitic philology. This latter tendency will surely prove harmful to the establishment of the study of biblical women and their literature on an objective, scientific foundation.[22]

The nucleus of this bibliography is the sets of references, which I collected in the course of researching and preparing for publication my various studies on women and womanhood in the biblical world.[23] Noticing (1) the stubborn refusal of many otherwise competent biblical scholars to recognize feminist scholarship as a legitimate branch of biblical research and women in the biblical world as a subject worthy of inquiry; (2) the unfortunate tendency of many scholars to know and to quote only the work of their own teachers, classmates, and students; (3) the growing tendency in the literary study of biblical narrative to ignore the well of genuine information from ancient Israel's neighbors, I decided to compile this *Guide*. I believe that this *Guide* demonstrates not only that the subject of women in the biblical world is worthy of inquiry but also that it is a field which has already engaged the minds of outstanding scholars in the fields of archaeology, literature, philology, history, and theology. For students and teachers who come to the Bible from the fields of literature and/or theology this *Guide* is meant to place under a single umbrella materials relevant to women in the biblical world from such diverse disciplines as Assyriology,[24] Ugaritology,[25] and the history of medicine.[26]

Professor Carol Meyers of Duke University kindly supplied me with a copy of the mimeographed 29-page "Women in the Bible: A Bibliography," prepared by Harriet V. Leonard, Reference Librarian at the Library of the Duke Divinity School in 1977. The latter bibliography, which covers both the Old and the New Testaments, is limited to books and articles available seventeen years ago in the libraries of Duke University. It contains a little more than two pages of articles in languages other than English and French. Professor Martha T. Roth of the Oriental Institute of the University of Chicago kindly supplied me with her 5½ page "Women in Mesopotamia: A Bibliography of Secondary Sources," dated October 10, 1991, and Professor Phyllis Trible of Union Theological Seminary in New York City provided me with Angela Bauer, "Feminist Interpretation of Hebrew Scriptures: A Bibliography" (New York: Union Theological Seminary, 1990). The latter bibliography, comprising twenty-four pages is to be commended to students of the subject at hand because it lists for each book of Hebrew Scripture from 1 (Malachi) to

twenty-six (Gen. 12–50) bibliographical entries as well as thirty-eight
entries for [feminist] hermeneutics and method (pp. 5–7) and twenty-
nine monographs (pp. 3–4). Prof. Zafrira Ben-Barak of the Dept. of
Bible at the University of Haifa; Dr. Athalya Brenner, Professor of
Feminism and Christianity at the Catholic University of Nijmegen;
and Dr. Nicholas Wyatt of the University of Edinburgh kindly
supplied me with lists of their own publications concerning the
subject at hand. Ms. Naomi Graetz, Senior Teacher in the
Department of English as a Foreign Language at Ben-Gurion
University shared with me the bibliography she collected for her
research on feminist perspectives in Judaism. Especially useful were
Religious Books 1876–1982, vol. 3: Subjects (New York and London:
R. R. Bowker, 1983), the annual book lists published by the British
Society for Old Testament Study, and the bibliographies found at the
end of Barbara S. Lesko, ed., *Women's Earliest Records from Ancient
Egypt and Western Asia.*[27] However, most of the materials, which I
was able to assemble here, were culled from the painstaking work of
going through festschriften, memorial volumes, publishers'
catalogues, the standard periodicals in biblical and Near Eastern
studies, and the standard indices such as *Annual Egyptological
Bibliography,*[28] the Keilschriftbibliographie published annually in the
periodical *Orientalia, Old Testament Abstracts,*[29] *Elenchus
Bibliographicus,*[30] and *Internationale Zeitshcriftenschau für
Bibelwissenschaft und Grenzgebiete.*[31] It should be noted that the
latter two indices include categories such as women or feminism
beginning only in the most recent volumes while the former indices
do not list such categories even in the most recent volumes.

This *Guide* differs from the various bibliographies concerning
women in the Bible and the ancient Near East referred to above in
that it refers to a significant body of research on women in the biblical world in the two important living languages of the Bible lands—
Modern Hebrew and Modern Arabic. Readers will also note that I
have recorded not only articles in so-called scientific refereed journals
but also articles in popular and semi-popular magazines. With respect
to the subject at hand neither type of journal has a monopoly on
either wisdom or foolishness.

I am most grateful to the American Theological Library Association for the generous grant, which enabled me to begin work on this
project and to Prof. Kenneth E. Rowe, Editor of the ATLA Bibliography Series for his encouragement and support throughout the
preparation of this *Guide.* I wish to record my thanks to Prof. Rivkah
Harris of the School of the Art Institute of Chicago and to my
teacher, Prof. David Marcus of the Jewish Theological Seminary of
America, for their having recommended me for the ATLA
Bibliography Grant. The Committee on Research and Publications of

the Faculty of Humanities and Social Sciences of Ben-Gurion University awarded me a very generous grant toward the cost of the preparation of the camera-ready copy produced by WordByte. Sincere thanks are due Margo and Amiel Schotz of WordByte for their painstaking efforts in the preparation of this volume. Special thanks are due Ben-Gurion University of the Negev for granting me sabbatical leave during the summer of 1990 and again in the fall of 1991 for work on this project. I am especially grateful to Mr. R. P. Carr, University Librarian and Keeper of the Brotherton Library at Leeds University in England for arranging for me a Visiting Scholar appointment at the Brotherton Library during the summer of 1990, Prof. Wadad Kadi, Chairman of the Dept. of Near Eastern Languages and Civilizations at the University of Chicago, for arranging for me an appointment as Visiting Scholar in that Department during the fall of 1991 and Prof. Byron L. Sherwin, Vice-President for Academic Affairs, for arranging for me an appointment as Ezra Sensibar Visiting Professor of Biblical Studies at Spertus College of Judaica for the fall semester of 1991.

I am also most grateful to have been able to make use of the libraries of the Hebrew University of Jerusalem, Tel-Aviv University, the Bodleian Library at Oxford University, the University Library at Cambridge University, and Ben-Gurion University of the Negev in Beersheva.

I intended to surprise my dear wife Judith with the dedication to her of this volume. In the midst of its preparation, however, Judith was summoned to the Academy on High. In recognition of her encouragement, loving devotion, help, and sage counsel I dedicate this first volume of *Women in the Biblical World: A Study Guide* to her memory.

I pray that God Almighty, who has enabled me to complete this volume, will enable me also to complete other projects, and that this volume will serve to create renewed respect for Sacred Scripture and for womankind.

Mayer I. Gruber
Ben-Gurion University of the Negev
Beersheva, Israel
November 1994

NOTES

1. See Sir Frederic Kenyon, *The Bible and Archaeology* (London: George G. Harrap & Co., Ltd., 1940), 58–80; Peter A. Clayton, *The Rediscovery of Ancient Egypt* (London: Thames and Hudson, 1982).

2. See S. N. Kramer, *The Sumerians* (Chicago: University of Chicago Press, 1963), 3–32; Sir E. A. Wallis Budge, *The Rise and Progress of Assyriology* (London: Martin Hopkinson & Co., 1925).

3. Sir Leonard Woolley, *Excavations at Ur* (New York: Thomas Y. Crowell, 1954), 78; contrast C. H. Gordon, "Abraham and the Merchants of Ura," *JNES* 17 (1958), 28–31.

4. I.e., Northern Iraq, which is mentioned by name in Hebrew Scripture 150 times.

5. I.e., Southern Iraq, which is mentioned by name in Hebrew Scripture 286 times.

6. Concerning the Amorites in general see M. Liverani, "The Amorites," in *Peoples of Old Testament Times,* ed. D. J. Wiseman for the Society for Old Testament Study (Oxford: Clarendon Press, 1973), 100–133. Concerning Mari see Abraham Malamat, *Mari and the Early Israelite Experience,* The Schweich Lectures of the British Academy, 1984 (Oxford: Oxford University Press for the British Academy, 1989).

7. Concerning the Canaanites see A. R. Millard, "The Canaanites," in *Peoples of Old Testament Times* (see previous note), pp. 29–52. Concerning Ugarit see Margaret S. Drower, "Ugarit," in *The Cambridge Ancient History,* vol. 2, pt. 2, 3d ed. (Cambridge: Cambridge University Press, 1975), 130–160.

8. See Sir Leonard Woolley, *A Forgotten Kingdom* (Baltimore, Md.: Penguin Books, 1953).

9. For extensive bibliography concerning Emar see *Meskéné-Emar: Dix ans de travaux 1972–1982* (Paris: Editions Recherches sur les civilisations, 1982).

10. For a brief survey of these inscriptions see Donald Harden, *The Phoenicians* (London: Thames and Hudson, 1962). For an up-to-date edition of the inscriptions with translation, commentary, and bibliography see John C. L. Gibson, *Textbook of Syrian Semitic Inscriptions, vol. 3: Phoenician Inscriptions* (Oxford: Clarendon Press, 1982).

11. See O. R. Gurney, *The Hittites* (London: Penguin Books, 1952); J. G. Macqueen, *The Hittites and Their Contemporaries in Asia Minor,* rev. ed. (London: Thames and Hudson, 1986).

12. See Gernot Wilhelm, *The Hurrians,* trans. Jennifer Barnes (Warminster: Aris & Phillips, 1989).

13. On the emergence of Jewish studies as a recognized academic discipline see Arnold J. Band, "Jewish Studies in American Liberal-Arts Colleges and Universities," *American Jewish Year Book* 67 (1966), 3–30; Jacob Neusner, "Two Settings for Jewish Studies," *Conservative Judaism* 27 (1972–73), 27–40.

14. See Berenice A. Carroll, ed., *Liberating Women's History: Theoretical and Critical Essays* (Urbana: University of Illinois Press, 1976), xi and passim in that anthology.

15. See Ellen Messer-Davidow, *(En)Gendering Knowledge: Feminists in Academia* (Knoxville: University of Tennessee Press, 1991); Sneja Gunew, ed., *Feminist Knowledge: Critique and Construct* (London and New York: Routledge, 1990).

16. See Barbara S. Lesko, ed., *Women's Earliest Records from Ancient Egypt and Western Asia,* Brown Judaic Studies, 166 (Atlanta: Scholars Press, 1989), xiii.

17. Cf. ibid., p. xv.

18. See below, pp. xxiii.

19. Cf. Rivkah Harris, "Independent Women in Ancient Mesopotamia?" in Lesko, *Women's Earliest Records,* p. 145.

20. E.A. Speiser, *Genesis,* The Anchor Bible, vol. 1 (Garden City, N.Y.: Doubleday & Co., 1965), 266.

21. See, e.g., Meir Sternberg, *The Poetics of Biblical Narrative* (Bloomington: Indiana University Press, 1985), 445–475, which has inspired additional studies by Ararat and by Fewell and Gunn; q.v.

22. See, e.g., Sharon Pace Jeansonne, *The Women of Genesis: From Sarah to Potiphar's Wife* (Minneapolis: Fortress Press, 1990), 3, and contrast my review in *AJS Review* 17 (1992), 281–284.

23. See below, pp. 89–90.

24. The study of the languages and literatures of ancient Iraq, i.e., Babylonia and Assyria. Since the first great corpora of texts from ancient Iraq, which were deciphered, came from Northern Mesopotamia, i.e., Assyria, the study of all aspects of the language, literature, and culture of ancient Iraq came to be called Assyriology.

25. I.e., the study of the language, literature, and culture of ancient Ugarit; see above, n. 7.

26. See, for example, the study published in *Obstetrics and Gynecology* by Harer and el-Dwakhly, which is listed below under "Women and Womanhood in Ancient Egypt: Articles," p. 170, #2185.

27. See there, pp. 319–344.

28. (Leiden: International Association of Egyptologists in cooperation with the Nederlands Instituut voor het Nabije Oosten).

29. (Washington, D.C.: Catholic Biblical Association and Catholic University of America).

30. (Rome: Biblical Institute Press).

31. (Düsseldorf: Patmost Verlag).

INTRODUCTION

For a general orientation to the study of women in the world of Hebrew Scripture, commonly called the Old Testament, readers are urged to consult entries such as "Women," "Women in the Old Testament," and "Women in the Ancient Near East," and the like in such standard reference works as *The Interpreter's Dictionary of the Bible* (4 vols.; New York and Nashville: Abingdon, 1962); *The Interpreter's Dictionary of the Bible Supplementary Volume* (New York and Nashville: Abingdon, 1975); *Harper's Bible Dictionary*, ed. Paul J. Achtemeier (San Francisco: Harper & Row, 1985); *The International Standard Bible Dictionary*, ed. Geoffrey W. Bromley (4 vols.; Grand Rapids: Eerdmans, 1979–1988); *The Anchor Bible Dictionary* (New York: Doubleday & Co., 1992); and the like, as well as general, Catholic and Jewish encyclopedias.

The entries in the standard Bible dictionaries concerning biblical books, in which women play an especially significant role often provide useful information, insights, and bibliography. Commentaries in the standard series of Bible commentaries, especially on those biblical books or parts of books, in which women play an important role (Gen. 1–3; 6; 12–50; Ex. 1–15; 21–22; 38:8; Lev. 12; 15; Num. 5–6; Deut. 15; 21–25; Judg. 13–21; Samuel; Kings; Isaiah; Jeremiah; Ezekiel; Hosea 1–4; Zephaniah; Ps. 45; Job. 1–3; 31; 42; Song of Songs [also called Canticles]; Ruth; Esther) should be utilized. Readers should expect that *some* commentaries published since the mid-1970s will pay more attention to women and to feminist interpretations. Some readers may, likewise, be pleasantly surprised that women were never completely ignored in the better biblical commentaries from antiquity until now.

For information and bibliography concerning named goddesses referred to in Hebrew Scripture the reader is referred to the *Dictionary of Deities and Demons*, ed. K. van der Toorn, et al. (Leiden: E. J. Brill, 1995).

Standard Bible commentary series, which should be consulted include The Anchor Bible (Garden City, N.Y.: Doubleday) Hermeneia (Minneapolis: Fortress Press); The International Critical Commentary (Edinburgh: T. & T. Clark/New York: Scribner's); The Jewish Publication Society Torah Commentary (Philadelphia: Jewish Publication Society); The New International Commentary on the Old Testament (Grand Rapids: Eerdmans); Das Alte Testament Deutsch (Goettingen: Vandenhoeck und Ruprecht); Handbuch zum Alten Testament (Tübingen: Mohr); Handkommentar zum Alten Testament (Goettingen: Vandenhoeck und Ruprecht); The Word Bible Commentary (Waco Texas: Word Books, Inc.); etc. Readers should note that the commentaries listed below under "Hebrew Scripture— Books" are individual commentaries on books, which are especially relevant to the subject at hand, and which are not found in any of the aforementioned series.

Readers are likewise urged to consult Bible dictionaries and the standard Bible commentaries with respect to the various named and unnamed women in the Bible. A list of the unnamed women, who play a role in Hebrew Scripture, may be compiled from a concordance by examining the entries under "mother of," "daughter of," "sister of," and "wife of." As for the women named in Hebrew Scripture—some few of whom merit entries in the standard biblical encyclopedias,[1] there are 111, whose names are as follows: (1) Abi (2 Kgs. 18:2), who is also called Abijah (2 Ch. 29:1), (2) Abigail the wife of Nabal and later of David; (3) Abigail the daughter of Nahash, who was also sister of Zeruiah, and mother of Joab and Amasah (2 Sam. 17:25); (4) Abigail the sister of David (1 Ch. 2:16–17);[2] (5) Abihail the wife of Abishur (1 Ch. 2:29); (6) Abihail the wife of Jerimoth and mother of Mahalath and the wife of Rehoboam (2 Ch. 11:18); (7) Abital wife of David (2 Sam. 3:4; 1 Ch. 3:3); (8) Abishag (1 Kgs. 1–2); (9) Achsah, daughter of Caleb and wife of Othniel (Josh. 15; Judg. 1; 1 Ch. 2:49); (10) Adah I, one of the two wives of Lamech (Gen. 4:23); (11) Adah II, the Hittite wife of Esau (Gen. 36); (12) Ahinoam the wife of Saul (1 Sam. 14:50); (13) Ahinoam the wife of David (1 Sam. 25 etc.); (14) Anah, the daughter of Zibeon the Hivite and mother of Oholibamah [see below] (Gen. 36:2); (15) Asenath (Gen. 41); (16) Atarah, the wife of Jerahmeel (1 Ch. 2:26); (17) Queen Athaliah; (17) Azubah, one of the four wives of Caleb son of Hezron (1 Ch. 2:18); (18) Bilhah; (19) Baara, one of the two wives of Shaharaim [the other was Hushim] (2 Ch. 8:8); (20) Basemath, the Hittite wife of Esau (Gen. 26:34); (21) Basemath, the Ishmaelite wife of Esau (Gen. 36:3ff.); (22) Basemath the daughter of King Solomon, who married Ahimaaz (1 Kgs. 4:15); (23) Bathsheba the mother of King Solomon, who is called Bathshua the daughter of Ammiel in 1 Ch. 3:5; (24) Bithiah the daughter of Pharaoh who married Mered (1 Ch. 4:18); (25) Dinah; (26) Delilah; (27) Ephrath, third wife of Caleb son of Hezron (2 Ch. 2:19); (28) Ephrath wife of Caleb (1 Ch. 2:19); (29) Esther (Hadassah); (30) Eve; (31) Gomer (Hos. 1:3); (32) Hagar; (33) Hagith wife of David and mother of Adonijah (2 Sam. 3:4; etc.); (34) Hammolecheth (1 Ch. 7:18); (35) Hanutal (also called Hanital) the wife of King Josiah and the mother of Kings Jehoahaz and Zedekiah (2 Kgs. 23; 24; Jer. 52); (36) Hannah; (37) Hephzibah the mother of King Manasseh (2 Kgs. 21:1); (38) Hazlelponi their sister (1 Ch. 4:3); (39) Helah (1 Ch. 4:5,

7); (40) Hodesh (1 Ch. 8:9); (41) Hoglah, one of the five daughters of Zelophehad (Num. 26; 27; 36; Josh. 17); (42) Huldah; (43) Hushim [see above under Baara]; (44) Iscah daughter of Haran and niece of Abram (Gen. 11:29) (45) Jael; (46) Jehoaddan of Jerusalem, the mother of King Amaziah son of Joash (2 Kgs. 14:2; 2 Ch. 25:1); (47) Jecoliah of Jerusalem, the mother of King Azariah (2 Kgs. 15:2; 2 Ch. 26:3); (48) Jehosheba daughter of Joram and the wife of Jehoiada the priest (2 Kgs. 11:2) [she is called Jehoshabath in 2 Ch. 22:1]; (49) Jemimah daughter of Job (Job. 42:14); (50) Jerioth, the second wife of Caleb son of Hebron (1 Ch. 2:18); (51) Jochebed; (52) Jerusha, the mother of King Jotham (2 Kgs. 15:33; 2 Ch. 27:1); (53) Jezebel; (54) Judith, the Hittite wife of Esau (Gen. 26:34); (55) Keturah; (56) Kessiah daughter of Job (Job. 42:14); (57) Leah; (58) Lo-Ruhamah, daughter of Hosea and Gomer (Hos. 1:6, 8); (59) Maacah I, the concubine of Caleb (1 Ch. 2; 7; 8); (60) Maacah II, the wife of David and mother of Absalom (2 Sam. 3:3; 1 Ch. 3:2); (61) Maacah III, the daughter of Absalom (1 Kgs. 15; 2 Ch. 11); (62) Mahalath the wife of Esau (Gen. 28:9); (63) Mahalath the wife of King Rehoboam (2 Ch. 11:18); (64) Mahlah I, one of the five daughters of Zelophehad [see above under Hoglah]; (65) Mahlah II the daughter of Hammolecheth (1 Ch. 7:18); (66) Matred, the mother-in-law of Hadar [also called Hadad] King of Edom (Gen. 36:39; 1 Ch. 1:50); (67) Mehetabel the daughter of Matred the daughter of Me-zahab (Gen. 36:39); (68) Merab (1 Sam. 14; 18); (69) Me-zahab (Gen. 36:39; 1 Ch. 1:50); (70) Meshulemeth wife of King Manasseh and mother of King Amnon (2 Kgs. 21:19); (71) Micaiah mother of King Abijah (2 Ch. 13:2); (72) Michal daughter of Saul and wife of David; (72) Milcah daughter of Nahor (Gen. 11; 22; 24); (73) Milcah one of the five daughters of Zelophehad [see above under Hoglah]; (74) Miriam; (75) Naamah I, the sister of Tubal-cain (Gen. 4:22); (76) Naamah II, the mother of King Rehoboam (1 Kgs. 14:21; 2 Ch. 12:13); (77) Naarah, one of the two wives of Ashhur [see above under Helah] (1 Ch. 4:5–6); (78) Naomi; (79) Nehushta, the wife of King Jehoiachin (2 Kgs. 24:8); (80) Noah, one of the five daughters of Zelophehad [see above under Hoglah]; (81) Noadiah, the last named prophetess in Hebrew Scripture Neh. 6:14; (82) Ohalibamah the wife of Esau (Gen. 36); (83) Puah; (84) Rachel; (85) Rahab; (86) Rebecca; (87) Reumah the concubine of Nahor (Gen. 22:24); (88) Rizpah (2 Sam. 3; 21); (89) Ruth; (90) Sarai/Sarah; (91) Serah daughter of Asher (Gen. 46; Num. 26; 1 Ch. 7:30); (92) Sheerah daughter of Ephraim (1 Ch. 7:24); (93) Shimeath, mother of one of the murderers of Joash (2 Kgs. 12:22; 2 Ch. 24:26); (94) Shimrith, mother of one of the murderers of Joash (2 Ch. 24:26); (95) Shiphrah; (96) Shlomith I (Lev. 24:11); (97) Shlomith II (1 Ch. 3:19); (98) Tamar I (Gen. 8); (99) Tamar II (2 Sam. 13); (100)

Taphath daughter of Solomon who married Ben-abinadab (1 Kgs. 4:11); (101) Timnah I, the sister of Lotan (Gen. 36, 12, 22); (102) Timnah II, the concubine of Eliphaz (1 Ch. 1:39); (103) Tirzah, one of the five daughters of Zelophehad [see above under Hoglah]; (104) Vashti; (105) Zeresh; (106) Zeruah the mother of Jeroboam (2 Kgs. 11:26); (107) Zeruiah, the sister of King David and the mother of Joab, Abishai, and Asahel (108) Zibiah of Beersheba, the mother of King Jehoash (1 Kgs. 12:2; 2 Ch. 24:1); (109) Zillah, one of the two wives of Lamech [see above under Adah]; (110) Zilpah; (111) Zipporah.

Concerning women in ancient Egypt and ancient Mesopotamia readers are urged first and foremost to consult the entries "Women" in the *Lexikon der Aegyptologie* (Wiesbaden: Harrassowitz, 1975–) and the *Reallexikon der Assyriologie* (Berlin: Walter de Gruyter, 1928–) respectively and the several entries concerning "Private Life" in *Civilizations of the Ancient Near East,* ed. Jack M. Sasson (New York: Scribners, forthcoming). Such reference works in biblical and ancient Near Eastern studies should also be consulted for information and bibliography concerning topics such as prophetess and prostitute.

Readers are likewise urged to examine the books listed below under General Works and the anthologies compiled respectively by Durand, Grimal, and Lesko, which are listed under Ancient Near East and the various books and anthologies of feminist biblical scholarship listed below under Hebrew Scripture—Books.

Scholarly literature up to 1975 in the entire field of cuneiform studies, can easily be located with the help of Rykle Borger, *Handbuch der Keilschriftliteratur* (3 vols.; Berlin and New York: Walter de Gruyter, 1967–1975). The latter work includes indices to references to named monarchs and deities in both the cuneiform texts and the secondary literature.

The present *Guide* contains in addition to the Preface, Introduction, and indices eighteen divisions. The first division, "General Works on Women in Antiquity" lists books published between 1779 and the present era, which are valuable for three reasons: (1) They demonstrate that the study of the history of women in antiquity is most assuredly not a passing fad of the last quarter of the twentieth century; (2) they demonstrate that the use of data recovered from the ancient Near East for the understanding of the roles of women in human history goes back to the very beginnings of archaeological research in the Near East in the Napoleonic era; (3) they provide extremely useful information concerning insights into and approaches to the study of women in both the Bible and the civilizations of ancient Israel's neighbors.

The second division, "Women in the Ancient Near East: Books, Articles, and Dissertations," lists (1) anthologies, which contain sem-

inal studies on women in a variety of ancient cultures in the lands of
the Bible. The most important of these are the books edited by
Durand, Grimal, and Lesko; (2) books and articles, which attempt to
deal with women or aspects of the life and experiences of women in
the ancient Near East as a whole; (3) books and articles, which deal
with the life of women in areas of the ancient Near East, for which
there is no separate division among the eighteen divisions of the
present *Guide.*

The third division of this *Guide,* "Women in the Art and Archaeology of the Ancient Near East: Books, Articles, and Dissertations," lists materials which discuss archaeological finds from the land
of Israel as well as from the other lands of the ancient Near East
which a) shed light on women or womanhood in the biblical world;
and b) cannot be related to specific non-Israelite cultures of the ancient Near East.

By including in the fourth division of this *Guide,* "Women and
Womanhood in Hebrew Scripture—Books," anthologies as well as
issues of periodicals, which contain three or more articles referring to
women in Hebrew Scripture it was possible to avoid listing any collective work concerned significantly with the subjects of women in
ancient Israel or feminist interpretation of Hebrew Scripture more
than once. With respect to a number of works, whose connection
with these subjects may be less than obvious from their titles, I have
cited the specific relevant subjects touched upon in these books.

Division 5, "Women and Womanhood in Hebrew Scripture—
Articles," lists articles found in both periodicals and collective volumes. This section lists articles that deal in some significant way with
a) women or womanhood in Hebrew Scripture; b) feminist interpretation of Hebrew Scripture; c) the history of feminist interpretation
of; or d) the critique of feminist interpretation of Hebrew Scripture.
Readers will note the following: a) a few subjects such as the identity
of the virgin or young woman mentioned in Isaiah 7 are discussed
during every era from antiquity to the present; b) a few subjects such
as Huldah the prophetess and women in the Israelite cult are discussed both in the 1890s and the latter part of the twentieth century;
and c) a few subjects, such as feminine similes applied to God in
Isaiah 4–66, are the subject of quite a number of studies during the
1980s.

Division 6 lists as yet unpublished masters essays and doctoral
dissertations dealing with women or aspects of the life and
experience of women in Hebrew Scripture. I highly recommend the
perusal of masters theses and doctoral dissertations on women in
Hebrew Scripture for two reasons. The first is the wealth of
bibliography contained in many of these. The second is the frequency
with which published scholars who are careful to quote everything

published are found to have, as it were, labored in vain to come up with a new idea, which was already presented in an unpublished thesis or dissertation.

Divisions 7–17 of this *Guide* (see Contents) deal variously with books, articles in periodicals and collective volumes, and dissertations, which touch upon a) specific named women in specific cultures of the ancient Near East; b) the role or roles of women in specific cultures of the ancient Near East.

Division 18 is a comprehensive bibliography of studies concerning Asherah prepared by Prof. Steve A. Wiggins as a by-product of the research leading to his book, *A Reassessment of Asherah*, AOAT 235 (Kevelaer: Butzon & Bercker/Neukirchen-Vluyn: Neukirchener Verlag, 1993). Asherah, it should be noted, is sometimes a cult object but often a goddess, or possibly, for some ancient Israelites the female consort of God. Unquestionably, interest in this deity was aroused by the discovery of references to her in a number of ancient Israelite inscriptions. There should, however, be no doubt that it was the combination of two factors, (a) the discovery of these inscriptions during the 1970s precisely when interest in woman in the biblical world increased tremendously; and (b) that dramatic interest in our subject, which account for the phenomenal number of scholarly books and articles dealing with A/asherah.

NOTES

1. For the more well-known personalities, who are likely to be discussed at length in the encyclopedia articles, commentaries, and in books or articles cited in Divisions 4 and 5 of this *Guide* I have provided no biblical references.
2. According to 1 Ch. 2:16–17 this is the same Abigail, who is described as the mother of Joab and Amasa in 2 Sam. 17:25.

ABBREVIATIONS

AAAS	*Annales Archéologiques Arabes Syriennes*
ADOG	Abhandlungen der Deutschen Orient-Gesellschaft
AF	*Aegyptologische Forschungen*
AfO	*Archiv für Orientforschung*
AJA	*American Journal of Archaeology*
AJSL	*American Journal of Semitic Languages & Literatures*
AOAT	Alter Orient und Altes Testament
AoF	*Altorientalische Forschungen*
ARCE	American Research Center in Egypt
ARM	*Archives royales de Mari*
ArOr	*Archiv Orientální*
ASAE	*Annales du Service des Antiquités de l'Égypte*
ASAW	Abhandlungen der Sächsischen Akademie der Wissenschaften
AuOr	*Aula Orientalis*
AUSS	*Andrews University Seminary Studies*
BA	*Biblical Archaeologist*
BAR	*Biblical Archaeology Review*
BASOR	*Bulletin of the American Schools of Oriental Research*
BES	*Bulletin of the Egyptological Seminar*
BIFAO	*Bulletin de l'Institut Français d'Archéologie Orientale*
BJRL	*Bulletin of the John Rylands Library*
BM	*Beth Mikra*
BMFA	*Bulletin of the Museum of Fine Arts*
BN	*Biblische Notizen*
BO	*Bibliotheca Orientalis*
BSFE	*Bulletin de la Société Française d'Égyptologie*
BTB	*Biblical Theology Bulletin*
BZ	*Biblische Zeitschrift*
BZAW	Beihefte zur ZAW
CBQ	*Catholic Biblical Quarterly*
CCAR	Central Conference of American Rabbis
CdE	*Chronique d'Egypte*
CRAIBL	*Comptes rendus de l'Académie des inscriptions et belles-lettres*
CT	*Cuneiform Texts from Babylonian Tablets in the British Museum*
CTA	Andrée Herdner, *Corpus des tablettes en cunéiformes alphabetiques découvertes à Ras Shamra-Ugarit de 1929 à 1939*
DBAT	*Dielheimer Blätter zum Alten Testament*
DD	*Dor le Dor, the Jewish Bible Quarterly*
EI	*Eretz Israel*

EstBib	*Estudios bíblicos*
ETL	*Ephemerides theologicae Lovanienses*
EVKomm	*Evangelische Kommentare*
GM	*Göttinger Miszellen*
HAR	*Hebrew Annual Review*
HSM	Harvard Semitic Monographs
HSS	Harvard Semitic Series
HTR	*Harvard Theological Review*
HUCA	*Hebrew Union College Annual*
IEJ	*Israel Exploration Journal*
IFAO	Institut Français d'Archéologie Orientale
IMJ	*Israel Museum Journal*
JAAR	*Journal of the American Academy of Religion*
JANES	*Journal of the Ancient Near Eastern Society*
JAOS	*Journal of the American Oriental Society*
JARCE	*Journal of the American Research Center in Egypt*
JBL	*Journal of Biblical Literature*
JBQ	*Jewish Bible Quarterly*
JCS	*Journal of Cuneiform Studies*
JEA	*Journal of Egyptian Archaeology*
JEOL	*Jaarbericht van het Vooraziatsisch-Egyptisch Genootschap, "Ex Oriente Lux"*
JFSR	*Journal of Feminist Studies in Religion*
JESHO	*Journal of the Economic and Social History of the Orient*
JJS	*Journal of Jewish Studies*
JLA	*Jewish Law Annual*
JNES	*Journal of Near Eastern Studies*
JNSL	*Journal of Northwest Semitic Languages*
JQR	*Jewish Quarterly Review*
JRAS	*Journal of the Royal Asiatic Society*
JSJ	*Journal for the Study of Judaism*
JSOT	*Journal for the Study of the Old Testament*
JSS	*Journal of Semitic Studies*
JSSEA	*Journal of the Society for the Study of Egyptian Antiquities*
JTS	*Journal of Theological Studies*
KTU	M. Dietrich, O. Loretz, and J. Samartin, eds., *Die keilalphabetischen Texte aus Ugarit*
KUB	Keilschrifturkunden aus Boghazköi
MARI	*Mari, Annales de Recherches Interdisciplinaires*
MDAIK	*Mitteilungen des Deutschen Archäologischen Instituts Abteilungen Kairo*
MDB	*Le Monde de la Bible*
MIFAO	*Memoires de l'Institut Français d'Archéologie Orientale*
MIO	*Mitteilungen des Instituts für Orientforschung*
MMJ	*Metropolitan Museum Journal*

MSL	Materialien zum sumerischen Lexikon
n.f.	neue folge
n.s.	new series
OBO	Orbis biblicus et orientalis
OBT	Overtures to Biblical Theology
OLZ	*Orientalistische Literaturzeitung*
OrAnt	*Oriens Antiquus*
o.s.	old series
OTS	*Old Testament Studies*
PEQ	*Palestine Exploratin Quarterly*
RA	*Revue d'Assyriologie*
RB	*Revue Biblique*
RdE	*Revue d'Égyptologie*
REJ	*Revue des études juives*
RHD	*Revue historique de droit Français et étranger*
RHR	*Revue de l'Histoire des Réligions*
RIDA	*Revue Internationale des Droits de l'Antiquité*
RivB	*Rivista Biblica*
RSF	*Rivista di Studi Fenici*
RSO	*Rivista degli studi orientali*
RSR	*Recherches de science religieuse/ Religious Studies Review*
RT	*Recueil de travaux rélatifs à la philologie et à l'archéologie égyptiennes et assyriennes*
SAOC	Studies in Ancient Oriental Civilizations
SAK	*Studien zur Altägyptischen Kultur*
SASAE	Suppléments aux Annales du service des Antiquités de l'Égypte
SBAP	*Proceedings of the Society of Biblical Archaeology*
SBL	Society of Biblical Literature
SEL	*Studi Epigrafici e Linguistici*
SR	*Sciences Religieuses*
STTh	*Studia Theologica*
SWBAS	Social World of Biblical Antiquity Series
TBT	*The Bible Today*
TGUOS	*Transactions of the Glasgow University Oriental Society*
TS	*Theological Studies*
TZ	*Theologische Zeitschrift*
UF	*Ugarit-Forschungen*
USQR	*Union Theological Seminary Quarterly Review*
VT	*Vetus Testamentum*
VTS	Vestus Testamentum Supplements
WJT	*Westminster Journal of Theology*
WO	*Die Welt des Orients*
WZKM	*Wiener Zeitschrift für die Kunde des Morgenlandes*
ZA	*Zeitschrift für Assyriologie*
ZAS	*Zeitschrfit für Aegyptische Sprache und Altertumskunde*

ZAW   *Zeitschrift für die alttestamentliche Wissenschaft*
ZDPV   *Zeitschrift des deutschen Palästina-Vereins*
ZEE   *Zeitschrift für Evangelische Ethik*

1. GENERAL WORKS ON WOMEN IN ANTIQUITY

1. Adelman, Joseph. *Famous Women: An Outline of Feminine Achievement Throughout the Ages with Life Stories of Five Hundred Noted Women.* New York: Pictorial Review, 1926.

2. Alexander, William, M. D. of Edinburgh. *The History of Women from the Earliest Antiquity; Giving Some Account of Almost Every Interesting Particular Concerning That Sex among All Nations Ancient and Modern.* 2 vols. London: n.p., 1779; 3d ed.; 2 vols. London: n.p., 1782 Vol. 1, p. A of "Advertisement" reads as follows: "Work was composed solely for the amusement and instruction of the Fair Sex; in order to render it the more intelligible, we have studied the utmost plainness and simplicity of language; have totally excluded almost every word that is not English, and even, as much as possible, avoided every technical term."

3. Bachofen, Johann Jacob. *Das Mutterrecht: Eine Untersuchung über die Gynaikokratie der alten Welt nach ihrer religiosen Natur.* Stuttgart: Krais & Hoffmann, 1861. The thesis: that matriarchy preceded patriarchy; Semiramis; Egypt (pp. 92–193).

4. Backer, Louis de. *Le Droit de la Femme dans l'Antiquité: Son Devoir au Moyen Age.* Paris: Claudin, 1880.

5. Ballow, Patricia K. *Women: A Bibliography of Bibliographies.* Boston: G. K. Hall, 1986.

6. Bardèche, Maurice. *Histoire des Femmes.* Paris: Stock, 1968.

7. Basserman, Lujo. *The Oldest Profession: A History of Prostitution.* Translated by James Cleugh. New York: Stein & Day, 1968.

8. Beard, Mary R. *Woman as Force in History: A Study in Traditions and Realities.* New York: Macmillan, 1946.

9. —. *On Understanding Women.* New York: Greenwood, 1968.

1

10. Beauvoir, Simone de. *The Second Sex.* Translated by H. M. Parshley. New York: Bantam, 1970.

11. Betty, R. *Who's Who in the Ancient World.* Harmondsworth: Penguin Books, 1973.

12. Beyer, Johanna, et al. *Frauenhandlexikon.* Munich: C. H. Beck, 1983.

13. Birt, Theodor. *Frauen der Antike.* Leipzig: Quelle & Meyer, 1932.

14. Bridenthal, Renata; Koonz, Claudia; and Stuart, Susan M., eds. *Becoming Visible: Women in European History.* Boston: Houghton Mifflin, 1987.

15. Briffault, Robert. *The Mothers: A Study of the Origins of Sentiments and Institutions.* 3 vols. New York: Macmillan, 1927.

16. Bullough, Vern L. *The History of Prostitution.* New Hyde Park, New York: University Books, 1964.

17. Bullough, Vern L., and Bullough, Bonnie. *The Subordinate Sex: A History of Attitudes toward Women.* Urbana: University of Illinois Press, 1973.

18. Davis, Elizabeth Gould. *The First Sex.* New York: G. P. Putnam's Sons, 1971.

19. de Koven, Anna. *Women in the Cycles of Culture: A Study of "Women Power" Through the Centuries.* New York: G. P. Putnam, 1941.

20. D'Oriega, Guy. *Histoire et Géographie de la femme.* Paris: Editions du Scorpion, 1958.

21. Duché, Jean. *Le premier sexe.* Paris: Editions Robert Leffont, 1972.

22. Dupouy, Edmond. *La Prostitution dans l'Antiquité: Étude d'Hygiene Sociale.* Paris: Librairie Meuvillon, 1887.

23. Foucault, M. *Histoire de la sexualité.* Paris: Gallinard, 1984.

24. Hale, Sara Josepha. *Women's Record; or, Sketches of All Distin-*

guished Women, from the Creation to A.D. 1854. 2 vols. New York: Source Book Press, 1970; reprint of the 1855 edition.

25. Heiler, Friedrich. *Die Frau in der Religion des Menschheit.* Berlin: Walter de Gruyter, 1977.

26. Henry, Sondra, and Taitz, Emily. *Written Out of History.* New York: Bloch, 1978.

27. Heywood, Thomas. *Nine Books of Various History Concerning Women.* London: n.p., 1624; reissued 1657 as *The General History of Women.*

28. Hoch-Smith, Judith, and Spring, Anita. *Women in Ritual and Symbolic Roles.* New York & London: Plenum Press, 1978.

29. Ireland, Norma. *Index to Women of the World from Ancient to Modern Times.* Westwood, Mass.: Faxon, 1970.

30. Jacobson, Anita. *Marriage and Money.* Lund: Berlingski Boktruckeriet, 1967.

31. King, William C., comp. *Woman: Her Position, Influence, and Achievement Throughout the Civilized World: Her Biography, Her History, from the Garden of Eden to the Twentieth Century.* Springfield, Mass.: King-Richardson, 1902.

32. Lacroix, Paul. *History of Prostitution among All the Peoples of the World, from the Most Remote Antiquity to the Present Day.* Translated by Smaule Putnam. 3 vols. Chicago: Pascal Corici, 1926.

33. Langdon-Davies, John. *A Short History of Women.* New York: Viking Press, 1927. Chapter 3: Asia and Egypt

34. Leipoldt, Johannes. *Die Frau in der antiken Welt und im Urchristentum.* Gütersloh: Gütersloher Verlagshaus, 1953. Egypt, Israel

35. Letourneau, Charles. *La Condition de la femme dans les diverses races et civilisations.* Paris: V. Girad & E. Brière, 1903.

36. Lévy, Edmond, ed. *La femme dans les sociétés antiques.* Strasbourg: AECR, 1983.

37. Lissner, Anneliese, et al., eds. *Frauenlexikon.* Freiburg: Herder, 1988.

38. Mair, Lucy Philip. *Marriage.* 2d ed. London: Scolar, 1977.

39. Miquell, Violetta. *Woman in Myth and History.* New York: Vantage Press, 1962.

40. O'Faolain, Julian, and Martines, Lauro, eds. *Not in God's Image: Women in History from the Greeks to the Victorians.* New York: Harper & Row, 1973.

41. Ochshorn, Judith. *The Book of the Goddess: Past and Present.* New York: Crossroad, 1985.

42. Peradotto, John, and Sullivan, J. P., eds. *Women in the Ancient World: The Arethusa Papers.* SUNY Series in Classical Studies. Albany: State University of New York Press, 1984.

43. Ritchie, Maureen. *Women's Studies: A Check List of Bibliographies.* London: Mansell, 1980.

44. Rosaldo, M. Z., and Lamphere, L. *Women, Culture, and Society.* Stanford: Stanford University Press, 1974.

45. Seltman, Charles. *Women in Antiquity.* New York: St. Martin's Press, 1956.

46. Stone, Merlin. *The Paradise Papers: The Suppression of Women's Rites.* London: Virago, in association with Quartet Books, 1977.

47. Wahrmund, Ludwig. *Das Institut der Ehe im Altertum.* Weimar: H. Böhlaus, 1933.

48. Wakeman, Mary K. "Feminist Revision of the Matriarchal Hypothesis." *Anima* 7 (1981), 83–96.

49. Westermarck, E. *The History of Human Marriage.* 3d. ed. London: Macmillan, 1894.

50. Wieth-Knudsen, K. A. *Understanding Women: A Popular Study of the Question from Ancient Times to the Present Day.* Translated from the Danish by Arthur G. Chater. New York: Elliot Holt, 1921. Anti-feminist.

51. Winter, Alice Ames. *The Heritage of Women.* New York: Minton Balch, 1927.

52. Wormser-Migot, Olga. *Les Femmes dans l'Histoire.* Paris: Corrêa, 1952.

2. WOMEN IN THE ANCIENT NEAR EAST: BOOKS, ARTICLES, AND DISSERTATIONS

53. Attridge, Harold A., and Oden, Robert A. *The Syrian Goddess.* SBL Texts and Translations, 9. Missoula, Montana: Scholars Press, 1976.

54. Beckman, Gary. "Three Tablets from the Vicinity of Emar." *JCS* 40 (1988), 61–68.

55. Ben-Baraq, Zafrira. "Inheritance by Daughters in the Ancient Near East." *JSS* 25 (1980), 22–33.

56. Bowman, C. H. "The Goddess 'Anatu in the Ancient Near East." Ph.D. diss., Graduate Theological Union, 1978.

57. Brin, G. "Studies in the Law of Inheritance of the Biblical Period—A Comparative Study." *Diné Israel* 6 (1975), 231–249.

58. Cameron, A., and Kuhrt, A., eds. *Images of Women in Antiquity.* rev. ed. London: Rowtledge, 1993.

59. Caquot, André. "La déesse Segal." *Semitica* 4 (1951–1953), 55–58.

60. Cazelles, Henri. "Consécrations d'enfants et de femmes." In *Miscellanea Babylonica: Mélanges offerts à Maurice Birot,* pp. 45–49. Edited by J.-M. Durand & J.-R. Kupper. Paris: Éditions Recherche sur les Civilisations, 1985.

61. Dacquino, Pretro. "La 'Redenzione' del Matrimonio." *Bibbia e Oriente* 11 (1969), 145–148.

62. Deger-Halkotzy, S. "The Women of PY An. 607." *Minos,* n.s., 13 (1972), 137–160.

63. Derousseaux, Louis, ed. *La création dans l'orient ancien.* Paris: Cerf, 1987.

64. Descamps, P. "La Situation de la femme chez les anciens Sémites." *Revue Internationale de Sociologie* 37 (1929), 23–40.

65. Durand, J.-M., ed. *La femme dans le proche-orient antique.* Compte rendu de la 33ᵉ rencontre assyriologique internationale. Paris: Éditions Recherche sur les Civilisations, 1987.

66. Egender, D. "Le culte de la Mère de Dieu en Orient." *Terra Sainte* 5 (1972), 135–140.

67. Ellermeier, F. *Sibyllen, Musikanten, Haremsfrauen.* Theologische und Orientalische Arbeiten 2. Herzberg: Jungfer, 1970.

68. Farnell, Lewis R. "Sociological Hypothesis Concerning the Position of Women in Ancient Religion." *Archiv für Religionwissenschaft* 7 (1904), 70–94.

69. Feinstein, B. "The Faerie Queen and the Cosmologies of the Near East." *Journal of the History of Ideas* 29 (1968), 531–550.

70. Fensham, F. Charles. "Widow, Orphan, and the Poor in Ancient Near Eastern Legal and Wisdom Literature." *JNES* 21 (1962), 129–139.

71. Fildes, Valerie A. *Breasts, Bottles, and Babies.* Edinburgh: Edinburgh University Press, 1986. Pp. 3–13 deal with the ancient Near East.

72. Fleishman, Joseph. "Studies Pertaining to the Legal Status of the Child in the Bible and in the Ancient Near East." Ph.D. diss., Bar-Ilan University, 1989.

73. Fontaine, Carole R. "A Heifer from Thy Stable: On Goddesses and the Status of Women in the Ancient Near East." *USQR* 43 (1989), 67–91.

74. Frymer-Kensky, Tikva S. "The Judicial Ordeal in the Ancient Near East." Ph.D. diss., Yale University, 1977.

75. Gaster, T. H. *Thespis.* rev. ed. New York: Doubleday & Co., 1961.

76. Gray, Elmer L. "Capital Punishment in the Ancient Near East." *Biblical Illustrator* 13 (Fall 1986), 65–67.

77. Grimal, Peter, ed. *Histoire mondial de la femme: préhistoire et antiquité.* Paris: Nouvelle Librairie de France, 1965.

78. Hacket, Jo Ann. "Can a Sexist Model Liberate Us? Ancient Near Eastern 'Fertility' Goddess." *JFSR* 5 (1989), 65–76.

79. Heimpel, Wolfgang. "A Catalogue of Near Eastern Venus Deities." *Syro-Mesopotamian Studies* 4, no. 3 (December 1982), 9–22.

80. Hoffner, Harry. "Symbols for Masculinity and Femininity (Their Use in Ancient Near Eastern Sympathetic Magic Bowls)." *JBL* 85 (1966), 326–334.

81. —. "Incest, Sodomy and Bestiality in the Ancient Near East." In *Orient and Occident: Essays Presented to C. H. Gordon,* pp. 81–90. Edited by H. A. Hoffner. AOAT 22. Kevelaer: Butzon & Bercker/Neukirchen-Vluyn: Neukirchener Verlag, 1973.

82. Huehnergard, John. "Five Tablets from the Viciniy of Emar." *RA* 77 (1983), 11–43.

83. Ide, Arthur Frederick. *Women in the Ancient Near East.* Mesquito, Texas: Ide House Inc., 1982.

84. Johnson, Buffie. *Lady of the Beasts: Ancient Images of the Great Goddess and Her Sacred Animals.* San Francisco: Harper & Row, 1988.

85. Kinal, F. "Die Stellung der Frau im Alten Orient." *Belleten* 20 (1956), 367–378.

86. Knapp, A. B. *The History and Culture of Ancient Western Asia and Egypt.* Chicago: Dorsey Press, 1988.

87. Kornfeld, W. "L'adultère dans l'Orient antique." *RB* 57 (1950), 92–109.

88. Lackenbacher, S. "Une nouvelle attestation d'*Ištar Hurri* dans un contrat trouvé à Banijas (Syrie)." In *Miscellanea Babylonica: Mélanges offerts à Maurice Birot,* pp. 153–160. Edited by J.-M. Durand & J.-R. Kupper. Paris: Éditions Recherches sur les Civilisations, 1985.

89. Lesko, B. S., ed. *Women's Earliest Records from Ancient Egypt and Western Asia.* Brown Judaic Studies, no. 166. Atlanta: Scholars Press, 1989.

90. Lieberman, A. I. "Studies in the Trial by River Ordeal in the Ancient Near East During the Second Millenium B.C.E." Ph.D. diss., Brandeis University, 1969.

91. Lieberman, S. R. "The Eve Motif in Ancient Near Eastern and Classical Greek Sources." Ph.D. diss., Boston University Graduate School, 1975.

92. Lipínski, E., ed. *State and Temple Economy in the Ancient Near East.* 2 vols. Leuven: Departement Oriëntalistiek, 1979.

93. —. "The Wife's Right to Divorce in the Light of an Ancient Near Eastern Tradition." *JLA* 4 (1981), 9–27.

94. MacDonald, Elizabeth Mary. *The Position of Women as Reflected in Semitic Codes of Law.* Toronto: University of Toronto Press, 1931.

95. McComiskey, Thomas E. "The Status of the Secondary Wife; Its Development in Ancient Near Eastern Law." Ph.D. diss., Brandeis University, 1965.

96. Meier, Samuel A. "Women and Communication in the Ancient Near East." *JAOS* 111 (1991), 540–547.

97. Mendelsohn, I. "Slavery in the Ancient Near East." *BA* 9 (1946), 74–88.

98. —. "The Family in the Ancient Near East." *BA* 11 (1948), 24–40.

99. —. *Slavery in the Ancient Near East.* New York: Oxford University Press, 1949.

100. —. "On Marriage in Alalakh." In *Essays on Jewish Literature and Thought Presented in Honor of S. W. Baron*, pp. 351–357. Edited by J. L. Blau. New York: Columbia University Press, 1959.

101. Möbius, H. "Die Göttin mit dem Löwen." In *Festschrift W. Eilers,* pp. 450–468. Edited by Gernot Wiessner. Wiesbaden: Harrassowitz, 1967.

102. Moscati, Sabatino, ed. *Le Antiche Divinità.* Studi Semitici. Rome: Centro di Studi Semitici, 1958.

103. Naaman, N. "The Ishtar Temple at Alalakh." *JNES* 39 (1980), 209–214.

104. "The Position of Women in Barbarism and among the Ancients." *Westminster Review* 64 (1855), 378–436.

105. Powell, Marvin A. *Labor in the Ancient Near East.* New Haven: American Oriental Society, 1987.

106. Rabinowitz, J. J. "A Legal Formula in the Susa Tablets, in an Egyptian Document of the Twelfth Dynasty, in the Aramaic Papyri, and in the Book of Daniel." *Biblica* 36 (1955), 74–77.

107. Rémy, P. "La condition de la femme dans les codes du Proche-Orient ancien et les codes d'Israel." *Sciences Ecclésiastiques* 16 (1964), 107–127; 291–320.

108. Renger, J. "mārat ilim: Exogamie bei den semitischen Nomaden des 2. Jahrtausends." *AfO* 24 (1973), 103–107.

109. Ringgren, Helmer. *Religions of the Ancient Near East.* Translated by John Sturdy. Philadelphia: Westminster, 1973.

110. Römer, W. H. Ph. "Einige Überlegungen zur 'heiligen Hochzeit' nach altorientalischen Texten." In *Von Kanaan bis Kerala,* pp. 411–428. Edited by W. C. Delsman, et. al. AOAT, vol. 211. Kevelaer: Butzon & Bercker/Neukirchen-Vluyn: Neukirchener Verlag, 1982.

111. Sayce, Archibald Henry. *The Religions of Ancient Egypt and Babylonia.* The Gifted Lectures. Edinburgh: University of Edinburgh Press, 1902.

112. Schipflinger, Th. "Die fraulich-mütterliche Aspekt im Göttlichen." *Anthropos* 62 (1967), 944–945.

113. Schretter, Manfred K. *Alter Orient und Hellas.* Innsbrucker Beiträge zur Kulturwissenschaft, Sonderheft 33. Innsbruck: Sprachwissenschaftlichen Seminars der Universität Innsbruck, 1974.

114. Seibert, Ilse. *Woman in the Ancient Near East.* Revised by George A. Shepperson. Translated by Marianne Herzfeld. New York: A. Schram, 1974.

115. Silver, Morris. *Economic Structures of the Ancient Near East.* London: Croom Helm, 1985.

116. Spyckett, Agnès. "Une grande déesse élamite retrouve son visage." *Syria* 45 (1968), 67–73.

117. Strenge, John H. "The Ancient Position of Women." *Lutheran Church Review* 34 (1915), 410–417.

118. Strika, F. I. "Prehistoric Roots: Continuity in the Image and Rituals of the Great Goddess Cult in the Near East." *RSO* 57 (1983), 1–41.

119. Thomas, Edward. "On the Position of Women in the East in Olden Times." *JRAS,* 1879, pp. 1–60.

120. Vaux, Roland de. "Sur le roile des femmes dans l'Orient ancien." *RB* 44 (1935), 397–412.

121. "Women in Antiquity." *Methodist Review* 78 (1896), 314–317.

3. WOMEN IN THE ART AND ARCHITECTURE
OF THE ANCIENT NEAR EAST:
BOOKS, ARTICLES, AND DISSERTATIONS

122. Al-Gailani-Werr, Lamia, and al-Jadir, Walid. "Seal Impressions from Sippar." *Sumer* 37 (1981), 129–144.

123. Al-Gailani-Werr, Lamia, with the assistance of Shakir, Burhan, and Salman, Salah. "Catalogue of the Cylinder Seals from Tell Suliemeh-Himrin." *Sumer* 38 (1982), 68–88.

124. Albenda, Pauline. "Western Asiatic Women in the Iron Age: Their Image Revealed." *BA* 46 (1983), 82–88.

125. Amiran, Ruth. "Reflections on the Deity at the EB II and EB III Temples at Ai." *BASOR,* no. 208 (1972), 9–13 + 2 fig. the goddess Bilulu.

126. Amiran, Ruth, and Tadmor, Miriam. "A Female Cult Statuette from Chalcolithic Beer-sheva." *IEJ* 30 (1980), 137–139.

127. 'Amr, Abdel-Jalil. "A Nude Female Statue with Astral Emblems." *PEQ* 117 (1985), 104–111.

128. —. "Four Unique Double-Faced Female Heads from the Amman Citadel." *PEQ* 120 (1988), 55–63.

129. —. "Ten Human Clay Figurines from Jerusalem." *Levant* 20 (1988), 185–196.

130. Arensburger, B., and Rak, Y. "Jewish Skeletal Remains from the Period of the Kings of Judea." *PEQ* 117 (1985), 30–34.

131. Avigad, N. "The Seal of Jezebel." *IEJ* 14 (1964), 274–276.

132. —. "Two Ammonite Seals Depicting the Dea Nutrix." *BASOR,* no. 225 (1977), 63–66.

133. —. "The King's Daughter and the Lyre." *IEJ* 28 (1978), 146–151. The seal of Ma 'adonah the king's daughter.

134. —. "Some Decorated West Semitic Seals." *IEJ* 35 (1985), 1–7. 6th cent. B.C.E. seal l'byḥy bt 'zy'

135. —. "Two Seals of Women and Other Hebrew Seals." *EI* 20 (1989), 90–96; 197.

136. Barnett, R. D. "'Anath, Ba'al and Pasargadae." *Mélanges de l'Université Saint-Joseph* 45 (1969), 405–422.

137. —. "The Earliest Representation of Anath." *EI* 14(1978), 28–31.

138. —. "A Winged Goddess of Wine on an Electrum Plaque." *Anatolian Studies* 30 (1980), 169–178.

139. Barrelet, Marie-Thérèse. "Un inventaire de Kar-Tukulti-Ninurta: Textiles Décorés Assyriens et Autres." *RA* 71 (1977), 51–92.

140. Beck, Perahya. "A Head of a Goddess from Qitmit." *Qadmoniyot* 19 (1986), 79–81 (in Hebrew).

141. Ben-Arie, Sarah. "A Clay Mold of a Goddess." *Qadmoniyot* 16 (1983), 123–124 (in Hebrew).

142. —. "A Mould for a Goddess Plaque." *IEJ* 33 (1983), 72–77.

143. Ben-Tor, A. "Cylinder Seals of the Early Bronze Age in Eretz-Israel." *Qadmoniyot* 11 (1978), 2–5 (in Hebrew).

144. Bertman, Stephen. "Tassled Garments in the Ancient East Mediterranean." *BA* 24 (1961), 119–128.

145. Blakely, J. A., and Hurton, F. L. "South Palestinian 'Bes' Vessels of the Persian Period." *Levant* 18 (1956), 111–119.

146. Brun, François. "Deux statuettes qatabanites." *Semitica* 35 (1985), 97–98.

147. Brunner-Traut, Emma. "Gravidenflasche. Das Salben des Mutterliebes." *Archäologie und das Altes Testament: Festschrift für Kurt Galling,* pp. 35–48. Edited by Arnulf Kuschke & Ernst Kutsch. Tübingen: J. C. B. Mohr, 1970.

148. —. "*Das Muttermilchkrüglein Ammen mit Stillumhang und Mondamulett.*" *WO* 5 (1970), 145–164.

149. Clamer, Christa. "A Gold Plaque from Tel Lachish." *Tel Aviv* 7 (1980), 152–162. A goddess.

150. Collun, D. *First Impressions: Cylinder Seals in the Ancient Near East.* London: British Museum, 1987.

151. Contenau, G. *Manuel d'archéologie orientale.* 3 vols. Paris: Editions A. & J. Picard, 1927–1940.

152. Crocker, P. T. "An Assyrian Royal Tomb." *Buried History* 25 (1989), 92–95.

153. Crüsemann, F. "Ein israelitisches Ritualbad aus vorexilischer Zeit." *ZDPV* 94 (1978), 68–75.

154. Cullican, W. "Dea Tyra Gravida." *Australian Journal of Biblical Archaeology* 1 (1969), 35–50. Terracotta figurines of pregnant goddesses 600 B.C.E.

155. Danmanville, J. "Iconographie d'Ištar-Saušga en Anatolie ancienne." *RA* 56 (1962), 113–131; 175–190.

156. Davis, D., and Kloner, A. "A Burial Cave of the Late Israelite Period on the Slopes of Mt. Zion." *Qadmoniyot* 11 (1978), 16–19 (in Hebrew). Hammi'ohel daughter of Menahem; 1/3 of the burials are women.

157. Dessel, J. P. "An Iron Age Figurine from Tel Halif." *BASOR,* no. 269 (1988), 59–64. A goddess.

158. Dothan, Trude. "A Female Mourner Figurine from the Lachish Region." *EI* 9 (1969), 42–46 (in Hebrew).

159. ——. "Another Mourning—Woman Figurine from the Lachish Region." *EI* 11 (1973), 120–121; 4 figs. (in Hebrew).

160. Finkel, D. J. "The Dynamics of Middle Eastern Skeletal Populations (3100 B.C.–A.D. 200)." Ph.D. diss., University of Oregon, 1974.

161. Fuhr, I. *Ein altorientalisches Symbol.* Wiesbaden: Harrassowitz, 1967.

162. Gitin, S., and Dever, W. G. *Recent Excavations in Israel. Studies in Iron Age Archaeology.* Winona Lake: Eisenbrauns for the American Schools of Oriental Research, 1989.

163. Giveon, Raphael. "Remarks on the Tel Qarnayim Goddess."
      BN 33 (1986), 7–9.

164. Görg, Manfred. "Die Königstochter und die Leier." *BN* 14
      (1981), 7–10. The seal of Ma 'adonah the king's daughter.

165. ——. "'Mein Schiff is YHWH.' Zur Dekoration eines hebräis-
      chen Siegels." *BN* 25 (1984), 7–9. Merab in 6th century
      B.C.E. seal from Jerusalem.

166. Gubel, Eric, and Bordreuil, Pierre. "Statuette fragmentaire
      portant le nom de la Baalat Gubal." *Semitica* 35 (1985), 5–
      11.

167. Haines, Richard C. "A Report of the Excavations at Nippur
      during 1960–1961." *Sumer* 17 (1961), 67–70 + plates.

168. Hančar, Franz. "Der Kult der Grossen Mutter im kupfer-
      zeitlichen Kleinasien: Zur Deutung der Kultstandarten des
      Alaca Höjüks." *AfO* 13 (1939–1941), 289–298.

169. Hanfmann, G. M. A., and Balmuth, M. S. "The Image of an
      Anatolian Goddess at Sardis." *Jahrbuch für kleinasiatische
      Forschung* 2 (1967), 361–369.

170. Hillers, D. H. "The Goddess with the Tambourine."
      Concordia Theological Monthly 41 (1970), 606–619.

171. Jack, J. W. "Nedabiah in the Lachish Letters." *Expository
      Times* 47 (1935–1936), 430–431.

172. James, E. O. *The Cult of the Mother Goddess: An Archaeo-
      logical and Documentary Study.* London: Thames &
      Hudson, 1959.

173. "A Jerusalem Celebration of Temple and Bamot." *BAR* 3, no. 3
      (1977), 22–24.

174. Kaplan, J. "Archaeological Survey on the Left Bank of the Yar-
      kon River." *IEJ* 22 (1953), 157–160. Neolithic clay statue of
      fertility goddess.

175. Keel, Othmar. "The Peculiar Headrests for the Dead in First
      Temple Times." *BAR* 13, no. 4 (1987), 50–53.

176. Kühne, H. "Bemerkungen zu einigen Glasreliefs des 2. Jahrtausend v. Chr. aus Syrien und Palästina." *ZA* 59 (1969), 299–318. Naked woman or goddess.

177. Lawton, Robert. "Israelite Personal Names on Pre-Exilic Hebrew Inscriptions." *Biblica* 65 (1984), 340–346.

178. Lipínski, Edward. "The Syro-Palestinian Iconography of Woman and Goddess." *IEJ* 36 (1986), 87–96.

179. Matoušova-Rajmova, Maria. "Some Cylinder Seals from Dhiba'i and Harmal." *Sumer* 31 (1975), 49–66.

180. Matthiae, M. Paolo. "Nouvelles Fouilles á Ebla en 1987–1989." *CRAIBL*, 1990, 384–431.

181. Mazar, A. "Cylinder Seals of the Middle and Late Bronze Ages in Eretz-Israel." *Qadmoniyot* 11 (1978), 6–14 (in Hebrew).

182. —. "Clay Plaques Depicting a Goddess Standing in a Sanctuary Façade." *Qadmoniyot* 15 (1982), 113–115 (in Hebrew).

183. Mellaart, James. "Excavations at Çatal Hüyük, 1962." *Anatolian Studies* 13 (1961), 43–103.

184. Moscati, S. *Historical Art in the Ancient Near East.* Rome: Centro di Studi Semitici, 1963.

185. Naar, Karl J. "Mutterrechtliche Züge im Neolitikum (Zum Befund von Çatal Hüyük)." *Anthropos* 63 (1968/69), 409–420.

186. Perrot, Jean. "La 'Venus' de Beersheva." *EI* 9 (1969), 100–101.

187. Podella, Thomas. "Ein mediterraner Trauerritus." *UF* 18 (1986), 26–69. Four terra cotta figurines of barebreasted women bewailing the dead.

188. Pritchard, J. B. *Palestinian Figurines in Relation to Certain Goddesses Known Through Literature.* American Oriental Series, vol. 24. New Haven: American Oriental Society, 1943.

189. —. *The Ancient Near East in Pictures Related to the Old Testament.* 3d ed. Princeton: Princeton University Press, 1969.

190. Rashid, Fawzi. "Burying Daughters Alive and the Polygamy Tradition in Preshistoric Times." *Sumer* 36 (1980), 53–62 (in Arabic).

191. Schlossman, Betty L. "Portraiture in Mesopotamia in the Late Third and Early Second Millenium B.C." *AfO* 26 (1978/ 79), 56–77; 28 (1981–82), 143–170.

192. Schmitz, Bettina, and Steffgen, U., eds. *War sie nur schön? Die Frau im Spiegel der Jahrtausende.* Mainz, 1989.

193. Seger, Joe D. "Reflections on the Gold Hoard from Gezer." *BASOR,* no. 221 (1976), 133–140.

194. Shanks, Hershel. "Ancient Ivory—The Story of Wealth, Decadence, and Beauty." *BAR* 11, no. 5 (1985), 40–53. Includes Chalcolithic female figures from Sefadi.

195. Spyckett, A. *La Statuaire du Proche-Orient ancien.* Leiden: E. J. Brill, 1981.

196. Stager, L. "The Archaeology of the Family in Ancient Israel." *BASOR,* no. 260 (1985), 1–36.

197. Stern, Ephraim. "Two Phoenician Glass Seals from Tel Dor." *JANES* 16–17 (1984/85), 213–216. Sun emblem of Astarte

198. Tadmor, Miriam. "Female Relief Figurines during the Late Bronze Age in Canaan." *EI* 15 (1981), 79–84 (in Hebrew).

199. —. "Female Cult Figurines in Late Canaan and Early Israel: Archaeological Evidence." In *Studies in the Period of David and Solomon and Other Essays,* pp. 139–173. Edited by Tomoo Ishida. Winona Lake: Eisenbrauns, 1982.

200. Taha, Munir Yousif. "Sumerian Statues from Tell Ma'tuq." *Sumer* 26 (1970), 101–108 (in Arabic).

201. Taylor, J. Glen. "The Two Earliest Known Representations of Yahweh." In *Ascribe to the LORD: Biblical and Other Studies in Memory of Peter C. Craigie,* pp. 557–566. Edited by Lyle Eslinger and Glen Taylor. Sheffield: JSOT Press, 1988.

202. Toueir, Kassem. "The Syrian Archaeological Expedition to Tell al 'Abd Zrejehey: Clay Figurines of the Third Millenium

B. C." *Syro-Mesopotamian Studies* 2 (1978), 59–93. Mother goddess figurines

203.   Vandier, Jacques. "Une bronze de la déesse Ouadjet à Bologne." *ZÄS* 97 (1971), 126–129.

204.   Weiss, Harvey. "From Ebla to Damascus: Art and Archaeology of Ancient Syria." *Archaeology* 38, no. 5 (September/October 1985), 58–61.

205.   Williams, Ellen Reeder, and Heim, Suzanne. "Ebla to Damascus: Art and Archaeology of Ancient Syria." *BA* 48 (1985), 140–147.

206.   Winter, Irene J. "On the Problems of Karatepe: The Reliefs and Their Content." *Anatolian Studies* 29 (1979), 115–151. Women in art.

207.   Yakar, Jak. "The Twin Shrines of Beycesultan." *Anatolian Studies* 24 (1974), 151–161. Goddesses.

208.   Zivie, Alain-Pierre. "Portrait de femme: Une tête en bois stuqué récemment découverte à Saqqarah." *RdE* 39 (1988), 179–195 + pl. 7–11.

4. WOMEN AND WOMANHOOD IN HEBREW SCRIPTURE: BOOKS

209. Achetemeier, Elizabeth. *The Committed Marriage: Biblical Perspectives on Current Issues*. Philadelphia: Westminster Press, 1976.

210. Achtemeier, Paul J. *The Bible, Theology, and Feminist Approaches = Interpretation*, vol. 42, no. 1 (January 1988).

211. Adams, Charles. *Women of the Bible*. New York: Lane and Scott, 1851.

212. Adams, Queenie M. *Neither Male nor Female: A Study of the Scriptures*. Ilfracombe: Stockwell, 1973.

213. Adinolfi, M. *Il femminismo della Bibbia*. Spicilegium Pontificii Athenaei Antoniani 22. Rome: Antonianum, 1981.

214. Adinolfi, M., and Geraci, P. *Bibbia e ginecologia a confronto*. Casale Monferrato: Piemme, 1989.

215. Aguilar, Grace. *The Women of Israel, or, Characters and Sketches from the Holy Scriptures and Jewish History*. 2d ed. New York: Appleton, 1853.

216. Alexander, George M. *Handbook of Biblical Personalities*. New York: Seabury, 1981.

217. Alter, Robert. *The Art of Biblical Narrative*. New York: Basic Books, 1981.

218. Amram, D. W. *The Jewish Law of Divorce According to Bible and Talmud*. Philadelphia: E. Stern, 1896; repr. New York: Hermon Press, 1968.

219. Arnold, Patrick M. *Gibeah: The Search for a Biblical City*. JSOT Supplement Series, no. 79. Sheffield: Sheffield Academic Press, 1990. Pp. 61–87: The outrage at Gibeah; Judg. 19.

220. Aschkenasy, Nehama. *Eve's Journey.* Philadelphia: University of Pennsylvania Press, 1986.

221. Aston, Sophia. *The Mothers of the Bible.* Boston: Jk. E. Tilton, 1859.

222. Auffret, Pierre. *La sagesse a bâti sa maison.* Fribourg: Editions Universitaires/Göttingen: Vandenhoeck & Ruprecht, 1982. Gen. 2–3; 2 Sam. 13; Ps. 128; 123; 131

223. Augustinovich, Agustin. *El ocultismo y la Biblia.* Caracas: Tripode, 1977. 1 Sam. 28; the necromancer at Endor

224. Bach, Alice, ed. *The Pleasure of Her Text: Feminist Readings of Biblical and Historical Texts.* Philadelphia: Trinity Press International, 1990.

225. Bailey, R. C. *David in Love and War: The Pursuit of Power in 2 Samuel 10–12.* JSOT Supplementary Series, no. 75. Sheffield: Sheffield Academic Press, 1990.

226. Bakan, David. *And They Took Themselves Wives.* New York: Harper & Row, 1979.

227. Bal, Mieke. *Femmes imaginaires: L'ancien testament au risque d'une narratologie critique.* Utrecht: HES, 1986.

228. —. *Lethal Love: Feminist Literary Readings of Biblical Love Stories.* Bloomington, Indiana: Indiana University Press, 1987.

229. —. *Death and Dissymetry: The Politics of Coherence in the Book of Judges.* Chicago: University of Chicago Press, 1988.

230. —. *Murder and Difference: Gender, Genre, and Scholarship on Sisera's Death.* Bloomington: Indiana: Indiana University Press, 1988.

231. Bal, Mieke, ed. *Anti-Covenant: Counter-Reading Women's Lives in the Hebrew Bible.* Sheffield: Almond Press, 1989.

232. Bal, Mieke; van Dijk-Hemmes, Fokkelien; and van Ginneken, Grietje. *En Sara in haar tent lachte...: Patriarchaat en verzet in bijbelverhalen.* Utrecht: HES, 1984.

233. Baldwin, George Colfax. *Representative Women: From Eve...
to Mary.* New York: Sheldon & Co./Boston: Gould &
Lincoln, 1855.

234. Balz-Cochois, Helgard. *Gomer. Der Höhenkult Israels im
Selbstverständnis der Volksfrömmigkeit.* Frankfurt: P. Lang,
1982.

235. Bar-Efrat. S. *Narrative Art in the Bible.* Translated from the
Hebrew by D. Shefer-Vanson in conjunction with the
author. JSOT Supplementary Series, no. 70; Bible and Literature Series, no. 17. Sheffield: JSOT Press, 1989.

236. Barnard, David. *Biblical Women.* Giving a correct biographical
description of every female mentioned in Scripture, with ex-
planatory remarks. Cincinnati: Hart & Col., 1863.

237. Batten, J. Rowena. *Women Alive: Twenty-Five Talks on Wom-
en of the Bible.* Grand Rapids: Zondervan, 1965.

238. Baudissin, Wolf Wilhelm Friedrich. *Die Geschichte des alttestamentlichen Priesterthums.* Stuttgart: S. Hirzel, 1889.
Ex. 38:8

239. Bauer-Kayatz, Christa. *Studien zu Proverbien 1–9.* Wissenschaftliche Monographien zum Alten und Neuen Testament.
Neukirchen-Vluyn: Neukirchener Verlag, 1966.

240. Beer, Georg. *Die Soziale und Religiöse Stellung der Frau im
israelitischen Altertum.* Tübingen: J. C. B. Moor, 1919.

241. Benjamin, D. C. *Deuteronomy and City Life.* Lanham: University Press of America, 1983.

242. Berg, Sandra Beth. *The Book of Esther: Motifs, Themes, and
Structure.* SBL Dissertation Series, vol. 44. Missoula: Scholars Press, 1979.

243. Berlin, Adele. *Poetics and Interpretation of Biblical Narrative.*
Bible & Literature Series, no. 9. Sheffield: Almond, 1983.

244. *Bibliography on Biblical Feminism.* Minneapolis: Evangelical
Women's Caucus, 1975.

245. Bilezikian, Gilbert. *Beyond Sex Roles: A Guide for the Study of*

Female Roles in the Bible. Grand Rapids: Baker House, 1985.

246. Bitter, S. *Die Ehe des Propheten Hoseas.* Göttinger Theologische Arbeiten, no. 3. Göttingen: Vandenhoeck & Ruprecht, 1975.

247. Bloesch, Donald G. *Is the Bible Sexist?* Westchester, Illinois: Crossway, 1982.

248. Bloom, Harold. *The Book of J.* New York: G. Weidenfeld, 1990.

249. Boecker, Hans Jochen. *Frau und Mann.* Erblauliche Reden, no. 6. Neukirchen-Vluyn: Neukirchener Verlag, 1977.

250. Boer, C. Den. *Man en vrouw in bijbels perspectief.* Kampen: Kok., 1985.

251. Boer, P. A. H. de. *Fatherhood and Motherhood in Israelite and Judean Piety.* Leiden: E. J. Brill, 1974.

252. Bohlen, Reinhold. *Der Fall Naboth, Hintergrund und Werdegung einer alttestamentlichen Erzählung (1 Kön 21).* Trier Theologische Studien, 35. Trier: Paulinus-Verlag, 1978. Athaliah, Jezebel

253. Boström, Gustav. *Proverbiastudien: die Weisheit und das fremde Weib in Spruche 1–9.* Lunds Universitets Årsskrift 30, 3. Lund: Gleerup, 1935.

254. Brenner. Athalya. *The Israelite Woman: Social Role and Literary Type in Biblical Narrative.* JSOT Supplements, no. 21. Sheffield: JSOT Press, 1985.

255. —.*The Song of Songs.* Old Testament Guides. Sheffield: JSOT Press, 1989.

256. Brim, Charles. *Medicine in the Bible.* New York: Froben Press, 1936.

257. Briscoe, Jill. *Prime Rib and Apple.* Grand Rapids: Zondervan, 1976.

258. Broch, Yitzhak, I. *Ruth.* New York: Feldheim, 1983.

259. Brownmiller, Susan. *Against Our Will*. New York: Bantam Books, 1975. This classic study of the phenomenology of rape includes treatment of biblical rape narratives and relevant biblical law.

260. Bruns, J. Edgar. *God as Woman, Woman as God*. New York: Paulist Press, 1973.

261. Buchanan, Isabelia Reid. *Women of the Bible*. Minneapolis: Colwell, 1924.

262. Bull, G. T. *Love Songs in Harvest: An Interpretation of the Book of Ruth*. Glasgow: Pickering, 1972.

263. Burchard, Samuel. *The Daughters of Zion*. New York: J. S. Taylor, 1853.

264. Burgess, E. T. *Other Women of the Bible*. Little Rock, Arkansas: Baptist Publications, 1964.

265. Burke, J. Ashleigh. *The X-rated Book: Sex and Obscenity in the Bible*. Houston: J.A.B., 1983.

266. Burns, Rita J. *Has the Lord Indeed Spoken Only Through Moses? A Study of the Biblical Portrait of Miriam*. SBL Dissertation Series, no. 84. Atlanta: Scholars Press, 1987.

267. Burrows, Millar. *The Basis of Israelite Marriage*. New Haven: American Oriental Society, 1938.

268. Burton, Juliette T. *The Five Jewels of the Orient*. New York: Masonic Publishing Co., 1872.

269. Busch, E. *Frauen wie wir: biblische Frauengestalten*. Gladbeck: Schriftenmissions-Verlag, 1976.

270. Bushnell, Katherine C. *God's Word to Women: One Hundred Bible Studies on Woman's Place in the Divine Economy*. 2d ed. Oakland, Calif.: By the author, 1923.

271. Caird, G. B. *The Language and Imagery of the Bible*. Philadelphia: Westminster, 1980.

272. Callaway, Mary. *Sing O Barren One: A Study in Comparative Midrash*. SBL Dissertation Series, no. 91. Atlanta: Scholars Press, 1986.

273. Calvocoressi, Peter. *Who's Who in the Bible.* London: Viking, 1987.

274. Camp, Claudia V. *Wisdom and the Feminine in the Book of Proverbs.* Bible and Literature Series, no. 11. Sheffield: Almond, 1985.

275. Carmichael, Calum M. *The Laws of Deuteronomy.* Ithaca, N.Y. and London, Eng.: Cornell University Press, 1974.

276. —. *Woman, Law, and the Genesis Traditions.* Edinburgh: Edinburgh University Press, 1979.

277. —. *Law and Narrative in the Bible.* Ithaca, N.Y. and London, Eng.: Cornell University Press, 1985.

278. Carmody, Dennis Lardner. *Biblical Women: Contemporary Reflections on Biblical Texts.* New York: Crossroad, 1988.

279. Cassuto, Umberto. *Biblical and Oriental Studies.* 2 vols. Jerusalem: Magnes, 1973–1975.

280. Chappell, Clovis Gilham. *Feminine Faces.* New York and Nashville: Abingdon-Cokesbury, 1942.

281. Clapp, Marie W. *The Old Testament as It Concerns Women.* New York: Methodist Book Concern, 1934.

282. Clines, David J. A. *What Does Eve Do to Help? And Other Readerly Questions to the Old Testament.* JSOT Supplement Series, no. 94. Sheffield: JSOT Press, 1990.

283. Clines, David J. A., and Eskenazi, Tamara C. *Telling Queen Michal's Story.* Sheffield: Sheffield Academic Press, 1991.

284. Cody, A. I. *A History of the Old Testament Priesthood.* Analecta Biblica 35. Rome: Pontifical Biblical Institute, 1969.

285. Cole, William Graham. *Sex and Love in the Bible.* New York: Association Press, 1959.

286. Collins, Adela Yarboro, ed. *Feminist Perspectives on Biblical Scholarship.* SBL Biblical Scholarship in North America 10. Chico: Scholars Press, 1985.

287. Collins, Stanley. *Courage and Submission: A Study of Ruth and Esther.* Glendale, CA.: Regal, 1975.

288. Conroy, Charles. *Absalom Absalom! Narrative and Language in 2 Sam. 13–20.* Analecta Biblica, 81. Rome: Biblical Institute Press, 1978. Tamar

289. Coote, R. B., and Ord, D. R. *The Bible's First Historian: From Eden to the Court of David with the Yahwist.* Philadelphia: Fortress, 1989.

290. Cosby, Michael R. *Sex in the Bible.* Englewood, N.J.: Prentice Hall, 1984.

291. Cox, Francis August. *Female Scripture Biography.* 2 vols. Boston: Lincoln & Edmands, 1831.

292. Crenshaw, James L. *Samson: A Secret Betrayed, A Vow Ignored.* Atlanta: John Knox Press, 1978. the women in Samson's life

293. Cross, Earle Bennett. *The Hebrew Family. A Study in Historical Sociology.* Chicago: University of Chicago Press, 1927.

294. Cross, Frank Moore, Jr. *Canaanite Myth and Hebrew Epic: Essays in the History of the Religion of Israel.* Cambridge: Harvard University Press, 1973.

295. Crotwell, Helen, ed. *Women and the Word: Sermons.* Philadelphia: Fortress, 1977.

296. Crüseman, F., and Thyen, H., eds. *Als Mann und Frau geschaffen. Exegetische Studien zur Rolle der Frau.* Gelnhausen/ Berlin: Burckhardthaus-Stein, 1978.

297. Culley, Robert C. *Studies in the Structure of Hebrew Narrative.* Philadelphia: Fortress, 1980.

298. Daly, Mary. *Beyond God the Father: Toward a Philosophy of Women's Liberation.* Boston: Beacon Press, 1973.

299. Danker, Albert. *Heroines of Olden Times.* New York: Chapple and Tozer, 1875.

300. Darr, Katheryn Pfisterer. *Far More Precious Than Jewels: Perspectives on Biblical Women.* Louisville: Westminster/ John Knox, 1991. Sarah, Hagar, Ruth, Esther

301. Davis, Elizabeth Gould. *The First Sex.* New York: Putnam, 1971.

302. Day, Peggy L., ed. *Gender and Difference in Ancient Israel.* Minneapolis: Fortress, 1989.

303. Deen, Elizabeth. *Family Living in the Bible.* New York: Harper & Row, 1963.

304. —. *The Bible's Legacy for Womanhood.* Garden City, N.Y.: Doubleday, 1969.

305. —. *Wisdom from Women in the Bible.* San Francisco: Harper & Row, 1978.

306. —. *All of the Women of the Bible.* San Francisco: Harper & Row, 1988.

307. Demers, Patricia. *Women as Interpreters of the Bible.* Mahwah, N. J.: Paulist Press, 1992.

308. Detrick, R. Blaine. *Favorite Women of the Bible.* Lima, Ohio: CSS, 1988.

309. Diesel, P. M. L. *Adam and Eve and the Universe.* New York: Exposition Press, 1971.

310. Dillow, J. *Solomon on Sex.* Nashville: Thomas Nelson, 1977.

311. Döller, Johannes. *Die Reinheits—und Speisegesetze des alten Testament.* Münster: Aschendorff, 1917.

312. —. *Das Weib im alten Testament.* Münster: Aschendorff, 1920.

313. Drimmer, Frederick. *Daughters of Eve.* Illustrations by Hal Frenck. Norwalk, Conn.: C. R. Gibson, 1975.

314. Dryburgh, B. *Lessons for Lovers in the Song of Solomon.* New Canaan, Conn.: Keats, 1975.

315. Eberharter, A. *Das Ehe- und Familienrecht der Hebräer mit Rücksicht auf die ethnologische Forschung dargestellt.* Münster: Aschendorff, 1914.

316. Eider, Dorothy. *Women of the Bible Speak to Women of Today.* Marina del Ray, CA.: De Vorss, 1986.

317. Eller, Vernard. *The Language of Canaan and the Grammar of Feminism.* Grand Rapids: Eerdmans, 1982.

318. Emswiler, Sharon Neufer. *The Ongoing Journey: Women and the Bible.* New York: Women's Division, Board of Global Ministries, United Methodist Church, 1977.

319. Engelken, Karen. *Frauen im alten Israel.* BWANT 120. Stuttgart: W. Kohlhammer, 1990.

320. Engelsman, Joan Chamberlain. *The Feminine Dimension of the Divine.* Philadelphia: Westminster, 1979.

321. Engert, Thadaeus. *Ehe- und familien Recht der Hebräer:* Munich: J. Lenner, 1905.

322. Epstein, L. M. *Marriage Laws in the Bible and the Talmud.* HSS, vol. 12. Cambridge: Harvard University Press, 1942.

323. —. *Sex Laws and Customs in Judaism.* New York: Bloch, 1948; repr. with an introduction by Ari Kiev. New York: Ktav, 1967.

324. Epting, Ruth. *Für die Freiheit frei.* Zürich: Theologischer Verlag, 1972.

325. Evans, Mary T. *Woman in the Bible.* Downers Grove, Illinois: InterVarsity Press, 1983.

326. Exum, J. Cheryl, ed. *Signs and Wonders.* Atlanta: Scholars Press, 1989.

327. Exum, J. Cheryl, and Bos, J. W. eds. *Reasoning with Foxes: Female Wit in a World of Male Power.* Semeia 42. Atlanta: Scholars Press, 1988.

328. Falk, Marcia. *Love Lyrics from the Bible. A Translation and Literary Study of the Song of Songs.* Bible and Literature Series, no. 4. Sheffield: Almond Press, 1982.

329. Falk, Ze'ev. *Hebrew Law in Biblical Times.* Jerusalem: Wahrmann Books, 1964.

330. Faulhaber, Michael von. *The Women of the Bible.* Westminster, Md.: Newman Press, 1955.

331. Faulkner, James. *Romances and Intrigues of the Women of the Bible.* New York: Vantage, 1975.

332. Fiorenza, Elizabeth Schüssler. *In Memory of Her.* New York: Crossroad, 1983.

333. —. *Bread Not Stone: The Challenge of Feminist Biblical Interpretation.* Edinburgh: T. & T. Clark, 1990.

334. Fisch, Harold. *Poetry with Purpose: Biblical Poetics and Interpretation.* Indiana Studies in Biblical Literature. Bloomington: Indiana University Press, 1988.

335. Fischer, Clare Benedicks, et al. *Women in a Strange Land.* Philadelphia: Fortress, 1974.

336. Foh, Susan T. *Women and the Word of God.* Grand Rapids: Baker Book House, 1979.

337. Fohrer, G. *History of Israelite Religion.* Nashville & New York: Abingdon, 1972.

338. Fokkelman, J. P. *Narrative Art and Poetry in the Books of Samuel.* 3 vols. Assen: Van Gorcum, 1980–1986.

339. Fox, Everett. *In the Beginning: A New English Rendering of the Book of Genesis.* New York: Schocken Books, 1983.

340. Fox, Michael V. *The Song of Songs and the Ancient Egyptian Love Songs.* Madison: University of Wisconsin Press, 1985.

341. —. *Qoheleth and His Contradictions.* JSOT Supplement Series, no. 71. Sheffield: JSOT Press, 1989.

342. Fraine, Jean de. *Women of the Old Testament.* Translated by Forrest L. Ingram. De Pere, Wisconsin: St. Norbert Abbey Press, 1968.

343. Frankiel, Tamar. *The Voice of Sarah: Feminist Spirituality and Traditional Judaism.* San Francisco: Harper & Row, 1990.

344. Frazer, Sir James George. *Folklore in the Old Testament.* London: Macmillan, 1919.

345. Freedman, D. N., and Graff, D. F., eds. *Palestine in Transition.* Sheffield: Almond Press, 1983.

346. Frick, F. *The Formation of the State in Ancient Israel.* Sheffield: Almond Press, 1985.

347. Frymer-Kensky, Tikva. *In the Wake of the Goddesses: Women, Culture, and the Biblical Transformation of Pagan Myth.* New York: Free Press, 1992.

348. Gadala, Marie-Thérèse. *Le féminisme de la Bible.* 2 vols. Paris: Geuthner, 1930–1951.

349. Gammie, John G., and Perdue, Leo G., eds. *The Sage in Israel and the Ancient Near East.* Winona Lake: Eisenbrauns, 1990.

350. Garbini, G. *History and Ideology in Ancient Israel.* London: SCM, 1988.

351. Garsiel, Moshe. *The First Book of Samuel: A Literary Study of Comparative Structures, Analogies and Parallels.* Ramat Gan: Revivim, 1985.

352. —. *Midrashic Name Derivations in the Bible.* Ramat Gan: Revivim, 1987.

353. Gaspari, Christof. *Ein plus eins ist eins; Leitbilder für Mann und Frau.* Wiesbaden: Herold, 1985.

354. Gaster, Theodor H. *The New Golden Bow.* New York: Criterion Books, 1959.

355. —. *Myth, Legend, and Custom in the Old Testament.* New York: Harper & Row, 1969.

356. Gerber, Aaron H. *Biblical Attitudes on Human Sexuality.* Great Neck, N.Y.: Todd & Honeywell, 1982.

357. Gerstenberger, Erhard S., and Schrage, Wolfgang. *Frau und Mann.* Kohlhammer Taschenbücher Biblische Konfrontationen 1013. Stuttgart: Kohlhammer, 1980.

358. Gibert, P. *Bible, Mythes et Récits de Commencement.* Paris: Editions du Seuil, 1986.

359. Gilbert, Maurice, ed. *La sagesse de l'ancien testament.* Leuven: University Press, 1979.

360. Gilliland, Dolores Scott. *Selected Women of the Scriptures of Stamina and Courage.* Illustrated by Gael Scott. Spearfish, South Dakota: Honor Books, 1978.

361. Ginsberg, H. L. *The Israelian Heritage of Judaism.* New York: Jewish Theological Seminary, 1982.

362. Glickman, S. Craig. *A Song for Lovers.* Downers Grove, Ill.: InterVarsity Press, 1976. Canticles

363. Goldingay, John. *Songs from a Strange Land: Psalms 42–51.* Leicester: Inter-Varsity Press, 1978.

364. Gottwald, Norman. *The Tribes of Yahweh: A Sociology of the Religion of Liberated Israel 1250–1050 B.C.* Maryknoll: Orbis Books, 1979.

365 —. *The Hebrew Bible. A Socio-Literary Introduction.* Philadelphia: Fortress, 1985

366. Goulder, Michael D. *The Song of Fourteen Songs.* JSOT Supplement, no. 36. Sheffield: University of Sheffield Press, 1986.

367. Granqvist, Hilma. *Child Problems among the Arabs.* Helsinki/Copenhagen: Soderstrom & Co., 1950.

368. Graves, Robert, and Patai, Raphael. *Hebrew Myth: The Book of Genesis.* New York: Greenwich House, 1973.

369. Grelot, Pierre. *Man and Wife in Scripture.* New York: Herder & Herder, 1964.

370. —. *Le couple humain dans l'Ecriture.* Paris: Editions du Cerf, 1969.

371. Griffith, K. A. *Come and Meet Adam and Eve: The Story of Gen. 1–4.* Grand Rapids: Zondervan, 1977.

372. Gross, R. M., ed. *Beyond Androcentrism: New Essays on Women and Religion*. Missoula: Scholars Press, 1977.

373. Gunn, David M. *The Story of King David: Genre and Interpretation*. JSOT Supplementary Series 6. Sheffield: Sheffield University Press, 1978.

374. Gunn, David M., ed. *Narrative Novella in Samuel*. Sheffield: Almond Press, 1991.

375. Hadas, Pamela White. *In Light of Genesis*. Philadelphia: Jewish Publication Society, 1980.

376. Hallet, Mary Thomas. *Their Names Remain: Seventeen Women of Old Testament Days*. New York: Abingdon Press, 1938.

377. Harrison, Eveleen. *Little-known Women of the Bible*. New York: Round Table Press, 1936.

378. Hartmann, Anton T. *Die Hebräerin am Putztische und als Braut*. 3 vols. Amsterdam: Kunst-und-Industrie-Comptoir, 1809–1810.

379. Hartsoe, Colleen Ivey. *Dear Daughter: Letters from Eve and Other Women of the Bible*. Wilton, Conn.: Morehouse-Barlow, 1981.

380. Haytes, M. *The New Eve in Christ: The Use and Abuse of the Bible in the Debate about Women in the Church*. London: SPCK, 1987. Gen. 1:27; female metaphors for God; feminist hermeneutics

381. Headley, Phineas Camp. *Historical and Descriptive Sketches of the Women of the Bible, from Eve of the Old Testament to the Marys of the New Testament*. Auburn: Derby Miller & Co., 1850.

382. Heidt, William G. *The Canticle of Canticles: The Book of Wisdom*. Collegeville, Minn.: Human Life Center, 1977. Female authorship of Canticles.

383. Heister, Maria-Sybilla. *Frauen in der biblischen Glaubengeschichte*. Göttingen: Vandenhoeck & Ruprecht, 1984.

384. Hentschel, Georg. *Die Elijaerzählungen*. Erfurter Theologische Studien, 33. Leipzig: St. Benno Verlag, 1977. Jezebel

385. Herr, Ethel L. *Chosen Women of the Bible*. Chicago: Moody, 1976.

386. Hess, Margaret. *Esther: Courage in Crisis*. Wheaton, Illinois: Victor Books, 1980.

387. Hoek, J. *Man en vrouw naar Gods beeld; een bijbelse bezinning*. Kampen: Kok, 1984.

388. Honeywell, Betty. *Living Portraits*. Chicago: Moody, 1965.

389. Hopkins, D. *The Highlands of Canaan*. Sheffield: Almond Press, 1985.

390. Horner, Thomas M. *Sex in the Bible*. Rutland, Vt.: C.E. Tuttle, 1974.

391. Hurley, James B. *Man and Woman in Biblical Perspective*. Grand Rapids: Zondervan, 1981.

392. Hyers, C. *And God Created Laughter: The Bible as Divine Comedy*. Atlanta: John Knox, 1987.

393. Ide, Arthur Frederick. *Woman in Ancient Israel*. Mesquito, Texas: Ide House Inc., 1982.

394. —. *Sex, Woman, and Religion*. Dallas: Monument, 1984.

395. Jacobsen, Dan. *The Rape of Tamar: The Trap and a Dance in the Sun*. London: Secker & W., 1980.

396. Janzen, Waldemar. *Still in the Image: Essays in Biblical Theology and Anthropology*. Newton, Kansas: Faith and Life Press/Winnipeg: CMBC Publications, 1982. sexuality, female roles

397. Jay, William. *Lectures on Female Scripture Characters*. New York: Carter & Bros., 1854.

398. Jeansonne, Sharon Pace. *The Women of Genesis*. Minneapolis: Fortress, 1990.

399. Jensen, Mary E. *Bible Women Speak to Us Today*. Minneapolis: Augsburg, 1983.

400. Jobling, David. *The Sense of Biblical Narrative: Structural Analyses in the Hebrew Bible II.* JSOT Supplement, no. 39. Sheffield: JSOT Press, 1986. Gen. 2–3

401. Johanan, J. D. *Joseph and Potiphar's Wife in World Literature.* Norfolk, Conn./New York: New Directions, 1968.

402. Jones, G. H. *The Nathan Narratives.* JSOT Supplement Series, no. 80. Sheffield: Sheffield Academic Press, 1990.

403. Jüngling, H.-W. *Richter 19.* Analecta Biblica, no. 84. Rome: Biblical Institute Press, 1981.

404. Junsson, Gunnlauger A. *The Image of God: Genesis 1:26–28 in a Century of Old Testament Research.* Coniectanea Biblica. Old Testament Series, 96. Lund: Almquist & Wiksell, 1988.

405. Karssen, G. *Frau, Mensch und Mutter in der Bible (1 Mose 2, 23).* Neuhausen & Stuttgart: Hänssler, 1976.

406. Keay, Kathy. *Men, Women, and God.* Basingstoke: Marshall Pickering, 1987.

407. Kellerman, D. *Die Priesterschrift von Numeri 1:1 bis 10:10 literarkritisch und traditionsgeschichtlich untersucht.* BZAW, no. 120. Berlin: Walter de Gruyter, 1970. Num. 5

408. Kennet, R. H. *Ancient Hebrew Social Life and Custom as Indicated in Law, Narrative, and Metaphor.* London: Humphrey Milford, 1933.

409. Kilian, R. *Die Verhiessung Immanuels Jes. 7, 14.* Stuttgarter Bibelstudien, 35. Stuttgart: Verlag Katholisches Bibelwerk, 1968.

410. Kirk, Martha Ann. *Celebrations of Biblical Women's Stories; Tears, Milk and Honey.* Kansas City: Sheed, 1987.

411. Klein, L. R. *The Triumph of Irony in the Book of Judges.* Bible and Literature Series, no. 14. Sheffield: Almond Press, 1988.

412. Kraus, H. J. *Gottesdienst in Israel.* 2d ed.; Munich: Kaiser, 1962.

413. Kroeze, J. H. *Adam en Eva.* Johannesburg: Boekhandel De Jong, 1974.

414. Kruse, Ingeborg. *Unter dem Schleier ein Lachen: Neue Frauengeschichthen aus dem Alten Testament.* Stuttgart: Kreuz, 1986.

415. Kubler, Franz. *Her Children Call Her Blessed.* New York: Stephen Daye Press, 1955.

416. Kugel, James L. *In Potiphar's House.* Cambridge: Harvard University Press, 1991.

417. Kulow, Nelle Wahler. *Even as You and I: Sketches of Human Women from the Divine Book.* Columbus, Ohio: Wartburg Press, 1955.

418. Kuyperk, Abraham. *Women of the Old Testament; fifty meditations.* Grand Rapids: Zondervan, 1936.

419. Lachs, Rosalyn. *Women and Judaism.* Garden City, N.Y.: Doubleday, 1980. Women in Hebrew Scripture, pp. 88–118

420. Lacocque, André. *The Feminine Unconventional: Four Subversive Figures in Israel's Tradition.* OBT. Minneapolis: Fortress, 1990.

421. Laffey, Alice L. *An Introduction to the Old Testament: A Feminist Perspective.* Philadelphia: Fortress, 1988.

422. Landy, Francis. *Paradoxes of Paradise. Identity and Difference in the Song of Songs.* Bible and Literature Series. Sheffield: Almond Press, 1983.

423. Lang, Bernhard. *Frau Weisheit.* Düsseldorf: Patmos, 1975.

424. —. *Die einzige Gott. Die Geburt des biblischen Monotheismus.* Munich: Kösel-Verlag, 1981. Hosea, Shaddai, Lady Wisdom, Prov. 1–9

425. —. *Wisdom and the Book of Proverbs.* New York: Pilgrim, 1986.

426. Langer, Heidemarie et al. *Wir Frauen in Ninive. Gesprache mit Iona.* Stuttgart: Kreuz, 1984.

427. Lawler, G. L. *'Almah—Virgin or Young Woman?* Des Plaines, Ilinois: Regular Baptist Press, 1973.

428. Leggett, D. A. *The Levirate and Goel Institutions in the Old Testament with Special Attention to the Book of Ruth.* Cherry Hill, N.J.: Mack Publishing Co., 1974.

429. Legrand, Lucien. *The Biblical Doctrine of Virginity.* New York: Sheed & Ward, 1963.

430. Levin, Christoph. *Der Sturz der Königin Atalya.* Stuttgart: Stuttgarter Biblestudien, 1982.

431. Lewis, Ethel Clark. *Portraits of Bible Women.* New York: Vantage, 1956.

432. Licht, Jacob. *Storytelling in the Bible.* Jerusalem: Magnes, 1978.

433. Limburg, James. *Old Stories for a New Time.* Atlanta: John Knox, 1983.

434. Loades, Ann, ed. *Feminist Theology: A Reader.* London: SPCK/ Louisville: Westminster/John Knox, 1990.

435. Locher, Clemens. *Die Ehre einer Frau in Israel.* OBO, 70. Freiburg: Universitätsverlag/Göttingen: Vandenhoeck & Ruprecht, 1986. Deut. 22:13–21; *betula.*

436. Lockerbie, J. *Esther: Das Buch der Versehung Gottes.* Marburg: Francke, 1980.

437. Lockyer, Herbert. *The Women of the Bible.* Grand Rapids: Zondervan, 1971.

438. Lofts, N. *Women in the Old Testament: Twenty Psychological Studies.* New York: Macmillan, 1950.

439. Löhr, Max. *Die Stellung des Weibes zu Jahwe-Religion und -Kult.* Leipzig: Hinrichs, 1908.

440. Long, Burke O. *Images of Man and God: Old Testament Short Stories in Literary Focus.* Bible and Literature Series, no. 1. Sheffield: Almond Press, 1981.

441. Lundholm, Algot Theodore. *Women of the Bible.* 2 vols. Rock, Island, Ill.: Augustana Book Concern, 1923–1926.

442. McAllister, Grace Edna. *God Portrays Women.* Chicago: Moody, 1954.

443. —. *God Portrays More Women.* Chicago: Moody, 1956.

444. Mace, David R. *Hebrew Marriage: A Sociological Study.* London: Epworth Press, 1953.

445. MacHaffie, Barbara J. *Her Story: Women in Chirstian Tradition.* Philadelphia: Fortress, 1986. survey of feminist biblical hermeneutics

446. Maertens, Thierry. *The Advancing Dignity of Woman in the Bible.* De Pere, Wisconsin: St. Norbert Abbey Press, 1969.

447. Maillot, Alphonse. *Eve, Ma Mère: Étude sur la femme dans l'Ancien Testament.* Paris: Letouzey & Ané, 1989.

448. Marble, Annie Russell. *Women of the Bible.* New York & London: Century, 1923.

449. Marcus, David. *Jephthah and His Vow.* Lubbock, Texas: Texas Tech Press, 1986.

450. Marshall, Zona Bays. *Certain Women.* New York: Exposition Press, 1960.

451. Martyn, Sarah Towne. *Women of the Bible.* New York: American Tract Society, 1868.

452. Mason, Maggie. *Women Like Us: Learn More about Yourself through Studies of Biblical Women.* Waco Texas: Word Books, 1978.

453. Matheson, George. *The Representative Women of the Bible.* New York: A. C. Armstrong, 1907.

454. Matthews, Victor H. *Manners and Customs in the Bible.* rev. ed. Peabody, Mass: Hendrickson, 1991.

455. Mayes, A. D. H. *Judges.* Old Testament Guides. Sheffield: JSOT Press, 1990.

456. Mendenhall, G. *The Tenth Generation.* Baltimore: Johns Hopkins University Press, 1973.

457. Mesters, Carlos. *Abraâo e Sara*. Pétropolis: Vozes, 1978.

458. Meyers, Carol. *Discovering Eve: Ancient Israelite Women in Context*. New York: Oxford: 1988.

459. Mollenkott, Virginia. *Women, Men, and the Bible*. Nashville: Abingdon, 1977.

460. —. *The Divine Feminine: The Biblical Imagery of God as Female*. New York: Crossroad, 1983.

461. Mondersohn, Ernst. *Die Frauen des Alten Testament*. Neuhaussen: Hänssler, 1982.

462. Moore, Carey A. *Studies in the Book of Esther*. The Library of Biblical Studies. New York: Ktav, 1982.

463. Morton, Henry Cnova Vollam. *Women of the Bible*. New York: Dodd, Mead & Co., 1941.

464. Müller, Hans-Peter. *Vergleich und Metaphor im Hohenlied*. OBO 56. Freiburg: Universitätsverlag/Göttingen: Vandenhoeck & Ruprecht, 1984.

465. Mulliken, Frances Hartman, and Salts, Margaret. *Women of Destiny in the Bible*. Independence, Mo.: Herald Publishing House, 1978.

466. Musgrave, Peggy. *Who's Who among Bible Women*. Springfield, Mo.: Gospel Publishing House, 1981.

467. Neal, Hazel G. *Bible Women of Faith*. Anderson, Indiana: Warner Press, 1955.

468. Neufeld, Ephraim. *Ancient Hebrew Marriage Laws*. London: Longmans Green, 1944.

469. Neveu, Louis. *Avant Abraham (Genèse I–XI)*. Angiers: Université Catholique de l'Ouest, 1984.

470. Newsom, Carol A., and Ringe, Sharon H., eds. *The Women's Bible Commentary*. London: SPCK, 1992.

471. Nichol, Charles Ready. *God's Woman*. Clifton Texas: Mrs. C. R. Nichol, 1938.

472. Niditch, Susan. *Underdogs and Tricksters*. New Voices in Biblical Studies. San Francisco: Harper & Row, 1987.

473. *Notable Women of Olden Times*. Philadelphia: American Sunday School Union, 1852.

474. Nunnally-Cox, Janice. *Foremothers*. New York: Seabury, 1981.

475. O'Reilly, Bernard. *Heroic Women of the Bible and the Church*. New York: J.B. Ford & Co., 1878.

476. Ochshorn, Judith. *The Female Experience and the Nature of the Divine*. Bloomington: Indiana University Press, 1981.

477. Ockenga, Harold J. *Women in the Bible*. Grand Rapids: Zondervan, 1962.

478. —. *Women Who Made Bible History*. Grand Rapids: Zondervan, 1972.

479. Oduyoye, Modupe. *The Sons of the Gods and the Daughters of Men*. Maryknoll, N.Y.: Orbis Books, 1984. Gen. 1–11

480. Ohler, A. *Frauen gestalten der Bibel*. Würzburg: Echter Vorlag, 1987. Rachel, Leah, Tamar, Miriam, Miriam.

481. Otwell, John H. *And Sarah Laughed*. Philadelphia: Westminster, 1977.

482. Pagels, Elaine. *Adam, Eve, and the Serpent*. New York: Random House, 1988.

483. Palmer, B. ed. *Medicine and the Bible*. Exeter: Paternoster Press for the Christian Medical Fellowship, 1986.

484. Pardes, Ilana. *Countertraditions in the Bible: A Feminist Approach*. Cambridge, Mass. & London, Eng.: Harvard University Press, 1992.

485. Patai., Raphael. *Sex and Family in the Bible and the Middle East*. Garden City, N.Y.: Doubleday, 1959.

486. —. *The Hebrew Goddess*. New York: Ktav, 1967.

487. Patte, Daniel, ed. *Genesis 2 and 3: Kaleidoscopic Structural Readings.* = *Semeia,* vol. 18. Chico: Society of Biblical Literature, 1980.

488. Paul, S. M. *The Covenant Code in the Light of Cuneiform and Biblical Law.* VTS, vol. 18. Leiden: E. J. Brill, 1971.

489. Pease, Alice Campbell. *Significant Women of the Bible.* Introduction by Helen Brett Montgomery. Grand Rapids: Zondervan, 1941.

490. Pedersen, Johannes. *Israel: Its Life and Culture.* 4 vols. London: Oxford University Press, 1926–1940.

491. Peters, Norbert. *Die Frau im alten Testament.* Düsseldorf: 1926.

492. Pfister, Herta. *Der an uns Gefallen findent. Frauen im Alten Testament.* Freiburg: Herder, 1986.

493. Phillips, Anthony. *Ancient Israel's Criminal Law.* Oxford: B. Blackwell, 1970.

494. Phillips, John A. *Eve: The History of an Idea.* San Francisco: Harper & Row, 1984.

495. Phipps, William E. *Genesis and Gender: Biblical Myths of Sexuality and Their Cultural Impact.* Westport, Conn.: Greenwood Press/Praeger Publishers, 1989.

496. Piper, Otto A. *The Biblical View of Sex and Marriage.* New York: Scribners, 1960.

497. Pitt-Rivers, Julian. *The Fate of Shechem or the Politics of Sex: Essays in the Anthropology of the Mediterranean.* Cambridge: Cambridge University Press, 1977.

498. Plaskow, Judith, and Romero, Joan A., eds. *Women and Religion: Papers of the Working Groups on Women and Religion, 1972–1973.* rev. ed. Missoula: Scholars Press, 1974.

499. Plaut, W. Gunther. *The Torah: A Modern Commentary.* 4th ed. New York: UAHC, 1981.

500. Pobee, John S., and Wartenberg-Potter, Barbel von., eds. *New*

Eyes for Reading: Biblical and Theological Reflections by Women from the Third World. Geneva: World Council of Churches, 1986.

501. Polzin, Robert. *Moses and the Deuteronomist. A Literary Study of the Deuteronomic History, Part One: Deuteronomy, Joshua, Judges.* New York: Seabury, 1980.

502. —. *Samuel and the Deuteronomist. A Literary Study of the Deuteronomic History, Part Two: 1 Samuel.* San Francisco: Harper & Row, 1989.

503. Porter, Joshua. *The Extended Family in the Old Testament.* London: Edutext Publishers, 1967.

504. Preston, James J., ed. *Mother Worship: Theme and Variations.* Chapel Hill, N.C.: University of North Carolina Press, 1982.

505. Price, Eugenia. *The Unique World of Women, in Bible Times and Now.* Grand Rapids: Zondervan, 1969.

506. Raurell, Frederic. *Mots sobre l'Home.* Barcelona: Publicacions de l'Abadia de Montserrat, 1984.

507. —. *Lineamenti di antropolgia biblica.* Casale Monferrato: Piemme, 1986.

508. Redford, D. R. *A Study of the Biblical Story of Joseph (Genesis 37–50).* VTS, vol. 20. Leiden: E. J. Brill, 1970.

509. Reik, Theodor. *The Creation of Woman.* New York: Braziller, 1960.

510. Reiser, W. *Eine Frau wie Ruth. Ein biblisches Buch wird aktuell.* Zürich: Theologisches Verlag, 1972.

511. Remy, Nahida. *The Jewish Woman.* Authorized translation by Louise Mannheimer with a preface by Prof. Dr. Lazarus. 4th ed. New York: Bloch, 1923. Contains a chapter on biblical women.

512. Reuther, Rosemary Radford. *Sexism and God-Talk: Toward a Feminist Theology.* Boston: Beacon Press, 1983.

513. Reviv, Hanoch. *The Elders in Ancient Israel.* Translated by Lucy Plitmann. Jerusalem: Magnes, 1983. Deut.; Ruth.

514. Richards, Alberta Rae. *Women of the Bible.* Gastonia, N.C.: Geographical Publications Co., 1962.

515. Robbins, Gregory Allen, ed. *Genesis 1–3 in the History of Exegesis: Intrigue in the Garden.* Studies in Women and Religion, no. 27. Lewiston, N.Y. & Queenston, Ont.: Mellen, 1988.

516. Roddy, Lee. *Women in the Bible.* Chappaqua, N.Y.: Christian Herald Books, 1980.

517. Roellenbleck, E. *Magna Mater im Alten Testament.* Darmstadt: Wissenschaftliche Buchgesellschaft, 1974.

518. Rofé, Alexander. *Introduction to Deuteronomy.* Jerusalem: Akademon, 1988 (in Hebrew).

519. Rogerson, J. W. *Anthropology and the Old Testament.* Oxford: Clarendon, 1978.

520. Rolston, H. *Personalities Around David.* Richmond: John Knox, 1968.

521. Romaniuk, Kazimierz. *Matzenstwo; rodzina w Biblii.* Katawice: Sw. Jacka, 1981.

522. Rosenberg, David, ed. *Congregation: Contemporary Writers Read the Jewish Bible.* New York and London: Harcourt, Brace, Jovanovich, 1987.

523. Rosenberg, Z. *The World of Words. The Truth about the Scroll of Ruth. The Message of Logography.* New York: Philosophical Library, 1973.

524. Rost, L. *The Succession to the Throne of David.* Historic Texts & Interpretations Series, vol. 1. Sheffield: Almond Press, 1982.

525. Rusche, Helga. *They Lived By Faith: Women of the Bible.* Translated by Elizabeth Williams. New York: Helicon, 1963.

526. Russell, Letty M. *Human Liberation in a Feminist Perspective: A Theology.* Philadelphia: Westminster, 1974.

527. —. *The Liberating Word: A Guide to Nonsexist Interpretation of the Bible.* Philadelphia: Westminster, 1977.

528. —. *The Future of Partnership.* Philadelphia: Westminster, 1979.

529. Russell, Letty M., ed. *Feminist Interpretation of the Bible.* Philadelphia: Westminster, 1985.

530. Sakenfeld, Katherine Doob. *Faithfulness in Action.* Philadelphia: Fortress, 1985.

531. Salvoni, Fausto. *Sesso e amore nella Bibbia.* Genova: Ed. Lanterna, 1969.

532. Sangster, Margaret Elizabeth. *The Women of the Bible: A Portrait Gallery.* New York: Christian Hearld, 1911.

533. Sapp, S. *Sexuality, the Bible, and Science.* Philadelphia: Fortress, 1977. Gen. 1–3; Cant.

534. Sasson, Jack M. *Ruth. A New Translation.* With a Philological Commentary and a Formalist-Folklorist Interpretation. 2d ed. Biblical Seminar Series, no. 10. Sheffield: JSOT Press, 1990.

535. Saussy, Carroll. *God Images and Self Esteem: Empowering Women in a Patriarchal Society.* Louisville: Westminster/John Knox, 1991.

536. Scanzoni, Letha. *All W're Meant to Be: A Biblical Approach to Women's Liberation.* Waco, Texas: Word Books, 1974.

537. Schäfer, P. W. *Dein Gott ist mein Gott: Ruth, die Moabiterin.* Neuffen: Sennenweg Verlag, 1973.

538. Schelkle, Karl Hermann. *The Spirit and the Bride: Women in the Bible.* Translated by Matthew J. O'Connell. Collegeville, Minn.: Liturgical Press, 1979.

539. Scheppes, David. *Remarkable Women of Scripture.* Philadelphia: Dorrance & Co., 1976.

540. Schilling, Othmar. *Das Mysterium Lunae und die Erschaffung der Frau, nach Gn. 2, 21f.* Paderborn: F. Schoningh, 1963.

541. Schley, D. C. *Shiloh: A Biblical City in Tradition and History.* JSOT Supplement Series. Sheffield: JSOT Press, 1989.

542. Schmidt, Eva Renate; Korenhof, Mieke; and Jost, Renate, eds. *Feministisch gelesen.* 2 vols. Stuttgart: Kreuz, 1988–89.

543. Schottroff, Luise, and Schottroff, Willy. *Die Macht der Auferstehung: Sozialgeschichtliche Bibelauslegungen.* Munich: Kaiser, 1988.

544. Schroer, Silvia. *In Israel gab es Bilder: Nachrichten von darstellender Kunst im Alten Testament.* OBO 74. Freiburg: Universitätsverlag /Göttingen: Vandenhoeck & Ruprecht, 1987.

545. Schüngel-Straumann, Helen. *Die Frau am Anfang.* Freiburg: Herder, 1989.

546. Schüssler-Fiorenza, Elisabeth. *Bread Not Stone: The Challenge of Feminist Biblical Interpretation.* Boston: Beacon, 1984.

547. Sell, Henry Thorne. *Studies of Famous Bible Women.* New York: Fleming H. Revell, 1925.

548. Sheres, Ita. *Dinah's Rebellion: A Biblical Parable for Our Time.* New York: Crossroads Continuum, 1991.

549. Smith, Joyce Marie. *A Woman's Priorities.* Wheaton, Ill.: Tyndale House, 1976. Bible biography with bibliography.

550. Smith, Judith Florence. *In Our Lady's Library: Character Studies of the Women of the Old Testament.* Forward by Dom Savinine Louismet. London: Longmans, Green, & Co., 1923.

551. Smith, Mark S. *The Early History of God.* San Francisco: Harper & Row, 1990.

552. Sölle, Dorothee, and Schottroff, Luise. *Mijn broeders hoedster; vrouwen lezen de bijbel.* Baarn: Ten Haven, 1986.

553. Song, Theo. *Ehe und Familie; biblische Perspektiven.* Stuttgart: Calmer, 1981.

554. Sprague, William Buell, ed. *Women of the Old and New Testament: A Series of Portraits.* 2d ed. New York: D. Appleton & Co./Philadelphia: G. S. Appleton, 1851.

555. Stanton, Elizabeth Cady. *The Woman's Bible.* New York: European Publishing Co., 1895–1898.

556. Starr, Lee Anna. *The Bible Status of Women.* New York: Fleming Revell, 1926.

557. Staton, Julia. *What the Bible Says About Women.* Joplin, Mo.: College, 1980.

558. Steck, O. H. *Die Paradieserzählung. Eine Auslegung von Gen 2, 4b–3, 24.* Biblische Studien, Heft 60. Neukirchen-Vluyn: Neukirchener Verlag, 1970.

559. Stedman, R. C. *The Queen and I: Studies in Esther.* Waco Texas: Word Books, 1977.

560. Steele, Eliza R. *Heroines of Sacred History.* 2d ed. New York: J. S. Taylor & Co., 1842.

561. Stendahl, Krister. *The Bible and the Role of Women: A Case Study in Hermeneutics.* Philadelphia: Fortress, 1966.

562. Sternberg, Meir. *The Poetics of Biblical Narrative.* Bloomington: Indiana University Press, 1985.

563. Stone, Merlin. *When God Was a Woman.* New York: Dial Press, 1976.

564. Stowe, Harriet Elizabeth Beecher. *Woman in Sacred History.* New York: J. B. Ford, 1873.

565. Strus, Andrzej. *La stylistique sonore des noms propres dans le Pentateuque.* Analecta Biblica, no. 80. Rome: Biblical Institute Press, 1978.

566. Sudlow, Elizabeth W. *Career Women of the Bible.* New York: Pageant Press, 1951.

567. Swartley, Willard M. *Slavery, Sabbath, War, and Women.* Scottdale, Pa. & Waterloo, Ont.: Herald Press, 1983.

568. Swidler, Leonard J. *Women in Judaism.* Metuchen: Scarecrow, 1976.

569. —. *Biblical Affirmations of Women.* Philadelphia: Westminster, 1985.

570. Terrien, Samuel. *Till the Heart Sings: A Biblical Theology of Manhood and Womanhood.* Philadelphia: Fortress, 1985.

571. Teubal, Savina J. *Sarah the Priestess: The First Matriarch of Genesis.* Athens, Ohio: Swallow, 1984.

572. —. *Hagar the Egyptian: The Lost Tradition of the Matriarchs.* San Francisco: Harper & Row, 1990.

573. Thomas, Metta Newman. *Women of the Bible: A Study of Life and Character.* Nashville: Twentieth Century Christian, 1956.

574. Thompson, Henry Adams. *Women of the Bible.* Dayton, Ohio: U. B. Publishing House, 1914.

575. Thompson, Lucy Gertsch. *Women of the Bible: A Book Telling the Life Stories of Twenty Prominent Women of the Old and New Testaments.* Salt Lake City: Deseret Book Co., 1957.

576. Tillion, Germaine. *Le Harem et les Cousins.* Paris: Seuill, 1966.

577. Tinney, Ethel. *Women of the Bible, in Verse.* New York: Pageant Press, 1953.

578. Tischler, Nancy Marie Patterson. *Legacy of Eve: Women of the Bible.* Atlanta: John Knox Press, 1977.

579. Tolbert, Mary Ann, ed. *The Bible and Feminist Hermeneutics.* Semeia 28. Chico: Scholars Press, 1983.

580. Tosato, A. *Il matrimonio israelitico. Une teoria generale.* Analecta Biblica, no. 100. Rome: Biblical Institute Press, 1982.

581. Tournay, Raymond Jacques. *Word of God, Song of Love: A Commentary on the Song of Songs.* Translated by J. Edward Crowley. New York and Mahwah: Paulist Press, 1988.

582. Trible, Phyllis. *God and the Rhetoric of Sexuality*. Philadelphia: Fortress, 1978.

583. ——. *Texts of Terror: Literary Feminist Readings of Biblical Narratives*. Philadelphia: Fortress, 1984.

584. Trible, Phyllis, ed. *The Effects of Women's Studies on Biblical Studies = JSOT* 22. Sheffield; JSOT, 1982.

585. Utzschneider, Helmut. *Hosea. Prophet vor dem Ende*. OBO, 31. Freiburg: Universitätsverlag/Göttingen: Vandenhoeck & Ruprecht, 1980.

586. Van der Toorn, Karel. *Van haar wieg tot haar graf: De rol van de godsdienst in het leven van de Israëlitische en de Babylonische vroux*. Baarn: Ten Have, 1987. Includes revisionist discussion of the issue of cultic prostitution

587. Van Wolde, E. J. *A Semiotic Analysis of Genesis 2–3*. Studia Semitica Neerlandica, 25. Assen: Maastrict & Van Gorcum, 1989.

588. Vander Velde, Frances. *She Shall Be Called Woman*. Grand Rapids: International Publications, 1957.

589. Vanel, Jean. *Le livre de Sara*. Paris: Éditions du Cerf, 1984.

590. Vaux, Roland de. *Ancient Israel*. Translated by John McHugh, 2 vols. 2d ed. New York: McGraw Hill, 1965.

591. Viberg, Åke. *Symbols of Law: A Contextual Analysis of Legal Symbolic Acts in the Old Testament*. Coniectanea Biblica, Old Testament Series 34. Stockholm: Almqvist & Wiksell, 1992. Deut. 25:9; Ezek. 16:8; Ruth 3:9; 4:8, 16.

592. Visser 't Hooft, Willem Adolph. *The Fatherhood of God in an Age of Emancipation*. Philadelphia: Westminster, 1982.

593. Vonier, Anscar. *L'Ésprit et l'Épouse*. Paris: Éditions du Cerf, 1947.

594. Vos, Clarence J. *Women in Old Testament Worship*. Delft: Judel & Brinkman, 1968.

595. Wacker, Marie-Therese. *Der eine Gott und die Göttin*. Freiburg: Herder, 1991.

596. Wacker, Marie-Therese, ed. *Der Gott der Männer und die Frauen*. Düsseldorf: Patmost Verlag,1987.

597. Walker, Barbara G. *The Woman's Dictionary of Symbols and Sacred Objects*. San Francisco: Harper & Row, 1988.

598. Wallace, Howard N. *The Eden Narrative*. HSM, no. 32. Atlanta: Scholars Press, 1985.

599. Walter, Karin, ed. *Frauen entdecken die Bibel*. Freiburg: Herder, 1986.

600. —. *Zwischen Ohnmacht und Befreiung. Biblische Frauengestalten*. Freiburg: Herder, 1988.

601. —, and Bartolomei, M. C. *Donne alla riscoperta della Bibbia*. Brescia: Queriniana, 1988.

602. Webb, B.-G. *The Book of Judges: An Integrated Reading*. JSOT Supplement Series, no. 46. Sheffield: Sheffield Academic Press, 1987.

603. Weems, Renita J. *Just a Sister Away: A Womanist Vision of Women's Relationships in the Bible*. San Diego: LuraMedia, 1988.

604. Weiler, Gerda. *Ich werfe im Lande die Kriege: Das verborgene Matriarchat im Alten Testament*. Munich: Frauenoffensive, 1984.

605. —. *Das Matriarchat im Alten Israel*. Stuttgart, Berlin and Cologne: Kohlhammer, 1989.

606. Weinfeld, Moshe. *Deuteronomy and the Deuteronomic School*. Oxford: Clarendon Press, 1972.

607. Weld, Horatio H. *The Women of the Old and New Testaments*. Philadelphia: Lindsay and Blakiston, 1848.

608. Wenham, G. J. *The Biblical View of Marriage and Divorce*. London: Third Way Publications, 1982.

609. Werner, Hazen G. *The Bible and the Family*. Nashville: Abingdon, 1966.

610. Westbrook, R. *Studies in Biblical and Cuneiform Law.* Cahiers de la Revue Biblique, no. 26. Paris: Gabalda, 1988.

611. —. *Property and the Family in Biblical Law.* JSOT Supplement Series, no. 113. Sheffield: JSOT Press, 1991.

612. Westermann, Claus. *Genesis.* 3 vols. Translated by John J. Scullion. Minneapolis: Augsburg, 1984.

613. White, John B. *A Study of the Language of Love in the Song of Songs and Ancient Egyptian Love Poetry.* SBL Dissertation Series, no. 38. Missoula: Scholars Press, 1978.

614. Whybray, R. N. Wisdom in Proverbs. London: SCM Press, 1965.

615. Wijk-Bos, Johanna van. *Reformed and Feminist: A Challenge to the Church.* Louisville: Westminster/John Knox, 1991.

616. Wijngaarden, W. D. van. *Die sociale positie van de vrouw bij Israël in den vóór- en na-exilischen tijd.* Leiden: E. J. Brill, 1991.

617. Williams, James G. *Women Recounted: Narrative Thinking and the God of Israel.* Bible and Literature Series, no. 6. Sheffield: Almond, 1982.

618. Wilson, Elizabeth. *A Scriptural View of Women's Rights and Duties.* Philadelphia: W. S. Young, 1849.

619. Winter, Urs. *Frau und Göttin: Exegetische und ikonographische Studien zum weiblichen Gottesbild im Alten Israel und in dessen Umwelt.* OBO, no. 53. Friburg: Universitätsverlag/Göttingen: Vandenhoeck & Ruprecht, 1983.

620. Wolff, Hans Walter. *Die Hochzeit der Hure: Hosea heute.* Munich: Kaiser, 1979.

621. —. *Anthropology of the Old Testament.* Philadelphia: Fortress, 1981.

622. Woodrow, Ralph. *Woman's Adornment: What Does the Bible Really Say?* Riverside, CA.: Woodrow, 1976.

623. Wright, David P. *The Disposal of Impurity.* SBL Dissertation Series, no. 101. Atlanta: Scholars Press, 1987.

624. Wurmnest, Karl F. *Die Rolle des Individuums innerhalb von Familie und Ehe im alten Israel.* Cologne: Kleikamp, 1979.

625. Zschokke, Hermann. *Das Weib im Alten Testament.* Vienna: H. Kirsch, 1883.

5. WOMEN AND WOMANHOOD IN HEBREW SCRIPTURE: ARTICLES

626. Abel, F.-M. "L'anathème de Jéricho et la maison de Rahab." *RB* 57 (1950), 321–330.

627. Abramowitz, Chaim. "The Story of Creation—The Garden of Eden." *DD* 10 (1982) 3–9; 187–190; 234–242.

628. —. "Hosea's True Marriage." *DD* 15 (1986/87), 79–83

629. Abrams, Judith Zabarenko. "Rachel: A Woman Who Would Be a Mother." *JBQ* 18 (1989–90), 213–221.

630. Abramsky, S. "The Woman Who Looked Out the Window." *BM* 25 (1980), 114–124 (in Hebrew).

631. Abschlag, W. "Jungfrau oder Junge Frau." *Anzeiger für die katholische Geistlichkeit* 83 (1974), 200–285. Isa. 7:14

632. Ackerman, James S. "Prophecy and Warfare in Early Israel: A Study of the Deborah and Barak Story." *BASOR,* no. 220 (1975), 5–13.

633. —. "Knowing Good and Evil: A Literary Analysis of the Court History in 2 Samuel 9–20 and 1 Kings 1–2." *JBL* 109 (1990), 41–60.

634. Ackroyd, Peter A. "The Teraphim." *Expository Times* 62 (1950/51), 378–380. He sees them as mother goddesses.

635. —. "The Succession Narrative (so-called)." *Interpretation* 35 (1981), 383–396.

636. Adinolfi, M. "Il ripudio secundo Mal. 2, 14–16." *Bibbia e Oriente* 12 (1970), 247–256.

637. —. "La coppia nel Cantico ꞌdei Cantici." *Bibbia e Oriente* 22 (1980), 3–29.

638. Aharoni, R. "Concerning Three Similar Stories in the Book of

Genesis (Gen 12, 20, 26)." *BM* 24 (1979), 213–223 (in Hebrew).

639. Aharoni, Y. "Jael the Wife of Heber the Kenite and Shamgar the son of Anath." In *All the Land of Naphtali. The Twenty-fourth Archaeological Convention, October 1966,* pp. 55–61. Edited by H. Z. Hirschberg. Jerusalem: Israel Exploration Society, 1967.

640. Ahlström, G. W. "I Samuel 1, 15." *Biblica* 60 (1979), 254.

641. Ahuvyah, A. "And Hannah Prayed." *BM* 26 (1981), 318–324 (in Hebrew).

642. —. "'If you are prophets of the Lord… (Num 12)'—How the Bible Responds to the Question 'Who Has Heard His Word and Obeyed?'" *BM* 26 (1981), 115–128 (in Hebrew).

643. —. "And when pleased they maim oxen." *BM* 35 (1989–90), 227–236 (in Hebrew). Gen. 34; 49:6; Num. 30:2–17

644. Aitken, Kenneth T. "The Wooing of Rebekah." *JSOT* 30 (1984), 3–23.

645. Albertz, Rainer, "Das Ueberleben der Familie sichern." *Lutherische Monatsheft* 25 (1986), 401–405.

646. Aletti, Jean-Noël. "Proverbs 8, 22–31. Etude de Structure." *Biblica* 57 (1976), 25–37.

647. —. "Séduction et Parole en Proverbs I–IX." *VT* 27 (1977), 129–144.

648. Alexander, T. D. "The Hagar Traditions in Genesis XVI and XXI." In *Studies in the Pentateuch,* pp. 131–148. Edited by J. A. Emerton. VTS, vol. 16. Leiden: E. J. Brill, 1990.

649. Allen, C. G. "On me be the curse my son." In *Encounter with the Text,* pp. 159–172. Edited by Martin J. Buss. Semeia Supplements, no. 8. Philadelphia: Fortress, 1979. Rebekah; Gen. 23–29

650. Alter, Robert. "How Conventions Help Us Read: The Case of the Bible's Annunciation Type-Scene." *Prooftexts* 3 (1983), 115–130.

651. Altpeter, Gerda. "II Sam 12, 1–15a. Eine strukturalistische Analyse." *TZ* 38 (1982), 46–52.

652. Alvarez Oses, J. A. "La mujer y la serpiente." *Caesaraugusta* 2 (1964), 49–74.

653. Amit, Yairah. "The Story of Amnon and Tamar: Reservoir of Sympathy for Absalom." *Hasifrut* 32, no. 9 (1983), 80–87 (in Hebrew).

654. —. "'There was a man...and his name was...'—Editorial Variations and Their Tendenz." *BM* 30 (1984/85), 388–391 (in Hebrew). Deals with feminist hermeneutics, Hannah, Manoah's wife.

655. —. "Judges 4: Its Contents and Form." *JSOT* 39 (1987), 89–111.

656. Amsler, S. "La sagesse de la femme." In *La sagesse de l'Ancien Testament,* pp. 112–116. Edited by M. Gilbert. Louvain: Genbloux, 1979.

657. Anbar, Moshe. "The History of Composition of the Story of Rahab and the Spies." *BM* 29 (1983/84), 255–257 (in Hebrew).

658. —. "'He gave her as a dowry for his daughter' (1 Kgs. 9:16)." *SHNATON* 9 (1985), 233 (in Hebrew).

659. Anderlini, Giampaoh. "'ešet zenunim (Os. 1, 2)." *Bibbia e Oriente* 30 (1988), 169–182.

660. Anderson, A. A. "The Marriage of Ruth." *JSS* 23 (1978), 171–183. Contends that Ruth is not about levirate marriage.

661. Anderson, Berhard W. "'The Lord Has Created Something New'— A Stylistic Study of Jer. 31:15–22." *CBQ* 40 (1978), 463–478.

662. Anderson, F. "Israelite Kinship Terminology and Social Structure." *Biblical Translator* 20 (1970), 29–34.

663. Anderson, Gary. "Celibacy or Consummation in the Garden? Reflections on Early Jewish and Christian Interpretations of the Garden of Eden." *HTR* 82 (1989), 121–148.

664. Anderson, I. David. "Renaming and Wedding Imagery in Isa 62." *Biblica* 67 (1986), 75–80.

665. Andreason, Niels-Erik. "The Role of the Queen Mother in Israelite Society." *CBQ* 45 (1983), 179–194.

666. Andriolo, K. R. "A Structural Analysis of Genealogy and World View in the Old Testament." *American Anthropologist* 75 (1973), 1657–1669.

667. Apostolos-Cappadona, Diane. "Scriptural Women Who Danced." In *Dance as Religious Studies*, pp. 95–108. Edited by Doug Adams and Diane Apostolos-Cappadona. New York: Crossroad, 1990.

668. —. "Martha Graham and the Quest for the Feminine in Eve, Lilith, and Judith." In *Dance as Religious Studies,* pp. 118–133. Edited by Doug Adams and Diane Apostolos-Cappadona. New York: Crossroad, 1990.

669. Aptowitzer, V. "La création de l'homme d'après les anciens interprètes." *REJ* 75 (1922), 1–15.

670. Ararat, Nissan. "Reading According to the 'Seder' in Biblical Narrative: To Balance the Reading of the Dinah Episode." *Hasifrut* 27 (1978), 15–34 (in Hebrew).

671. —. "Deception and Guile in the Stories of Genesis (ct'd)." *BM* 26 (1981), 137–147 (in Hebrew). Gen. 38; Tamar and Judith; Esther and Book of Esther

672. —. "The Story of Amnon and Tamar—A Sequential Reading." *BM* 28 (1982/83), 331–357.

673. Arnold, P. M. "Hosea and the Sin of Gibeah." *CBQ* 51 (1989), 447–460.

674. Arom, N. "'For Rachel, Your Younger Daughter'—'She Is Leah'? A 'False' Statement of Identity Reflecting a False Situation." *BM* 30 (1984/85), 541–549 (in Hebrew).

675. Arpali, Boaz. "Caution: A Biblical Story." *Hasifrut* 2 (1970), 580–597 (in Hebrew).

676. Aschkenasy, Nehama. "A Non-Sexist Reading of the Bible." *Midstream* 27, no. 6 (1981), 51–55.

677. Aschliman, Sylvia Albrecht. "A New Look at Women of Old." *TBT* 28 (1990), 353–357.

678. Asensio, F. "Tradicion subre un pecado sexual en el paradiso?" *Gregorianum* 30 (1949), 49–520; 31 (1950), 35–61; 136–191; 362–390.

679. Asmussen, Jes Peter. "Matriarchalische Remkniszenen im AT?" *Dansk Teologiske Tiddskrift* 17 (1954), 242–248.

680. Astour, Michael C. "Tamar the Hierodule: An Essay on the Method of Vestigial Motifs." *JBL* 85 (1966), 185–196.

681. Augustin, Matthias. "Die Inbesitznahme der schönen Frau aus der unterschiedlichen Sichtt der Schwachen und der Mächtigen." *BZ* 27 (1983), 145–154.

682. Aviezer, Nathan. "Esther's Plan to Save the Jews: Overall Strategy, Initial Failure, Ultimate Success." *DD* 11 (1983), 153–158.

683. Avigad, Nahman. "Oniahu's Ship—A Hebrew Seal Decorated with a Sailing Ship." *Qadmoniyot* 16 (1983), 124–125 (in Hebrew).

684. Bach, Alice. "The Pleasure of Her Text." *USQR* 43 (1989), 41–58. 1 Sam. 25; David's wives: Abigail, Michal, Bathsheba

685. Bailey, J. A. "Initiation and the Primal Woman in Gilgamesh and Genesis 2–3." *JBL* 89 (1970), 137–150.

686. Bakon, Shimon. "Saul and the Witch of Endor." *DD* 5 (1976), 16–23.

687. —. "Hosea—His Marriage." *DD* 15 (1986/87), 88–96.

688. Bal, Mieke. "The Rhetoric of Subjectivity." *Poetics Today* 5 (1984), 337–376.

689. —. "Sexuality, Sin, and Sorrow: The Emergence of Female Character." In *The Female Body in Western Culture*, pp. 317–338. Edited by Susan Rubin Suleiman. Cambridge: Harvard University Press, 1986. Also in *Poetics Today* 6 (1985), 21–42.

690. Baldensperger, Ph. J. "Woman in the East." *Palestine Exploration Fund Quarterly Statement,* 1899, pp. 132–160; 1900, pp. 171–190; 1901, pp. 66–90, 167–184, 252–273.

691. Ball, C. J. "Israel and Babylon." *SBAP* 16 (1893–94), 188–200. Naamah sister of Tubal-cain (Gen. 4:22)

692. Baltzer, Klaus. "Women and War in Qoheleth 7:23–8:1a." *HTR* 80 (1987), 127–132.

693. Balz-Cochois, Helgard. "Gomer oder die Macht der Astarte." *Evangelische Theologie* 42 (1982), 37–65.

694. Bar-Asher, Mordechai. "The Gender of Nouns in Biblical Hebrew." *Semitics* 6 (1978), 1–14. Lists the 106 nouns in biblical Hebrew which have both masculine and feminine forms.

695. Barilqo, H. "One Small Question." *BM* 30 (1984/85), 305–311 (in Hebrew). Abishag, Bathsheba

696. Barron, Mary Catherine. "Davidic Diminishment: Something to do with Love." *TBT* 19 (1981), 222–227.

697. Barstad, Hans M. "The Old Testament Personal Name *rāḥāb.* An Onomastic Note." *Svensk exegetisk årsbok* 54 (1989), 43–49.

698. Bartimus, Rüdiger. "Tempus als Strukturprinzip. Anmerkungen zur stilistischen und theologischen Relevenz des Tempusgebrauchs im 'Lied der Hanna' (1 Sam. 2, 1–10)." *BZ* 31 (1987), 15–35.

699. Barton, George A. "Ashtoreth and Her Influence in the Old Testament." *JBL* 10 (1891), 73–91.

700. Baskin, Judith R. "Rabbinic Reflections on the Barren Wife." *HTR* 82 (1989), 101–114.

701. Bass, Dorothy C. "Women's Studies and Biblical Studies: An Historical Perspective." *JSOT* 22 (1982), 6–12.

702. Batten, L. W. "Hosea's Message and Marriage." *JBL* 48 (1929), 257–273.

703. Beattie, D. R. G. "Kethib and Qere in Ruth IV 5." *VT* 21 (1971), 490–494.

704. —. "The Book of Ruth as Evidence for Israelite Legal Practice." *VT* 24 (1974), 251–267.

705. —. "A Midrashic Gloss in Ruth 2:7." *ZAW* 89 (1977), 122–124.

706. —. "Ruth III." *JSOT* 5 (1978), 39–48; 49–51.

707. —. "Ruth 2, 7 and Midrash." *ZAW* 99 (1987), 422–423.

708. Becker, Joachim. "Das Elterngebot." *Internationale katholische Zeitschrift, ' Communio'* 8 (1979), 289–299.

709. Beek, M. A. "Rahab in the Light of Jewish Exegesis." In *Von Kanaan bis Karala. Festschrift für Prof. Mag. Dr. Dr. J. P. M. van der Ploeg O. P. zur Vollendung des siebzigsten Lebensjahres am 4. Juli 1979*, pp. 37–44. Edited by W. C. Delsman et al. AOAT, vol. 211. Kevelaer: Butzon & Bercker, Neukirchen/Vluyn: Neukirchener Verlag, 1982.

710. Beeston, A. F. L. "One Flesh." *VT* 36 (1986), 115–117.

711. Begrich, J. "Atalja, die Tochter Omris." *ZAW* 53 (1939), 78–79.

712. Bekkenkamp, Jonneke. "Het Hooglied: een vrouwenlied in een mannentraditie." In *Ik zing mijn lied voor al wie met me gat*, pp. 72–89. Edited by Ria Lemaire. Utrecht: HES, 1986.

713. Belkin, S. "Levirate and agnate marriage in rabbinic and cognate literature." *JQR* 60 (1970), 275–379.

714. Bellefontaine, Elizabeth. "Deuteronomy 21:18–21: Reviewing the Case of the Rebellious Son." *JSOT* 13 (1979), 13–31.

715. —. "Customary Law and Chieftainship: Judicial Aspects of 2 Samuel 14.4–21." *JSOT* 38 (1987), 47–72.

716. Ben-Baraq, Zafrira. "The Legal Background to the Restoration of Michal to David." In *Studies in the Historical Books of the Old Testament*, pp. 15–29. Edited by J. A. Emerton. VTS, vol. 30. Leiden: E. J. Brill, 1979.

717. —. "The Story of Meribaal and the System of Land Grants in Israel." *BM* 25 (1979), 48–62 (in Hebrew).

718. —. "The Case of the Daughters of Zelophehad in Light of a New Document from Nuzi." *SHNATON* 3 (1979), 116–123 (in Hebrew).

719. —. "Inheritance by Daughters in the Ancient Near East." *JSS* 25 (1980), 22–33. Job's daughters, daughters of Zelophehad

720. —. "Meribaal and the System of Land Grants in Ancient Israel." *Biblica* 62 (1981), 73–91. Meribaal, inheritance by women, daughters of Zelophehad

721. —. "The Status and Rights of the Gebirah." *JBL* 110 (1991), 23–34.

722. —. "The Daughters of Job Against the Background of Inheritance Practices in Israel and Mesopotamia. *EI* 2 4 (1993), 41–48 (in Hebrew).

723. Ben-Reuven, S. "David—From Abigail to Bathsheba." *BM* 27 (1981/82), 244–245 (in Hebrew).

724. —. "*'elem and 'almâ* in the Bible." *BM* 28 (1982/83), 320–321 (in Hebrew).

725. Ben-Yasher, M. "Examination of the Pericope Concerning Rispah daughter of Aya (2 Sam. 21)." *BM* 11 (1965), 34–41 (in Hebrew).

726. Benjamin, Don C. "Israel's God: Mother and Midwife." *BTB* 19 (1989), 115–120.

727. —. "The Persistent Widow." *TBT* 28 (1990), 213–219.

728. Bennett, Anne McGrew. "Overcoming the Biblical and Traditional Subordination of Women." *Radical Religion* 1 (1971), 26–31.

729. —. "The Woman's Bible: Introduction." In *Women and Religion: 1973. Proceedings,* pp. 39–43. Edited by Joan Arnold Romero. Tallahassee: American Academy of Religion, 1973.

730. Bennett, Anne McGrew, et al. "The Women's Bible: Review

and Perspectives." In *Women and Religion: 1973. Proceedings,* pp. 39–78. Edited by Joan Arnold Romero. Tallahassee: American Academy of Religion, 1973.

731. Berg, Werner. "Die Identität der 'jungen Frau' in Jes 7, 14. 16." *BN* 3 (1980), 7–13.

732. ——. "Der Sündenfall Abrahams und Sarahs nach Gen 16, 1–6." *BN* 19 (1982), 7–14.

733. Bergant, Dianne. "Symbolic Names in Hosea." *TBT* 20 (1982), 159–160.

734. ——. "Women in the Bible." *Emmanuel* 91 (1985), 153–155, 161.

735. ——. "Might Job Have Been a Feminist?" *TBT* 28 (1990), 336–341.

736. Bergerk, P. R. "Zum Hosea bereit bis hin zu einer Runleib Brot: Prov 6, 26." *ZAW* 99 (1987), 98–106.

737. Bergin, Helen; McKinley, Judith; and Mitchell, Sarah. "Sexism Ancient and Modern: Turning a Male World Upside Down." *Pacifica* 3 (1990), 157–171.

738. Berlin, Adele. "Grammatical Aspects of Biblical Parallelism." *HUCA* 50 (1979), 17–43.

739. ——. "Characterization in Biblical Narrative: David's Wives." *JSOT* 23 (1982), 69–85.

740. ——. "Literary Exegesis of Biblical Narrative: Between Poetics and Hermeneutics." In *Not in Heaven: Coherence and Complexity in Biblical Narrative,* pp. 120–128; 239–241. Edited by Jason P. Rosenblatt and Joseph C. Sitterson, Jr. Indiana Studies in Biblical Literature. Bloomington & Indianapolis: Indiana University Press, 1991.

741. Bernstein, Moshe J. "Two Multivalent Readings in the Ruth Narrative." *JSOT* 50 (1991), 15–26.

742. Bertman, Stephen. "Symbolic Design in the Book of Ruth." *JBL* 84 (1965), 165–168.

743. Beuken, W. A. M. "I Sam. 28: The Prophet as 'Hammer of the Witches'." *JSOT* 6 (1978), 3–17.

744. —. "No Wise King Without a Wise Woman (1 Kings III, 16–28)." *OTS* 25 (1989), 1–10.

745. Beyerle, Stefan. "Feministische Theologie und alttestamentliche Exegese." *BN* 59 (1991), 7–11.

746. Beylin, Z. "Studies in the Book of Hosea." *BM* 27 (1981/82), 164–167 (in Hebrew).

747. Biale, David. "The God with Breasts: El Shaddai in the Bible." *History of Religions* 20 (1982), 241–256.

748. Biddle, Mark E. "The 'Endangered Ancestress' and the Blessing for Nations." *JBL* 109 (1990), 599–611. Concerns Gen. 12: 10–20; 20: 1–18; 26:1–11

749. Bigger, Stephen F. "The Family Laws of Leviticus 18 in their Setting." *JBL* 98 (1979), 187–203.

750. Bird, Phyllis. "Images of Women in the Old Testament." In *Religion and Sexism*, pp. 41–88. Edited by Rosemary Radford Reuther. New York: Simon & Schuster, 1974.

751. —. "'...,ő ʃ†Δί⟩ °Δ,." *Deltio Biblikon Meleton,* n.s., 1 (1980), 41–59 (in Modern Greek).

752. —. "'Male and Female He Created Them': Gen 1:27b in the Context of the Priestly Account of Creation." *HTR* 74 (1981), 129–159.

753. —. "Genesis I–III as a Source for a Contemporary Theology of Sexuality." *Ex Audito* 3 (1987), 31–44.

754. —. "The Place of Women in the Israelite Cultus." In *Ancient Israelite Religion: Essays in Honor of Frank M. Cross,* pp. 397–419. Edited by Paul D. Hanson, Patrick D. Miller, Jr., and S. Dean McBride. Philadelphia: Fortress, 1987.

755. —. "Translating Sexist Language as a Theological and Cultural Problem." *USQR* 42 (1988), 89–95.

756. —. "The Harlot as Heroine; Narrative Art and Social Presup-

position in Three Old Testament Texts." *Semeia* 46 (1989), 119–140.

757. Black, Edith. "Why Women Cannot be Ordained: Biblical Arguments." *Homiletic and Pastoral Review* 80 (1980), 21–31.

758. Bledstein, Adrien Janis. "The Genesis of Humans: The Garden of Eden Revisited." *Judaism* 20 (1977), 187–200.

759. —. "The Trials of Sarah." *Judaism* 30 (1981), 411–417.

760. —. So J was a woman?" *Sh'ma* 21/407, Feb. 8, 1991, pp. 49–51. Review of Harold Bloom, *The Book of J.*

761. —. "A Feminist Responds to *The Book of J.*" *Lilith* 16 (Summer 1991), 28.

762. Blenkinsopp, J. "The Social Context of the 'Outsider Woman' in Proverbs 1–9." *Biblica* 72 (1991), 457–473.

763. Blondheim, S. H., and Blondheim, Menahem. "The Obstetrical Complication of Benjamin's Birth." *DD* 13 (1984/85), 88–92.

764. Bockel, Pierre. "Les deux rires de Sara: du désespoir à l'amour." *Bible et Terre Sainte* 70 (1965), 17–18.

765. —. "L'Egypte et la Bible de Joseph à l'Exode." *MDB* 41 (Nov.–Dec. 1985), 3.

766. Bohlen, R. "Alttestamentliche Kunstprosa als Zeitkritik." *Trierer Theologische Zeitschrift* 87 (1978), 192–202.

767. Bonora, Antonio. "Jefte sacrifica sua figlia vergine (Gdc 11, 29–40)." *Parola, Spiritue Vita* 12 (1985), 20–30.

768. —. "La via dell' amore in Pr 30, 18–20." *RivB* 35 (1987), 51–55.

769. Booij, Th. "Hagar's Words in Gen XVI 13b." *VT* 30 (1980), 1–7.

770. Borbone, Pier Giorgio. "Il terzo incomodo. L'interpretazione del testo masoretivco di Osea 3, 1." *Henoch* 7 (1985), 151–160.

771. Boss, J. "The Character of Childbirth According to the Bible." *Journal of Obstetrics & Gynaecology* 69 (1962), 508–513.

772. Bossman, David. "Ezra's Marriage Reform: Israel Redefined." *BTB* 9 (1979), 32–38.

773. —. "Kinship and Religious System in the Prophet Malachi." In *Religious Writings and Religious Systems*, vol. 1, pp. 127–141. Edited by Jacob Neusner et al. Atlanta: Scholars Press, 1989.

774. Bottini, G. Claudio. "Gezabele, una figura drammatica." *Terra Santa* 60 (1984), 99–103.

775. Braslavi, Y. "A Bridegroom of Blood (Ex. 4, 26)." *BM* 8 (1963), 108–115 (in Hebrew).

776. —. "Gen. 30:14ff and Ex. 21:10." *BM* 9 (1964), 79–83 (in Hebrew).

777. Bratcher, R. G. "A Study of Isaiah 7:14." *Bible Translator* 9 (1958), 97–126.

778. Bravmann, M. M. "Concerning the Phrase '. . . and shall cleave unto his wife' (Gen 2. 24)." *Muséon* 85 (1972), 269–274.

779. Brennan, J. P. "Virgin and Child in Is 7, 14." *TBT* 1 (1964), 968–974.

780. Brenner, A. B. "Onan, the levirate marriage and the genealogy of the Messiah." *Journal of the American Psychoanalytic Association* 10 (1962), 701–721.

781. Brenner, Athalya. "Esther Through the Looking Glass" *BM* 86 (1981), 267–278 (in Hebrew).

782. —. "My Beloved is Fair and Ruddy: On the Song of Songs 5: 10–11." *BM* 89 (1982), 168–173 (in Hebrew).

783. —. "Aromatics and Perfumes in the Song of Songs." *JSOT* 25 (1983), 75–81.

784. —. "Jezebel." *SHNATON* 5–6 (1983), 27–39 (in Hebrew).

785. —. "Naomi and Ruth." *VT* 33 (1983), 387–397.

786. —. "Biblical Attitudes Toward Foreign Women and Exogamic Marriages." *BM* 30 (1984), 179–185 (in Hebrew).

787. —. "Female Social Behaviour: Two Descriptive Patterns within 'The Birth of the Hero' Paradigm." *VT* 36 (1986), 257–273.

788. —. "Self Denial as a Means for Self Assertion: On the Social Situation of Women in Ancient Israel." *Mara: A Journal for Feminism and Theology* 2 (1988), 19–30 (in Hebrew).

789. —. "'Come Back, Come Back the Shulammite' (The Song of Songs 7.1–10): A Parady of the *wasf* Genre." In *On Humour and the Comic in the Hebrew Bible,* pp. 275–293. Edited by Y. T. Radday and A. Brenner. Sheffield: Sheffield Academic Press and Almond Press, 1990.

790. —. "A Triangle and a Rhombus in Narrative Structure: A Proposed Integrative Reading of Judges IV and V." *VT* 40 (1990), 129–137.

791. —. "Qoheleth 3.1–9: A Framed Erotic Poem? In *H. M. Gevariahu Memorial Volume,* pp. 9–23. Edited by B-Z. Luria. Jerusalem: The Israel Society of Biblical Research, 1990 (in Hebrew).

792. Bressan, G. "Il Cantico di Anna (I) (1 Sam. 2, 1–10)." *JBL* 32 (1951), 503–521.

793. Breyfogle, C. "The Religious Status of Woman in the Old Testament." *Biblical World* 35 (1910), 405–419.

794. —. "The Social Status of Woman in the Old Testament." *Biblical World* 35 (1910), 107–116. She explains (p. 107) that she was motivated to explore this question by "the present movement of woman for equality."

795. Brichto, Herbert Chanan. "The Case of the Sota and Biblical Law." *HUCA* 46 (1975), 55–70.

796. Briend, J. "Contexte biblique: Joseph." *MDB* 41 (Nov.–Dec. 1985), 28–30.

797. Briggs, Belinda M. "The Bible Estimate of Woman." *Methodist Review* 103 (1920), 879–896.

798. Brin, Gershon. "Mother's First Born and Father's First Born in the Bible." In *Ben-Zion Lurie Festschrift,* pp. 31–50. Edited by Y. Avishur et al. Jerusalem: Israel Society for Biblical Research, 1979 (in Hebrew).

799. Broadrib, D. "Thoughts on the Song of Solomon." *Abr-Naharain* 3 (1961/62), 11–36.

800. Brock, Sebastian. "Genesis 22: Where Was Sarah?" *Expository Times* 96 (1984), 14–17.

801. Brodie, Louis. "The Children and the Prince: The Structure, Nature and Date of Isaiah 6–12." *BTB* 9 (1979), 27–31.

802. Bronner, Leila Leah. "Gynomorphic Imagery in Exilic Isaiah." *DD* 12 (1983/84), 71–83; also published in *South African Judaica* 1 (1984), 21–39.

803. Bronznick, Norman M. "More on *hlk 'el* ." *VT* 35 (1985), 98–99 Am. 2:7; also *b' 'l* ; Gen. 16:2; 30:3; 38:8; 2 Sam. 16:21

804. Brooks, B. S. "Fertility Cult Functionaries in the Old Testament." *JBL* 60 (1941), 227–253.

805. Brown, John Pairman. "The Role of Women and the Treaty in the Ancient World." *BZ* 25 (1981), 1–28.

806. —. "The Mediterranean Seer and Shamanism." *ZAW* 93 (1981), 399. The necromancer at En-Dor (1 Sam. 28)

807. Brueggemann, W. "Of the Same Flesh and Bone." *CBQ* 32 (1970), 532–542. Concerns Gen. 2.

808. —. "Israel's Social Criticism and Yahweh's Sexuality." *JAAR* 45 (1977), 349.

809. —. "Will our faith have children? Will our children have faith?" *Word & World* 3 (1983), 272–283. Gen. 11:30; Isa. 54:1–3; Jer. 31:15

810. Bruin, Elizabeth. "Judaism and Womanhood." *Westminster Review* 180 (1913), 125–132.

811. Brunet, Gilbert. "L'hébreu keleb." *VT* 35 (1985), 485–488. Deut. 23:19.

812. Bruppacher, Hans. "Die Bedeutung des Namens Ruth." *TZ* 22 (1960), 12–18.

813. Bryce, Mary Charles. "Ruth: For a Beginning." *TBT* 20 (1982), 209–214.

814. Burden, J. J. "'n 'Prostituut' doen reg; die Juda-Tamar-verhaal." *Theologica Evangelica* 13 (1980), 42–52. Gen. 38

815. Burns, Dan E. "Dream Form in Genesis 2.4b–3.24: Asleep in the Garden." *JSOT* 37 (1987), 3–14.

816. Burrows, Millar. "The Complaint of Laban's Daughters." *JAOS* 57 (1937), 259–276.

817. —. "The Ancient Oriental Background of Hebrew Levirate Marriage." *BASOR*, no. 77 (1940), 2–15.

818. —. "Levirate Marriage in Israel." *JBL* 59 (1940), 23–33.

819. —. "The Marriage of Boaz and Ruth." *JBL* 59 (1940), 445–454.

820. Buxenbaum, Yaakov. "Shear-Yashub (On Isaiah 7–8)." *BM* 33 (1987/88), 35–50 (in Hebrew). Terms for "have sex"; "be barren"; 1 Sam. 8:3.

821. Cades, J. "La femme dans l'Ancient Testament." *RSR* 12 (1922), 115–116.

822. Cady, D. R. "The Biblical Position of Woman." *Congregational Quarterly* 12 (1870), 370–377.

823. Callaway, Phillip R. "Deut. 21:18–21: Proverbial Wisdom and Law." *JBL* 103 (1984), 341–352.

824. Camp, Claudia V. "The Wise Women of 2 Samuel: A Role Model for Women in Early Israel." *CBQ* 43 (1981), 14–29.

825. —. "Female Voice, Written Word: Women and Authority in Hebrew Scripture." In *Embodied Love: Sensuality and Relationship as Feminist Values,* pp. 97–113. Edited by Paula M. Cooey, Sharon A. Farmer, and Mary Ellen Ross. San Francisco: Harper & Row, 1987.

826. —. "Woman Wisdom as Root Metaphor: A Theological Consideration." In *The Listening Heart. Essays in Wisdom and the Psalms in Honor of Roland E. Murphy, O Carm,* pp. 45–76. Edited by Kenneth G. Hoglund, et al. JSOT Supplementary Series, no. 58. Sheffield: JSOT Press, 1987.

827. —. "Wise and Strange: An Interpretation of the Female Imagery in Proverbs in Light of Trickster Mythology." *Semeia* 42 (1988), 14–36.

828. —. "The Female Sage in Ancient Israel and in the Biblical Wisdom Literature." In *The Sage in Israel and the Ancient Near East,* pp. 185–203. Edited by John G. Gammie and Leo G. Perdue. Winona Lake: Eisenbrauns, 1990.

829. Campbell, Antony. "The Old Testament and Women Today." *Compass* 15 (1981), 1–9.

830. Campbell, E. F., Jr. "Moses and the Foundation of Israel." *Interpretation* 29 (1975), 141–151.

831. Campbell, K. M. "Rahab's Covenant; a short note on Joshua 2:9–21." *VT* 22 (1972), 243–244.

832. Campbell, T. "Eve, Esther, Ruth, Rebecca, Mary, Martha. . . ." *U S Catholic* 40 (Nov. 1975), 32–34.

833. Cañellas, Gabriel. "El celibato en el Antiguo Testamento." *Biblia y Fe* 5 (1979), 241–253.

834. —. "El Magnificat, origen y mensaje." *Biblia y Fe* 9 (1983), 229–237.

835. Carmichael, Calum M. "A Ceremonial Crux: Removing a Man's Sandal as a Female Gesture of Contempt." *JBL* 96 (1977), 321–336.

836. —. "A Common Element in Five Supposedly Disparate Laws." *VT* 29 (1979), 129–142.

837. —. "'Treading' in the Book of Ruth." *ZAW* 92 (1980), 248–266.

838. —. "Forbidden Mixtures." *VT* 32 (1982), 394–415.

839. Carmo, José Manuel Sanchez. "Esdras, Nemias y los origenes del judaismo." *Salamanticensis* 32 (1985), 5–34.

840. Carmody, J. "Lessons of Hosea 1–3." *TBT* 40 (1969), 2773–2778.

841. Carr, G. Lloyd. "Is the Song of Songs a 'Sacred Marriage Drama'?" *Journal of the Evangelical Theology Society* 22 (1979), 103–114.

842. Carroll, Michael P. "Myth, Methodology, and Transformation in the Old Testament: The Stories of Esther, Judith, and Susanna." *SR* 12 (1983), 301–312.

843. Cartledge, Tony W. "Were Nazirite Vows Unconditional?" *CBQ* 51 (1989), 409–422.

844. Caspi, Mishael. "Who Makes the Barren Housewife a Joyful Mother of Children." *BM* 25 (1980), 365–366 (in Hebrew).

845. —. "The Story of the Rape of Dinah: The Narrator and the Reader." *Hebrew Studies* 26 (1985), 25–45.

846. —. "I have *qnh* a Man with the Lord." *BM* 33 (1987/88), 29–35 (in Hebrew).

847. Castelnuovo, A. "Evoluzione psicologica di Ester." *Rassegna mensile di Israel* 43 (1977), 92–111.

848. Cavalcanti, Tereza. "The Prophetic Ministry of Women in the Hebrew Bible." In *Through Her Eyes: Women's Theology from Latin America*, pp. 118–139. Edited by Elsa Tamez. Maryknol, N.Y.: Orbis, 1989.

849. Cazelles, H. "Fille de Sion et theologie mariale dans la Bible." *Bulletin de la Société Française d'Etudes Mariales* 21 (1964), 51–74.

850. —. "La maternité royale dans l'Ancien Testament." *MDB* 32 (Jan–Feb 1984), 3–4.

851. Chamberlayne, John H. "Kinship Relations Among the Early Hebrews." *Numen* 10 (1963), 159.

852. Charbel. Antonio. "Gen 2, 18.20: Una polemica sottintesa dello Jahvista." *Bibbia e Oriente* 22 (1980), 233–235.

853. Chesire, J. Blunt, Jr. "Jael the Wife of Heber the Kenite." *Protestant Episcopal Review* 2 (1888–1889), 277–284.

854. Chotzner, J. "On the Life and Social Position of Hebrew Women in Biblical Times." *SBAP* 6 (1883–1884), 137.

855. Christ, Carol P. "Heretics and Outsiders: The Struggle Over Female Power in Western Religion." *Soundings* 61 (1978), 260–280.

856. Christenson, Duane L. "Huldah and the Men of Anatoth." In *Society of Biblical Literature 1984 Seminar Papers*, pp. 399–404. Edited by K. H. Richards. Chico, California: Scholars Press, 1984.

857. Clark, David J. "Sex-related Imagery in the Prophets." *Bible Translator* 33 (1982), 409–413.

858. —. "The perils of pictures." *Bible Translator* 34 (1983), 440–441. Zech. 5:7

859. Clarkson, Shannon. "Laughing About God." *SR* 18 (1989), 38–49.

860. Clines, David J. A. "Hosea 2: Structure and Interpretation." In *Studia Biblica 1978 I. Papers on Old Testament and Related Themes*, pp. 83–103. JSOT Supplement Series, no. 11. Sheffield: JSOT Press, 1979.

861. —. "Story and Poem: The Old Testament as Literature and as Scripture." *Interpretation* 34 (1980), 115–127.

862. —. "Reading Esther from Left to Right: Contemporary Strategies for Reading a Biblical Text." In *The Bible in Three Dimensions. Essays in Celebration of the Fourtieth Anniversary of the Department of Biblical Studies, University of Sheffield*, pp. 31–52. Edited by David J. A. Clines, Stephen C. Fowl, and Stanley E. Porter. JSOT Supplements, no. 87. Sheffield: JSOT Press, 1990.

863. Coats, G. W. "Widow's Rights; A Crux in the Structure of Genesis 38." *CBQ* 34 (1972), 461–466.

864. —. "Critical Comments: On Narrative Criticism." *Semeia* 3 (1975), 139–140. Hagar; Gen. 16; 21

865. —. "Parables, Fables and Anecdotes: Storytelling in the Succession Narrative." *Interpretation* 35 (1981), 368–382.

866. —. "A Threat to the Host." In *Saga, Legend, Tale, Novella, Fable: Narrative Forms in Old Testament Literature,* pp. 71–81. Edited by George W. Coats. JSOT Supplements, no. 35. Sheffield: JSOT Press, 1985. Gen. 12:10–20; 20:1–18; 26:1–16

867. —. II Samuel 12:17a." *Interpretation* 40 (1986), 170–175.

868. Cogan, Mordechai. "'Ripping Open Pregnant Women' in Light of an Assyrian Analogue." *JAOS* 103 (1983), 755–757. Am. 1:13

869. —. "The Expulsion of Ishmael—No Laughing Matter." *Conservative Judaism* 41, no. 2 (1988), 29–33.

870. Coggins, Richard. "The Contribution of Women's Studies to Old Testament Studies: A Male Reaction." *Theology (London)* 91 (1988), 5–16.

871. Cohen, Chayim. "The 'Widowed' City." *JANES* 5 (1973), 75–81.

872. —. "The Semantic Range of the Terms ʾamâ and *šipĕḥâ.*" SHNATON 5–6 (1978/79), XXV–LIII.

873. —. "Jewish Medieval Commentary on the Book of Genesis and Modern Biblical Philology Part I: Gen. 1–18." *JQR* 81 (1990), 1–11. Includes discussion of Gen. 18, 10, 14

874. Cohen, D. "But His Father Called Him Benjamin." *BM* 23 (1978), 239–41 (in Hebrew).

875. Cohen, G. H. "The Names in the Book of Ruth." *Amsterdamse Cahiers voor Exegese en Bijbelse Theologie* 1 (1980), 62–75.

876. Cohen, H. H. "David and Bathsheba." *Journal of Bible and Religion* 23 (1965), 142–148.

877. Cohen, M. "*Maqṭîrôt ûmezabbeḥôt lēhlōhêhen* (1 Rois X 8b)." *VT* 41 (1991), 332–341.

878. Cohen, Shaye J. D. "From the Bible to the Talmud: The Prohibition of Intermarriage." *HAR* 7 (1983), 23–29.

879. —. "Solomon and the Daughter of Pharaoh: Intermarriage, Conversion, and the Impurity of Women." *JANES* 16–17 (1984–85), 23–37.

880. Cohn, Robert L. "Form and Perspective in 2 Kings V." *VT* 33 (1983), 171–184.

881. Collins, Adela Yarboro. "An Inclusive Biblical Anthropology." *Theology Today* 34 (1977), 358–369.

882. Collins, Raymond F. "The Bible and Sexuality." *BTB* 7 (1977), 149–167; 8 (1978), 3–18.

883. Conzelmann, Hans. "The Mother of Wisdom." In *The Future of Our Religious Past,* pp. 230–243. Edited by J. A. Robinson. New York: Harper & Row, 1971.

884. Coogan, Michael David. "A Structural and Literary Analysis of the Song of Deborah." *CBQ* 40 (1978), 143–166.

885. Cook, Johann. "Hannah and/or Elkanah on their way home (1 Sm 2:11): A Witness to the Complexity of the Tradition History of the Samuel Texts." *Old Testament Essays (Journal of the Old Testament Society of South Africa)* 3 (1990–), 247–262.

886. Cooper, Alan. "The Euphemism in Numbers 12:12—A Study in the History of Interpretation." *JJS* 32 (1981), 56–64.

887. —. "A Note on the Vocalization of Ashtoreth." *ZAW* 102 (1990), 98–100.

888. Cooper, Alan, and Goldstein, Bernard R. "Biblical Literature in the Iron(ic) Age: Reflections on Literary-Historical Method." *Hebrew Studies* 32 (1991), 45–60. Review article concerning Harold Bloom, *The Book of J;* deals with larger issues concerning women in ancient Israel.

889. Copher, C. B. "Blacks and Jews in Historical Interaction." *Journal of the Interdenominational Research Center* 3 (1975), 9–16. Moses and the Cushite woman; Num. 12:1.

890. Coppens, J. "La soumission de la femme à l'homme d'après Gen. 3, 16b." *ETL* 14 (1937), 632–640.

891. —. "La Prophétie d'Emmanuel." *Recherches bibliques, L'Atteinte du Messie,* 1954, 39–50.

892. —. "La Prophétie de la 'Almah (Is VII, 14–17)." *ETL* 28 (1954), 648–678.

893. —. "La nudité des protoplastes." *ETL* 46 (1970), 380–383.

894. Cortese, Enzo. "La nudità in Lv 18 e 20." *Parola Spirito e Vita* 20 (1989), 53–62.

895. Costas, Orlando E. "The Subversiveness of Faith: Esther as a Paradigm for Liberating Theology." *Ecumenical Review* 40 (1988), 66–78.

896. Couroyer, Bernard. "La tablette du coeur." *RB* 90 (1983), 416–434.

897. Couturier, Guy. "Débora: une autorité politoco-religieuse aux origines d'Israël." *SR* 18 (1989), 213–228.

898. Cowling, G. "Women in the Old Testament." *Ancient Society* 9 (1979), 96–115.

899. Coxon, Peter W. "A Note on 'Bathsheba' in 2 Samuel 12, 1–6." *Biblica* 62 (1981), 247–250.

900. —. "Was Naomi a Scold?" *JSOT* 45 (1989), 25–37.

901. Craghan, John F. "Esther, Judith, and Ruth: Paradigm for Human Liberation." *BTB* 12 (1982), 11–19.

902. —. "Esther: A Fully Liberated Woman." *TBT* 24 (1986), 6–11.

903. Craigie, Peter C. "Deborah and Anat: A Study of Poetic Imagery." *ZAW* 90 (1978), 374–381.

904. —. "Psalm 113." *Interpretation* 39 (1985), 70–74.

905. Crane, T. "God and the Woman." *TBT* 66 (1973), 1195–2000.

906. Craven, Toni. "Women Who Lied for the Faith." In *Justice and the Holy. Essays in Honor of Walter Harrelson,* pp. 35–49. Edited by Douglas A. Knight and Peter J. Paris. Atlanta: Scholars Press, 1989.

907. Crawley, Joann. "Faith of Our Mothers: The Dark Night of Sara, Rebekah, and Rachel." *Review for Religious* 45 (1986), 531–537.

908. Crenshaw, James L. "Education in Ancient Israel." *JBL* 104 (1985), 601–615.

909. —. "A Mother's Instruction to Her Son (Proverbs 31:1–9)." In *Perspectives on the Hebrew Bible: Essays in Honor of Walter J. Harrelson*, pp. 9–22. Edited by James L. Crenshaw. Macon, GA.: Mercer University Press, 1988.

910. Criado, R. "La mujer en el AT." *Miscelánea de Estudias Arabes y Hebráicos* 11 (1962), 19–42.

911. Croce, Lucia. "La *niddâ* nel pensiero biblico e mišnico." *Egitto e Vicino Oriente* 6 (1983), 235–245 Lev. 15:19–25; menstruation

912. Crocker, P. T. "Apothecaries, Confectionaries, and a New Discovery at Qumran." *Buried History* 25 (1989), 36–46. Discusses the use of perfumes in Hebrew Scripture

913. Croix-Rosse, Andre de la. "La femme au temps des Juges." *Bible et Vie Chrétienne* 1 (1953), 40–50.

914. Crook, Margaret B. "The Marriageable Maiden of Prov. 31:10–31." *JNES* 13 (1954), 137–140.

915. Cropp, Johannes. "Die Perikope von Canaanäischen Weibe." *Theologische Studien und Kritiken* 43 (1870), 125–134.

916. Cross, Earle Bennett. "Traces of the Matronymic Family in the Hebrew Social Organization." *Biblical World* 36 (1910), 407–414.

917. Cross, Frank M., Jr., and Freedman, David Noel. "The Song of Miriam." *JNES* 14 (1955), 237–250.

918. Cross, Nancy. "Those Poor Misquoted Scriptures." *Homiletic and Pastoral Review,* 84, no. 10 (1986), 57–60.

919. Cruveilhier, P. "Le levirat chez les hebreux et chez les assyriens." *RB* 34 (1925), 524–546.

920. —. "Les droit de la femme dans la Genèse et dans le receuil de lois assyriennes." *RB* 36 (1927), 350–376.

921. Cunchillos, J. L. "Los běne ha'elohîm en Gen 6, 1–4." *Est Bib* 28 (1969), 5–31.

922. Curtis, A. H. "Marriage in the Bible and the Early Christian Church." *Expository Times* 59 (1947), 42–44.

923. Danelius, Eva. "Shamgar Ben 'Anath." *JNES* 22 (1963), 191–193.

924. Daniélou, J. "Rahab, figure de l'Église." *Irénikon* 22 (1949), 26–45.

925. —. "La typologie de la femme dans l'Ancien Testament." *La Vie Spirituelle* 80 (1949), 491–510.

926. Darr, Kathryn Pfisterer. "Like Warrior, Like Woman: Destruction and Deliverance in Isaiah 42:10–17." *CBQ* 49 (1987), 560–571.

927. Davidson, Richard M. "The Theology of Sexuality in the Beginning: Genesis 1–2." *AUSS* 26 (1986), 5–24.

928. —. "The Theology of Sexuality in the Beginning: Genesis 3." *AUSS* 26 (1988), 121–131.

929. —. "The Theology of Sexuality in the Song of Songs: Return to Eden." *AUSS* 27 (1989), 1–12.

930. Davies, Eryl N. "Inheritance Rights and the Hebrew Levirate Marriage." Part 1. *VT* 31 (1981), 138–44; Part 2. *VT* 31 (1981), 257–268.

931. —. "Ruth IV 5 and the Duties of the Go'el." *VT* 33 (1983), 231–234.

932. Davis, M. Stephen. "Polygamy in the Ancient World." *Biblical Illustrator* 14 (1987), 34–36.

933. Davis, Steve. "Stories of the Fall in the Ancient Near East." *Biblical Illustrator* 13 (1986), 36–40.

934. De Pury, A. "Genèse XXXIV et l'histoire." *RB* 71 (1969), 5–49.

935. Deem, Ariella. "The Goddess Anath and Some Biblical Hebrew Cruces." *JSS* 23 (1978), 25–30.

936. —. "Cupboard Love: The Story of Amnon and Tamar." *Ha-Sifrut* 8 (1979), 100–107 (in Hebrew).

937. —. "The Great Woman of Shunem." In *Proceedings of the Eighth World Congress of Jewish Studies, Divison A*, pp. 21–25. Jerusalem: World Union of Jewish Studies, 1982.

938. Del Olmo Lete, Gregorio. "'ʾaḥar šillûḥèā' (Ex 18,2)." *Biblica* 51 (1970), 414–416.

939. Delcor, M. "Astarte et la fecondité des troupeaux en Deut. 7:13 et parallèles." *UF* 6 (1974), 1–5.

940. —. "La vision de la femme dans l'Epha de Zach. 5:5–11 a la lumière de la litterature hittite." *RHR* 187 (1975), 137–145.

941. —. "Allusions à la déesse en Nahum 2, 8." *Biblica* 58 (1977), 73–83.

942. —. "Le culte de la 'Reine du Ciel' selon Jer 7, 18; 44, 17–19.25 et son survivances." In *Von Kanaan bis Kerala*, pp. 101–122. Edited by W. C. Delsman et al. AOAT 211. Kevaler: Butzon & Bercker/Neukirchen-Vluyn: Neukirchener Verlag, 1982.

943. DeMerv, I. "La creation de la femme." *Bible et Vie Chretienne* 28 (1959), 9–13.

944. Dempster, Stephen G. "Mythology and History in the Song of Deborah." *Westminster Theological Journal* 41 (1978), 33–53.

945. Deroche, Michael. "Israel's 'Two Evils' in Jeremiah II 13." *VT* 31 (1981), 369–372. Discusses well as symbol for wife in Jer., Prov., and Cant.

946. —. "Structure, Rhetoric, and Meaning in Hosea IV 4–10." *VT* 33 (1983), 185–198.

947. Derret, J. D. M. "The Disposal of Virgins." *Man* 9 (1974), 23–30.

948. Deuerloo, K. A. "After God's Likeness: Male and Female (Gen. 5:2, 3; 1:27)." *Amsterdamse Cahiers voor Exegese en Bijbelese Theologie* 6 (1985), 36–42.

949. —. "TŠWQH 'dependency,' Gen 4, 7." *ZAW* 99 (1987), 405–406.

950. —. "Die Gefährdung der Ahnfrau (Gen 20)." *DBAT* 25 (1988), 17–27.

951. —. "The King's Wisdom in Judgment: Narration as Example (I Kings III)." *OTS* 25 (1989), 11–21.

952. Diamond, J. A. "The Deception of Jacob. A New Perspective on an Ancient Solution of the Problem." *VT* 34 (1984), 211–213. Rachel and Leah

953. Diebner, B. J. "Deborahs Tod 35, 8: 'schwierig' und 'unverständlich'?" *DBAT* 25 (1988), 172–184.

954. —. "... er hatte sich nämlich ein kuschitische Frau genommen (Num 12, 1)." *DBAT* 25 (1988), 74–79.

955. —. "For He Had Married a Cushite Woman." *Nubica* I/II (1990), 499–504.

956. Diebner, B., and Schult, H. "Die Ehen der Erzväter." *DBAT* 8 (1975), 2–10.

957. Diest, Ferdinand. "Prov. 31:1—A Case of Constant Mistranslation." *JNSL* 6 (1978), 1–3. The mother of Lemuel

958. Dijk-Hemmes, Fokkelien Van. "Als H/hij tot haar hart spreekt. Een visie op (visies op) Hosea 2." In *Door het oog van de tekst. essays voor Mieke Bal over visie*, pp. 121–139. Edited by Ernst van Alphen and Irene de Jong. Muiderberg: Continuo, 1988.

959. —. "The Imagination of Power and the Power of Imagination." *JSOT* 44 (1989), 75–88. Cant.; Hos. 2.

960. Dion, Paul, E., O.P. "Did Cultic Prostitution Fall into Oblivion During the Poxtexilic Era? Some Evidence from Chronicles and the Septuagint." *CBQ* 43 (1981), 41–48.

961. Dohmen, Christoph. "Das Immanuelzeichen. Ein jesajanisches Drohwort und seine inneralttestamentliche Rezeption." *Biblica* 68 (1987), 305–329.

962. Domeris, W. R. "Biblical Perspectives on the Role of Women." *Journal of Theology for Southern Africa* 55 (1986), 58–61.

963. Donaldson, Mara E. "Kinship Theory in the Patriarchal Narratives: The Case of the Barren Wife." *JAAR* 49 (1981), 77–87.

964. Donner, H. "Art und Herkunft der Königinmutter im Alten Testament." In *Festschrift Johannes Friedrich zum 65. Geburtstag*, pp. 105–145. Heidelberg: Winter, 1959.

965. Dresner, Samuel. "Rachel and Leah: Sibling Tragedy or the Triumph of Piety and Compassion." *Bible Review* 6, no. 1 (1990), 22–27; 40–42.

966. Driver, G. R. "Hebrew Mothers (Exodus 1:19)." *ZAW* 67 (1955), 246–248.

967. Dubarle, A.-M. "L'amour humain dans le Cantique des Cantiques." *RB* 61 (1954), 67–86.

968. —. "Amour et fécondité dans la Bible." *Recherches et Débats* 43 (1963), 105–121.

969. —. "Les chromosomes, Adam et Eve: un nouveau concordisme." *Revue de sciences philosophiques et théologiques* 61 (1977), 429–436.

970. —. "Le jugement de Salomon: un coeur à l'écoute." *Revue de sciences philosophiques et théologiques* 63 (1979), 419–427.

971. Duman, Marcel. "Language sexiste et traductions de la Bible." *Eglise et théologie* 19/2 (1988), 241–253.

972. Dumas, A. "Similitude et diversitédes sexes dans le plan de Dieu." *Etudes et Recherches* 40 (1965), 97–108.

973. Dumbrell, W. J. "The Role of Women: A Reconsideration of the Biblical Evidence." *Interchange* 4 (1977), 14–22.

974. Dus, Jan. "Die Geburtslegende Samuels I Sam. 1." *RSO* 43 (1968), 163–194.

975. Duvshani, M. "The Images of Women and Children in Isaiah and Jeremiah." *BM* 22 (1967), 83–93 (in Hebrew).

976. —. "Artistic Traits in the Stories about Samuel's Birth and the Crowning of Saul (I Sam 1 and 6–9)." *BM* 26 (1981), 362–369 (in Hebrew).

977. Eakins, J. Kenneth. "Anthropomorphisms in Isaiah 40–55." *Hebrew Studies* 20/21 (1979–80), 47–50.

978. Ehrlich, Z. H. "The Inheritance of Hoglah, Daughter of Zelophehad." *BM* 28 (1982/83), 232–235 (in Hebrew).

979. Ellington, John. "Man and Adam in Genesis 1–5." *Bible Translator* 30 (1979), 201–205.

980. —. "Miscarriage or Premature Birth." *Bible Translator* 37 (1986), 334–337. Concerning Ex. 21:22ff.

981. Ellis, Bob R. "An Annotated Bibliography for the Book of Malachi." *Southwestern Journal of Theology* 30 (1987), 48–49.

982. Ellison, H. L. "The Meaning of Hosea in the Light of His Marriage." *Evangelical Quarterly* 41 (1969), 3–9.

983. Emanueli, Moshe. "Dinah, Leah's Daughter" *BM* 17 (1972), 442–450 (in Hebrew).

984. —. "Tamar, Judah's Wife (Gen. 38): *BM* 18 (1972), 25–32 (in Hebrew).

985. —. "Abraham, Sarah, and Hagar." *BM* 20 (1974), 554–561 (in Hebrew).

986. —. "The Sons of God Took Wives Whomever They Chose (Gen. 6, 1–4)." *BM* 20 (1974), 150–152; 165–166 (in Hebrew).

987. Emerton, J. A. "Some Problems in Genesis XXXVIII." *VT* 25 (1975), 357–360.

988. —. "An Examination of a Recent Structuralist Interpretation of Gen. 38." *VT* 26 (1976), 79–98.

989. —. "Judah and Tamar." *VT* 29 (1979), 403–415.

990. Emmerson, G. I. "Women in Ancient Israel." In *The World of Ancient Israel,* pp. 371–394. Edited by R. E. Clements. Cambridge, Eng.: Cambridge University Press, 1989.

991. Engar, Ann. W. "Old Testament Women as Tricksters." *Bucknell Review,* vol. 33, pt. 2 (1990), 143–157.

992. Escudero, M. "El matrimonio, Figura de la Alianza den los Profetas." *Revista Teologica Limense* 6 (1972), 49–71.

993. Eslinger, Lyle. "A Contextual Identification of the *bene ha'elohim* and *benoth ha'adam* in Genesis 6:1–4." *JSOT* 13 (1979), 65–73.

994. —. "The Case of an Immodest Lady Wrestler in Deuteronomy XXV 11–12." *VT* 31 (1981), 269–281.

995. —. "More Drafting Techniques in Deuteronomic Laws." *VT* 34 (1984), 221–226.

996. Exum, J. Cheryl. "Promise and Fulfillment: Narrative Art in Judges 13." *JBL* 99 (1980), 43–59.

997. —. "'You Shall Let Every Daughter Live': A Study of Exodus 1:8–2:10." *Semeia* 28 (1983), 63–82.

998. —. "The Mothers of Israel: The Patriarchal Narratives from a Feminist Perspective." *Bible Review,* vol. 2, no. 1 (1986), 60–67.

999. —. "Murder They Wrote: Ideology and the Manipulation of Female Presence in Biblical Narrative." *USQR* 43 (1989), 19–39.

1000. —. "The Tragic Vision and Biblical Narrative: The Case of Jephthah." *Semeia* 34 (1989), 59–83.

1001. Exum, J. Cheryl, and Whedbee, J. William. "Isaac, Samson, and Saul: Reflections on the Comic and Tragic Visions." *Semeia* 32 (1984), 5–40.

1002. Eybers, I. H. "The Matrimonial Life of Moses." *Ou-Testamentiese Werkgemeenskap in Suid-Afrika* 5 (1964/65), 11–34.

1003.   —. "The Matrimonial Life of Hosea." *Ou-Testamentiese Werkgemeenskap in Suid-Afrika* 7 (1966) 11–34.

1004.   Eynde, Pierre van den. "Le mystere d'Anne, la sterile." *Bible et Vie Chrétienne* 34 (1960), 29–37.

1005.   Fabretti, N. "La Terre Sainte, terre des femmes." *Terre Sainte* 5 (1973), 166–167.

1006.   Falasca, M. "L'instituto matrimoniale premosaico nella Sacra Scrittura." *Euntes Docete* 18 (1965), 381–422.

1007.   Falk, Z. W. "Jeremiah's Marriage." *BM* 15 (1970), 431–440 (in Hebrew).

1008.   —. "Über die Ehe in der biblischen Propheten." *Zeitschrift der Savigny-Stiftung für Rechtsgeschichte Romanistische Abteilung* 90 (1973), 36–44.

1009.   —. "Concerning Marriage in Hosea and Malachi." *BM* 21 (1975), 211–216 (in Hebrew).

1010.   —. "Addenda to *Hebrew Law in Biblical Times*." *Diné Israel* 8 (1977), 33–48.

1011.   Feilschuss-Abir, A. S. "...da werden eure Augen geöffnet und ihr werdet sein wie Gott wissend Gutes und Böses (Gen 3, 5)." *Theologie und Glaube* 74 (1984), 190–203.

1012.   —. "Erschaffung, Bestimmung und Stellung der Frau in der Urgeschichte in anthropologischen Sicht." *Theologie und Glaube* 76 (1986), 399–423.

1013.   Feinberg, Charles L. "The Virgin Birth in the Old Testament and Isaiah 7, 14." *Bibliotheca Sacra* 119 (1962), 251–258.

1014.   Fensham, F. C. "Aspects of Family Law in the Covenant Code in Light of Ancient Near Eastern Parallels." *Diné Israel* 1 (1969), V–XXV.

1015.   —. "The Son of a Handmaid in Northwest Semitic." *VT* 19 (1969), 312–321.

1016.   —. "Genesis XXXIV and Mari." *JNSL* 4 (1975), 71–78.

1017. —. "The Marriage Metaphor in Hosea for the Covenant Relationship Between the Lord and His People (Hos 1:2–9)." *JNSL* 12 (1984), 71–78.

1018. Festorazzi, Franco. "Le Figlie di Lot. Gen 19, 30–38. Valore della vita o vergogna dell'incesto?" *Parola Spirito e Vita* 20 (1989), 33–39.

1019. Feuillet, André. "Dier Sieg der Frau nach dem Protoevangelium." *Internationale Katholische Zeitschrift* 7 (1978), 26–35.

1020. —. "Le drama d'amour du Cantique des Cantiques remis en son contexte prophétique." *Nova et Vetera 63* (1988), 81–136.

1021. Fewell, Danna Nolan. "Feminist Reading of the Hebrew Bible: Affirmation, Resistance, and Transformation." *JSOT* 39 (1987), 77–87.

1022. Fewell, Danna Nolan, and Gunn, David M. "Is Coxon a Scold? On Responding to the Book of Ruth." *JSOT* 45 (1989), 39–43.

1023. Fewell, Danna Nolan, and Gunn, David M. "Controlling Perspectives: Women, Men, and the Authority of Violence in Judges 4 and 5." *JAAR 58* (1990), 389–411.

1024. Fewell, Danna Nolan, and Gunn, David M. "Tipping the Balance: Sternberg's Reader and the Rape of Dinah." *JBL* 110 (1991), 193–211.

1025. Firestone-Seghi, Laya. "Ruth's Story: Renewal of the Feminine." *Reconstructionist* 49, no. 7 (1983), 11–15, 26.

1026. Fisch, A. H. "A Structuralist Approach to the Stories of Ruth and Boaz." *BM* 24 (1979), 260–265 (in Hebrew).

1027. Fisch, Harold. "Ruth and the Structure of Covenant History." *VT* 32 (1982), 425–437.

1028. Fischer, Alexander. "David und Batseba. Ein literarkritischer und motivgeschichtlicher Beitrag zu II Sam. 11." *ZAW* 101 (1989), 50–59.

1029.   Fischer, Georg. "Die Redewegung *dibber 'al leb* im AT—Ein
        Beitrag zum Verständnis von Jes 40, 2." *Biblica* 65 (1984),
        244–250.

1030.   Fishbane, M. "Accusations of Adultery: A Study of Law and
        Scribal Practice in Numbers 5:11–31." *HUCA* 45 (1974),
        25–45.

1031.   Fisher, Eugene. "Cultic Prostitution in the Ancient Near
        East: A Reassessment." *BTB* 6 (1976), 229–236.

1032.   Fitzgerald, Aloysius. "The Mythological Background for the
        Presentation of Jerusalem as a Queen and False Worship
        as Adultery in the Old Testament." *CBQ* 34 (1972), 403–
        416.

1033.   Florentin-Smyth, Françoise. "Ce que la Bible ne doit pas de
        la femme." *Les Etudes Théologiques et Religieuses* 40
        (1965), 75–89.

1034.   Flügge, P. "Lamechs Tochter Naema." *ZAW* 62 (1950), 314.

1035.   Flusser, D. "'Do not commit adultery,' 'do not murder'."
        Textus 4 (1964), 220–224.

1036.   Foh, Susan T. "What Is the Woman's Desire?" *Westminster
        Theological Journal* 37 (1975), 376–383. Interpretation of
        Gen. 3:16; 4:7

1037.   Follis, Elaine R. "The Holy City as Daughter." In *Directions
        in Biblical Hebrew Poetry*, pp. 173–184. JSOT Supple-
        ments, vol. 40. Edited by Elaine R. Follis. Sheffield: JSOT
        Press, 1987.

1038.   Fontaine, Carole. "The Bearing of Wisdom on the Shape of 2
        Samuel 11–12 and 1 Kings 3." *JSOT* 34 (1986), 61–77.

1039.   Fox, Michael V. "Love, Passion, and Perception in Israelite
        and Egyptian Love Poetry." *JBL* 102 (1983), 219–228.

1040.   —. "Scholia to Canticles." *VT* 33 (1983), 199–206.

1041.   Franklin, Cecil L. "Sexuality and Gender in the Bible." *Iliff
        Review* 35, no. 2 (1978), 19–27.

1042. Franklin, Paul. "The Sayings of Agur in Proverbs 30: Piety or Scepticism?" *ZAW* 95 (1983), 239–252.

1043. Fransen, P.-I. "L'hégire d'Agar, fuite ou appel?" *Bible et Terra Sainte* 141 (1982), 5–7.

1044. Franson, Frederik. "Prophesying Daughters." *Covenant Quarterly* 34 (Nov. 1976), 21–40

1045. Freedman, David Noel. "Psalm 113 and the Song of Hannah." *EI* 14 (1978), 56–69.

1046. Freedman, R. David. "Woman, A Power Equal to Man." *BAR* 9, no. 1 (1983), 56–58.

1047. Frieden, Abtei Maria. "Die Jungfraulichkeit in der Heiligen Schrift." *Erbe und Auftrag* 54 (1978), 133–144; 217–255.

1048. Friedman, Joni. "Miriam the Prophetess: A Feminist Perspective." *Philadelphia Jewish Exponent*, Friday Forum, April 26, 1974.

1049. Friedman, Mordechai A. "Israel's Response in Hosea 2:17b: 'You are my Husband'." *JBL* 99 (1980), 199–204.

1050. Friedman, Norman. "Esther hamalka, the Royal Mistress and Mordecai Hayehudi, the Jewish Judge." *DD* 6 (1977), 111–117.

1051. Friedman, Richard Elliot. "Deception for Deception." *Bible Review* 2, no. 1 (1986), 22–31, 68.

1052. —. "Is Everybody a Bible Exegete?" *Bible Review* 7 (April 1991), 16–18, 50–51. Review of Harold Bloom, *The Book of J.*

1053. Friedman, Theodore. "The Shifting Role of Women, From the Bible to the Talmud." *Judaism* 36 (1987), 479–487.

1054. Friedmann, Meir. "Mitwirkung von Frauen beim Gottesdienste." *HUCA* 8–9 (1931–32), 511–523. Discusses women singers in Hebrew Scripture

1055. Frost, Francis. "Homme et femme à l'image de Dieu; signification humaine et chrétienne de la féminité." *Mélanges de Science Religieuse* 38 (1981), 161–176.

1056. Frost, Stanley B. "Judgment on Jezebel, or a Woman Wronged." *Theology Today* 20 (1964), 503–517.

1057. Frotstig-Adler, N. H. "La storia di Jefte." *Annuario di Studi Ebraici* 2 (1964), 9–30.

1058. Frye, Roland M. "Language for God and Feminist Language." *Interpretation* 43 (1989), 45–57.

1059. Frymer-Kensky, Tikva. "Patriarchal Family Relationships and Near Eastern Law." *BA* 44 (1981), 209–214.

1060. —. "Pollution, Purification, and Purgation in Biblical Israel." In *The Word of the Lord Shall Go Forth: Essays in Honor of David Noel Freedman in Celebration of His Sixtieth Birthday*, pp. 399–414. Edited by Carol L. Meyers and M. O'Connor. Winona Lake, Indiana: Eisenbrauns for the American Schools of Oriental Research, 1983.

1061. —. "The Strange Case of the Suspected Sotah (Numbers V, 11–31)." *VT* 34 (1984), 11–26.

1062. —. "The Trial Before God of an Accused Adulteress." *Bible Review* 2, no. 3 (1986), 46–49.

1063. —. "The Ideology of Gender in the Bible and the Ancient Near East." In *DUMU-E$_2$—DUB-BA-A: Studies in Honor of Åke W. Sjöberg*, pp. 185–191. Edited by Hermann Behrens, Darlene Loding, and Martha T. Roth. Philadelphia: Occasional Publications of the Samuel Noah Kramer Fund, 1989.

1064. —. "Law and Philosophy: The Case of Sex in the Bible." *Semeia* 45 (1989), 89–102.

1065. Fubini, Guido. "Gli ebrei e il divorzio." *La Rassegna Mensile di Israel* 36 (1970), 355–365.

1066. Fuchs, Esther. "Status and Role of Female Heroines in the Biblical Narrative." *Mankind Quarterly* 23 (1982), 149–160.

1067. —. "Structure and Patriarchal Functions in the Biblical Betrothal Type-Scene: Some Preliminary Notes." *JFSR* 3 (1987), 7–13.

1068.   —. "'For I have the Way of Women': Deception, Gender, and Ideology in Biblical Narrative." *Semeia* 42 (1988), 68–83.

1069.   —. "The Literary Characterization of Mothers and Sexual Politics in the Hebrew Bible." *Semeia* 46 (1989), 151–166.

1070.   —. "Marginalization, Ambiguity, Silencing: The Story of Jephthah's Daughter." *JFSR* 5 (1989), 33–45.

1071.   Fuchs-Kreimer, Nancy. "Feminism and Scriptural Interpretation: A Contemporary Jewish Critique." *Journal of Ecumenical Studies* 20 (1983), 534–548.

1072.   Furman, Nelly. "His Story Versus Her Story: Male Genealogy and Female Strategy in the Jacob Cycle." *Semeia* 46 (1989), 141–150.

1073.   Gabel, J. B., and Wheeler, C. B. "The Redactor's Hand in the Blasphemy Pericope of Leviticus XXIV." *VT* 30 (1980), 227–229.

1074.   Gablenz, Clara von. "Frauengestellten im AT." *EvKomm* 21 (1988), 418.

1075.   Garbini, Giovanni. "'Narrativa della successione' o 'storia dei re'?" *Henoch* 1 (1979), 19–41. Deals with erotic situations and the importance of women in 2 Sam 9–20 and 1 Kgs 1–2

1076.   —. "Gli Ebrei in Palestina: Yahvismo e religione fenicia." In *Forme di Contatto e Processi di Transformazione nelle Societa Antiche*, pp. 899–910. Pisa and Rome: Scuola Normale Superíore/École Française de Rome, 1983.

1077.   —. "Poesia alessandrina e 'Cantico dei Cantici'." *Alessandriaed il Mondo Ellenistico-Romano: Studi in Onore di Achille Andriani*. Rome: "L'Erma," 1983.

1078.   —. "Calchi lessicali greci nel 'Cantico dei Cantici'." *Rendiconti dell' Accademia Nazionale dei Lincei* 39 (1984), 149–160.

1079.   Gardiner, Anne. "Genesis 2:4b–3: A Mythological Paradigm of Sexual Equality or of the Religious History of Pre-exilic Israel?" *Scottish Journal of Theology* 43 (1990), 1–18.

1080.   Garnot, Moshe. "The Prophecy in the Book of Judges." *BM*
        25 (1979), 256–258 (in Hebrew). Deborah

1081.   Garrett, Duane A. "Votive Prostitution Again: Comparison
        of Proverbs 7:13–14 and 21:28–29." *JBL* 109 (1990),
        681–682.

1082.   Garsiel, Moshe. "A Review of Recent Interpretations of the
        Story of David and Bathsheba, 2 Sam. 11." *Immanuel* 2
        (1973), 18–20.

1083.   —. "David and Bathsheba." *DD* 5 (1976), 24–28; 85–90;
        134–137.

1084.   Gaugel, K. H. "Toward a Biblical Theology of Marriage and
        Family." *Journal of Psychology and Theology* 5 (1977),
        150–162.

1085.   Gehrke, R. "The Biblical View of the Sexual Polarity." *Con-
        cordia Theological Monthly* 41 (1970), 195–205.

1086.   Gelander, S. "On the Book of Ruth, The Relation Between
        the Framework and the Content as Indicative of its Mean-
        ing." *BM* 28 (1982/83), 150–155 (in Hebrew).

1087.   Gelin, A. "Le mariage d'après l'Ancien Testament." *Lumière
        et Vie* 4 (1952), 7–20.

1088.   Geller, Stephen A. "The Sack of Shechem: The Use of Ty-
        pology in Biblical Covenant Religion." *Prooftexts* 1 0
        (1990), 1–15.

1089.   Gendler, Mary. "Male and Female Created He Them: A
        Feminist View." *Jewish Heritage* 13 (Winter 1971–72),
        24–29. Deals with Gen. 1:27

1090.   Gerl, Hanna-Barbara. "Gott-Vater und Mutter." *Erbe und
        Auftrag* 66 (1990), 5–16.

1091.   Gerleman, G. "Die Bildsprache des Hohenliedes und die alt-
        ägyptische Kunst." *Annual of the Swedish Theological In-
        stitute* 1 (1962), 24–30.

1092.   Gerstenberger, Erhard S. "Dominar ou Amar: O Relaciona-
        mento de Homen e Mulher no Antigo Testamento." *Estu-
        dios Teológicos* 23 (1983), 42–56.

1093. —. "Bibelexegese und biblische Theologie angesichts feministischer Kritik." *Deutsches Pfarrerblatt* 88 (1988), 6–9.

1094. Gevirtz, S. "The Reprimand of Reuben (Gen 49, 3–4)." *JNES* 30 (1971), 87–98.

1095. Geyer, Marcia L. "Stopping the Juggernaut: A Close Reading of 2 Samuel 20:13–22." *USQR* 41 (1987), 33–42.

1096. Gilbert, Maurice "'Une suele chair' (Gn 2, 24)." *Nouvelle Revue Théologique* 100 (1978), 66–89.

1097. Giménez, Clementina M. "La mujer en la Biblia." *Cultura Biblica* 221 (1968), 230–234.

1098. Ginsberg, H. L. "Studies in Hosea 1–3." In *Yehezkel Kaufmann Jubilee Volume*, pp. 50–69. Edited by Menahem Haran. Jerusalem: Magnes, 1960.

1099. —. "Lexicographical Notes." In *Hebräische Wörtforschung*, pp. 71–82. VTS, vol. 16. Leiden: E. J. Brill, 1967. Hos. 4

1100. Girardet, Giorgio M. "La famiglia nell' Antico Testamento." *Protestatesimo* 9 (1954), 98–113.

1101. Gitay, Zefira. "Hagar's Expulsion—A Tale Twice Told in Genesis." *Bible Review* 2, no. 4 (1986), 26–32.

1102. Glazier-McDonald, Beth. "Malachi 2:12: 'er wĕ'ōneh— Another Look." *JBL* 105 (1986), 295–298.

1103. —. "Intermarriage, Divorce, and the bat-'ēl-nēkār: Insights into Mal. 2:10–16." *JBL* 106 (1987), 603–611.

1104. Glück, J. J. "Prov. 30, 15a." *VT* 14 (1964), 367–370.

1105. —. "Merab or Michal." *ZAW* 77 (1965), 72–81.

1106. Görg, Manfred. "Fremdsein in und für Israel." *Münchener theologische Zeitschrift* 37 (1986), 217–232.

1107. —. "Mirjam—ein weiterer Versuch." *BZ* 23 (1979), 285–289.

1108. —. "Piggul und pilaegaeš—Experimente zur Etymologie."
       BN 10 (1979), 7–11.

1109. —. "Die 'Sänfte Salomos' nach HL 3, 9f." BN 18 (1982), 15–
       25.

1110. —. "Das Wort zur Schlenge (Gen 3, 14f)." *BN* 19 (1982),
       121–140. Deals, *inter alia*, with Isa. 7:14 and Gen. 3:14

1111. —. "'Travestie' im Hohen Lied. Eine kritische Betrachtung
       am Beispiel von HL 1, 5f." *BN* 21 (1983), 101–115.

1112. —. "Der Spiegeldienst der Frauen (Ex 38, 8)." *BN* 23 (1984),
       9–13. Deals with women in the cult, serving women of Ex.
       38:8; 1 Sam. 2:22 and Egyptian parallels

1113. —. "Weisheit als Provokation." *Wissenschaft und Weisheit* 49
       (1986), 81–98. Deals with Gen. 2:25–3:7 and 1 Kgs. 10

1114. Goitein, S. D. "Women as Creators of Biblical Genres."
       Translated from the Hebrew by Michael Carasik. *Proof-
       texts* 10 (1988), 1–33.

1115. Goldfarb, S. D. "Jacob's Love for Rachel (Gen. 29–10–11)."
       BM 4 (1975), 289–292 (in Hebrew).

1116. —. "Sex and Violence in the Bible." *DD* 4 (1975), 125–130.

1117. Goldingay, John. "The Bible and Sexuality." *Scottish Journal
       of Theology* 39 (1986), 175–188.

1118. Good, Edwin M. "Deception and Women: A Response."
       Semeia 42 (1988), 117–132.

1119. Gordis, Robert. "'My Mother and My Sister'—A Note on
       Job 17, 14." *Lěšonénu* 26 (1971), 71–72 (in Hebrew).

1120. —. "Love, Marriage, and Business in the Book of Ruth." In *A
       Light unto my Path: Old Testament Studies in Honor of
       Jacob Myers*, pp. 241–264. Edited by Howard N. Bream,
       Ralph D. Neim, and Carey H. Moore. Philadelphia: Tem-
       ple University Press, 1974.

1121. —. "Religion, Wisdom, and History in the Book of Esther—
       A New Solution to an Ancient Crux." *JBL* 100 (1981),
       359–388.

1122. —. "More on mrḥm bn bṭnh (Isa. 49:15)." *Tarbiz* 53 (1983/ 84), 137–138 (in Hebrew).

1123. —. "Personal Names in Ruth—A Note on Biblical Etymologies." *Judaism* 35 (1986), 298–299.

1124. Gordon, Cynthia. "Hagar: A Throw-Away Character Among the Matriarchs?" *SBL Seminar Papers*, No. 24 (1983), 273.

1125. Gordon, Cyrus. H. " Almah in Isaiah 7, 14." *Journal of Bible and Religion* 21 (1953), 106.

1126. —. "The Patriarchal Age." *Journal of Bible and Religion* 21 (1953), 238–243.

1127. Gorgulho, L-B. "Ruth et la 'fille de Sion' mère du Messie." *Revue Thomiste* 63 (1963), 5601–514.

1128. Goto, K. "Ezekiel 8, 14: Tammuz-Ishtar." *Seishe-gaku ronshu* 7 (1970), 58–62 (in Japanese).

1129. Gottlieb, Freema. "Three Mothers." *Judaism* 30 (1981), 194–203.

1130. Gottlieb, I. B. "Light and Darkness in Perpual Round: Genesis 18 and 19." In *On the Path of Knowledge: Essays on Jewish Culture: Festschrift for Aharon Mirsky*, pp. 181–198. Edited by Zvi Malachi. Lod, Israel: Haberman Institute, 1986.

1131. Gow, Murray D. "Ruth Quoque—A Conquette (Ruth 4:5)." *Tyndale Bulletin* 41 (1990), 302–311.

1132. Graetz, Naomi. "Miriam: Guilty or Not Guilty." *Judaism* (1991), 184–192.

1133. —. "The Haftarah Tradition and the Battering of Hosea's Wife." *Conservative Judaism* 45, no. 1 (1992), 29–42.

1134. Granot, Alison M. "*'adam* and *'ish*: Man in the Old Testament." *Australian Bible Review* 25 (1977), 2–11.

1135. — . "The Image of Woman in the Bible." *BM* 27 (1981/82), 127–132 (in Hebrew).

1136.   Graupner, Axel. "Zum Verhältnis der beiden Dekalogfass-
        ungen Ex 20 und Dtn 5. Ein Gespräch mit Frank-Lothar
        Hossfeld." *ZAW* 99 (1987), 308–329. Argues that Deut. 5:
        21 constitutes a more respectful stance on woman vis-a-vis
        Ex. 20:17 as the latter puts 'house' before 'wife'.

1137.   Green, Alberto R. "Solomon and Siamon: A Synchronism
        Between Early Dynastic Israel and the Twenty-First Dynas-
        ty of Egypt." *JBL* 97 (1978), 353–367. Solomon's Egyp-
        tian wife

1138.   —. "Israelite Influence at Shishak's Court?" *BASOR,* no. 233
        (1979), 59–62.

1139.   Green, Barbara. "The Plot of the Biblical Story of Ruth."
        JSOT 23 (1982), 55–68.

1140.   Greenberg, Moshe. "Another Look at Rachel's Theft of the
        Teraphim." *JBL* 81 (1962), 239–248.

1141.   —. "The Vision of Jerusalem in Ezekiel 8–11: A Holistic In-
        terpretation." In *The Divine Helmsman: Studies on God's
        Control of Human Events: Presented to Lou H. Silberman,*
        pp. 143–164. Edited by James L. Crenshaw and Samuel
        Sandmel. New York: Ktav, 1980.

1142.   —. "Ezekiel 16: A Panorama of Passions." In *Love and Death
        in the Ancient Near East: Essays in Honor of Marvin H.
        Pope,* pp. 143–150. Edited by J. H. Marks, and R. M.
        Good. Guilford, Conn.: Four Quarters 1987.

1143.   Greenspahn, Frederick E. "A Typology of Biblical Women."
        Judaism 32 (1983), 43–50.

1144.   Greenstein, Edward L. "The Riddle of Samson." *Prooftexts* 1
        (1981), 237–260.

1145.   —. "The Scroll of Esther: A New Translation." *Fiction* 9, no.
        3 (1990), 52–81.

1146.   Grelot, P. "The Institution of Marriage: Its Evolution in the
        Old Testament." *Concilium* 6, no. 5 (1970), 39–50.

1147.   Grey, Mary C. "'Be My Witness'; Women in the Bible Re-
        considered." *Scripture Bulletin* 15 (1984), 12–14.

1148. Grober, S. F. "The hospitable lotus: A cluster of metaphors: An Inquiry into the Problem of Textual Unity in the Song of Songs." *Semitics* 9 (1984), 86–112.

1149. Gross, Walter, and Hunhold, Gerfried. "Die Ehe im Spiegel biblischer und kulturgeschichtlicher Uberlieferungen." *Theologische Quartalschrift* 167 (1987), 82–95.

1150. Grossberg, Daniel. "Canticles 3:10 in the Light of a Homeric Analogue and Biblical Poetics." *BTB* 11 (1981), 74–76.

1151. —. "Sexual Desire: Abstract and Concrete." *Hebrew Studies* 22 (1981), 59–60.

1152. Grottanelli, Cristiano. "The King's Grace and the Helpless Woman: A Comparative Study of the Stories of Ruth, Charila and Sita." *History of Religions* 22 (1982), 1–24.

1153. Gruber, Mayer I. "The Midrash in Biblical Research." In *The Solomon Goldman Lectures: Perspectives in Jewish Learning*, vol. 2, pp. 69–80. Edited by Nathaniel Stampfer. Chicago: Spertus College of Judaica Press, 1979.

1154. —. "'Will a Woman Forget her Infant?'" *Tarbiz* 51 (1982), 491–492 (in Hebrew).

1155. —. "The Motherhood of God in Second Isaiah." *RB* 90 (1983), 351–359.

1156. —. "Feminine Similes Applied to God in Second Isaiah." *Beer Sheva* 2 (1985), 75–84 (in Hebrew).

1157. —. "Hebrew *qĕdēšāh* and her Canaanite and Akkadian Cognates." *UF* 18 (1986), 133–148.

1158. —. "The Double Three-Part Question in the Book of Micah." *Tarbiz* 56 (1987), 583–584 (in Hebrew).

1159. —. "The *qĕdēšāh*—What Was her Function?" *Beer Sheva* 3 (1988), 45–51 (in Hebrew).

1160. —. "The Phenomenal Growth of the Israelite Population in Egypt." *BM* 33 (1988), 171–176 (in Hebrew).

1161. —. "Breast-Feeding Practices in Biblical Israel and in Old Babylonian Mesopotamia." *JANES* 19 (1989), 61–83.

1162.   —. "The Reality Behind Ruth 4:16." In *Festschrift for Prof. Haim Gevariahu,* pp. 233–235. Edited by B-Z. Lurie and S. Avramsky. Jerusalem: Israel Society for Biblical Research, 1990 (in Hebrew).

1163.   —. "The Reality Behind the Hebrew Expression *kā'ēt ḥāyāh.*" *ZAW* 103 (1991), 271–274.

1164.   Gunn, David M. "Traditional Composition in the 'Succession Narrative'." *VT* 26 (1976), 214–229.

1165.   —. "New Directions in the Study of Biblical Hebrew Narrative." *JSOT* 39 (1987), 65–75.

1166.   Gunnel, André. "En annan kvinna eller en annans kivinna? Ett översättningsproblem i ordspråksboken." *Svensk Exegetisk Årsbok* 50 (1985), 33–48.

1167.   Haag, Herbert. "Die Themata der Sündenfall-Geschichte." In *Lex tua veritas. Festschrift für Herbert Junker,* pp. 101–111. Edited by Heinrich Gross and Franz Mussner. Trier: Paulinus Verlag, 1991.

1168.   Hacket, Jo Ann. "Women's Studies and the Bible." In *The Future of Biblical Studies. The Hebrew Scriptures,* pp. 141–164. Edited by Richard Elliott Friedman. Semeia. Atlanta: Scholars Press, 1987.

1169.   Hagan, Harry. "Deception as Motif and Theme in 2 Sam 9–20; 1 Kgs 1–2." *Biblica* 60 (1979), 301–326.

1170.   Halevy, B. " 'And Sarah Oppressed Her' (Gen. 16, 6)." *BM* 11 (1965), 111–116 (in Hebrew).

1171.   —. "Sexual and Fire Metaphors in Hosea." *BM* 22 (1977), 473–476 (in Hebrew).

1172.   Halivni, David Weiss. "The Use of *qnh* in Connection with Marriage." *HTR* 57 (1964), 244–248.

1173.   Hall, Gary. "Origin of the Marriage Metaphor." *Hebrew Studies* 23 (1982), 169–171.

1174.   Hallo, William W. "As The Seal Upon Thy Heart." *Bible Review* 1, no. 1(1985), 20–27.

1175. —. "The First Purim." *BA* 46 (1983), 19–29.

1176. Halpern, Baruch. "The Resourceful Israelite Historian: The Song of Deborah and Israelite Historiography." *HTR* 76 (1983), 379–402.

1177. Hambrick-Stowe, Charles E. "Ruth the New Abraham, Esther the New Moses." *Christian Century* 100 (1983), 1130–1134.

1178. Hamiel, H. Y. "The Mother of Jacob and Esau (Gen. 28:6)." *BM* 32 (1986/87), 332–344 (in Hebrew).

1179. Hamill, Thomas. "The Bible and Its Imagination: A Modest Sounding of Its Harlot's Evaluation." *Irish Theological Quarterly* 52 (1986), 96–108.

1180. Hansen, Tracy. "My Name Is Tamar." *Priest and People* 4 (1990), 315–318. 2 Sam. 13

1181. Hanson, P. "Masculine Metaphors for God and Sex-Discrimination in the Old Testament." *Ecumenical Review* 27 (1975), 316–324.

1182. Hardesty, Nancy. "Women: Second Class Citizens?" *Eternity* 22, no. 1 (January 1971), 14–16; 24–29.

1183. Harris, Rivkah. Review of Pierre Grimal, ed., *Histoire mondiale de la femme, Préhistoire et Antiquité. JESHO* 9 (1966), 308–309.

1184. Harter, L. Blagg. "The Theme of the Barren Woman in the Patriarchal Narratives." *Concern* (Nov. 1971), 20–24; (Dec. 1971), 18–23.

1185. Hartmann, K. C. "More About the RSV and Is. 7:14." *Lutheran Quarterly* 7 (1955), 344–347.

1186. Hauser, Alan J. "Judges 5: Parataxis in Hebrew Poetry." *JBL* 99 (1980), 23–41.

1187. —. "Linguistic and Thematic Links Between Genesis 4:1–16 and Genesis 2–3." *Journal of the Evangelical Theological Society* 23 (1980), 297–305.

1188. Heindl, Edith. "Eine bekannte Frau, die Propheten Huldah."
       Skripten des Lehrstuhls für Theologie des Alten Testaments
       7 (1985), 123–132.

1189. Heitzmann, Alfonso Alegre. "El Cantar de los Cantares:
       Poesia y Rituel de la Pascua (Cant. I, 4–VII, 5)." *EstBib* 43
       (1985), 321–330.

1190. Held, Moshe. "Studies in Biblical Lexicography in the Light
       of Akkadian." *EI* 16 (1982), 76–85 (in Hebrew). Jer. 7:18;
       44:17–25; Isa. 47; the queen of heaven

1191. Heller, Jan. "Die Priesterin Rahab." *Communio Viatorum* 8
       (1965), 113–117.

1192. Heltzer, Michael. "A New Approach to the Question of the
       'Alien Wives' in the Book of Ezra and Nehemiah."
       SHNATON 10 (1990), 83–92 (in Hebrew).

1193. Hendel, Ronald S. "Of Demigods and the Deluge: Towards
       an Interpretation of Genesis 6:1–4." *JBL* 106 (1987), 13–
       26.

1194. —. "When the Sons of God Consorted with the Daughters
       of Men." *Bible Review* 3, no. 2 (1987), 8–13, 37. Gen.
       6:1–4.

1195. Henry, A.-M. "Le mystère de l'homme et de la femme." *La
       Vie Spirituelle* 80 (1949), 463–490.

1196. —. "Eve et son destin." *L'Anneau d'Or* 57–58 (1954), 189–
       201.

1197. Herrman, Wolfram. "Die Göttersöhne." *Zeitschrift für Reli-
       gion und Geistesgeschichte* 12 (1960), 242–251.

1198. Herzog, Kristin. "Die friedfertige Frau?" *Evangelische Theo-
       logie* 47 (1987), 60–82.

1199. Hess, R. S. "Splitting the Adam: The Usage of *'ādām* in Gen-
       esis I-V." In *Studies in the Pentateuch*, pp. 1–16. Edited by
       J. A. Emerton. VTS, vol. 16. Leiden: E. J. Brill, 1990.

1200. Higgins, Jean M. "Anastasius Sinaita and the Superiority of
       Woman." *JBL* 97 (1978), 253–256. Gen. 3:1–6; feminist
       hermeneutics

1201.   —. "The Myth of Eve the Temptress." *JAAR* 44 (1976), 639–647.

1202.   Hindson, E. E. "Development of the Interpretation of Isa 7:14." *Grace Journal* 10 (1969), 19–25.

1203.   Hirschberger, R. "Image et resemblance dans la tradition sacerdotale Gn 1, 26–28; 5, 1–3; 9:6b." *Revue des Sciences Religieuses* 59 (1985), 185–199.

1204.   Höffken, Peter. "Notizen zum Textcharakter von Jesaja 7, 1–17." *TZ* 36 (1980), 321–337.

1205.   Hoffner, Harry. "Symbols for Masculinity and Femininity." *JBL* 85 (1966), 326–334.

1206.   Hoftijzer, J. "Absalom and Tamar: A Case of Fratriarchy?" In *Festschrift for W. H. Gispen,* pp. 54–61. Kampen: Kok, 1970.

1207.   —. "David and the Tekoite Woman." *VT* 20 (1970), 419–444. 2 Sam. 14:1–24.

1208.   Holladay, William L. "Jer XXXI 22B Reconsidered: The Woman Encompasses the Man." *VT* 16 (1966), 236–239.

1209.   —. "Jeremiah and Women's Liberation." *Andover Newton Quarterly* 12 (1971–72), 213–223.

1210.   Holzinger, H. "Ehe und Frau im vordeuteronomischen Israel." In *Studien zur semitischen Philologie und Religionsgeschichte Julius Wellhausen,* pp. 227–241. ZAW Beihefte 27. Giessen: A Töpelmann, 1914.

1211.   Hongisto, Leif. "Literary Structure and Theology in the Book of Ruth." *AUSS* 23 (1985), 19–28.

1212.   Hoogewoud, F. J. "Juda en Tamar: Een poging tot kontekstueel lezen (Gen 38)." In *Verkenningen en een stroumgebied,* pp. 20–29. Amsterdam: University of Amsterdam Press, 1974.

1213.   Hopkins, Ian W. J. "The 'Daughters of Judah' Are Really Rural Satellites of an Urban Center." *BAR* 6, no. 5 (1980), 44–45. Ps. 48:11; 97:8.

1214.   Hoppe, Leslie J. "The Bible on Women: Patterns of Interpretation." *TBT* 28 (1990), 330–335.

1215.   Horowitz, Maryanne C. "The Image of God in Man—Is Woman Included?" *HTR* 72 (1979), 175–206. Gen. 1:27

1216.   Horton, F. L. "Form and Structure in Laws Relating to Women, Lv. 18, 6–18." *SBL Seminar Papers* 109 (1973), 20–33.

1217.   Hoshino, Mitsuo. "Divorce in the Bible." *Studies in the Christian Religion* 40 (1977), 125–150 (in Japanese). Gen. 16:4–14; 2 Sam. 3:14–16; Deut. 22: 13–19, 28; 24:1–4.

1218.   House, H. Wayne. "Miscarriage or Premature Birth: Additional Thoughts on Exodus 21, 22–25. *Westminster Theological Journal* 41 (1978), 108–213.

1219.   Houtman, C. "Exodus 4:24–26 and Its Interpretation." *JNSL* 11 (1983), 81–105. Zipporah.

1220.   Huber, Elaine C. "They Weren't Prepared to Hear: A Closer Look at the Woman's Bible." *Andover Newton Quarterly* 16 (1976), 271–276.

1221.   Huehnergard, John. "Biblical Notes on Some New Akkadian Texts from Emar (Syria)." *CBQ* 47 (1985), 428–434. teraphim; levirate marriage; Hos. 2:4–5.

1222.   Huey, F. B., Jr. "An Exposition of Malachi." *Southwestern Journal of Theology* 30 (1987), 12–21. Mal. 2:10–16; mixed marriage, divorce.

1223.   Hull, William E. "Woman in Her Place: Biblical Perspectives." *Review and Expositor* 72 (Winter 1975), 5–17.

1224.   Humphrey, W. L. "The Story of Jephthah and the Tragic Vision: A Response to J. Cheryl Exum." In *Signs and Wonders*, pp. 85–96. Edited by J. Cheryl Exum. Atlanta: Scholars Press, 1989.

1225.   Hurvitz, Avi. "Ruth 2, 7—'A Midrashic Gloss'?" *ZAW* 95 (1983), 121–123.

1226.   Hutter, Manfred. "Das Ehebruch-Verbot im altorientalischen und alttestamentlischen Zusammenhang." *Bibel und Liturgie* 59 (1986), 96–104.

1227. Hyman, Frieda C. "Women of the Bible." *Judaism* 5 (1956), 338–347.

1228. —. "The Education of a Queen." *Judaism* 137 (1986), 78–85. Queen Esther.

1229. Hyman, Ronald T. "Questions and the Book of Ruth." *Hebrew Studies* 24 (1983), 17–25.

1230. —. "Questions and Changing Identity in the Book of Ruth." *USQR* 39 (1984), 189–201.

1231. Ihromi. "Die Koeniginmutter und der 'amm ha'arez im Reich Juda." *VT* 24 (1974), 421–429.

1232. Iriarte, María Eugenia. "Mujer y ministerio. Antiguo Testamento." *Biblia y Fe* 16 (1990), 29–50.

1233. Isser, Stanley. "Two Traditions: The Law of Exodus 21:22–23 Revisited." *CBQ* 52 (1990), 30–45.

1234. Istavrides, Vasil T. "The concept of the nature of men and women which allows us to envisage partnership." *Greek Orthodox Theological Review* 7, nos. 1–2 (1961/62), 14–21.

1235. Jackson, B. S. "Reflections on Biblical Criminal Law." *JJS* 24 (1973), 8–38.

1236. Jacob, Edmond. "Feminisme ou Messianisme? A propos de Jérémie 31, 22." In *Beiträge zur alttestamentliche Theologie. Festschrift für Walther Zimmerli*, pp. 179–184. Edited by Herbert Donner, Robert Hanhart, and Rudolf Smend. Göttingen: Vandenhoeck & Ruprecht, 1977.

1237. —. "Les premiers chapitres de la Genèse." *MDB* 9 (May–June–July 1979), 5–10. Gen. 1–2

1238. Jacob, Paul F. "'Cows of Bashan'— A Note on the Interpretation of Amos 4:1." *JBL* 104 (1985), 109–110.

1239. Jacobson, Diane. "What is Wisdom; Who is She?" *Word and*

World 7 (1987), 241–244.

1240. Jacobson, H. "A Legal Note on Potiphar's Wife." *HTR* 69 (1976), 177. Gen. 39:10–18.

1241. Japhet, Sara. "The Relationship Between the Legal Corpora in the Pentateuch in the Light of Manumission Laws." In *Studies in Bible*, pp. 63–89. Scripta Hierosylamitana, no. 31. Edited by Sara Japhet. Jerusalem: Magnes, 1986.

1242. Jagendorf, Zvi. "'In the Morning, Behold, It Was Leah': Genesis and the Reversal of Sexual Knowledge." *Prooftexts* 4 (1984), 187–192. Gen. 29:25; Leah; Eve (Gen. 2–3), Lot's daughters; Tamar (Gen. 38); Rachel.

1243. Janzen, J. Gerald. "A Certain Woman in the Rhetoric of Judges 9." *JSOT* 38 (1987), 33–37.

1244. Jasper, G. "Polygamy in the Old Testament." *Africa Theological Journal* 2 (1969), 27–57.

1245. Jay, Nancy. "Sacrifice, Descent, and the Patriarchs." *VT* 38 (1988), 52–70.

1246. —. "Sacrifice as Remedy for Having Been Born a Woman." In *Immaculate and Powerful*, pp. 283–309. Edited by C. W. Atkinson et al. Boston: Beacon Press, 1985.

1247. Jeansonne, Sharon Pace. "Images of Rebekah: From Modern Interpretations to Biblical Portrayal." *Biblical Research* 34 (1989), 33–52.

1248. Jenny, H. "Le mariage dans la Bible." *Maison-Dieu* 50 (1957), 5–29.

1249. Jensen, Jans Jørgen Lundager. "Die Frauen der Patriarchen und der Raub der Subinerinnend." *Scandinavian Journal of Theology* 1 (1986), 103–108.

1250. —. "Die Frauen der Patriarchen und der Raub der Sabinerinnen. Eine Bemerkung zur Entstehung der Völker und der Struktur der Identität." *Scottish Journal of Theology* 1 (1987), 104–109.

1251. Jentgens, Gerhard. "Die Heilige Schrift und die Frauen."

1251. Jentgens, Gerhard. "Die Heilige Schrift und die Frauen." *Bibel und Kirche* 2 (1954), 34–46.

1252. Jepsen, Alfred. "Amah and Schiphchah." *VT* 8 (1958), 293–297.

1253. —. "Die Nebiah in Jes. 8:3." *ZAW* 72 (1960), 267–268.

1254. Jobling, David. "Mieke Bal on Biblical Narrative." *RSR* 17, no. 1 (1991), 1–10.

1255. Johnson, Elizabeth A. "The Incomprehensibility of God and the Image of God Male and Female." *TS* 45 (1984), 441–465.

1256. —. "Feminist Hermeneutics." *Chicago Studies* 27 (1988), 123–135.

1257. Jones, B. W. "Two Misconceptions about the Book of Esther." *CBQ* 39 (1977), 171–181.

1258. —. "The So-Called Appendix to the Book of Esther." *Semitics* 6 (1978), 36–43.

1259. Jones, David Clyde. "Malachi on Divorce." *Presbyterion* 15 (1989), 16–22.

1260. —. "A Note on the LXX of Malachi 2:16." *JBL* 109 (1990), 683–685.

1261. Jongeling, B. "hz't n'my (Ruth i 19)." *VT* 28 (1978), 474–477.

1262. Jongeling, K. "Joab and the Tekoite Woman." *JEOL* 30 (1987–88), 116–122.

1263. Joüon, P. "Les unions entre les 'Fils de Die' et les 'Filles des Hommes'." *RSR* 29 (1939), 108–114. Gen. 6:1–4

1264. Julian, A. K. "God as a Mother; Is. 49:14–26 and Tiruvacaken." *Indian Theological Studies* 20 (1983), 109–136.

1265. Junker, H. "Die Frau im alttestamentlischen Ekstatischen Kult." *Theologie und Glaube* 21 (1929), 68–74.

Image of Daughter Zion as Speaker in Biblical Poems of Suffering." *Journal of Religion* 67 (1987), 164–182. Jer. 4; Lam 2; mother bereft of children; pollutant female

1267.   Kaiser, Walter C. "Divorce in Malachi 2:10–16." *Criswell Theological Review* 2 (1987), 73–84.

1268.   Kamesar, Adam. "The Virgin of Isaiah 7:14: The Philological Argument from the Second to the Fifth Century." *JTS*, n.s., 41 (1990), 51–75.

1269.   Kaplan, Lawrence. "'And the Lord Sought to Kill Him' (Exod 4:24): Yet Once Again." *HAR* 5 (1981), 65–74. Zipporah

1270.   Katzenstein, H. J. "Who Were the Parents of Athaliah?" *IEJ* 5 (1955), 194–197.

1271.   Katzoff, Louis. "What's in a Biblical Name?' *DD* 9 (1981), 148–149. Leah, Zilpah, Rachel, Bilhah, Dinah

1272.   —. "From the Nuzi Tablets." *DD* 13 (1985), 216–219. Sarah, Rebekah, Hagar; Gen. 12; 16; 20; 26

1273.   —. "Hosea and the Fertility Cult." *DD* 15 (1986/87), 84–87. Hos.; 2 Kgs. 23:7

1274.   Kearney, Peter J. "Marriage and Spirituality in the Song of Songs." *TBT* 25 (1987), 144–149. Gen. 2–3; Cant.

1275.   Keel, O. "Die Stellung der Frau in der Erzählung von Schöpfung und Sündenfall. Gen 2 v. 3." *Orientierung* 39 (1975), 74–76.

1276.   Kellenbach, Katharina von. "Antisemitismus in biblischer Matriarchatsforschung?" *Berliner theologische Zeitschrift* 3 (1986), 144–147. Review of Gerda Weiler, *Ich verwerfe im Lande die Kriege.*

1277.   Keller, Carl A. "Die Gefährung der Ahnfrau." *ZAW* 66 (1955), 181–191.

1278.   Kelly, William. "First and Second Samuel." *TBT* 100 (1979), 1885–1892. David's wives, Tamar

1279. Kessler, Martin. "Genesis 34—An Interpretation." *Reformed Review* 19 (1965), 3–8.

1280. —. "The Law of Manumission in Jer 34." *BZ*, NF, 15 (1971), 105–108.

1281. Kessler, Rainer. "Benenung des Kindes durch die israelitische Mutter." *Wort und Dienst* 19 (1987), 25–35.

1282. —. "Die Frau als Gehilfin des Mannes? Gen 2, 18.20 und das biblische Verständnis von 'Hilfe'." *DBAT* 24 (1987), 120–126.

1283. Keukens, Karlheinz H. "Richter 11, 37f.: Rite de passage und Übersetzungsprobleme." *BN* 19 (1982), 41–42. Judg. 11:37–38; Jephthah's daughter, *betulim*

1284. Kevers, Paul. "Étude littéraire de Genèse XXXIV." *RB* 87 (1980), 38–86. Gen. 34; Dinah

1285. —. "Les 'fils de Jacob' a Sichem." In *Pentateuchal and Deuteronomistic Studies: Papers Read at the XIIIth IOSOT Congress Leuven 1989*, pp. 41–46. Edited by C. Brekelmans and J. Lust. Leuven: University Press and Uitgeverij Peeters, 1990. Gen. 34; Dinah

1286. Kieffer, René. "Feministteologi och exegetik." *Svensk Teologisk Kvartalskrift* 61 (1985), 115–122.

1287. Kikawada, I. "Two Notes on Eve." *JBL* 91 (1972), 33–37.

1288. Kilian, R. "Die Geburt des Immanuel aus der Jungfrau, Jes. 7, 14." In *Zum Thema Jungfraugeburt*, pp. 9–35. Stuttgart: Kath. Bibelwerk, 1970.

1289. Kimball, Gayle. "A Theology of Femininity: The Woman's Bible." In *Women and Religion: 1973 Proceedings*, pp. 75–78. Edited by Joan Arnold Romero. Tallahassee: American Academy of Religion, 1973.

1290. King, Philip J. "Hosea's Method of Hope." *BTB* 12 (1982), 91–95. Hos. 1–2

1291. Kipper, J. Balduino. "O problema da *almah* nos estudo recentes (I)." *Revista de Cultura Biblica* 7 (1963), 80–92; n.s., 1 (1964), 180–195. Isa. 7:14; *'almah*

1292. —. "A mulher no Antigo Testamento." *Revista de Cultura Biblica* 39/40 (1986), 8–28.

1293. Kitchen, K. A. "Proverbs and Wisdom Books of the Ancient Near East: The Factual History of a Literary Form." *Tyndale Bulletin* 28 (1977), 69–114. Prov. 1–24; 25–29; 30; 31

1294. Klaus, Natan. "Abigail's Speech—A Literary Analysis." *BM* 32 (1986/87), 320–331 (Heb.).

1295. Klein, Hans. "Natur und Recht. Israels Umgang mit dem Hochzeitsbrauchtum seiner Umwelt." *TZ* 37 (1981), 3–18. Virginity, marriage regulations, Canaan, Gen. 2–3; 34; 38; Judg. 21; Hos. 1–4; Cant. 3:8

1296. Klein, Ralph W. "'The Song of Hannah' (1 Sam 2, 1–10)." *Concordia Theological Monthly* 41 (1970), 674–684.

1297. Kleinig, John W. "The Banquet of Wisdom—An Exegetical Study of Proverbs 9:1–12." *Lutheran Theological Journal* 17 (1983), 24–28.

1298. Knierim, Rolf. "The Role of the Sexes in the Old Testament." *Lexington Theological Quarterly* 10, no. 4 (1975), 2–10.

1299. Knight, Douglas A. "Moral Values and Literary Traditions: The Case of the Succession Narrative (2 Samuel 9–20; 1 Kings 1–2)." *Semeia* 34 (1985), 7–23.

1300. Knox, W. L. "The Divine Wisdom." *JTS* 38 (1937), 230–237.

1301. Kogut, S. "She Shall Be Called *'iššâ* Because She Was Taken Out of *'iš* (Gen. 2:23)—A Folk Etymology." *Tarbiz* 51 (1982), 293–298 (in Hebrew).

1302. König, Eduard. "Deborah and Hannah." *Homiletic Review* 51 (1906), 130.

1303. —. "Die Sexualität im Hohenlied und ihre Grenze." *Zeitschrift für Sexualwissenschaft* 9 (1922), 1–4.

1304. Kornarakis. John. "·Δί fl,íº÷∫™¶º†‡≤ˆs 'fi‡≤í∫≤fi‡Δ,

†∫†‡∆s'." *Deltio Biblikon Meleton*, n.s. 1 (1980), 29–40. Lot's wife; Gen. 19:12–28

1305. Kosmala, H. "The Bloody Husband." *VT* 12 (1962), 14–18. Ex. 4:24–26; Zipporah

1306. Kottackal, Joseph. "Morality of Sex in the Old Testament." *Bible Bhashyam* 7 (1981), 147–159.

1307. Kraeling, Emil G. "The Significance and Origin of Gen 6:1–4." *JNES* 6 (1947), 193–208.

1308. Kramer, S. N. "The biblical 'Song of Songs' and the Sumerian love songs." *Expedition* 5, no. 1 (1962), 25–31.

1309. Krause, Martin. "II Sam 11⁴ und das Konzeptionsoptimum." *ZAW* 95 (1983), 434–437. Lev. 15:19–28; conception; gynecology

1310. Krebs, Walter. "Lilith—Adams erste Frau." *Zeitschrift für Religions-und Geistesgeschichte* 27, no. 2 (1975), 141–152.

1311. Kreuzer, Siegfried. "Gott als Mutter in Hos 11?" *Theologische Quartalschrift* 169 (1989), 123–132.

1312. Krinetzki, Leo. "Die erotische Psychologie des Hohen Lieds." *Theologische Quartalschrift* 150 (1970), 404–416.

1313. Kronholm, Tryggve. "Polygami och monogami i Gamla Testamentet." *Svensk Exegetisk Årsbok* 47 (1982), 48–92.

1314. Kruger, P. A. "Israel the Harlot (Hos. 2:4–9)." *JNSL* 11 (1983), 107–116.

1315. —. "The Hem of the Garment in Marriage. The Meaning of the Symbolic Gesture in Ruth 3:9 and Ezek. 16:9." *JNSL* 12 (1984), 79–86.

1316. —. "Promiscuity or Marriage Fidelity? A Note on Prov. 5:15–18." *JNSL* 13 (1987), 61–68. metaphors for vagina

1317. Kruse, H. "Alma Redemptoris Mater." *Trierer Theologische Zeitschrift* 74 (1965), 15–36.

1318.   Kutler, Laurence. "A Strong Case for Hebrew MAR." *UF* 16
        (1984), 111–118. Marah (Ruth 1:10), Miriam

1319.   Labuschagne, C. J. "The Similes in the Book of Hosea." *Ou-
        Testamentiese Werkgemeenskap in Suid-Afrika* (1964/65),
        64–76.

1320.   Lacheman, Ernst R. "Apropos of Isaiah 7, 14." *Journal of
        Bible and Religion* 22 (1954), 42.

1321.   Lachs, Samuel T. "Hadassah That Is Esther." *JSJ* 10 (1979),
        219–220.

1322.   Lambert, G., S. J. "Le drame du jardin d'Eden." *Nouvelle
        Revue Théologique* 76 (1954), 917–948; 1044–1072.

1323.   Lambert, J. "Un-fettering the Word: a call for coarcial
        interpretaion of the Bible." *Covenant Quarterly* 32 (May
        1974), 3–26.

1324.   Landau, Lazare. "Rachel et Lea." *MDB* 30 (Aug.–Sep. 1983),
        50–51.

1325.   Landy, Francis. "The Song of Songs and the Garden of
        Eden." *JBL* 98 (1979), 513–528. Contends that Cant. is a
        commentary on Gen. 2–3. Also refers to Lev. 18; 19.

1326.   —. "Beauty and the Enigma: An Inquiry into Some Inter-
        related Episodes of the Song of Songs." *JSOT* 17 (1980),
        55–106.

1327.   Lang, Bernhard. "Die sieben Säulen der Weisheit (Sprüche IX
        1) in Licht israelitischer Architektur." *VT* 33 (1983), 488–
        491. Refers to Dame Wisdom.

1328.   Langemeyer, Bernhard. "Versuche einer Integration der
        kanaanäischen Fruchtbarkeitsreligion in der Glauben an
        Jahwe." *Franziskanische Studien* 69 (1987), 69–78. Anat.

1329.   Langlamet, F. "Josué II, et les traditions de l'Hexateuque. III.
        Rahab et les espions." *RB* 78 (1971), 321–354.

1330.   —. "Absalom et les concubines de son père. Recherches sur II
        Sam. XVI, 21–22." *RB* 84 (1977), 161–209.

1331. Lanser, Susan S. "(Feminist) Criticism in the Garden: Inferring Genesis 2–3." *Semeia* 41 (1988), 67–68.

1332. Lasine, Stuart. "Guest and Host in Judges 19, Lot's Hospitality in an Inverted World." *JSOT* 29 (1984), 37–59.

1333. ——. "Jehoram and the Cannibal Mothers (2 Kings 6:24–33): Solomon's Judgment in an Inverted World." *JSOT* 50 (1991), 27–53.

1334. Lattey, Cuthbert. "The Term *'Almah* in Is. 7:14." *CBQ* 9 (1947), 89–95.

1335. ——. "Various Interpretations of Is. 7:14." *CBQ* 9 (1947), 147–154.

1336. Lawlor, John I. "Theology and Art in the Narrative of the Ammonite War (2 Samuel 10–12)." *Grace Theological Journal* 3 (1982), 193–205.

1337. Lawton, Robert B., S.J. "Genesis 2:24: Trite or Tragic?" *JBL* 105 (1986), 97–98.

1338. ——. "1 Samuel 18: David, Merab, and Michal." *CBQ* 51 (1989), 423–425.

1339. Le Déaut, R. "Miryam soeur de Moise, et Maria mère de Messie." *Biblica* 45 (1964), 198–219.

1340. Ledrus, M. "Rebecca o della benevolenza." *Rivista del Clero Italiano* 47 (1966), 189–205.

1341. Lee, G. M. "Song of Songs V 16, 'My beloved is white and ruddy'." *VT* 21 (1971), 609.

1342. Legrand, L. "Biblical Anthropology or Anthropologies." *Indian Theological Studies* 14 (1977), 349–367.

1343. ——. "Virginity in the Bible." *Bible Bhashyam* 3 (1977), 178–191.

1344. Lehmann, M. R. "Biblical Oaths." *ZAW* 81 (1969), 74–92.

1345. Lehming, S. "Zur Erzählung von der Geburt der Jakobssöhne." *VT* 13 (1963), 74–81. Rachel, Leah, Zilpah, Bilhah, Dinah, Gen. 29:31–30:24

1346. Leibowitz, Eliyahu, and Leibowitz, Gilah. "Solomon's Judgment." *BM* 35 (1989–90), 242–244 (in Hebrew). 1 Kgs. 3:16–28

1347. Lemche, N. P. "Rachel and Lea. Or: On the Survival of Outdated Paradigms in the Study of the Origin of Israel, I." *Scandinavian Journal of the Old Testament* 1–2 (1987), 127–153.

1348. Leonard, Jeanne M. "La femme de Teqoa et le fils de David: étude de 2 Samuel 14:1–20." *Communio Viatorum* 23 (1980), 135–148.

1349. Lettinga, J. P. "Das alttestamentliche Magnifikat." In *Seine Stimme gehört und keinen Fabeln gefolgt. Festschrift für Samuel R. Külling zum 60. Geburtstag = Fundamentum*, Sondernummer, Heft 1. Edited by Reinhard Möller. Basel: Immanuel, 1984. 1 Sam. 2:1–10; Hannah

1350. Levenson, Jon D. "1 Samuel 25 as Literature and as History." *CBQ* 40 (1978), 11–28. Abigail, Bathsheba

1351. Levenson, Jon D., and Halpern, Baruch. "The Political Impact of David's Marriages." *JBL* 99 (1980), 502–518.

1352. Levenson, Paul H. "David and Michal: A Tragic Marriage." *CCAR Journal* 16, no. 4 (1969), 79–82.

1353. Leviant, Curt. "The Narrative Art of the Book of Esther." *National Jewish Monthly* 93 (March 1979), 55–56.

1354. Levinas, E. "Judaism and the Feminine Element." *Judaism* 18 (1969), 30–38.

1355. Levine, B. A. "In Praise of the Israelite Mišpāḥâ: Legal Themes in the Book of Ruth." In *The Quest for the Kingdom of God: Studies in Honor of George E. Mendenhall*, pp. 95–106. Edited by H. B. Huffmon, F. A. Spina, and A. R. W. Green. Winona Lake: Eisenbrauns, 1983.

1356. Levine, M. H. "Irony and Morality in Bathsheba's Tragedy." *CCAR Journal* 22, no. 3 (1975), 69–77.

1357. —. "A Biblical Protest Against the Violation of Women." *DD* 8 (1979), 194–196.

1358.   —. "A Protest Against Rape in the Story of Deborah." *BM* 25 (1979), 83–84 (in Hebrew).

1359.   —. "Hălālâ." *BM* 29 (1983/84), 180–181 (in Hebrew). Argues that the word means "dancing girl."

1360.   Levoratti, Armondo J. "Observaciones sobre Gen 2." *RivB* 25 (1963), 12–17.

1361.   Levy, Ludwig. "Sexualsymbolik in der Simsonsage." *Zeitschrift für Sexualwissenschaft* 3 (1916), 256–271.

1362.   Levy-Bruhl, H. "Le mariage de Booz." *Evidences* 17 (1951), 29–33. Ruth; Deut. 25:5–10

1363.   Lichtenstein, Murray H. "Chiasm and Symmetry in Proverbs 31." *CBQ* 44 (1982), 202–211.

1364.   Lindars, Barnabas. "'Rachel Weeping for her Children'—Jeremiah 31:15–22." *JSOT* 12 (1979), 47–62.

1365.   —. "Deborah's Song: Women in the Old Testament." *BJRL* 65 (1982–83), 158–175.

1366.   Linder, Helgo. "Spricht Gen 2, 24 von der Ehe?" *Theologische Beiträge* 19 (1988), 23–32.

1367.   Lipínski, E. "Psalm 68, 7 and the Role of the Košarot." *Annali dell' Instituto Orientale di Napoli* 21 (1971), 532–537.

1368.   Liptzin, Sol. "Lady Asenath." *DD* 7 (1978), 51–61.

1369.   —. "Solomon and the Queen of Sheba." *DD* 7 (1978), 172–185.

1370.   —. "Princess Hagar." *DD* 8 (1979), 114–126.

1371.   —. "The Love of David and Michal." *DD* 10 (1981), 48–58.

1372.   —. "Rahab of Jericho." *DD* 9 (1981), 111–119.

1373.   Livingston, Dennis H. "The Crime of Leviticus XXIV, 11." *VT* 36 (1986), 352–354.

1374.   Livio, Jean-Bernard. "Ruth, la moabite mère en Israël." *MDB* 30 (Aug.–Sept.–Oct. 1983), 30–31.

1375.   Ljung, Inger. "Tolkning av GT: s utsagor om kvinnor." *Svensk Exegetisk Årsbok* 49 (1984), 44–57. Gen. 1–3; I Kgs. 9:20–38; 2 Ch. 8:7–18; foreign women, exclusion of women from the cult; feminist hermeneutics

1376.   Loader, J. A. "Esther as a Novel with Different Levels of Meaning." *ZAW* 90 (1978), 417–421.

1377.   Loewenstamm, Samuel E. "The Laws of Adultery and Murder in Biblical and Mesopotamian Law." In *Comparative Studies in Biblical and Ancient Oriental Literatures,* pp. 146–153. AOAT 24. Edited by S. E. Loewenstamm. Neukirchen-Vluyn: Neukirchener Verlag/Kevelaer: Butzon & Bercker, 1980.

1378.   —. "The Laws of Adultery and Murder in Biblical and Mesopotamian Law." *BM* 8–9 (1962), 55–59 (in Hebrew).

1379.   —. "Exodus XXI 22–25." *VT* 22 (1977), 352–360. abortion

1380.   Lohfink, Norbert. "Die Gattung der 'Historischen Kurzgeschichte' in den letzten Jahren von Juda und in der Zeit des babylonischen Exils." *ZAW* 90 (1978), 319–347. Huldah

1381.   —. "War Kohelet ein Frauenfeind? Ein Versuch, die Logik und den Gegenstand von Koh., 7, 23–8, 1a herauszufinden." In *La Sagesse de l'Ancien Testament,* pp. 259–287. Edited by Maurice Gilbert. Leuven: Leuven University Press and Peeters, 1990.

1382.   Long, Burke O. "A Darkness Between Brothers: Solomon and Adonijah." *JSOT* 19 (1981), 79–94. Bathsheba, Tamar, succession narrative

1383.   López, Félix Garcia. "Del 'Yahwista' al 'Deuteronomisto.' Estudio critico de Génesis 24 (fin)." *RB* 87 (1980), 514–559. Rebekah

1384.   Loretz, Oswald. "Theme of the Ruth Story." *CBQ* 22 (1960), 391–399.

1385.   —. "Zum Problem des Eros im Hohenlied." *BZ* 8 (1964), 191–216.

1386.   —. "Götter und Frauen (Gen 6, 1–4). Ein Paradigma zu: Altes Testament-Ugarit." *Bibel und Leben* 8 (1967), 120–127.

1387.   "Lot's Wife: A Study in Detachment." *Expository Times* 28 (1916/1917), 445–449.

1388.   Lucas, Fr. Maria, O.F.M. CAP. "Origin of Marriage in the Bible." *Bible Bhashyam* 3 (1977), 161–177. J, P, Enkidu and Gilgamesh.

1389.   Luke, A. B. "Juda and Tamar (Gen 38)." *Scriptura* 17 (1965), 52–61.

1390.   Luke, K. "Abraham and Sarah in Egypt." *Indian Ecclesiastical Review* 4 (1965), 3–19.

1391.   —. "The Rape of Dinah." *The Living Word* 80 (1974), 99–113.

1392.   —. "Human Love: the Tradition of the Old Testament." *Jeevadhara* 8 (1978), 413–431.

1393.   —. "Two Birth Narratives in Genesis." *Indian Theological Studies* 17 (1980), 155–180. Gen. 25:19–26; 38:27–30

1394.   —. "The Nephilim were on the Earth (Gen 6:4)." *Bible Bhashyam* 9 (1983), 279–301.

1395.   —. "Indo-European Parallels to Genesis 19:30–38." *Indian Theological Studies* 21 (1984), 322–342. Lot's daughters

1396.   —. "The Queen of Sheba (1 Kg. 10:1–13)." *Indian Theological Studies* 23 (1986), 248–272.

1397.   Luria, Y. "Feminism in the Bible." *Congress Bi-Weekly* 41 (Dec. 6, 1974), 17–19.

1398.   Lurie, B-Z. "Gezer—šilluḥîm for Pharaoh's Daughter." *BM* 28 (1982/83), 103–106 (Hebrew).

1399.   Lyons, Ellen Louise. "A Note on Proverbs 31:10–31." In *The*

Listening Heart. Essays in Wisdom and the Psalms in Honor of Roland E. Murphy, O. Carm., pp. 237–245. Edited by Kenneth G. Hoglund, et al. JSOT Supplementary Series, no. 58. Sheffield: JSOT Press, 1987.

1400.   Lys, Daniel. "Le cantique des cantiques. Pour une sexualité non-ambigué." *Lumière et Vie* 28 (1979), 39–53.

1401.   McBride, Mary. "Daughters of Eve: The Role of Women in 'Fortunate Falls' among Biblical Heroes." *Response in Worship, Music, and the Arts* 15, nos. 2 and 3 (1975), 20–22.

1402.   McCarter, P. Kyle, Jr. "Plots, True or False: The Succession Narrative as Court Apologetic." *Interpretation* 35 (1981), 355–367.

1403.   McCarthy, Carmel. "The David Genealogy in the Book of Ruth." *Proceedings of the Irish Biblical Association* 9 (1985), 53–62.

1404.   McCreesh, T. "Wisdom as Wife: Proverbs 31:10–31." *RB* 92 (1985), 25–46.

1405.   MacDonald, J. R. B. "The Marriage of Hosea." *Theology* 67 (1964), 149–156.

1406.   MacDonald, John. "The Status and Role of the Na'ar in Israelite Society." *JNES* 35 (1976), 147–170. Discusses also *na'arah* and *'almah*.

1407.   McEvenue, Sean S. "Comparison of Narrative Styles in the Hagar Stories." *Semeia* 3 (1975), 64–80.

1408.   McGee, Daniel B. "Hosea: The Man and His Message." *Biblical Illustrator* 13 (Spring 1987), 25–29.

1409.   McGrath, B. "Reflections on Psalm 45." *TBT* 26 (1966), 1837–1842.

1410.   McHatten, Mary T. "Biblical Roots of Women." *Emmanuel* 89 (1983), 392–395. Gen. 1–4; Sarah, Rebecca, Rachel, Deborah, Judith, Esther

1411.   —. "The Prophetic Call to Women: Isaiah, Jeremiah, and

Ezekiel." *Emmanuel* 96 (1990), 398–403. Isa. 3:16–4:1; 32:9–14; Jer. 44:15–30; Ezek. 13:17–23

1412. McKane, W. "Ruth and Boaz." *TGUOS* 19 (1963), 29–40.

1413. —. "Poison, Trial By Ordeal, and the Cup of Wrath." *VT* 30 (1980), 474–492.

1414. McKay, J. W. "Helel and the Dawn-goddess: A Re-examination of the Myth in Isaiah XIV 12–15." *VT* 20 (1970), 451–464.

1415. McKeating, Henry. "Sanctions Against Adultery in Ancient Israelite Society, with some reflections on Methodology in the study of Old Testament Ethics." *JSOT* 11 (1979), 57–72.

1416. McKenzie, J. L. "The Elders in the Old Testament." *Biblica* 40 (1959), 522–540. Deut. 22:13–21

1417. McPheeters, W. M. "Women in the Ancient Hebrew Cult." *Christian Faith and Life,* o.s., 3 (1899), 72–74.

1418. Maccoby, Hyam. "Sex According to the Song of Songs." *Commentary* 67, no. 6 (1979), 53–59.

1419. Macht, David I. "A Scientific Appreciation of Leviticus 12:1–5." *JBL* 52 (1933), 253–260.

1420. Magonet, J. "The Liberal and the Lady: Esther Revisited." *Judaism* 29 (1980), 167–176.

1421. Maigret, J. "Samuel, Saül et la sorcière d'En-Dor." *Bible et Terre Sainte* 124 (1970), 7.

1422. Maillot, A. "Sexe dans la Bible." *Foi et Vie* 74, no. 4 (1975), 53–75.

1423. —. "Misogynie et Ancien Testament." *Foi et Vie* 75, no. 2 (1976), 36–47.

1424. Malkiel, Sh. "A Propos of Reading." *Lěšonénu* 47 (1982/83), 293 (in Hebrew). Hos. 2:4; *mippānêhā* a euphemism for genitals.

1425. Mannheimer, Louise. "Jewish Women of Biblical and Medieval Times." In *Papers of the Jewish Women's Congress Held at Chicago, September 4, 5, 6, and 7, 1893*, pp. 15–25. Philadelphia: Jewish Publication Society, 1894.

1426. Manor, Dale W. "A Brief History of Levirate Marriage as It Relates to the Bible." *Restoration Quarterly* 27 (1984), 129–142. Gen. 38; Deut. 25; Ruth

1427. Marcus, David. "The Barren Woman of Psalms 113:9 and the Housewife: An Antiphrastic Dysphemism." *JANES* 11 (1979), 81–84.

1428. Margalith, Othniel. "Dor and En-Dor." *ZAW* 97 (1985), 109–111.

1429. —. "More Samson Legends." *VT* 36 (1986), 397–405. Manoah's wife

1430. —. "Samson's Riddle and Samson's Magic Locks." *VT* 36 (1986), 225–234.

1431. —. "The Legends of Samson/Heracles." *VT* 37 (1987), 63–70. Delilah

1432. Margulies, H. "Das Rätsel der Beine im Alten Testament." *VT* 24 (1974), 56–76. Deborah

1433. Marocco, Giuseppe. "Alcuni studi recenti sul Cantico dei Cantici." *RivB* 35 (1987), 69–77.

1434. Marrs, Rick. "The Sons of God (Genesis 6:1–4)." *Restoration Quarterly* 23 (1980), 218–224.

1435. Marshall, J. "Remarks on Dr. Chotzner's Paper 'On the Life and Social Position of Hebrew Woman in Biblical Times'." *SBAP* 6 (1883–84), 222–224.

1436. Martin, D. C. "Human Sexuality in the Old Testament." *Biblical Illustrator* 12 (Summer 1986), 35–37.

1437. Marzel, Y. "The Sons of God and the Daughters of Man: Development and Destruction." *BM* 27 (1981/82), 203–219 (in Hebrew).

1438. Mathon, G. "Luxure; La sexualité humaine dans l'AT et NT." *Catholicisme* 8 (1977), 9–18.

1439. Mauldin, F. Louis. "Singularity and a Pattern of Sin, Punishment, and Forgiveness." *Perspectives in Religious Studies* 10 (1983), 41–50. Sarai, barren wife stories, Hagar

1440. May, H. G. "The Fertility Cult in Hosea." *AJSL* 48 (1932), 73–98

1441. —. "Ruth's Visit to the High Place at Bethlehem." *JRAS*, 1939, pp. 75–78. Claims that there underlies Ruth 3 cultic coitus in a holy place

1442. Meek, James. "Canticles and the Tammuz Cult." *AJSL* 39 (1922–23), 1–14.

1443. Meer, W. van der. "De lofzang van Hanna." *Gereformeerd Theologisch Tijdschrift* 76 (1976), 193–204. 1 Sam. 2:1–10.

1444. Meier, Samuel A. "Linguistic Clues on the Date and Canaanite Origin of Genesis 2:23–24." *CBQ* 53 (1991), 18–24.

1445. Meijer, Alexander, and Meijer, Amos. "Matrimonial Influence in the Bible." *DD* 13 (1984/85), 81–87, 97.

1446. Meilvitz, A. "The Fast of Esther." *Sinai* 64 (1969), 215–242 (in Hebrew).

1447. Meinhold, Arndt. "Zu Aufbau und Mitte des Estherbuches." *VT* 33 (1983), 435–445.

1448. —. Vierfaches: Strukturprinzip und Häufigkeitsfigur in Prov 1–9." *BN* 33 (1986), 53–79.

1449. Meller, Vilma. "Homer and Judges." *Bible Bhashyam* 9 (1983), 95–103.

1450. Mendelsohn, I. "The Conditional Sale into Slavery of Free-Born Daughters in Nuzi and in the Law of Ex. 21:7–11." *JAOS* 55 (1935), 190–195.

1451. Mendenhall, George E. "Law and Covenant in Israel and the Ancient Near East." *BA* 17 (1954), 26–46; 50–76.

1452. —. "The Hebrew Conquest of Canaan." *BA* 25 (1962), 66–87.

1453. —. "Social Organization in Early Israel." In *Magnalia Dei: The Mighty Acts of God*, pp. 132–151. Edited by Frank Moore Cross, Jr.; Werner E. Lemke, and Patrick D. Miller, Jr. Garden City, N.Y.: Doubleday, 1976.

1454. Merli, Dino. "La creazione e la dignita della donna." *Bibbia e Oriente* 12 (1970), 97–103.

1455. Merodie, Marie de. "'A Helper Fit for Him': Gen. 2:18–24." *Revue théologique de Louvain* 8 (1977), 329–352.

1456. Mettinger, Tryggve N. D. "Eva och revbenet. Manligt och kvinnligt i exegetisk belysning." *Svensk Teologisk Kvartalskrift* 54 (1978), 55–64. Gen. 1:26–31; 2–3; Sum. Enki and Ninhursag

1457. —. "The Study of the Gottesbild. Problems and Suggestions." *Svensk Exegetisk Årsbok* 54 (1989), 109–117. Gen. 1:27

1458. Meyers, Carol L. "The Roots of Restriction: Women in Early Israel." *BA* 41 (1978), 91–103.

1459. —. "Procreation, Production, and Protection: Male-Female Balance in Early Israel." *JAAR* 51 (1983), 569–593.

1460. —. "Gender Imagery in the Song of Songs." *HAR* 10 (1986), 209–223.

1461. —. "Gender Roles and Genesis 3:16 Revisited." In *The Word of the Lord Shall Go Forth: Essays in Honor of David Noel Freedman*, pp. 337–354. Edited by Carol L. Meyers and M. O'Connor. Winona Lake: Eisenbrauns, 1983.

1462. —. "Of Drums and Damsels: Women's Performance in Ancient Israel." *BA* 54 (1991), 16–27.

1463. —. "Text Without Context: On Bloom's Misreading of J." *Iowa Review* 21 (1991), 60–65.

1464. —. "'To Her Mother's House': Considering a Counterpart to the Israelite *Bêt 'āb*." In *The Bible and the Politics of Exegesis: Essays in Honor of Norman K. Gottwald on His*

Sixty-fifth Birthday, pp. 39–51; 304–307. Edited by David Jobling, Peggy L. Day and Gerald T. Sheppard. Cleveland: Pilgrim Press, 1991.

1465.   Michaelson, W. "Neither Male nor Female: The Thanksgiving Conference on Biblical Feminism." *Sojourners* 5 (Jan. 1976), 10–12.

1466.   "Michal." *Expository Times.* 29 (1917–1918), 221–224.

1467.   Michel, Walter L. "Btwlh, 'Virgin' or 'Virgin (Anath)' in Job 31:1?" *Hebrew Studies* 23 (1982), 59–66.

1468.   —. "A Theological Colloquium on *An Inclusive Language Lectionary:* Anthropology and Theology of the Old Testament." *DIALOG* 24 (1985), 42–49. Critique of feminist hermeneutics; matriarchs; Gen. 1:1–2:3

1469.   Middlekoop, P. "The Significance of the Story of the 'Bloody Husband' (Ex. 4:24–26)." *South East Asia Journal of Theology* 8 (1966), 34–38.

1470.   Milgrom, Jacob. "The Case of the Suspected Adulteress, Num. 5:11–31: Redaction and Meaning." In *The Creation of Sacred Literature,* pp. 69–75. Edited by Richard Elliot Friedman. Berkeley: University of California Press, 1981.

1471.   Miller, Clyde M. "Maidenhood and Virginity in Ancient Israel." *Restoration Quarterly* 22 (1979), 242–246.

1472.   Miller, John W. "Depatriarchalizing in Biblical Interpretation." *CBQ* 48 (1986), 609–616. Critique of Trible's article by the same title, q.v. Num. 23:19; 1 Sam. 15:29; Hos. 11:9

1473.   Mills, Watson E. "Childbearing in Ancient Times." *Biblical Illustrator* 13 (Fall 1986), 54–56.

1474.   Milne, Pamela J. . "Eve and Adam: Is a Feminist Reading Possible?" *Bible Review* 4, no. 3 (June 1988), 12–21, 39. Feminist hermeneutics and Gen. 2–4

1475.   —. "The Patriarchal Stamp of Scripture." *JFSR* 5 (1989), 17–34. Gen. 2–3

1476. Minc, Rachel. "Le rôle du choeur féminin dans le 'Livre de Ruth'." *Bible et Vie Chrétienne* 77 (1967), 71–76.

1477. ——. "Job et son épouse." *Israelitisches Wochenblatt* 71 (1971), 54–55.

1478. Mink, Hans-Aage. "Indtil døden shiller jer ad." In *Teksten & Tolkninger*, pp. 155–174. Edited by K. Jeppesen and F. H. Cryer. Amis: Aarhus, 1986.

1479. Minkoff, Harvey, and Melamed, Evelyn B. "Was the First Feminist Bible in Yiddish?" *Moment* 16, no. 3 (June 1991), 28–33, 52.

1480. Miscall, Peter D. "Literary Unity in Old Testament Narrative." *Semeia* 15 (1979), 27–44. Gen. 12:10–13; 20; 26: 1–11; 1 Sam. 25; 2 Sam. 11

1481. Mitchell, Mike. "The Go'el: Kinsman Redeemer." *Biblical Illustrator* 13 (Fall 1986), 13–15. Ruth

1482. Mittwoch, H. "The Story of the Blasphemer Seen in a Wider Context." *VT* 15 (1965), 386–389. Lev. 24:10–23

1483. Molin, G. "Die Stellung der Gebira im Staate Juda." *TZ* 10 (1954), 161–175. queen mother; gebira

1484. Mollenkott, Virginia R. "Women and the Bible: A Challenge to Male Interpretation." *Sojourners* 5 (Feb. 1976), 20–25.

1485. Moltmann, Jürgen. "Die Bibel und das Patriarchat: offene Fragen zur Diskissuion über feministische Theologie." *Evangelische Theologie* 42 (1982), 480–484.

1486. Moncure, John. "Sarah and Milkah." *Review and Expositor* 27 (1930), 62–64.

1487. Monlobou, Louis. "Modernité de la femme biblique." *Bulletin de littérature ecclésiastique* 82 (1981), 243–262.

1488. Moore, Carey A. "Archaeology and the Book of Esther." *BA* 38 (1975), 62–79 + 8 fig.

1489. ——. "Esther Revisited Again: A Further Examination of Certain Esther Studies of the Past Ten Years." *HAR* 7 (1983), 169–186.

1490.   —. "Eight Questions Most Frequently Asked About the Book of Esther." *Bible Review* 3, no. 1 (1987), 16–31.

1491.   Morag, S. "On Semantic and Lexical Features in the Language of Hosea." *Tarbiz* 53 (1983/84), 489–511 (in Hebrew).

1492.   Moreno, Antonio C. "Significado de la sexuelidad en el Antiguo Testamento." *Teología y Vida* 18 (1977), 251–268.

1493.   —. "La exégesis de Génesis 2,4b–3,24." *Teología y Vida* 19 (1978), 259–278.

1494.   Morey, Ann-Janine. "American Myth and Biblical Interpretation in the Fiction of Harriet Beecher Stowe and Mary E. Wilkins Freeman." *JAAR* 55 (1987), 741–763.

1495.   Morgenstern, Julian. "Beena Marriage in Ancient Israel and Its Historical Implications." *ZAW* 47 (1929), 91–110; 48 (1931), 46–58.

1496.   —. "The 'Bloody Husband' (?) Ex 4, 24–26 Once Again." *HUCA* 34 (1963), 35–70.

1497.   Morlan, Gail. "Toward a Biblical Understanding of Womanhood." *Ministry* 8 (1968), 3–9.

1498.   Morrison, Martha A. "The Jacob and Laban Narrative in Light of Near Eastern Sources." *BA* 46 (1983), 155–164. Rachel, Leah

1499.   Mosca, Paul G. "Who Seduced Whom? A Note on Joshua 15:18/Judg. 1:14." *CBQ* 46 (1984), 18–22. Achsah

1500.   Motyer, J. A. "Context and Content in the Interpretation of Isaiah 7, 14." *Tyndale Bulletin* 21 (1970), 118–125.

1501.   Müller, Hans-Peter. "Mann und Frau im Wandel der Wirklichkeitersfahrung Israels." *Zeitschrift für Religions und Geistesgeschichte* 17 (1965), 1–19. Gen. 29; 1 Sam. 19; Judg. 14; 16.

1502.   Müller, Iris, and Ramingo, Ida. "Women and Judaism." *Orientierung* 51 (1987), 30–32; reprinted in *Theology Digest* 34 (1987), 216–218. Gen. 1:27; Deut. 24:1–4

1503.   Mulder, Martin Jay. "Versuch zur Deutung von sokènèt in 1 Kon 1 2, 4." *VT* 22 (1972), 43–54.

1504.   Mulier, Stockton. "The Woman: A Biblical Theme." *Australian Journal of Biblical Archaeology* 6 (1973), 106–112.

1505.   Mullo-Weir, C. J. "The Alleged Hurrian Wife-Sister Motif in Genesis." *TGUOS* 22 (1967), 14–25.

1506.   Muntingh, L. H. "Married Life in Israel According to the Book of Hosea." *Ou-Testamentiese Werkgemeenskep in Suid-Afrika* 7 (1964/65), 77–84.

1507.   Murnion, P. J. "The Bible Teaching on Sexuality." *Dunwoodie Review* 7 (1967), 162–176.

1508.   Murphy, Roland E. "The Unity of the Song of Songs." *VT* 29 (1979), 436–443.

1509.   —. "Wisdom and Creation." *JBL* 104 (1985), 3–11.

1510.   —. "Cant. 2:8–17—A Unified Poem?" In *Mélanges bibliques et orientaux en l'honneur de M. Mathias Delcor*, pp. 305–310. Edited by A. Caquot, S. Legasse, and M. Tardieu. AOAT 215. Neukirchen-Vluyn: Neukirchener Verlag/ Kevelacr: Butzon & Bercker, 1985.

1511.   —. "Proverbs and Theological Exegesis." In *The Hermeneutical Quest: Essays in Honor of James Luther Mays*, pp. 87–95. Edited by D. G. Miller. Princeton Theological Monographs 4. Allison Park, Pa.: Pickwick, 1986. Lady Wisdom

1512.   —. "Wisdom's Song in Proverbs 1:20–33." *CBQ* 48 (1986), 456–460.

1513.   —. "Dance and Death in the Song of Songs." In *Love and Death in the Ancient Near East: Essays in Honor of Marvin H. Pope*, pp. 117–119. Edited by J. H. Marks and R. M. Good. Guilford, Conn.: Four Quarters, 1987. Cant. 7:1ff; 8:6

1514.   Murray, D. F. "Narrative Structure and Technique in the Deborah-Barak Story, Judges IV, 4–22." In *Studies in the Historical Books of the Old Testament*, pp. 155–189. Edited by J. A. Emerton. VTS, vol. 30. Leiden: E. J. Brill, 1979.

1515.   Mussell, Mary-Louis. "Guile and Power in the Lives of the Wives of the Patriarchs." *Proceedings, Eastern Great Lakes and Midwest Biblical Societies* 7 (1987), 173–181.

1516.   Myers, A. E. "The Use of *'almah* in the Old Testament." *Lutheran Quarterly* 7 (1955), 137–140.

1517.   Nadel, M. "Male and Female." *BM* 23 (1977), 80–85 (in Hebrew). Gen. 1:27; 2:7–22.

1518.   Nagy, Antal. "Die gesellschaftliche Situation und die allgemeine und hervorragende Stellung der Frauen im Alten Testament." *Theologiai Szemle* 25 (1982), 13–19.

1519.   Naor, M. "The Giants Were Then on Earth (Gen. 6, 1–4). *BM* 11 (1965), 26–33 (in Hebrew).

1520.   Neef, Heinz-Dieter. "Gottes Treue und Israels Untreue. Aufbauend Einheit von Jeremia 2, 2–13." *ZAW* 99 (1987), 37–58.

1521.   Neff, Robert Wilbur. "The Annunciations in the Birth Narrative of Ishmael." *Biblical Research* 17 (1972), 51–60. Hagar; Gen. 16:11–12; 21:8ff.

1522.   Neher, A. "Le symbolisme conjugal: expression de l'histoire dans l'Ancien Testament." *Revue d'Historie et de Philosophie Religieuses* 34 (1954), 30–49.

1523.   Nel, Philip. "The Riddle of Samson (Judg 14, 14. 18). *Biblica* 66 (1985), 534–545.

1524.   Nestle, Eb. "Tamar." *Expository Times* 15 (1903–04), 141.

1525.   Neu, Rainer. "Patrilokalität und Patrilinearität." *BZ* 3 4 (1990), 222–233.

1526.   Neveu, Louis. "Le paradis perdu(?). Recherches sur la structure littéraire de Genèse 2, 4b–3, 24." *Revue de l'Université Catholique de l'Ouest* 4 (1982), 27–74. Eve.

1527.   Newman, Murray L. "Rahab and the Conquest." In *Understanding the Word: Essays in Honor of Bernhard W. Anderson*, pp. 167–181. Edited by James T. Butler, Edgar W. Conrad and Ben C. Ollenburger. JSOT Supplement Series 37. Sheffield: JSOT Press, 1985.

1528. Nickels, Peter. "Wisdom's Table—Daily Bread." *TBT* 19 (1981), 168–172. Prov. 9.

1529. Nicol, George G. "Genesis XXIX. 32 and XXXV. 22a. Reuben's Reversal." *JTS* 31 (1980), 536–539. Bilhah, Rachel, Leah.

1530. —. "Bathsheba: A Clever Woman?" *Expository Times* 99 (1988), 360–363.

1531. Niditch, Susan. "The Wronged Woman Righted: An Analysis of Genesis 38." *HTR* 72 (1979), 143–149.

1532. —. "The 'Sodomite' Theme in Judges 19–20: Family, Community, and Social Disintegration." *CBQ* 44 (1982), 365–378.

1533. —. "Legends of Wise Heroes and Heroines." In *The Hebrew Bible and Its Modern Interpreters*, pp.445–463. Edited by Douglas A. Knight and Gene M. Tucker. Philadelphia: Fortress, 1985.

1534. —. "Portrayal of Women in the Hebrew Bible." In *Jewish Women in Historical Perspective*, pp. 25–42. Edited by Judith R. Baskin. Detroit: Wayne State University Press, 1991.

1535. Nielsen, Eduard. "Creation and the Fall of Man: A Cross-Disciplinary Investigation." *HUCA* 43 (1972), 1–22. Gen. 1–3.

1536. —. "Sur la théologie de l'auteur de Gn 2–4." *De la Tôrah au Messie. Mélanges Henri Cazelles,* pp. 55–63. Edited by Maurice Carrez, Joseph Doré and Pierre Grelot. Paris: Desclée, 1981.

1537. —. "Le choix contre le droit dans le livre de Ruth. De l'aire de battage au tribunal." *VT* 35 (1985), 201–212.

1538. Nowell, Irene. "A Celebration of Love." *TBT* 25 (1987),140–143.

1539. —. "Roles of Women in the Old Testament." *TBT* 28 (1990), 364–368.

1540. Nur-el-Din, M. A. "Some remarks on the title *mwt-nsw.*" *Orientalia Lovaniensia Periodica* 11 (1980), 91–98. Royal mother; 1 Kgs. 2:19.

1541. O'Callaghan, Martin. "The Structure and Meaning of Genesis 38: Judah and Tamar." *Proceedings of the Irish Biblical Association* 5 (1981), 72–88.

1542. O'Connell, Robert H. "Proverbs VII 16–17: A Case of Fatal Deception in A 'Woman in the Window' Type-Scene." *VT* 41 (1991), 235–241.

1543. O'Connor, Kathleen M. "The Invitation of Wisdom Woman: A Feminine Image of God." *TBT* 29 (1991), 87–93. Prov. 9.

1544. O'Connor, M. "The Women in the Book of Judges." *HAR* 10 (1986), 277–293.

1545. O'Day, Gail. "Singing Woman's Song: A Hermeneutic of Liberation." *Currents in Theology and Mission* 12 (1985), 203–210. Ex. 15:21 (Miriam); 1 Sam. 2:1–10 (Hannah); Luke 1: 46–55 (Mary)

1546. O'Rourke, John J. "Eve's Formation from Adam in Modern Theology." *Revue de l'Université d'Ottawa* 35 (1965), 161–191.

1547. O'Shea, W. J. "Marriage and Divorce: The Biblical Evidence." *Australasian Catholic Record* 47 (1970), 89–109.

1548. Ogden, Graham S. "The Use of Figurative Language in Malachi 2.10–16." *Bible Translator* 39 (1988), 223–230. wife and daughter as metaphors

1549. Okure, Teresa. "Biblical Perspectives on Women." *Voices from the Third World* 8 (1985), 82–92.

1550. Oliver, Dennis. "Psalm 44, Royal Wedding Song." *Mount Carmel* 31 (1983), 94–101. In Protestant and Jewish Bibles this is Ps. 45.

1551. Olyan, Saul. "*Hăšālôm:* Some Literary Considerations of 2 Kings 9." *CBQ* 46 (1984), 652–668. Jezebel

1552.   —. "Some Observations Concerning the Identity of the Queen of Heaven." *UF* 19 (1987), 161–174. Jer. 7:17–18; 44:15–28; Hermopolis Letter 4.1

1553.   Oren, Elyashiv. "Concerning *šrh kswth w 'nth* (Ex. 21, 10)." *Tarbiz* 33 (1964), 317 (in Hebrew).

1554.   —. "The Samson Narratives." *BM* 25 (1979), 259–262 (in Hebrew).

1555.   "Orpah. A Study in Internationalism." *Expository Times* 28 (1916–1917), 508–512.

1556.   Osiek, Carolyn. "Inspired Texts: The Dilemma of the Feminist Believer." *Spirituality Today* 32 (1980), 138–147. misogynism; feminist hermeneutics; Prov. 21:9, 19; 27:15

1557.   —. "Jacob's Well: Feminist Hermeneutics." *TBT* 24 (1986), 18–19.

1558.   —. "Biblical Images of the Feminine: Some Alternative Considerations." *TBT* 28 (1990), 342–346.

1559.   Otto, E. "Zur Stellung der Frau in den ältesten Rechtstexten des Alten Testament (Ex 20, 14; 22, 15f)." *ZEE* 26 (1982), 279–305.

1560.   Ottosson, Magnus. "Rahab and the Spies." In *DUMU-E₂-DUB-BA-A*," *Studies in Honor of Åke W. Sjöberg,* pp. 419–427. Edited by Hermann Behrens, Darlene Loding, and Martha T. Roth. Philadelphia: Occasional Publications of the Samuel Noah Kramer Fund, 1989.

1561.   Ouellette, L. "Woman's Doom in Gen 3, 16." *CBQ* 12 (1950), 389–399.

1562.   Papayiannopoulos, Ioannis. "Matters of Medico-Legal Character Concerning the Generative Function in the Old Testament." *Theologia* 55 (1984), 1012–1024 (in Modern Greek). rape

1563.   Pardee, Dennis. "*Mārîm* in Numbers v." *VT* 35 (1985), 112–115.

1564.   Parijs, Paul van. "Marriage in the Old Testament." *East Asian*

1565. Parker, Margaret. "Exploring Four Persistent Prophetic Images." *Bible Review* 6, no. 5 (1990), 38–45.

1566. Parker, Simon B. "The Marriage Blessing in Israelite and Ugaritic Literature." *JBL* 95 (1976), 23–30.

1567. —. "Jezebel's Reception of Jehu." *Maarav* 1 (1978), 67–78. 2 Kgs. 9:30–37

1568. —. "The Vow in Ugaritic and Israelite Narrative Literature." *UF* 11 (1979), 693–700. Judg. 11:30–31; 1 Sam. 1:11; Jephthah's daughter; Hannah

1569. —. "The Birth Announcement." In *Ascribe to the Lord: Biblical and Other Studies in Memory of Peter C. Craigie,* pp. 134–147. Edited by Lyle Eslinger and Glen Taylor. JSOT Supplement Series, no. 67. Sheffield: JSOT Press, 1988.

1570. Parnas, Moshe. "So She Wrote Letters in Ahab's Name and Sealed Them with His Seal." *BM* 29 (1983/84), 154–157 (in Hebrew). 1 Kgs. 21:8; Jezebel; queen; RS 16.242

1571. Paterson, J. "Divorce and Desertion in the Old Testament." *JBL* 51 (1932), 161–170.

1572. Paton, Lewis Bayles. "Outline Studies of Obscure Prophets II: Aaron and Miriam." *Homiletic Review* 49 (1904), 197–198.

1573. Patterson, Richard D. "A Multiplex Approach to Psalm 45." *Grace Theological Journal* 6 (1985), 29–48.

1574. Paul, Shalom M. "Literary and Ideological Echoes of Jeremiah in Deutero-Isaiah." *Proceedings of the Fifth World Congress of Jewish Studies,* vol. 1, Division 1 (1969), 102–120.

1575. —. "Two Cognate Terms for Mating and Copulation." *VT* 32 (1982), 492–494. Gen. 21:10, 12; Am. 2:7; *'lh* 'to mount', *hlk 'l* 'have sex with'

1576. —. "Biblical Analogues to Middle Assryian Law." In *Religion and Law: Biblical-Judaic and Islamic Perspectives,* pp. 333–350. Edited by E. B. Firmage, B. G. Weiss, and J. W. Welch. Winona Lake: Eisenbrauns, 1990. Deut. 25:11–12; Lev. 24:10–23; Isa. 47:1–4; Ezek. 23:24–25

Welch. Winona Lake: Eisenbrauns, 1990. Deut. 25:11–12; Lev. 24:10–23; Isa. 47:1–4; Ezek. 23:24–25

1577. Payne, J. Barton. "Right Questions About Isaiah 7:14." In *The Living and Active Word of God: Studies in Honor of Samuel J. Schultz*. Edited by Morris Inch and Ronald Youngblood. Winona Lake: Eisenbrauns, 1983.

1578. Peifer, Claude J. "The Marriage Theme in Hosea." *TBT* 20 (1982), 139–144.

1579. Peirce, F. X. "Recent Bible Study. The Woman of Genesis 3:15." *American Ecclesiastical Review* 103 (1940), 95–101.

1580. Peritz, I. J. "Women in the Ancient Hebrew Cult." *JBL* 17 (1898), 111–148.

1581. Perkins, Pheme. "Women in the Bible and Its World." *Interpretation* 4 (1988), 33–44.

1582. Perugni, Cesare. "Cantico dei Cantici e lirica d'amore sumerica." *RivB* 31 (1983), 21–41. *hieros gamos*

1583. Petermann, Ina. "Travestie in der Exegese? Das Buch Ruth und seine Deutungen." *DBAT* 22 (1985), 74–117.

1584. Petersen, David L. "A Thrice-Told Tale in Genre, Theme, and Motif in Genesis 12, 20 and 26." *Biblical Research* 18 (1973), 30–43.

1585. —. "Genesis 6:1–4, Yahweh and the Organization of the Cosmos." *JSOT* 13 (1979), 47–64.

1586. Petrozzi, M. "La maga di Endor." *Terra Santa* 51 (1975), 300–306.

1587. Phillips, Anthony. "Some Aspects of Family Law in Pre-Exilic Israel." *VT* 23 (1973), 349–361.

1588. —. "Nebalah—A Term for Serious Disorderly and Unruly Conduct." *VT* 25 (1975), 237–241.

1589. —. "Another Example of Family Law." *VT* 30 (1980), 240–245. 1 Sam. 18:21.

1591. —. "The Book of Ruth—Deception and Shame." *JTS* 37 (1986), 1–17.

1592. Philotea, M. "Jeremiah, Prophet of Affliction." *TBT* 36 (1968), 2513–2516.

1593. Phipps, William E. "The Plight of the Song of Songs." *JAAR* 42 (1974), 82–100.

1594. —. "The Menstrual Taboo in the Jewish-Christian Tradition." *Journal of Religion and Health* 19 (1980), 298–303.

1595. —. "Eve and Pandora Contrasted." *Theology Today* 45 (1988), 34–48.

1596. —. "A Woman Was the First to Declare Scripture Holy." *Bible Review* 6, no. 2 (1990), 14–15, 44.

1597. Pirenne, Jacques. "Le Procès de Filles de Salphaad." *Académie Royale de Belgique, Bulletin de la Classes des Lettres* Ser 5 T 52/6 (1966), 249–264. Num. 27:1–11

1598. Plaskow, Judith. "Feminism and Religious Authority." *Tikkun* 5, no. 2 (March/April 1990), 39–40.

1599. Platt, Elizabeth Ellen. "Jewelry of Bible Times and the Catalogue of Isa. 3: 18–23—Part I." *AUSS* 17 (1979), 71–84; Part II. *AUSS* 17 (1979), 189–201.

1600. Plaut, W. G. " Thou art my sister." *CCAR Journal* 10, no. 1 (1962), 26–30. Gen. 12; 20, 26

1601. Plautz, Werner. "Zur Frage des Mutterrechts im Altes Testament." *ZAW* 74 (1962), 9–30.

1602. —. "Monogamie und Polygamie im Alten Testament." *ZAW* 75 (1963), 3–27.

1603. —. "Die Form der Eheschliessung im Alten Testament." *ZAW* 76 (1964), 298–318.

1604. Plum, Karin Friis. "Kviundehermeneutik og bibels eksegese." *Dansk Teologisk Tidsskrift* 50 (1987), 19–41.

1604.   Plum, Karin Friis. "Kviundehermeneutik og bibels eksegese."
        Dansk Teologisk Tidsskrift 50 (1987), 19–41.

1605.   —. "The Female Metaphor: The Definition of Male and
        Female—an Unsolved Problem." *StTh* 43 (1989), 81–89.

1606.   Pogrebin, Letty Cottin. "Anti-Semitism in the Women's
        Movement." *Ms*, June 1982, pp. 45–46 ff.

1607.   Polzin, Robert. "'The Ancestress in Danger' in Danger."
        Semeia 3 (1975), 81–98.

1608.   Pope, Marvin H. "Response to Sasson on the Sublime Song."
        Maarav 2 (1980), 207–214. Song of Songs

1609.   Porten, B. "Theme and Historiosophic Background of the
        Scroll of Ruth." *Gratz College Annual of Jewish Studies* 6
        (1977), 69–78.

1610.   Porter, J. R. "The Daughters of Lot." *Folklore* 89 (1978),
        127–141.

1611.   Poulssen, N. "De Mikalscène, 2 Sam 6, 16. 20–23."
        Bijdragen: Tijdschrift voor Filosofie en Theologie 39
        (1978), 32–58.

1612.   —. "An Hour with Rispah: Some Reflections on 2 Samuel
        21:10." In *Von Kanaan bis Karala. Festschrift für Prof.
        Mag. Dr. Dr. J. P. M. van der Ploeg O. P. zur Vollendung
        des siebzigsten Lebensjahres am 4. Juli 1979*, pp. 185–211.
        Edited by W. C. Delsman et al. AOAT 211. Kevelaer:
        Butzon & Bercker/Neukirchen-Vluyn: Neukirchener Ver-
        lag, 1982.

1613.   Power, E. "He Asked for Water, Milk She Gave." *Biblica* 9
        (1928), 47. Judg. 5:25

1614.   Press, R. "Das Ordal im alten Israel." *ZAW* 51 (1933), 121–
        140; 227–255.

1615.   Previn, Dory. "Sheba and Solomon." *USQR* 43 (1989), 59–
        66.

1616.   Priest, John. "Huldah's Oracle." *VT* 30 (1980), 366–368.
        Huldah; Judg. 2:10; 2 Kgs. 22:14–20.

1617. Prince, J. Dyneley. "Note on Vashti." *JBL* 33 (1914), 87–90.

1618. Pritchard, Linda. "The Woman's Bible: Women in Religion in Historical Contest." In *Women and Religion 1973: Proceedings,* pp. 44–50. Edited by Joan Arnold Romero. Tallahassee: American Academy of Religion, 1973.

1619. Puech, E. "Athalie, fille d'Achab et la chronologie des rois d'Israël et de Juda." In *Escritos de Biblia y Oriente. Miscelánea commemorativa del 25° aniversario del Instituto Español Biblico y Arqueológico (Casa de Santiago) de Jerusalém,* pp. 116–136. Edited by Rafael Aguirre and Félix García López. Salamanca: Universidad Pontificio, 1981.

1620. Qimron, Elisha. "A Note to *mrḥm* = Woman, Mother." *Tarbiz* 52 (1982/83), 509 (in Hebrew). Isa. 49:15; *mrḥm; rḥm*

1621. Quitslund, S. "In the Image of God." *TBT* 84 (April 1976), 786–793.

1622. Rabinowitz, Isaac. "Sarah's Wish (Gen. XXI 6–7)." *VT* 29 (1979), 362–363.

1623. Radday, Y. T., and Welch, G. W. "Structure in the Book of Ruth." *BM* 24 (1979), 180–187 (in Hebrew).

1624. Rae, Hugh Rose. "Had Moses a Scolding Wife?" *Homiletic Review* 42 (1901), 257–260.

1625. Rallis, Irene Kerasote. "Nuptial Imagery in the Book of Hosea: Israel as the Bride of Yahweh." *St. Vladimir's Theological Quarterly* 34 (1990), 197–219.

1626. Ramras-Rauch, Gila. "Fathers and Daughters: Two Biblical Narratives." *Bucknell Review* 33, no. 2 (1990), 169–197.

1627. Ramsey, George W. "Is Name–Giving an Act of Domination in Genesis 2:23 and Elsewhere?" *CBQ* 50 (1988), 24–35.

1628. Rand, Herbert. "Justice in Solomon's Court." *DD* 10 (1982), 170–176. 1 Kgs. 3:16–28.

1629. Rapaport, D. I. "L'Etude des Troubles Menstruals dans la Bible et le Talmud." *Revue de l'Histoire de la Médecine*

Hébraique 9 (1951), 31–34. Lev. 15:19–23.

1630.   Rast, Walter E. "Cakes for the Queen of Heaven." In *Scripture in History and Theology: Essays in Honor of J. Coert Rylaarsdaam*, pp. 167–180. Edited by Arthur L. Merrill and Thomas W. Overholt. Pittsburgh Theological Monograph Series, no. 17. Pittsburgh: Pickwick Press, 1977. Jer 7:18; 44:19

1631.   Ratner, Robert. "The 'Feminine Takes Precedence' Syntagm and Job 19, 15." *ZAW* 102 (1990), 238–251.

1632.   Rattray, Susan. "Marriage Roles, Kinship Terms, and Family Structures in the Bible." *SBL Seminar Papers* 26 (1987), 537–544.

1633.   Raurell, Frederic. "El plaer eròtic en el Cantic dels Cantics." *Revista Catalana de Teología* 6 (1981), 257–298.

1634.   —. "Erotic Pleasure in the 'Song of Songs'." *Laurentianum* 24 (1983), 5–45.

1635.   —. "Il mito della maschilità di Dio come problema ermeneutico." *Laurentianum* 25 (1984), 3–77. Gen. 1:27; Deut. 32:18; Hos. 11:1–4

1636.   Ravenna, A. "La poligamia presso gli Ebrei." *Rivista Italiana per le Scienze Giuridiche* 11 (1967), 377–379.

1637.   Rebera, Basil. "Translating Ruth 3:16." *Bible Translator* 38 (1987), 234–237.

1638.   Read, D. "The Ethical Quality of Life: The Human Sexual Context." *American Ecclesiastical Review* 164 (1971), 257–264. Gen. 2–3.

1639.   Rehm, Martin. "Das Wort *'almah* in Is 7, 14." *BZ* 8 (1964), 89–101.

1640.   Reid, S. B. "Violence and Vengeance: Ingredients for Tragedy." In *Encounter with the Text*, pp. 153–158. Edited by Martin J. Buss. Semeia Supplements, no. 8. Philadelphia: Fortress, 1979.

1641.   Reif, S. C. "What enraged Phinehas?— A Study of Numbers

25:8." *JBL* 90 (1971), 200–206.

1642. Reines, H. S. "The Acquiring of a Wife in the Torah and in the Talmud." *Sinai* 60 (1967), 276–282 (in Hebrew).

1643. Rembold, Annette. "'Und Mirjam nahm die Pauke in die Hand, eine Frau prophezeit und tanzt einem anderen Leben voran.' Das Alte Testament feministisch gelesen." In *Handbuch Feministische Theologie*, pp. 285–298. Edited by Christine Schaumberger and Monika Maassen. Münster: Morgana, 1986.

1644. Renaud, Bernard. "Fidelité humaine et fidelité de Dieu dans le livre d'Osée 1–3." *Revue de Droit Canonique* 33 (1983), 184–200.

1645. —. "Osée 1–3: analyse diachronique et lecture synchronique, problèmes de méthode." *RSR* 57 (1983), 249–260.

1646. Rendsburg, Gary A. "Notes on Genesis XXXV." *VT* 34 (1984), 361–366. Rebekah, Deborah the wetnurse; Gen. 24:59.

1647. —. "David and His Circle in Genesis XXXVIII." *VT* 36 (1986), 438–446. Gen. 38; Tamar; daughter of Shua; Bathsheba

1648. Reymond, Robert L. "Who is the '*almah* of Isaiah 7:14?" *Presbyterion* 15 (1989), 1–15.

1649. Rice, Gene. "A Neglected Interpretation of the Immanuel Prophecy." *ZAW* 90 (1978), 220–227. Isa. 7:14; '*almah.*

1650. Richter, Hans-Friedemann. "Zum Levirat im Buch Ruth." *ZAW* 95 (1983), 123–126. Ruth 4:14–15; Deut. 25:10; levirate marriage.

1651. Ridout, G. "The Rape of Tamar." In *Rhetorical Criticism: Essays in Honor of James Muilenberg*, pp. 75–84. Pittsburgh Theological Monographs Series, no. 1. Pittsburgh: Pickwick Press, 1974.

1652. Rigaux, B., O.F.M. "La Femme et son Lignage dans Genèse III, 14–15." *RB* 61 (1954), 321–348.

1654.   Ringeling, H. "Die biblische Begründung der Monogamie."
        ZEE 10 (1966), 81–102.

1655.   Ringgren, Helmer. "Skönhetsävlingen i Esthers bok." *Svensk
        Exegetisk Årsbok* 46 (1981), 69–73.

1656.   —. "The Marriage Motif in Israelite Religion." In *Ancient
        Israelite Religion: Essays in Honor of Frank Moore Cross*,
        pp. 412–428. Edited by Patrick D. Miller, Jr., Paul P.
        Hansen, and S. Dean McBride. Philadelphia: Fortress,
        1987.

1657.   Ritterspach, A. D. "Rhetorical Criticism and the Song of
        Hannah." In *Rhetorical Criticism: Essays in Honor of
        James Muilenberg*, pp. 68–74. Pittsburgh Theological
        Monograph Series, no. 1. Pittsburgh: Pickwick Press,
        1974.

1658.   Robertson, Noel. "The Ritual Background of the Dying God
        in Cyprus and Syro-Palestine." *HTR* 75 (1982), 313–360.
        2 Kgs. 9; Ezek. 8:14

1659.   Robinson, Bernhard P. "The Jealousy of Miriam: A Note on
        Num 12." *ZAW* 101 (1989), 428–432.

1660.   Robinson, Ira. "*bĕpetaḥ ʿênayim* in Genesis 38:14." *JBL* 96
        (1977), 569.

1661.   —. "Zipporah to the Rescue: A Contextual Study of Exodus
        IV 24–6." *VT* 36 (1986), 447–461. Zipporah, Rahab,
        Ruth, foreign women who put Israelites to shame

1662.   Rodd, Cyril S. "The Family in the Old Testament." *Bible
        Translator* 18 (1967), 22–23.

1663.   Römer, W. H. Ph." Randbemerkungen zur Travestie von
        Deut. 22, 5." In *Travels in the World of the Old Testa-
        ment: Studies Presented to Professor M. A. Beek on the
        Occasion of his 65th Birthday*, pp. 217–222. Edited by
        M. S. H. G. Heerma van Voss et al. Assen: Van Gorcum,
        1974. Deut. 22:5

1664.   Rofé, Alexander. "The Betrothal of Rebekah (Gen. 24)."
        Eshel Beer-Sheva I (1976), 42–67 (in Hebrew).

1664. Rofé, Alexander. "The Betrothal of Rebekah (Gen. 24)." *Eshel Beer-Sheva* I (1976), 42–67 (in Hebrew).

1665. —. "La composizione de Gen. 24." *Bibbia e Oriente* 23 (1981), 161–165. Rebekah.

1666. —. "The Laws of Warfare in the Book of Deuteronomy: Their Origins, Intent and Positivity." *JSOT* 32 (1985), 23–44. Deut. 21:10–14.

1667. —. "Family and Sex Laws in Deuteronomy and the Book of the Covenant." *Henoch* 9 (1987), 131–160. Ex. 21–22; Deut. 21–25.

1668. —. "The Vineyard and Naboth: The Origin and Message of the Story." *VT* 38 (1988), 89–104. Jezebel; 1 Kgs. 21:1–20

1669. Rosenberg, Joel W. "The feminine through a (male) glass darkly." *Response* 9 (Winter 1975/76), 67–88.

1670. —. "The Garden Story Forward and Backward: The non-narrative dimension of Gen. 2–3." *Prooftexts* 1 (1981), 1–27.

1671. Rosenzweig, Michael L. "A Helper Equal to Him." *Judaism* 35. no. 3 (1986), 277–280. Gen. 1:27; 2:18–24; 'ezer kěnegdô.

1672. Roth, Wolfgang W. "The Wooing of Rebekah: A Tradition-Critical Study of Genesis 24." *CBQ* 34 (1972), 177–187.

1673. Rothe, Rosa M. "Duas mulheres 'violentas,' Débora e Jael." *Est Bib* 6 (1984), 21–30.

1674. Rothschild, Max M. "Israelites and Aliens—IV." *DD* 11 (1983), 245–248. the foreign women in Ezra-Nehemiah.

1675. Rottenberg, Meir. "The Interpretation of Rebekah's Question 'lāmmâ zeh 'ānōkî.'" *BM* 29 (1983/84), 218–219 (in Hebrew). Gen. 25:22.

1676. —. "Did Job's Wife Really Use a Euphemism in Job 2:9?" *Lěšonēnu* 52 (1988), 176–177 (in Hebrew).

1677. Rouillard, H., and Tropper, J. *"trpym,* rituels de guérison et

culte des ancêtres d'après 1 Samuel XIX 11–17 et les
textes parallèles d'Assur et de Nuzi." *VT* 37 (1987), 340–
361. Michal.

1678. Rowley, H. H. "The Interpretation of the Song of Songs."
JTS 38 (1937), 337–363.

1679. —. "The Marriage of Hosea." *BJRL* 39 (1956), 200–233.

1680. Rozner, Fred. "The Ordeal of the Wayward Woman (Sotah):
Miracle or Natural Phenomenon." *Koroth* 32 (1984),
396–406.

1681. Rudolph, W. "Präparierte Jungfrauen?" *ZAW* 75 (1968), 65–
73. Hos. 1.

1682. —. "Zu Mal 2 10–16." *ZAW* 93 (1981), 85–90. monogamy,
divorce; Deut. 24.

1683. Ruether, Rosemary. "Women's Liberation in Historical and
Theological Perspective." *Soundings* 53 (Winter 1970),
363–373.

1684. —. "Feminism and Patriarchal Religion: Principles of
Ideological Critique of the Bible." *JSOT* 22 (1982), 54–66.

1685. —. "Prophetic Tradition and the Liberation of Women:
Premise and Betrayal." *Journal of Theology for Southern
Africa* 73 (1990), 24–33.

1686. Ruppert, Lothar. "Erwägungen zur Kompositions—und
Redaktionsgeschichte von Hosea 1–3." *BZ* 26 (1982),
208–233.

1687. Russell, Letty M. "Women and Freedom." *Lutheran World*
22, no. 1 (1975), 7–13.

1688. Rylaarsdam, J. Coert. "The Song of Songs and Biblical
Faith." *Biblical Research* 10 (1965), 7–18.

1689. Sacon, Kiyoshi K. "A Study of the Literary Structures of 'The
Succession Narrative'." In *Studies in the Period of David
and Solomon and Other Essays*, pp. 27–54. Edited by
Tomoo Ishida. Tokyo: Yamakawa-Shuppansha, 1982.

1690. Sadakata, H. "A Morphological Analysis of the Narrative of the Abandoned Child-Moses." *Bulletin of Christian Research Institute, Meiji Gakuin University,* 1978. pp. 1–17. Moses's mother, sister and adoptive mother.

1691. Sadgrove, M. "The Song of Songs as Wisdom Literature." In *Studia Biblica 1978. I. Papers on Old Testament and Related Themes,* pp. 245–248. JSOT Supplement Series, no. 11. Sheffield: JSOT Press, 1979.

1692. Sagan, Carl. "In Pain Shalt Thou Bring Forth Children." *BAR* 5, no. 1 (1979), 28.

1693. Sakenfeld, Katherine Doob. "The Bible and Women: Bane or Blessing." *Theology Today* 32 (1975), 222–233.

1694. —. "Old Testament Perspectives: Methodological Issues." *JSOT* 22 (1982), 13–20. feminist hermeneutics; inclusive language; feminine metaphors for God; Num. 27; 36; the daughters of Zelophehad

1695. —. "Loyalty and Love: The Language of Human Interconnections in the Hebrew Bible." *Michigan Quarterly Review* 22, no. 3 (1983), 190–204.

1696. —. "In the Wilderness, Awaiting the Land: The Daughters of Zelophehad and Feminist Interpretation." *Princeton Seminary Bulletin* 9 (1988), 179–186. Num. 27; 36

1697. —. "Feminist Perspectives on Bible and Theology." *Interpretation* 42 (1988), 5–18.

1698. —. "Zelophehad's Daughters." *Perspectives on the Hebrew Bible: Essays in Honor of Walter J. Harrleson,* pp. 37–47. Edited by J. L. Crenshaw. Macon, Ga.: Mercer University Press, 1988.

1699. Salkin, Jeffrey K. "Dinah: The Torah's Forgotten Woman." *Judaism* 35 (1986), 284–289.

1700. Salvoni, F. "La profezia di Isaia gulla 'Verginea' partoriente (Is 7, 14)." *Ricerche Bibliche e Religiose* 1 (1966), 19–40.

1701. —. "Sesso e amore nella Bibbia." *Ricerche Bibliche e Religiose* 4 (1969), 105–129.

1702. Sapp, S. "Biblical Perspectives on Human Sexuality." _Duke Divinity School Review_ 41 (1976), 105–122.

1703. Sarna, Nahum M. "The Ravishing of Dinah: A Commentary on Genesis Chapter 34." In _Studies in Jewish Education_, pp. 143–186. Edited by A. Shapiro and B. Cohen. New York: Ktav, 1984.

1704. —. "The Birth of Moses." _New Traditions_ 3 (1986), 84–85. wet-nursing

1705. —. "Exploring Exodus: The Oppression." _BA_ 49 (1986), 68–80. the midwives Shiphrah and Puah

1706. Sasson, Jack M. "The Issue of Ge'ullah in Ruth." _JSOT_ 5 (1978), 52–64.

1707. —. On M. M. Pope's _Song of Songs_ [AB 7c]." _Maarav_ 1 (1979), 177–196.

1708. —. "Unlocking the Poetry of the Song of Songs." _Bible Review_ 1, no. 1 (1985), 10–19.

1709. —. "_Wĕlō' yitbōšāšû_ (Gen 2, 25) and its implications." _Biblica_ 66 (1985), 418–421.

1710. —. "A Major Contribution to Song of Songs Scholarship." _JAOS_ 107 (1987), 733–789.

1711. —. "Who Cut Samson's Hair? (And Other Trifling Issues Raised by Judges 16)." _Prooftexts_ 8 (1988), 333–339.

1712. Sasson, Victor. "King Solomon and the Dark Lady in the Song of Songs." _VT_ 39 (1989), 407–414.

1713. Saucy, R. L. "The Husband of One Wife." _Bibliotheca Sacra_ 131 (1974), 229–240.

1714. Sauge, Kirsten. "Jael-tradisjonene i Dommerne 4 og 5." _Norsk Teologisk Tidsskrift_ 88 (1987), 109–113. Jael; Judges 4

1715. Saviv, S. "The Antiquity of Song of Songs, The Song of Songs' Influence on Isaiah and Jeremiah." _BM_ 29 (1983/84), 295–304 (in Hebrew).

1716. Sawyer, John F. A. "Daughter of Zion and the Servant of the Lord in Isaiah: A Comparison." *JSOT* 44 (1989), 89–107.

1717. Scanzoni, Letha. "The Feminists and the Bible." *Christianity Today* 17 (1973), 442–445.

1718. —. "The Early Feminists and the Bible: Do We Sin By Serving? In *What You Should Know about Women's Lib: A Christian Approach to Problems of Today,* pp. 8–17; 64–69. Edited by Miriam G. Moran. New York: Keats, 1974.

1719. Scharbert, J. "Ehe und Ehescheidung in der Rechtssprache des Pentateuch und beim Chronisten." In *Studien zum Pentateuch F. S. W. Kornfeld,* pp. 213–225. Edited by G. Braulik. Vienna: Herder, 1977.

1720. Schechter, Solomon. "Woman in Temple and Synagogue." In *Studies in Judaism: First Series,* pp. 313–325. Philadelphia: Jewish Publication Society, 1896.

1721. Schenker, Adrian. "Die Ehre einer Frau 'Heiratsschwindel' und Beweisverfahren in Israel." *Freiburger Zeitschrift für Philosphie und Theologie* 74 (1987), 237–242. Review of Locher, q.v.

1722. Schierling, Marla J. "Primeval Woman: A Yahwistic View of Woman in Genesis 1–11:9." *Journal of Theology for Southern Africa* 42 (1983), 5–9.

1723. Schildenberger, J. "Die Erschaffung des Menschen nach der Paradieserzählung." *Benediktinische Monatschrift* 7 (1951), 276ss.

1724. —. "Die Erzählung von Paradies und Sündenfall (Gen 2, 4b–3, 24)." *Bibel und Kirche* 1 (1951), 3 ss.

1725. —. "Das Buch Ruth als literarisches Kunstwerk und als religiöse Botschaft." *Bibel und Kirche* 18 (1963), 102–108.

1726. —. "Der Königspsalm." *Erbe und Auftrag* 56 (1980), 128–133. Ps. 45; Jezebel.

1727. Schmid, Herbert. "Die 'Mutter Erde' in der Schöpfungsgeschichte der Priesterschrift." *Judaica* 22 (1966), 237–243.

1728.   Schmidt, Anne. "Undviklingen i Israel og Juda 841–35 f. Kr.
        Som 2 Kong. 9–11 ser den." *Dansk Teologisk Tidsskrift* 46
        (1983), 1–21. Athalia

1729.   Schmidt, Klaus. "Dar bist du aufgestanden, Debora; Väter
        und Mütter in der Anfängen Israels." *Junge Kirche* 46
        (1985), 442–445.

1730.   Schmitt, John J. "The Gender of Ancient Israel." *JSOT* 26
        (1983), 115–125.

1731.   —. "The Motherhood of God and Zion as Mother." *RB* 92
        (1985), 557–569.

1732.   —. "The Wife of God in Hosea 2." *Biblical Research* 34
        (1989), 5–18.

1733.   —. "Israel and Zion—Two Gendered Images: Biblical Speech
        Patterns and Their Contemporary Neglect." *Horizons* 18
        (1991), 18–32.

1734.   —. "Like Eve, Like Adam; *mšl* in Gen 3, 16." *Biblica* 72
        (1991), 1–22.

1735.   —. "The Virgin of Israel: Referent and Use of the Phrase in
        Amos and Jeremiah." *CBQ* 53 (1991), 365–387.

1736.   Schottroff, Luise. "Das Bundnis mit der Ungerechtigkeit: die
        Stadt ist zur Hure geworden (Jes 1, 16–21)." In *Die
        Parteilichkeit Gottes*, pp. 69–77. Edited by Luise and Willy
        Schottroff. Munich: Kaiser, 1984.

1737.   —. "Bibelarbeit zu Jes 42, 1–9." In *Die Macht der Auferste-
        hung: Sozialgeschichtliche Bibelauslegungen*, pp. 27–38.
        Munich: Kaiser, 1988.

1738.   Schüngel-Straumann, Helen. "Zum Text von Gen 16, 13b."
        VT 21 (1971), 254–256. Hagar

1739.   —. "Tamar. Eine Frau verschafft sich ihr Recht." *Bibel und
        Kirche* 39 (1984), 148–157.

1740.   —. "Gott als Mutter in Hosea 11." *Theologische Quartal-
        schrift* 166 (1986), 119–134.

1741. —. "God as Mother in Hosea 11." *Theology Digest* 34 (1987), 3–8.

1742. Schüssler Fiorenza, Elisabeth. "Emerging Issues in Feminist Biblical Interpretation." In *Christian Feminism: Visions of a New Humanity*, pp. 33–54. Edited by Judith L. Weidman. San Francisco: Harper & Row, 1984.

1743. —. "To Set the Record Straight: Biblical Women's Studies." In *Mainstreaming: Feminist Research for Teaching Religious Studies*, pp. 21–31. Edited by Arlene Swidler and Walter E. Conn. Lanham, Md.: University Press of America, 1985.

1744. —. "The Ethics of Biblical Interpretation: Decentering Biblical Scholarship." *JBL* 107 (1988), 3–17.

1745. —. "Text and Reality—Reality as Text: The Problem of a Feminist Historical and Social Reconstruction Based on Texts." *StTh* 43 (1989), 19–34.

1746. Schunck, Klaus-Dietrich. "Das 9. und 10. Gebot-jüngstes Glied des Dekalogs?" *ZAW* 96 (1984), 104–109.

1747. Schwartz, B. J. "A Literary Study of the Slave-girl Pericope—Leviticus 19:20–22." *Studies in Bible*, pp. 241–256. Scripta Hierosolymitana, no. 31. Edited by Sara Japhet. Jerusalem: Magnes, 1986.

1748. Seebass, H. "Zum Text von Gen. 16, 13b." *VT* 21 (1971), 254–256. Hagar

1749. —. "Nathan and David in 2 Sam. 12." *ZAW* 86 (1974), 203–211.

1750. —. "Num XI, XII und die Hypothese des Jahwisten." *VT* 28 (1978), 214–233. Miriam, the Cushite wife

1751. —. "Gehörten Verheissungen zum ältesten Bestand der Väter-Erzählungen?" *Biblica* 64 (1983), 189–209.

1752. Segal, Benjamin J. "The Theme of the Song of Songs." *DD* 15 (1986/87), 106–113.

1753. —. "Double Meanings in the Song of Songs." *DD* 16 (1987/88), 249–55.

1754. —. "Four Repetitions in the Song of Songs." *DD* 16 (1987/88), 32–39.

1755. Segal, J. B. "The Jewish Attitude towards Women." *JJS* 30 (1979), 121–137. misogyny and monotheism

1756. Segal, M. H. "The Song of Songs." *VT* 12 (1962), 470–490.

1757. Segert, Stanislav. "Paranomasia in the Samson Narrative in Judges XIII–XVI." *VT* 34 (1984), 454–461. Delilah means "Flirtations."

1758. —. "Diptotic Geographical Feminine Names in the Hebrew Bible." *Zeitschrift für Althebraistik* 1 (1988), 99–102.

1759. Selman, M. J. "Comparative Customs and the Patriarchal Age." In *Essays on the Patriarchal Narratives*, pp. 93–138. Edited by A. R. Millard and D. J. Wiseman. Leicester: Inter-Varsity, 1980.

1760. Selms, A. van. "The Best Man and Bride—From Sumer to St. John. With a New Interpretation of Judges, Chapters 14 and 15." *JNES* 9 (1950), 65–75.

1761. Serra, Aristide. "Eva, donna dell' alleanza." *Parola Spirito e Vita* 13 (1986), 171–190.

1762. Shapira, D. S. "Biblical Researches." *Sinai* 54 (1963–64), 53–47 (in Hebrew). Hos. 1–3.

1763. Sharp, Donald B., S. J. "In Defense of Rebecca?" *BTB* 10 (1980), 164–168.

1764. Shashar, M. "Song of Songs and Bedouin Love Poetry." *BM* 31 (1985/86), 360–370 (in Hebrew).

1765. Sherlock, P. "Women and the Arguments from Creation." *Interchange* 20 (1976), 245–249.

1766. Shideler, M. M. "Male and Female Created He Them." *Religion in Life* 43 (Spring 1974), 60–67.

1767. Shrager, Miriam Y. "A Unique Biblical Law." *DD* 15 (1986/87), 190–194. Deut. 25:11–12; MAL #8.

1768.   Siebert-Hommes, J. C. "Twelve Women in Exodus 1 and 2." *Amsterdamse cahiers voor Exegese en Bijbelse theologie* 9 (1988), 47–58.

1769.   Simms, Tom. "Solomon's Pillow Talk with His Egyptian Wife." *BAR* 14, no. 1 (1988), 67.

1770.   Simon, Uriel. "An Ironic Approach to a Biblical Story: On the Interpretation of the Story of David and Bathsheba." *HaSifrut* 2 (1970), 598–607 (in Hebrew).

1771.   —. "The Story of the Birth of Samuel." In *Studies in Bible and Exegesis* 2, pp. 57–110. Edited by U. Simon. Ramat-Gan: Bar-Ilan University Press, 1986 (in Hebrew).

1772.   Sjöberg, Åke. "Eve and the Chameleon." In *In the Shelter of Elyon: Essays on Ancient Palestinian Life and Literature in Honor of G. W. Ahlström*, pp. 217–225. Edited by W. Boyd Barrick and John R. Spencer. JSOT Supplement Series, no. 31. Sheffield: JSOT Press, 1984.

1773.   Ska, Jean-Louis. "'Je vais lui faire un allié qui soit son homologue' (Gn 2, 18): A propos du terme *'ezer* 'aide'." *Biblica* 65 (1984), 233–238.

1774.   —. "L'arbre de la tente: la fonction du décor en Gn 18, 1–15." *Biblica* 69 (1987), 383–389. Sarah.

1775.   —. "L'Ironie de Tamar (Gen 38)." *ZAW* 100 (1988), 261–263.

1776.   Smelik, K. A. D. "The Witch of Endor: I Samuel 28 in Rabbinic and Christian Exegesis till 800 A.D." *Vigiliae Christianae* 33 (1979), 160–179.

1777.   Snaith, N. H. "The Cult of Molech." *VT* 16 (1966), 123–124.

1778.   —. "The Daughters of Zelophahad." *VT* 16 (1966), 124–127. Num. 27:1–11; 36: 1–9; Josh. 17:1–16.

1779.   Soden, W. von "*Mīryām— Maria '(Gottes-) Geschenk.'*" *UF* 2 (1970), 269–272.

1780.   —. "Zum hebräischen Wörterbuch." *UF* 13 (1981), 157–

164. Ex. 21:10: 'ônâ = 'shelter'

1781. Soggin, J. A. "Osservazioni filologico-linguistiche al secundo capitolo della Genesi." *Biblica* 44 (1963), 521–530.

1782. —. "Bemerkungen zum Deboralied, Richter Kap. 5. Versuch einer neuen Übersetzung und eines Verstosses in die älteste Geschichte Israels." *TLZ* 106 (1981), 625–639.

1783. —. "Jezabel, oder die fremde Frau." In *Mélanges bibliques et orientaux en l'honneur de M. Henri Cazelles*, pp. 453–460. AOAT 212. Edited by K. Bergerhof, M. Dietrich, and O. Loretz. Kevelaer: Butzon & Bercker/Neukirchen-Vluyn: Neukirchener Verlag, 1981.

1784. Sole, Francesco. "Il matrimonio presso gli Israelite." *Palestra del Clero* 43 (1964), 1081–1094.

1785. Soleh, A. "The Artistic Structure of Jehu's Enthronement (2 Kings 9–10)." *BM* 28 (1982/83), 64–71 (in Hebrew). Jezebel.

1786. Souza, Luís de. "Magia na Biblia." *Revista de Cultura Biblica*, n.s., 9 (1985), 3–4. The witch of Endor

1787. Speiser, E. A. "The Wife-Sister Motif in Patriarchal Narratives." In *Biblical and Other Studies*, pp. 15–28. Edited by A. Altmann. Waltham: Brandeis University Press, 1963.

1788. —. "Leviticus and the Critics." In *Yehezkel Kaufmann Jubilee Volume*, pp. 28–45. Edited by Menahem Haran. Jerusalem: Magnes, 1960. Lev. 19:20–21.

1789. Spreafico, Ambrogio. "Possibilita elimiti di una ricera di antropologia biblica veterotestamentaria. Note in margine a une recente volume di F. Raurell." *Rivista Biblica* 35 (1987), 63–68.

1790. Stamm, J. J. "Hebräische Frauennamen." In *Hebräische Wortforschung. Festschrift für W. Baumgartner*, pp. 301–339. VTS, vol. 16. Leiden: E. J. Brill, 1967.

1791. Stecher, Reinhold. "Die persönliche Weisheit in den Proverbien Kap. 8." *Zeitschrift für Katholische Theologie* 75 (1953), 411–451.

1792. Steinberg, Naomi. "Gender Roles in the Rebekah Cycle." *USQR* 39 (1984), 175–188.

1793. Steiner, F. "Enslavement and the Early Hebrew Lineage System; an Explication of Genesis 47, 29–31; 48, 1–16." *Man* 54 (1954), 73–75.

1794. Steinmueller, John C. "The Etymology of the Biblical Usage of *'Almah.*" *CBQ* 2 (1940), 28–43.

1795. Steyn, J. "Simson in Gasa (Richters 16:1–3)." *Theologica Evangelica* 11/2–3 (1978), 13–21. Samson's women

1796. Stinespring, W. F. "No Daughter of Zion: A Study of the Appositional Genitive in Hebrew Grammar." *Encounter* 26 (1965), 133–141.

1797. Stitzinger, Michael F. "Genesis 1–3 and the Male/Female Role Relationships." *Grace Theological Journal* 2 (1981), 23–44

1798. Stockton, E. D. "The woman: A Biblical Theme." *Australian Journal of Biblical Archaeology* 2 (1973), 106–112.

1799. Stolz, Fritz. "Feministische Religiosität-Feministische Theologie. Religionswissenschaftliche Perspketiven." *Zeitschrift für Theologie und Kirche* 86, no. 4 (1989), 477–516.

1800. Strauss, Joseph. "Woman's Position in Ancient and Modern Jewry." *Westminster Review* 174 (1910), 620–628.

1801. Streefkerk, Nic. "Saul te Endor." *Homiletica en Biblica* 21 (1982), 248–252.

1802. Stuhlmueller, Carroll. "The Women of Genesis." *TBT* 28 (1990), 347–352.

1803. Stulman, Louis. "Encroachment in Deuteronomy: An Analysis of the Social World of the D Code." *JBL* 109 (1990), 613–632. mother, harlotry, adultery; Deut. 21; 22

1804. —. "Sex and Familial Crisis in the D Code: A Witness to Mores in Transition." *JSOT* 53 (1992), 47–64.

1805. Surberg, Raymond F. "The Place of Woman in the Old Testament." *The Springfielder* 33, no. 4 (March 1970), 27–32.

1806. Swanston, H. F. G. "Michal at the Window." *TBT* 48 (1970), 3312–3313.

1807. Swidler, Leonard. "In Search of Huldah." *TBT* 98 (Nov. 1978), 1780–1785.

1808. Tamez, Elsa. "The Woman Who Complicated the History of Salvation." *Cross Currents* 36 (1986), 129–135. Hagar; Gen. 16; 21

1809. Tångberg, K. Arvid. "Die Bewertung des ungeborenen Lebens im alten Israel und im alten Orient." *Scandinavian Journal of the Old Testament* 1 (1987), 51–65.

1810. —. "Vurderingen au det ufødte liv i det gamle Israel og Orienten." *Tidsskrift for Teologi og Kirke* 55 (1984), 212–221. Ex. 21:22; Job. 10; Ps. 139; abortion

1811. Taylor, A. B. "Liberation for Women: A Biblical View." *Japan Christian Quarterly* 40 (Spring 1974), 61–70.

1812. Taylor, J. Glen. "The Song of Deborah and Two Canaanite Goddesses." *JSOT* 23 (1982), 99–108.

1813. Terrien, Samuel. "The Omphalos Myth and Hebrew Religion." *VT* 20 (1970), 315–338.

1814. —. "Towards a Biblical Theology of Womanhood." *Religion in Life* 42, no. 3 (Autumn 1973), 322–333.

1815. Thompson, J. A. "Industry in Ancient Israel." *Buried History* 21, no. 1 (1985), 18–24.

1816. —. "Writing in Ancient Israel." *Buried History* 21, no. 2 (1986), 35–41.

1817. Thompson, Michael E. W. "Isaiah's Song of Immanuel." *Expository Times* 95 (1983), 67–71. Isa. 7:14; 'almah.

1818. Thompson, Th., and Thompson, D. "Some Legal Problems in the Book of Ruth." *VT* 18 (1968), 79–99.

1819. Thompson, Yaakov. "Samson in Timnah; Judges 14–15." *DD*

15 (1986/87), 249–255.

1820. Tijn, M. van. "Chawa-Eva (Gen 2, 20–23)." *Regelrecht 5* (1968), 20–24.

1821. Toeg, A. "Does Dt. 24, 1–4 Incorporate a General Law on Divorce?" *Diné Israel* 2 (1971), v–xxiv.

1822. Tolbert, Mary. "Defining the Problem: The Bible and Feminist Hermeneutics." *Semeia* 28 (1983), 113–126.

1823. —. "Protestant Feminists and the Bible: On the Horns of a Dilemma." *USQR* 43 (1989), 1–17.

1824. Toorn, Karel van der. "Judges XVI 21 in the Light of the Akkadian Sources." *VT* 32 (1986), 248–253. Women's work a humiliation

1825. —. "The Nature of the Biblical 'Teraphim' in the Light of the Cuneiform Evidence." *CBQ* 52 (1990), 203–222 Rachel; Michal; Gen. 31:19; 1 Sam. 19:11–17

1826. —. "Female Prostitution in Payment of Vows in Ancient Israel." *JBL* 108 (1989), 193–205.

1827. Tosato, Angelo. "Il linguaggio matrimoniale veterotestamentario: stato degli studi." *Annali dell' Instituto Orientali di Napoli* 43 (1983), 135–160.

1828. —. "The Law of Leviticus 18:18; A Reexamination." *CBQ* 46 (1984), 199–214.

1829. —. "L'onore di una donna in Israele." *Biblica* 68 (1987), 268–276. Deut. 22:13–21; review of Locher

1830. Tournay, Raymond-Jacques. "The Song of Songs and its Concluding Section." *Immanuel* 10 (1980), 5–14.

1831. Trible, Phyllis. "Depatriarchalizing in Biblical Interpretation." *JAAR* 41 (1973), 30–48.

1832. —. "Eve and Adam: Genesis 2–3 Reread." *Andover Newton Quarterly* 13 (1973), 251–258; reprinted in *Womanspirit Rising*, pp. 74–83. Edited by Carol P. Christ and Judith Plaskow. San Francisco: Harper & Row, 1979.

1833. —. "Good Tidings of Great Joy: Biblical Faith without Sexism." *Christianity and Crisis* 34 (February 4, 1974), 12–16.

1834. —. "The Bible Without Sexism." *Jewish Spectator,* 40, no. 1 (Spring 1978), 49–53.

1835. —. "Biblical Theology as Women's Work." *Religion in Life* 44, no. 1 (Spring 1975), 7–13.

1836. —. "Wisdom Builds a Poem: The Architecture of Proverbs 1:20–33." *JBL* 94 (1975), 509–518.

1837. —. "The Gift of a Poem: A Rhetorical Study of Jeremiah 31: 15–22." *Andover Newton Quarterly* 17 (1976–77), 271–280.

1838. —. "Two Women in a Man's World: A Reading of the Book of Ruth." *Soundings* 59 (1976), 251–279. 135.

1839. —. "A Meditation in Mourning: The Sacrifice of the Daughter of Jephthah." *USQR* 36, Supplement (1981), 59–73.

1840. —. "Feminist Hermeneutics and Biblical Studies." *The Christian Century* (Feb. 1982), 116–118.

1841. —. "A Daughter's Death: Feminism, Literary Criticism, and the Bible." *Michigan Quarterly Review* 22, no. 3 (1983), 178–189.

1842. —. "Huldah's Holy Writ: On Women and Biblical Authority." *Touchstone* 3, no. 1 (1985), 6–13.

1843. —. "The Other Woman: A Literary and Theological Study of the Hagar Narratives." In *Understanding the Word: Essays in Honor of Bernhard W. Anderson,* pp. 221–246. Edited by James T. Butler, Edgar W. Conrad, and Ben C. Ollenburger. JSOT Supplement Series, no. 37. Sheffield: JSOT Press, 1985.

1844. —. "Bringing Miriam out of the Shadows." *Bible Review* 5, no. 1 (1989), 14–25, 34.

1845. —. "Five Loaves and Two Fishes: Feminist Hermeneutics and Biblical Theology." *TS* 50 (1989), 279–295.

1846. —. "The Pilgrim Bible on a Feminist Journey." *Daughters of Sarah* 15 (1989), 4–7.

1847. —. "Subversive Justice: Tracing the Miriam Traditions." In *Justice and the Holy: Essays in Honor of Walter Harrelson*, pp. 99–109. Edited by Douglas A. Knight and Peter J. Paris. Atlanta: Scholars Press, 1989.

1848. Tsevat, Matitiahu. "Marriage and Monarchical Legitimacy in Ugarit and Israel." *JSS* 3 (1958), 237–243.

1849. —. "Two Old Testament Stories and their Hittite Analogues." *JAOS* 103 (1983), 321–326.

1850. Tsimariyon, Tsemah. "Shared Elements in the Books of Jonah, Ruth, and Judith." *BM* 32 (1986/87), 221–223 (in Hebrew).

1851. Tsmudi, Yosef. "Concerning the Scroll of Ruth." *BM* 35 (1989–90), 202–215 (in Hebrew).

1852. Tucker, Gene M. "The Rahab Saga (Joshua 2): Some Form-Critical and Traditio-Historical Observations." In *The Use of the Old Testament in the New and Other Essays. Festschrift for W. F. Stinespring*, pp. 66–86. Edited by James E. Efird. Durham, N.C.: Duke University Press, 1972.

1853. Tucker, N. "Genesis 24." *BM* 16 (1971), 326–338 (in Hebrew).

1854. Turner, Mary Donovan. "Rebekah: Ancestor of Faith." *Lexington Theological Quarterly* 20 (1985), 42–49.

1855. Turnham, Timothy J. "Ishmael." *Biblical Illustrator* 14 (Fall 1987), 15–17. Hagar, Sarah, Gen. 16; 21.

1856. —. "Male and Female Slaves in the Sabbath Year Laws of Exodus 21:1–11." *SBL Seminar Papers* 26 (1987), 545–549.

1857. Tuya, Manuel de. "La profecia de la 'almah (Is. 7, 14), un caso de 'tipologia redaccional'?" *Studium* 24 (1984), 231–267.

1858. Ubell, Lori. "Sarah's Voice." *Hadassah Magazine,* Aug/Sep. 1990, pp. 18–21. Hagar, Sarah.

1859. Ullendorff, Edward. "The Bawdy Bible." *BSOAS* 42 (1979), 425–456. Terms for sexual activity and sexual organs in Hebrew Scripture; includes index of biblical passages.

1860. Utzschneider, Helmut. "Patrilinerität im alten Israel. Eine Studie zur Familie und ihrer Religion." *BN* 56 (1991), 60–97.

1861. Uys, P. H. de V. "The Term *gᵉbîrâ* in the Book of Proverbs." *Ou-Testamentiese Werkgemeenskap in Suid-Afrika* 11 (1968), 83–85.

1862. Van Gemeren, Willem A. "Psalm 131:2—kegamul. The Problem of Meaning and Metaphor." *Hebrew Studies* 23 (1982), 51–57.

1863. Van Selms, A. "Hosea and Canticles." *Ou-Testamentiese Werkgemeenskap in Suid-Afrika* 7/8 (1964/65), 85–89.

1864. Van Seters, John. "The Problem of Childlessness in Near Eastern Law and the Patriarchs of Israel." *JBL* 87 (1968), 401–408.

1865. —. "Jacob's Marriages and Ancient Near Eastern Customs: A Reexamination." *HTR* 62 (1969), 377–395.

1866. Vasholz, P. Ivan. "You Shall Not Covet Your Neighbor's Wife." *Westminster Theological Journal* 42 (1987), 397–403. Ex. 20:17; Deut. 5:21; dowry

1867. Veijola, T. "David and Meribaal." *RB* 85 (1978), 338–361. Meribaal and Rizpah

1868. Vellanickal, Matthew. "Family Life in the Bible." *Bible Bhashyam* 33 (1977), 192–212.

1869. Vendrame, C. "Sentido coletivo da *Almah,* Is 7, 14 (parlog). *Revista de Cultura Biblica* 7 (1963), 10–16.

1870. Verkhovskoy, Serge. "Creation of Man and the Establishment of the Family in the Light of the Book of Genesis." *St. Vladimir's Seminary Quarterly* 8 (1964), 5–30.

1871. Vickrey, J. F. "Vision of Eve in *Genesis B.*" *Speculum* 44 (1969), 86–102.

1872. Villiers, D. W. de. "Not for Sale! Solomon and Sexual Perversion in the Song of Songs." *Old Testament Essays* 3 (1990), 317–324.

1873. Vogels, Walter. "It is not good that the *mensch* should be alone; I will make him/her a helper fit for him/her (Gen. 2:18)." *Eglise et Theologie* 9 (1978), 9–35.

1874. —. "'Osée—Gomer' car et comme 'Yahweh-Israël: Os. 1–3." *Nouvelle Revue Théologique* 103 (1981), 711–727. Gomer; Ruhamah.

1875. —. "Diachronic and Synchronic Studies of Hosea 1–3." *BZ* 28 (1984), 94–98.

1876. Wadsworth, Tom. "Is There a Hebrew Word for Virgin? *Bethulah* in the Old Testament." *Restoration Quarterly* 23 (1980), 161–171.

1877. Wagner, W. H. "The Demonization of Women." *Religion in Life* 42 (1974), 56–74.

1878. Wakeman, Mary K. "On Idolatry." In *Women and Religion: 1973 Proceedings,* pp. 51–55. Edited by Joan Arnold Romero. Tallahassee: American Academy of Religion, 1973.

1879. Waldman, Nahum M. "Concealment and Irony in the Samson Story." *DD* 13 (1984/85), 71–80.

1880. Walker, Norman. "'Adam' and 'Eve' and 'Adon'" *ZAW* 74 (1962), 66–68.

1881. Walle, R. Vande, S. J. "Esther and Judith: Two Valiant Women." *Bible Bhashyam* 9 (1983), 104–113.

1882. Walsh, Jerome T. "Genesis 2:4b–3:24: A Synchronic Approach." *JBL* 96 (1977), 161–177.

1883. Walters, Stanley D. "Hannah and Anna: The Greek and Hebrew Text of 1 Samuel 1." *JBL* 107 (1988), 385–412.

1884. Waltke, B. K. "The Old Testament and Birth Control: Family Planning under the Law." *Christianity Today* 13, no. 3 (1968), 99–102.

1885. Wander, Nathaniel. "Structure, Contradiction and 'Resolution' in Mythology: Father's Brother's Daughter Marriage and the Treatment of Women in Genesis 11–50." *JANES* 13 (1981), 75–99.

1886. Watson, Wilfred G. E. "Gender-Matched Synonymous Parallelism in the Old Testament." *JBL* 99 (1980), 321–341.

1887. Weber, S. C. "Ruth: The Understatement of a Lifetime." *TBT* 98 (Nov. 1978), 1750–1756.

1888. Webster, Edwin C. "Pattern in the Song of Songs." *JSOT* 22 (1982), 73–93.

1889. Weder, H. "Perspektive der Frauen?" *Evangelische Theologie* 43 (1983), 175–178.

1890. Weeks, Noel. "Man, Nuzi and the Patriarchs." *AbrNaharim* 16 (1975–76), 73–82.

1891. Weems, Renita J. "Gomer: Victim of Violence or Victim of Metaphor?" *Semeia* 47 (1989), 87–104.

1892. Weiler, Gerda. "Feminismus und Antisemitismus. Ein unvereinbar Widerspruch." *Berliner theologische Zeitschrift* 4 (1987), 312–316.

1893. Weinfeld, M. "The Worship of Molech and of the Queen of Heaven and its Background." *UF* 4 (1982), 133–154.

1894. —. "Sarah and Abimelech (Genesis 20) Against the Background of an Assyrian Law and the Genesis Apocryphon." In *Mélanges bibliques et orientaux en l'honneur de M. Mathias Delcor*, pp. 431–436. Edited by A. Caquot, S. Legasse and M. Tardieu. AOAT 215. Kevelaer: Butzon & Bercker/Neukirchen-Vluyn: Neukirchener Verlag, 1985.

1895. —. "Sarah and Abimelech (Genesis 20) Against the Background of Assyrian Law and the Genesis Apocryphon." *Tarbiz* 52 (1982/83), 639–641 (in Hebrew).

1896. Weingreen, J. "The Case of the Daughters of Zelophehad." *VT* 16 (1966), 518–522.

1897. Weiser, Asher. "The Family in the Bible." In *Ben-Zion Lurie Festschrift,* pp. 51–63. Edited by Y. Avishur et al. Jerusalem: Israel Society for Biblical Research, 1979 (in Hebrew).

1898. Weisman, Ze'ev. "šārôtêāh (Judges 5:29)." *VT* 26 (1976), 116–120.

1899. —. "Diverse Historical and Social Reflections in the Shaping of Patriarchal History." *Zion* 50 (1985), 1–13 (in Hebrew).

1900. Weitenmeyer, M. "Nabots vingård (1 Konig 21, 1–16)." *Dansk Teologisk Tidsskrift* 29 (1966), 129–143.

1901. Wenham, G. J. "*Bĕtûlāh* 'A Girl of Marriageable Age'." *VT* 22 (1972), 326–348.

1902. —. "The Restoration of Marriage Reconsidered." *JJS* 30 (1979), 36–40. Deut. 24:1–4

1903. —. "Why Does Sexual Intercourse Defile? (Lev. 15:15)." *ZAW* 95 (1983), 432–434.

1904. —. "The Perplexing Pentateuch." *Vox Evangelica* 17 (1987), 7–21.

1905. Wenham, G. J., and McConville, J. G. "Drafting Techniques in Some Deuteronomic Laws." *VT* 30 (1980), 248–252. Deut. 22:13–29 (women laws)

1906. Wesselius, J. W. "Joab's Death and the Central Theme of the Succession Narrative (2 Samuel IX–1 Kings II)." *VT* 40 (1990), 236–251.

1907. —. "De wijze vrouwen in 2 Samuel 14 en 20." *Nederlands Theologisch Tijdschrift* 45 (1991), 89–100.

1908. West, Angela. "Genesis and Patriarchy." Part I. *The New Blackfriars* 62 (1981), 17–32; Part II. *The New Blackfriars* 62 (1981), 420–432. feminist hermeneutics

1909. West, Stuart A. "The Rape of Dinah and the Conquest of

Shechem." *DD* 8 (1979), 144–156.

1910.   —. "Judah and Tamar—A Scriptural Enigma." *DD* 12
        (1984), 246–252.

1911.   Westbrook, R. "Lex talionis and Exodus 21, 22–25." *RB* 93
        (1986), 52–69.

1912.   —. "The Prohibition on Restoration of Marriage in Deu-
        teronomy 24:1–4." In *Studies in Bible*, pp. 387–405.
        Scripta Hierosylamitana, no. 31. Edited by Sara Japhet.
        Jerusalem: Magnes, 1986.

1913.   —. "1 Samuel 1:8." *JBL* 109 (1990), 114–115. Hannah

1914.   Westenholz, Joan Goodnick. "Tamar, Qĕdēšā, Qadištu, and
        Sacred Prostitution in Mesopotamia." *HTR* 82 (1989),
        245–266. Gen. 38

1915.   Wharton, James A. "A Plausible Tale: Story and Theology in
        II Samuel 9–20, 1 Kings 1–2." *Interpretation* 35 (1981),
        341–354. succession narrative; Bathsheba, Tamar; etc.

1916.   Whatham, Arthur E. "Cain's Wife." *Expository Times* 8
        (1896–97), 8.

1917.   White, Ernest. "Biblical Principles for Modern Family
        Living." *Review and Expositor* 75 (1978), 5–17. Positive
        aspects of Hebrew Scripture's attitudes toward women,
        sexual relationships, and marriage

1918.   White, Hugh C. "Initiation Legend of Ishmael." *ZAW* 87
        (1975), 267–306. Gen. 16 and 21:8–21; Hagar; Sarah

1919.   Whitelan, Keith W. "The Defence of David." *JSOT* 29
        (1984), 61–87. Bathsheba

1920.   Wickham, L. R. "The Sons of God and the Daughters of
        Men: Gen 6, 2 in Early Christian Exegesis." *OTS* 19
        (1974), 136–147.

1921.   Wifall, Walter. "Bone of my Bones and Flesh of my Flesh—
        The Politics of the Yahwist." *Currents in Theology and
        Mission* 10 (1983), 176–183.

1922.   Wildeboer, G. "De Vrouw in Israel." *Onze Eeuw* 10 (1910),

104–137.

1923. Willi-Plein, I. "Genesis 27 als Rebekkageschichte. Zu einem historiographischen Kunstgriff der biblischen Väter-geschichten." *TZ* 45 (1989), 315–334.

1924. Williams, James G. "The Beautiful and the Barren: Conventions in Biblical Type-Scenes." *JSOT* 17 (1980), 107–119. Gen. 12:10–20; 20; 24; 26; 29; Ex. 2:5–21; betrothal; wife-sister motif

1925. —. "Genesis 3." *Interpretation* 35 (1981), 274–279.

1926. Willis, J. T. "Cultic Elements in the Story of Samuel's Birth and Dedication." *Studia Theologica* 26 (1972), 33–61.

1927. —. "The Song of Hannah and Ps. 113." *CBQ* 35 (1973), 139–154.

1928. —. "The Meaning of Isaiah 7:14 and Its Application in Matthew 1:23." *Restoration Quarterly* 21 (1978), 1–18.

1929. Wiseman, D. J. "Rahab of Jericho." *Tyndale House Bulletin* 14 (1964), 8–11.

1930. Wöller, Ulrich. "Zu Gen 47." *ZAW* 96 (1984), 271–272.

1931. Wolmarans, H. P. "What does Malachi say about Divorce?" *Hervormde teologiese studies* 22 (1964), 46–47 (in Afrikaans).

1932. Wolters, Al. "Nature and Grace in the Interpretation of Proverbs 31:10–31." *Calvin Theological Journal* 19 (1984), 153–166.

1933. —. "Ṣôpiyyâ (Prov. 31:27) as Hymnic Participle and Play on Sophia." *JBL* 104 (1985), 577–587.

1934. Worden, T. "The Creation of Woman." *Scripture* 10 (1958), 60–61.

1935. —. "The Literary Influence of the Ugaritic Fertility Myth on the Old Testament." *VT* 3 (1951), 273–297.

1936. Wright, C. J. H. "The Israelite Household and the Decalogue: The Social Background and Significance of Some

Commandments." *Tyndale Bulletin* 30 (1979), 101–124.

1937. Wright, G. E. "Women and Masculine Theological Vocabulary in the Old Testament." In *Grace Upon Grace: Essays in Honor of Lester J. Kuyper,* pp. 64–69. Edited by James I. Cook. Grand Rapids: Eerdmans, 1975.

1938. Wright, G. R. H. "The Mother-Maid at Bethlehem." *ZAW* 98 (1986), 56–72. Ruth, Naomi, fertility cult

1939. Wyatt, N. "Araunah the Jebusite and the Throne of David." *StTh* 39 (1985), 39–53.

1940. —. "Cain's Wife." *Folklore* 97 (1986), 88–95; 232.

1941. —. "The Story of Dinah and Shechem: A Study in Comparative Religion." *UF* 22 (1990), 433–458.

1942. Yamauchi, Edwin M. "Tammuz and the Bible." *JBL* 84 (1965), 283–290.

1943. —. "Cultic Prostitution: A Case Study in Cultural Diffusion." In *Orient and Occident: Essays Presented to Cyrus Gordon on the Occasion of his Sixty-Fifth Birthday,* pp. 213–222. Edited by Harry A. Hoffner, Jr. AOAT 22. Kevelaer: Butzon & Bercker/Neukirchen-Vluyn: Neukirchener Verlag, 1973.

1944. Yaron, Reuven. "On Divorce in Old Testament Times." *RIDA* 3ᵉ serie 4 (1957), 117–128.

1945. —. "The Restoration of Marriage." *JJS* 17 (1966), 1–11.

1946. —. "'Go in unto my maid' (Gen. 16:1ff; etc.)." *Proceedings of the Fifth World Congress of Jewish Studies,* vol. 1 (1969), 5–9 (in Hebrew).

1947. Yee, Gale A. "An Analysis of Prov. 8:22–31 According to Style and Structure." *ZAW* 94 (1982), 48–65.

1948. —. "Literary Ambiguity in II Samuel 11." *Interpretation* 42 (1980), 240–253.

1949. —. "'I Have Perfumed My Bed with Myrrh': The Foreign Woman (*'iššâ zārâ*) in Proverbs 1–9." *JSOT* 43 (1989), 53–

68.

1950. —. "'Your Mother Was a Hittite': The Symbol of the Adulteress in Ezek. 16:1–43." [paper at 1988 CBA]

1951. Yeivin, S. "Philological Notes, XV." *Lěšonénu* 42 (1977), 60–63 (in Hebrew). Gen. 20:12; Sarah

1952. Yoshikoka, Barbara. "The Culture of Dissent: The Woman's Bible, the Female Witch, and the Female Sectarian Preacher." In *Women and Religion: 1973 Proceedings*, pp. 56–63. Edited by Joan Arnold Romero. Tallahassee: American Academy of Religion, 1973.

1953. Yubero, Galindo D. "La formacion de Eva en la Biblia y en la catequesis." *Lumen* 15 (1966), 44–55.

1954. Zakovitch, Yair. "The Threshing-Floor Scene in Ruth and the Daughters of Lot." *SHNATON* 3 (1978), 29–33 (in Hebrew). Ruth 3; Gen. 19:30–38

1955. —. "The Woman's Rights in the Biblical Law of Divorce." *JLA* 4 (1981), 28–46. Deut. 24:1–4; Judg. 19:3; Jer. 3:1

1956. —. "Assimilation in Biblical Narrative." In *Empirical Models for Biblical Criticism*, pp. 175–176. Edited by Jeffrey M. Tigay. Philadelphia: University of Pennsylvania Press, 1985. Gen. 34; 2 Sam. 13

1957. —. "The Woman in Biblical Narrative—An Outline." *BM* 32 (1986/87), 14–32 (in Hebrew).

1958. Zalcman, Lawrence. "Ambiguity and Assonance at Zephaniah II 4." *VT* 36 (1986), 365–371. On the personification of the Philistine cities as women

1959. Zalevsky, S. "Hannah's Vow and Its Fulfillment (1 Sam. 1)." *BM* 23 (1978), 304–326 (in Hebrew).

1960. Zappone, Katherine E. "A Feminist Hermeneutics for Scripture: The Standpoint of the Interpreter." *Proceedings of the Irish Bible Association* 8 (1984), 25–38.

1961. Zelechow, Bernard. "All About Eve: A Review Essay." *Shofar* 7, no. 4 (summer 1989), 59–64.

1962.   Ziderman, I. Irving. "Abraham's Servant." *DD* 14 (1985/86), 124–125. Gen. 24:11; Rebekah

1963.   Ziegenaus, Anton. "Als Mann und Frau erschofen sie (Gen. 1, 27)." *Münchener Theologische Zeitschrift* 31 (1980), 210–222.

1964.   Zimmerman, C. L. "The Chronology and Birth of Jacob's Children by Leah and Her Handmaid." *Grace Journal* 13 (1972), 3–12.

1965.   Zingg, E. "Israel's Privatrecht nach den Gesetzen des Moses." *Judaica* 18 (1962), 129–128.

1966.   —. "Ehe und Familie nach den Gesetzen des Moses." *Judaica* 20 (1964), 121–128.

1967.   Zipor, Moshe. "What is ḥălālâ ?" *BM* 33 (1987/88), 51–58 (in Hebrew). Lev. 19:29; 21:7, 9, 14; zônā

1968.   —. "Restrictions on Marriage for Priests (Lev 21, 7. 13–14)." *Biblica* 68 (1987), 259–267.

1969.   —. "Ezechiel 16, 7." *ZAW* 103 (1991), 99–100.

1970.   Ziv, Y. "The Marriage of Ahaz and Abiah daughter of Zechariah." *BM* 15 (1969), 68–71 (in Hebrew).

1971.   Zyl, A. H. van. "I Sam. 1:2–2:11—A Life-World Lament of Affliction." *JNSL* 12 (1984), 151–161. Hannah

6. WOMEN AND WOMANHOOD IN HEBREW SCRIPTURE: THESES AND DISSERTATIONS

1972. Adler, Elaine June. "The Background for the Metaphor of Covenant as Marriage in the Hebrew Bible." Ph.D. diss., University of California at Berkeley, 1990.

1973. Arbeli, Shoshana. "Women in the Bible in Positions of Privilege and Their Involvement in Social and Political Affairs: A Comparative Study Using Ancient Near Eastern Sources." Ph.D. diss., Hebrew University of Jerusalem, 1984 (in Hebrew).

1974. Balz-Cochois, Helgard. "Das Ehegleichnis Hoseas: Form, Kontext und Theologie; Hos. 2, 4–25 als grosser Eifersuchtsmonolog in Kontext von Hos 1, 2–5, 7." Ph.D. diss., München Fachbereich evangelische Theologie, 1980.

1975. Ben-Abu, David. "The Status of Woman in Israel and in the Ancient Near East." M.A. thesis, Bar-Ilan University, 1983 (in Hebrew).

1976. Bigger, S. F. "Hebrew Marriage and Family in the Old Testament Period." Ph.D. diss., University of Manchester, 1975.

1977. Burns, Camilla. "The Heroine with a Thousand Faces: Woman Wisdom in Proverbs 1–9." Ph.D. diss., Graduate Theological Union, 1990.

1978. Collins, Oral Edmond. "The Stem znh and Prostitution in the Hebrew Bible." Ph.D. diss., Brandeis University, 1977.

1979. Cowan, Margaret P. "Genesis 38: The Story of Judah and Tamar and Its Role in the Ancestral Narratives of Genesis." Ph.D. diss., Vanderbilt University, 1990.

1980. Gilner, David Jonathan. "The Legal Status of Women as Reflected in Pentateuchal Law." M.A. thesis, Emory University, 1972.

1981.   —. "The Status of Women in Ancient Israel." Ph.D. diss., Hebrew Union College, Cincinnati, 1989.

1982.   Hall, Gary H. "The Marriage Imagery in Jeremiah 2 and 3." Ph.D. diss., Union Theological Seminary, Richmond, Va., 1980.

1983.   Hooks, Stephen M. "Sacred Prostitution in Israel and the Ancient Near East." Ph.D. diss., Hebrew Union College, Cincinnati, 1985.

1984.   Kaithathara, J. "The Indissolubility of a Ratified, Consummated Marriage." Ph.D. diss., Pont. Univ. Urbanianae, Rome 1972.

1985.   Kellenbach, Katharine von. "Anti-Judaism in Christian Rooted Feminist Writings: An Analysis of Major U.S. and West-German Feminist Theologians." Ph.D. diss., Temple University, 1990.

1986.   Matthews, Edwin LeBron "The Use of the Adultery Motif in Hebrew Prophecy." Ph.D. diss., New Orleans Baptist Theological Seminary, 1987.

1987.   Neff, R. W. "The Announcement in Old Testament Birth Stories." Ph.D. diss., Yale University, 1969.

1988.   Olyan, Saul M. "Problems in the History of the Cult and Priesthood in Ancient Israel." Ph.D. diss., Harvard University, 1985.

1989.   Plautz, W. "Die Frau in Familie und Ehe. Ein Beitrag zum Problem ihrer Stellung im Alten Testament." Ph.D. diss., Kiel, 1959.

1990.   Poethig, E. B. "The Victory Song Tradition of the Women of Israel." Ph.D. diss., Union Theological Seminary, 1985.

1991.   Rauh, S. "Hebräische Familienrecht in vorprophetischen Zeit." Ph.D. diss., Berlin, 1907.

1992.   Schneeman, Gisela. "Deutung und Bedeutung der Beschneidung nach Ex. 4, 24–26." Ph.D. diss., Prague, 1979. Zipporah

1993. Sharp, D. B. "Sarah and Rebekah as Portrayed by the Yahwist Writer." Ph.D. diss., Innsbruck, 1976.

1994. Shout, W. R. "The Fertility Religion in the Thought of Amos and Micah." Ph.D. diss., University of California at Los Angeles, 1951.

1995. Stradling, F. S. "The Birth and Naming of the Children of Jacob in Genesis 29:32–30:24 and 35:16–20." Ph.D. diss., Manchester, 1972.

1996. Teachout, R. P. "The Use of Wine in the Old Testament." Ph.D. diss., Dallas Theological Seminary, 1976.

1997. White, J. B. "A Study of the Language of Love in the Song of Songs and Ancient Egyptian Poetry." Ph.D. diss., Duke University, 1975.

7. WOMEN AND WOMANHOOD IN ANCIENT EGYPT: BOOKS AND DISSERTATIONS

1998. Aldred, Cyril. *Akhenaten and Nefertiti: Art of the Amarna Period.* London: Thames & Hudson, 1974.

1999. Armstrong, A. H., ed. *Classical Mediterranean Spirituality: Egyptian, Greek, Roman.* World Spirituality: An Encyclopedic History of the Religious Quest 15. New York: Crossroad, 1986.

2000. Baer, Klaus. *Rank and Title in the Old Kingdom.* Chicago: University of Chicago Press, 1960.

2001. Baines, John. *Fecundity Figures: Egyptian Personification and the Iconology of a Genre.* Index by Lisa M. Letchy. Warminster: Aris & Phillips; Chicago: Bolchazy Carducci, 1985.

2002. Baines, J. and Màlek, J. *Atlas of Ancient Egypt.* Oxford: Clarendon Press, 1980. See pp. 204–208 for "Women in."

2003. Bakir, Abd el-Mohsen. *Slavery in Pharaonic Egypt.* Cairo: Imprimerie de l'Institut français d'archéologie orientale, 1952.

2004. Bedell, Ellen. *Criminal Law in the Egyptian Ramesside Period.* Ph.D. diss., Brandeis University, 1975.

2005. Bénédite, G. *Le Tombeau de la Reine Thihi.* Paris: Leroux, 1890.

2006. Bierbrier, Morris. *The Late New Kingdom in Egypt.* Warminster: Aris & Phillips, 1975.

2007. —. *The Tomb-Builders of the Pharaohs.* London: British Museum, 1982.

2008. Brunner-Traut, E. *Der Tanz im alten Aegypten.* Glückstadt: J. J. Augustin, 1958.

2009. Buttles, Janet R. *Queens of Egypt*. London: A. Constable, 1908.

2010. Černý, J. *Catalogue des ostraca hiératique non-littéraires de Deir el Médineh*. 6 vols. Cairo: IFAO, 1937–1970.

2011. —. *A Community of Workmen at Thebes in the Ramesside Period*. Cairo: IFAO, 1973.

2012. Desroches-Noblecourt, Christiane. *La femme au temps des Pharaons*. Paris: Pernoud, 1986.

2013. Desroches-Noblecourt, Christiane, and Kuentz, C. *Le petit temple d'Abou Simbel*. 2 vols. Cairo: Centre de documentation et d'étude sur l'ancienne Égypte, 1968.

2014. Donadoni Roveri, Anna Maria, ed. *Daily Life*. Egyptian Civilization, vol. 1. Milan: Egyptian Museum of Turin, 1987.

2015. Dondelinger, E. *Der Jenseitsweg der Nofretari*. Graz: Akadem. Druck und Verlaganstalt, 1973.

2016. Dunham, D., and Simpson, W. K. *The Mastaba of Queen Mersyankh III G 7530–7540*. Boston: Museum of Fine Arts, 1974.

2017. Erman, Adolf, and Ranke, Hermann. *Aegypten und Aegyptische Leben in Altertum*. Tübingen: J.C.B. Mohr, 1923.

2018. Fischer, Henry George. *Varia (Egyptian Studies I)*. New York: Metropolitan Museum of Art, 1976.

2019. —. *Egyptian Titles of the Middle Kingdom*. 3 parts. New York: Metropolitan Museum of Art, 1985.

2020. Galvin, M. *The Priestesses of Hathor in the Old Kingdom and the lst Intermediate Period*. Ph.D. diss., Brandeis University, 1981.

2021. Gitton, M. *L'épouse du dieu Ahmes Néfertary: Documentes sur la vie et son culte posthume*. Paris: Belles Lettres, 1975.

2022. —. *Les divines épouses de la 18e dynastie*. Paris: Belles Lettres, 1984.

2023.   Graefe, E. *Untersuchungen zur Verwaltung und Geschichte der Institution der Gottesgemahlin des Amun.* 2 vols. Weisbaden: Harrassowitz, 1981.

2024.   Green, L. "Queens and Princesses of the Amarna Period: Their Social, Political, Religious and Cultic Role." Ph.D. diss., University of Toronto, 1988.

2025.   Hari, R. *Horemheb et la reine Moutnedjemet ou la fin d'une dynastie.* Geneva: Editions de Belles Lettres/Imprimerie La Sirène, 1974.

2026.   Hart, George. *A Dictionary of Egyptian Gods and Goddesses.* London: Routledge & Kegan Paul, 1986.

2027.   Hayes, William C. *A Papyrus of the Late Middle Kingdom in the Brooklyn Museum.* Brooklyn, N.Y.: Brooklyn Museum, 1955.

2028.   James, T. G. H. *The Hekanakhte Papers and Other Early Middle Kingdom Documents.* New York: Metropolitan Museum of Art, 1962.

2029.   Jéquier, J. *Les pyramides des reines Neit et Apouit.* Cairo: IFAO, 1933.

2030.   Johnson, Sally Barber. *The Cobra Goddess of Ancient Egypt.* London: Kegan Paul, 1990.

2031.   Katan, Norma Jean. *Hieroglyphs: The Writing of the Ancient Egyptians.* Rev. ed. London: Trustees of the British Museum, 1985.

2032.   Keimer, L. *Remarques sur le tatouage dans l'Egypte ancienne.* Cairo: Institut Français, 1948.

2033.   Kitchen, K. A. *The Third Intermediate Period in Egypt.* Warminster: Aris & Phillips, 1973.

2034.   Kuchman(-Sabhaly), L. "The Development of the Titulary and Iconography of the Ancient Egyptian Queen from Dynasty One to Early Dynasty Eighteen." Ph.D. diss., University of Toronto, 1982.

2035.   Leca, L. *La Médicine Egyptienne aus temps des Pharaons.* Paris: Les Editions Rojer Dacosta, 1971.

2036.   Lesko, B. S. *The Remarkable Women of Ancient Egypt.* 2d ed. Providence, R.I.: Scribe Publications, 1987.

2037.   Lüddeckens, Erich. *Aegyptische Eheverträge.* Wiesbaden: Harrassowitz, 1960.

2038.   Manniche, Lise. *Sexual Life in Ancient Egypt.* Illustrated. London: Kegan Paul, 1987.

2039.   Menu, Bernadette. *La regime juridique des terres et du personnel attaché a la terre dans le Papyrus Wilbour.* Lille: Faculté des lettres et sciences humaines de l'université de Lille, 1970.

2040.   —. *Recherches sur l'histoire juridique, economique et sociale de l'ancienne Egypte.* Versailles: B. Menu, 1982.

2041.   Mertz, B. "Certain Titles of the Egyptian Queens and Their Bearing on the Hereditary Right to the Throne." Ph.D. diss., University of Chicago, 1952.

2042.   Millard, A. "The Position of Women in the Family and Society in Ancient Egypt with Special Reference to the Middle Kingdom." Ph.D. diss., University of London, University College 1976.

2043.   Müller, Hans Wolfgang. *Der Isiskult im antiken Benevent.* Berlin: B. Hessling, 1969.

2044.   Münster, Maria. *Untersuchungen zur Gottin Isis vom alten Reich biz zum Ende des neuen Reiches.* Berlin: B. Hessling, 1968.

2045.   Murray, Margaret Alice. *Priesthoods of Women in Egypt.* International Congress of History and Religons, vol. 1. Oxford: Clarendon, 1908.

2046.   Palmer, M. S. "The Position of Women in Ancient Egypt." M.A. thesis, University of Manchester, 1929.

2047.   Pestman, P. W. *Marriage and Matrimonial Property in Ancient Egypt. A Contribution to Establishing the Legal Position of the Women.* Leiden: E. J. Brill, 1961.

2048.   Pinch, G. *New Kingdom Votive Offerings to Hathor.* Warminster: Aris & Phillips, 1970.

2049. Pintore, Franco. *Il matrimino interdinastico nel Vicino Orientale durante i secoli XV–XIII.* Rome: Instituto per l'Oriente, 1978.

2050. Ratié, A. *La reine Hatchepsout.* Leiden: E. J. Brill, 1979.

2051. Redford, Donald R. *The Chronology of the Eighteenth Dynasty.* Toronto: University of Toronto Press, 1967.

2052. Reiser, Elfriede. *Die Köngliche Harim im alten Aegypten und seine Verwaltung.* Vienna: Notring, 1972.

2053. Robins, Gay. *Women in Ancient Egypt.* London: British Museum, 1993.

2054. Samson, J. *Nefertiti and Cleopatra.* London: Rubicon Press, 1985.

2055. Sander-Hansen, C. E. *Das Gottesweib des Amun.* Copenhagen: E. Munksgaard, 1940.

2056. Schoske, Sylvia; Wildung, Dietrich; Eggebrecht, Arne, eds. *Nofret-Die Schöne: Die Frau im alten Agypten.* 2 vols. Mainz: P. von Zabern, 1984–85.

2057. Schulze, Peter H. *Frauen im alten Agypten.* Gutau: Löbbe Verlag, 1987.

2058. Simpson, William K., and Dunham, Dows. *The Mastaba of Queen Meresankh III.* Boston: Museum of Fine Arts, 1974.

2059. Tefnin, R. *La statuaire d'Hatshepsout: pourtrait royal et politique sous la 18ᵉ dynastie.* Brussells: Fondation Egyptologique Reine Elisabeth, 1979.

2060. Thausing, G., and Goedicke, H. *Nofretari: Eine Documentation der Wandegemälde ihres Grabes.* Graz: Akkademische Druck und Verlagsanstalt, 1971.

2061. Trigger, Bruce, et al. *Ancient Egypt: A Social History.* Cambridge: Cambridge University Press, 1983.

2062. Troy, Lana. *Patterns of Queenship in Ancient Egyptian Myth and History.* Uppsala: University of Uppsala, 1986.

2063.   Valbelle, Dominique. *Les ouvriers de la tombe Deir el-Medineh à l'époque Ramesside.* Cairo: IFAO,1985.

2064.   Ward, William A. *Index of Egyptian Administrative and Religious Titles.* Beirut: American University of Beirut Press, 1982.

2065.   —. *Essays on Feminine Titles of the Middle Kingdom and Related Subjects.* Beirut: American University Press, 1986.

2066.   Wenig, Stephen. *Die Frau im Alten Aegypten.* Leipzig: Edition Leipzig, 1967.

2067.   Wente, Edward F. *Late Ramesside Letters.* SAOC, 33. Chicago: University of Chicago Press, 1967.

2068.   Werbrouck, Marcelle. *Les Pleureuses dans l'Egypte ancienne.* Brussels: Fondations Egyptologique Reine Elisabeth, 1938.

2069.   Winlock, H. E. *Bas-reliefs from the Temple of Rameses I at Abydos.* New York: Metropolitan Museum of Art, 1921.

2070.   —. *The Tomb of Queen Meryet-Amun at Thebes.* New York: Metropolitan Museum of Art, 1932.

2071.   —. *The Treasure of the Three Egyptian Princesses.* New York: Metropolitan Museum of Art, 1948.

8. WOMEN AND WOMANHOOD IN ANCIENT EGYPT: ARTICLES

2072. Aldred, Cyril. "Hairstyles and History." *BMFA* 15 (1957), 199.

2073. —. "Queen Mutnodjme—A Correction." *JEA* 56 (1970), 195–196.

2074. Allam, Schafik. "Zur Stellung der Frau im Alten Aegypten (in der Zeit des Neun Reiches 16.–10. Jhr. u Z)." *Das Altertum* 16 (1970), 67–81; *BiOr* 26 (1969), 155–159.

2075. —. "De l'adoption en Egypte pharaonique." *OrAnt* 11 (1972), 277–295.

2076. —. "Zur Adoption im pharaonischen Agypten." *Das Altertum* 19 (1973), 3–17.

2077. —. "An Allusion to an Egyptian Wedding Ceremony." *GM* 13 (1974), 9–11.

2078. —. "Les obligations et la famille dans la société égyptienne ancienne." *OrAnt* 16 (1977), 89–97.

2079. —. "Quelques aspects du marriage dans l'Egypte ancienne." *JEA* 67 (1981), 116–135.

2080. —. "La Vente dans l'Egypte ancienne (Particulièrement à l'époque du nouvel empire)." *RHD* 60 (1982), 377–393.

2081. —. "Eheschliessung und Scheidung im Altägypten." *Das Altertum* 29 (1983), 117–123.

2082. —. "Familie und Besitzverhaltnisse in der altägyptischen Arbeitersiedulung von Deir-el-Medineh." *RIDA* 30 (1983), 17–39.

2083. —. "Un contrat de marriage (Pap. Démotiaue Caire J. 68567)." *RdE* 35 (1984), 4–21.

2084. —. "Trois lettres d'affaires (P. Caire CG 58056, 58058, 58060)." *BdE* 97/I (1985), 19–30.

2085. —. "Sinuhe's Foreign Wife (Reconsidered)." *Discussions in Egyptology* 4 (1986), 15–16.

2086. —. "Zur Stellung der Frau im Altägypten." *Discussions in Egyptology* 5 (1986), 7–15.

2087. Allen, T. G. "A Unique Statue of Senmut." *AJSL* 44 (1928), 49–55.

2088. Altenmüller, H. "Die Stellung der Königsmutter Chentkaues beim Ubergang von der 4. zur 5. Dynastie." *CdE* 45 (1970), 223–235.

2089. —. "Tausret und Sethnacht." *JEA* 68 (1982), 107–115.

2090. —. "Das Grab der Königin Tausret im Tal der König." *SAK* 10 (1983), 15–20.

2091. Assman, Jan. "Eine Traumoffenbarung der Göttin Hathor: Zeugnisse 'Persönlicher Frömmigkeit' in thebanischen Privatgräbern der Ramessidenzeit." *RdE* 30 (1978), 22–50.

2092. Bakry, Hassan S. K. "The Discovery of a Statue of Queen Twosre (1207–1194? B.C.) at Medinet Naṣr, Cairo." *Revista degli Studi Orientali* 46 (1971), 109–117.

2093. Bardis, P. D. "Incest in Ancient Egypt." *Indian Journal of the History of Medicine* 12 (1967), 14–20.

2094. Barta, Winfried. "Bemerkungen zur Existenz der Rituale für Geburt und Krönung." *ZAS* 112 (1985), 1–13.

2095. Bergman, J. "Nut: Himmelsgöttin, Baumgöttin, Lebensgeberin." In *Humanitas Religiosa: Festschrift für Haralds Biezais zu seinen 70. Geburtstag*, pp. 53–69. Stockholm: Almquist Wiksell, 1979.

2096. Berlandini-Grenier, J. "Senenmout, Stoliste royal sur une statue-cube avec Neferouré." *BIFAO* 76 (1976), 111–132.

2097. Bernard-Delapierre, G. "Une nouvelle mention de la déesse Mafdat sous la Ire dynastie." *RdE* 4 (1936), 220–221.

2098. Bierbrier, Morris. "Terms of Relationship at Deir-el-Medina." *JEA* 66 (1980), 100–107.

2099. Blackman, A. M. "On the Position of Women in the Ancient Egyptian Hierarchy." *JEA* 7 (1921), 8–30.

2100. Blankenberg-van Delden, C. "Additional Remarks on Queen Ahhotep, Consort of Senakhtenre Tao I?." *GM* 49 (1981), 17–18.

2101. —. "Ahmes Merytamon and Ahhotep I, Consort of Senakhtenre Tao I?" *GM* 47 (1981), 15–19.

2102. —. "A Genealogical Reconstruction of the Kings and Queens of the Late 17th and Early 18th Dynasties." *GM* 54 (1982), 31–45.

2103. —. "Ahmes Satamon." *GM* 68 (1983), 37–39.

2104. Bleeker, C. J. "The Position of the Queen in Ancient Egypt." In *The Sacral Kingship,* pp. 261–268. Studies in the History of Religion, vol. 4. Leiden: E. J. Brill, 1959.

2105. Bockel, P. "L'Egypte et la Bible. La Fin des Pharaons. *MDB* 45 (Aug.-Sept.-Oct. 1986) 1.

2106. Borghauts, J. F. "Monthu and Matrimonial Squabbles." *RdE* 33 (1981), 11–22.

2107. Bosse-Griffiths, K. "The Great Enchantress in the Little Golden Shrine of Tut 'ankhamun." *JEA* 59 (1973), 100–108.

2108. Bryan, B. M. "Evidence of Female Literacy from Theban Tombs of the New Kingdom." *BES* 6 (1984), 17–32.

2109. —. "Non-Royal Women's Titles in the 18th Egyptian Dynasty." *ARCE Newsletter* 134 (1986), 13–16.

2110. —. "The Career and Family of Minmose, High Priest of Onuris." *CdE* 61 (1986), 5–30.

2111. Caminos, R. "The Nitocris Adoption Stela." *JEA* 50 (1964), 71–101.

2112.   Capart, J. "La reine Thenti-Hapi." *CdE* 16 (1941), 39–49.

2113.   Carter, H. "A Tomb Prepared for Queen Hatshepsut." *JEA* 50 (1964), 107–118.

2114.   Černý, J. "The Will of Naunakhte and the Related Documents." *JEA* 31 ((1945), 29–53.

2115.   —. "Consanguineous Marriages in Pharaonic Egypt." *JEA* 40 (1954), 23–29.

2116.   —. "A Note on the Ancient Egyptian Family." In *Studi in onore di A. Calderini e R. Paribeni* vol. 2, pp. 51-55. 2 vols. Milan: Ceschina, 1956–1957.

2117.   —, and Peet, T. E., "A Marriage Settlement of the Twentieth Dynasty." *JEA* 13 (1927), 30–39.

2118.   Coche, Christiane. "Une nouvelle statue de la déesse léonto-céphale Ouadjit wp t3wy." *RdE* 22 (1970), 51–62.

2119.   Cole, Dorothea. "The Role of Women in the Medical Practice of Ancient Egypt." *Discussions in Egyptology* 9 (1987), 25–29.

2120.   —. "The Woman of Ancient Egypt as a Child." *Discussions in Egyptology* 13 (1989), 29–38.

2121.   Condon, Virginia. "Two Account Papyri of the Late Eighteenth Dynasty (Brooklyn 35.1453 A and B)." *RdE* 35 (1984), 57–82. Numerous named women

2122.   Cruz-Uribe, Eugene. "On the Wife of Merneptah." *GM* 24 (1977), 23–31.

2123.   Daressy, G. "Inscriptions de la Chapelle d'Ameniritis ä Medinet-Habou." *RT* 23 (1901), 4–18.

2124.   —. "Une princesse inconnue d'époque Saite." *ASAE* 8 (1907), 280–281.

2125.   —. "La reine Aahmès-Henuttamehu." *ASAE* 9 (1908), 95–96.

2126.   —. "La stèle de la fille de Chéops." *RT* 30 (1908), 1–10.

2127. —. "Les parents de la reine Teta-Chera." *ASAE* 9 (1908), 137–138.

2128. —. "La tombe de la mère de Chefren." *ASAE* 10 (1910), 41–49.

2129. d'Auria, S. "The Princess Baketamnum." *JEA* 69 (1983), 161–169.

2130. David, A. R. "The Manchester Mummy Project." *Archaeology* 38, no. 6 (Nov./Dec. 1985), 40–47. mummy of a 14 year old girl

2131. Deines, H. von. "*Mwt rmṯ* Mutter der Menschen." *MIO* 4 (1956), 27–39.

2132. Desroches-Noblecourt, Christiane. "Concubines de Mort' et Mère de Famille au moyen empire à propos d'une supplique pour une naissance." *BIFAO* 53 (1953), 7–47.

2133. Dodson, A. M. "The Tombs of the Queens of the Middle Kingdom." *ZAS* 115 (1988), 123–136.

2134. Edwards, I. E. S. "A Relief of Qudshu-Astarte-Anath in the Winchester College Collection." *JNES* 14 (1955), 49–51.

2135. El-Amir, Mustafa. "Monogamy, Polygamy, Endogamy and Consanguinity in ancient Egyptian marriage." *BIFAO* 62 (1964), 103–167.

2136. El-Sayed, R. "Les rôles attribués à la déesse Neith dans certains textes des cercueils." *Orientalia,* n.s., 43 (1974), 275–294.

2137. Engelbach, R. "Recent Acquisitions in the Cairo Museum III. Sphinx of a Queen." *ASAE* 31 (1931), 128–129.

2138. Eyre, C. J. "Crime and Adultery in Ancient Egypt." *JEA* 70 (1984), 92–105.

2139. Fazzini, R. "Art from the Age of Akhenaton." *Archaeology* 26 (1973), 298–302 + 9 fig.

2140. Federn, Walter. "Dahanunzu (KBoV6iii8)." *JCS* 14 (1960), 33. The widow of Tutankhamon

2141.   Fischer, Henry George. "A Daughter of the Overlords of Upper Egypt in the First Intermediate Period." *JAOS* 76 (1956), 99–110.

2142.   —. "The Butcher *Ph-r-nfr*, IV. Additional Note: A Female Overseer of the 'im.3.t." *Orientalia,* n.s. 29 (1960), 187–190.

2143.   —. "The Nubian Mercenaries of Gebelein during the First Intermediate Period." *Kush* 9 (1961), 44–80.

2144.   —. "Three Old Kingdom Palimpsests in the Louvre." *ZÄS* 86 (1961), 21–31.

2145.   —. "The Cult and Nome of the Goddess Bat." *JARCE* 1 (1962), 7–23.

2146.   —. "Maquileuse en Egyptien." *RdE* 21 (1969), 150–151.

2147.   —. "Redundant Determinatives in the Old Kingdom." *MMJ* 8 (1973), 7–25.

2148.   —. "*Nbty* in Old Kingdom Titles and Names." *JEA* 64 (1974), 94–99.

2149.   —. "A feminine example of *wḏ ḥm.k 'thy majesty commands'* in the Fourth Dynasty." *JEA* 61 (1975), 246–247.

2150.   —. "Some Early Monuments from Busiris in the Egyptian Delta: The Fitzwillian Museum False Door." *MMJ* 11 (1976), 5–24.

2151.   —. "Boats manned with women (Westcar V, 1ff.)." In *Fragen an die altägyptische Literatur: Studien zum Gedenken an Eberhard Otto,* pp. 161–165. Edited by Jan Assmann, Erik Feucht, and Reinhard Grieshammer. Wiesbaden: L. Reichert, 1977.

2152.   —. "Quelques prétendues antiqutés de l'Ancien Empire." *RdE* 30 (1978), 78–95.

2153.   —. "The Request of a Wife to her Husband: An Unusual Expression of Asservation." *ZÄS* 105 (1978), 44–47.

2154.   —. "Addenda to 'The Request of a Wife to her Husband'." *ZÄS* 107 (1980), 86–87.

2155.   —. "Deux stèles villageoises du moyen empire." *CdE* 55 (1980), 13–15.

2156.   —. "Deux stèles curieuses de la première période inter- médiare." *Supplement au BIFAO* 81 (1981), 235–242.

2157.   —. "Notes on two tomb chapels at Gîza." *JEA* 67 (1981), 166–168.

2158.   Forgeau, A. "Enfant-Roi, Enfant-Dieu." *MDB* 45 (Aug.- Sept.-Oct. 1986), 13–15. Birth ceremonies, nursing, goddess, queen mother, etc.

2159.   Galvin, Marianne. "The Hereditary Status of the Titles of the Cult of Hathor." *JEA* 70 (1984), 42–49.

2160.   Gardiner, Alan H. "Adoption Extraordinary." *JEA* 26 (1940), 23–29.

2161.   —. "The Tomb of Queen Twosre." *JEA* 40 (1954), 40–44.

2162.   Gaster, Theodor H. "The Egyptian 'Story of Astarte' and the Ugaritic Poem of Baal." *BO* 9 (1952), 83–86.

2163.   Gauthier, H. "La titulature des reines des dynasties Mem- phites." *ASAE* 24 (1924), 198–209.

2164.   Gauthier-Laurent, M. "Les scénes de coiffure féminine dans l'Ancienne Egypte." In *Mélanges Maspero I,* pp. 673–696. Edited by Pierre Jouguet MIFAO 66. Cairo: Imprimerie de l'IFAO, 1938.

2165.   Ghalioungui, P. "Les plus anciennes femmes-médecins de l'histoire." *BIFAO* 75 (1975), 159–164.

2166.   Ghalioungui, P.; Khalil, S.; and Amar, A. L. "On an Ancient Egyptian Method of Diagonosing Pregnancy and Deter- mining Foetal Sex." *Medical History* 7 (1963), 2411– 2466.

2167.   Gitton, M. "Un monument de la reine Kheñsa à Karnak." *RdE* 19 (1967), 161–163; 184- 185.

2168.   —. "Le résiliation d'une fonction religieuse: Nouvelle inter- pretation de la Stéle de Donation d'Ahmes Néfertary." *BIFAO* 76 (1976), 65–89.

2169. —. "Le rôle des femmes dans le clergé dAmon à la 18ᵉ dynastie." *BSFE* 75 (1976), 31–46.

2170. Giveon, Raphael. "A New Kingdom Stela from Sinai." *IEJ* 31 (1981), 168-171.

2171. Godron, G. "A propos de la déesse Sédjémet-Nébet." *RSO* 43 (1968), 319–326.

2172. Goedicke, H. "An Approximate date for the Harem Investigation under Pepy I." *JAOS* 74 (1954), 88–89.

2173. —. "Die Laufbahn des *Mṯn*." *MDAIK* 21 (1966), 1–71.

2174. —. "Was Magic Used in the Harem Conspiracy Against Rameses III?" *JEA* 49 (1963), 71–92.

2175. Görg, Manfred. "Ein Kanaanäer im Sinai." *BN* 20 (1983), 19–21.

2176. Grapow, H. "Die Inschrift der Königin Katimala am Temple von Semne." *ZAS* 76 (1940), 24–41.

2177. Griffith, J. G. "The Pregnancy of Isis." *JEA* 56 (1970), 194–195.

2178. Grimm, Alfred. "Ein Porträt der Hatschepsut als Gottesfrau und Königin." *GM* 65 (1983), 33–38.

2179. Guentch-Ogloueff, M. "Astarté syrienne et le *ḏed* d'Osiris." *RdE* 1 (1933), 197–202.

2180. Guest, Edith M. "Women's Titles in the Middle Kingdom." *Ancient Egypt and the East* 11 (1926), 46–50.

2181. Habachi, L. "La reine Touy, femme de Séthi I et ses proches parents inconnus." *RdE* 21 (1969), 27–47.

2182. —. "The Tomb of the Princess Nebt of the VIII Dynasty Discovered at Qift." *SAK* 10 (1983), 205–213.

2183. Harari, I. "La fondation cultuelle: Notes sur l'organisation cultuelle dans l'ancien empire égyptien." *ASAE* 54 (1957), 317–344.

2184.   —. "La capacité juridique de la femme au Nouvel Empire."
        RIDA 30 (1983), 41–54.

2185.   Harer, W. Benson, Jr., and el-Dwakhly, Zenab. "Peseshet—
        The First Female Physician?" *Obstetrics and Gynecology*
        74, no. 6 (December 1989), 960–961.

2186.   Harris, J. R. "Neferneferuaten." *GM* 4 (1973), 15–17.

2187.   —. "Nefertiti Rediviva." *Acta Orientalia* 35 (1973), 5–13.

2188.   —. "Kiya." *CdE* 49 (1974), 25–30.

2189.   —. "Contributions to the History of the Eighteenth Dynas-
        ty." *SAK* 2 (1975), 95–101.

2190.   Hassenfuss, J. "Die Jungfrauengeburt in der Religions-
        geschichte." *Mariologische Studien* 4 (1969), 11–23.

2191.   Helck, Wolfgang. "Die Tochterheirat ägyptischer Könige."
        CdE 44 (1969), 22–25.

2192.   Hickmann, Hans. "Dieux et Déesses de la Musique." *Cahiers
        d'Hist. Egyptienne* Sér. Vi/1 (1954), 31–59.

2193.   Hoffman, I. "Die grosse Göttin des Osmittelmeerraumes in
        meroitischen Reich." *SAK* 5 (1977), 79–121.

2194.   Hohenwart-Gerlachstein, Anna. "The Legal Position of
        Women in Ancient Egypt." *Wiener Völkerkundliche Mitteil-
        ungen* 3, Jahrgang Nr. 1 (1955), 90ff.

2195.   Hollis, Susan T. "Women of Ancient Egypt and the Sky
        Goddess Nut." *Journal of American Folklore* 100 (1987),
        496–503.

2196.   Jacquet-Gordon, H. "A statuette of Ma'et and the Identity
        of the Divine Adoratress of Karomama." *ZAS* 94 (1967),
        86–93.

2197.   Janssen, J. J. "La reine Nefertari et la succession de Ramsès II
        par Merenptah." *CdE* 38 (1963), 30–36.

2198.   —. "An Allusion to an Egyptian Wedding Ceremony?" *GM*
        10 (1974), 25–28.

2199. —."The Rules of Legal Procedure in the Community of Necropolis Workmen at Deir el-Medina." *BO* 32 (1975), 291–296.

2200. —. "Absence from Work by the Necropolis Workmen of Thebes." *SAK* 8 (1980), 127–152.

2201. Janssen, Jac. J. & Pestman, P. W. "Burial and Inheritance in the Community of the Necropolis Workmen at Thebes." *JESHO* 11 (1968), 137–170.

2202. Jonckheere, Frans. "La durée de la gestation d'après les textes égyptiens." *CdE*. 30 (1955), 19–45. I.e., 9 mos. or 275 days.

2203. Kaplan, H. R. "The Problem of the Dynastic Position of Meryet-Nit." *JNES* 38 (1979), 23–27.

2204. Kaplony, P. "Denkmäler der Prinzessin Neferurê und der Königin Ti-mienêse in der Sammlung A. Ghertsos." *RdE* 22 (1970), 99–109.

2205. Kees, H. "Das Gottesweib Ahmes-Nofertere als Amon-priester." *Orientalia,* n.s., 23 (1954), 57–63.

2206. Keimer, L. "Remarques sur les 'cuillers à fard' du type dit à la nageuse." *ASAE* 52 (1952), 59–72.

2207. Kemp, Barry J. "The Harîm-Palace at Medinet el-Ghurab." *ZÄS* 105 (1978), 122–133.

2208. —. "Wall Paintings from the Workmen's Village at el-'Amarna." *JEA* 65 (1979), 47–53.

2209. Korr, Craig S. "Evidence of the Sign of the Goddess Tanit in the Theban Region of Egypt." *IEJ* 31 (1981), 95–96.

2210. Kuchman (-Sabhaly), L. "Titles of Queenship, parts I and II." *JSSEA* 7 (1977), 9–12; 9 (1979), 21–25.

2211. —. "The Titulary of Queens *Nbt* and *Hnwt*." *GM* 52 (1981), 37–42.

2212. Kuhlmann, K. P. "Ptolemais-Queen of Nectanebo I. Notes on the Inscription of an Unknown Princess of the XXXth Dynasty." *MDAIK* 37 (1981), 267–279.

2213. Leclant, M. J. "Tefnout et les divine adoratrices thébaines."
       MDAIK 15 (1957), 166-171.

2214. ⸺. "La Bible et l'Egypte au 1ᵉʳ Millenaire." *MDB* 45 (Aug.-
       Sept.-Oct. 1986), 2-3.

2215. ⸺. "Une nouvelle reine d'Egypt Noub-ounet." *CRAIBL*,
       1990, pp. 516-520.

2216. Leibovitch, Joseph. "Gods of Agriculture and Warfare in
       Ancient Egypt." *JNES* 12 (1953), 73-113.

2217. Lesko, B. S. "True Art in Ancient Egypt." *Egyptological
       Studies in Honor of Richard A. Parker,* pp. 85-97. Edited by
       Leonard H. Lesko. Hanover & London: University Press
       of New England for Brown University Press, 1986.

2218. ⸺. "Women of Egypt and the Ancient Near East." In *Be-
       coming Visible: Women in European History,* pp. 41-77.
       Edited by R. Bridenthal, C. Koon, and S. Stuard. 2d ed.
       Boston: Houghton-Mifflin, 1987.

2219. ⸺. "Women's Monumental Mark on Ancient Egypt." *BA* 54
       (1991), 4-15.

2220. Lesko, L. H. "A Little More Evidence for the End of the
       Nineteenth Dynasty." *JARCE* 5 (1966), 29-32.

2221. ⸺. "Three Late Egyptian Stories Reconsidered." In *Egypto-
       logical Studies in Honor of Richard A. Parker,* pp. 98-103.
       Edited by Leonard H. Lesko. Hanover & London: Uni-
       versity Press of New England for Brown University Press,
       1986.

2222. Lorton, David. "The Treatment of Criminals in Ancient
       Egypt." *JESHO* 20 (1977), 2-64.

2223. Málek, J. "Two Monuments of the Tias." *JEA* 60 (1974),
       161-167.

2224. ⸺. "Princess Inti, the Companion of Horus." *JSSEA* 10
       (1980), 229-241.

2225. Meltzer, Edmund S. "Queens, Goddesses, and other
       Women of Ancient Egypt." *JAOS* 110 (1990), 503-509.

2226. Menu, B. "La gestion du 'patrimoine' foncier d'Heka-nakhte." *RdE* 22 (1970), 111–129.

2227. —. "Quelques remarques à propos de l'étude comparée de la stèle juridique de Karnak et de la 'stèles' d'Ahmès-Néfertari." *RdE* 23 (1971), 155–163.

2228. —. "La 'stèle' d'Ahmès-Nefertari dans son contexte historique et juridique." *BIFAO* 77 (1977), 89–100.

2229. Midant-Reynes, B. "St-Imm 'femme' ou 'fille' d"Amon." *RdE* 28 (1976), 160–162.

2230. Millet, Nicholas B. "Social and Political Organisation in Meroe." *ZAS* 108 (1981), 124–141.

2231. Myśliwiec, Leslaw. "La mère, la femme, la fille et la variante féminine du dieu Atoum." *Études et Travaux* 13 (1983), 297–304.

2232. Newberry, P. E. "Queen Nitocris of the Sixth Dynasty." *JEA* 29 (1943), 51–54.

2233. Nims, C. "The Date of the Dishonoring of Hatshepsut." *ZAS* 93 (1966), 97–100.

2234. —. "Some Notes on the Family of Mereruka." *JAOS* 58 (1938), 638–647.

2235. Niwinski, Andrzey. "Some Remarks on Rank and Titles of Women in the Twenty-First Dynasty Theban 'State of Amun'." *Discusssions in Egyptology* 4 (1989), 79–90.

2236. Nord, D. "The Term *ḫar* 'harem' or 'musical performers'." In *Studies in Ancient Egypt, the Aegean and the Sudan in Honor of Dows Durham,* pp. 137–145. Edited by W. K. Simpson and W. M. Davis. Boston: Museum of Fine Arts,1981.

2237. Nur el-Din, M. A. "Some Remarks on the Title *mwt-nsw.*" *Orientalia Lovaniensia Periodica* 11 (1980), 91–98.

2238. Oded, B. "Egyptian References to the Edomite Deity Qaus." *AUSS* 9 (1977), 47–50.

2239. Ogdon, J. R. "The Desert of the Beautiful Goddess of the West." *JSSEA* 9 (1978), 107–110.

2240. —. "An Exceptional Family of Priests of the Early Fifth Dynasty at Gîza." *GM* 90 (1986), 61–65.

2241. Patrich, Yosef. "Earrings of the goddess El-'Uzza from Mampsis." *Qadmoniyot* 16 *Qadmoniyot* 16 (1983), 86–88 + 5 fig (in Hebrew).

2242. Peet, T. E. "Two Letters from Akhetaten." *Annals of Archaeology and Anthropology* 17 (1930), 82–97.

2243. Perdu, Olivier. "Khenemet-Nefer-Hedjet: Une Princesse et deux reines du moyen empire." *RdE* 29 (1977), 68–85.

2244. Pestman, P. W. "The Law of Succession in Ancient Egypt." In *Essays on Oriental Laws of Succession,* pp. 58–77. Edited by J. Brugman et al. Studia et Documenta ad iura orientis antiqui pertinentia, 9. Leiden: E. J. Brill, 1969.

2245. Pestman, P. W., and Janssen, J. J. "Burial and Inheritance in the Community of the Necropolis Workmen at Thebes." *JESHO* 11 (1968), 137–170.

2246. Pfluger, K. "The Private Funerary Stelae of the Middle Kingdom and their Importance for the Study of Ancient Egyptian History." *JAOS* 67 (1947), 127–135.

2247. Pillet, Marice. "Les scènes de naissance et de circoncision dans le tempel nord-est de mort à Karnak." *ASAE* 52 (1954), 77–104.

2248. Pinch, G. "Childbirth and Female Figurines at Deir el-Medina and el-'Amarna." *Orientalia,* n.s., 52 (1983), 405–414.

2249. Pirenne, J. "La statut de la femme dans l'ancienne Egypte." *Recueils de la Société Jean Bodin* 11 (1959), 63–77.

2250. Posner-Krieger, P. "Les chants d'amour de l'ancienne Egypte." *MDB* 45 (Aug.–Sept.–Oct. 1986), 42–43.

2251. Rabinowitz, Jacob J. "The 'Great Sin' in Ancient Egyptian Marriage Contracts." *JNES* 18 (1959), 73.

2252.   Radwan, A. "Rameses II und sein Mutter vor Osiris." *SAK* 6 (1978), 157–161.

2253.   Rammant-Peeters, Agnes. "Les couronnes de Nefertiti à el-Amarna." *Orientalia Lovaniensia Periodica* 16 (1985), 21–48.

2254.   Redford, Donald R. "The Monotheism of the Heretic Pharaoh." *BAR* 13, no. 3 (1987), 16–32.

2255.   Riefstahl, Elizabeth. "Doll, Queen, or Goddess." *Brooklyn Museum Journal* 2 (1943–1944), 7–23.

2256.   —. "Two Hairdressers of the Eleventh Dynasty." *JNES* 15 (1956), 10–17. Inu and Henut.

2257.   Robins, Gay. "The Relationships Specified by Egyptian Kingship Terms of the Middle and New Kingdoms." *CdE* 54 (1979), 197–217.

2258.   —. "Meritamum, daughter of Ahmose, and Meritamun daughter of Thutmose III." *GM* 56 (1982), 79–87.

2259.   —. "A Critical Examination of the Theory of the Right to the Throne of Ancient Egypt Passed through the Female Line in the 18th Dynasty." *GM* 62 (1983), 67–77.

2260.   Roccati, A. "Une légende égyptienne d'Anat." *RdE* 24 (1972), 152–159.

2261.   Samson, J. "Royal Names in Amarna History." *CdE* 56 (1976), 30–38.

2262.   —. "Nefertiti's Regality." *JEA* 63 (1977), 88–97. Nefertiti and her daughter.

2263.   —. "Akhenaten's Successor." *GM* 32 (1979), 83–97.

2264.   Satzinger, Helmut. "Zum Namen der Göttin Thermouthis." *OrAnt* 22 (1983), 235–245 + pl. viii–ix.

2265.   Schott, S. "Nut sprucht als Mutter und Sarg." *RdE* 17 (1965), 81–87.

2266.   Schulman, A. R. "Diplomatic Marriage in the Egyptian New Kingdom." *JNES* 38 (1979), 177–193.

2267. Silverman, D. P. "The Priestess of Hathor ʿnḫ-Ḥwt-Ḥr." *ZÄS* 110 (1983), 80–89.

2268. Simpson, W.K. "The Hyksos Princess Tany." *CdE* 34 (1959), 233–239.

2269. —. "A Relief of a Divine Votaress in Boston." *CdE* 57 (1982), 231–235.

2270. Smith, H. S. "Dates of the Obsequies of the Mothers of Apis." *RdE* 24 (1972), 176–187.

2271. —. "Society and Settlement in Ancient Egypt." In *Man, Settlement and Urbanism*, pp. 705–719. Edited by P. J. Ucko et al. London: Duckworth, 1972.

2272. Spalinger, A. "Remarks on the Family of Queen Ḫ'. s-nbw and the Problem of Kingship in Dynasty XIII." *RdE* 32 (1980), 95–116.

2273. Spiegelberg, W. "Notes on the Feminine Character of the New Empire." *JEA* 15 (1929), 199.

2274. Stavnik, É. "Une suggestion au sujet de la couronne de la princesse Sat-Hathor-Yount." *RdE* 2 (1934) 165–171.

2275. Stevens, John M. "Gynaecology from Ancient Egypt: The Papyrus Kahun: A Translation of the Oldest Treatise on Gynaecology that has Survived from the Ancient World." *Medical Journal of Australia* 63 (1975), 949–952.

2276. Tanner, R. "Untersuchungen zur Rechtsstellung der Frau im pharaonishchen Aegypten." *Klio* 46 (1965), 45–81.

2277. —. "Untersuchungen zur ehe- und erbrechtlichen Stellung der Frau im pharaonischen Aegypten." *Klio* 49 (1967), 5–37.

2278. Théoridès, A. "Du prestige de la procédure oraculaire parmi le personnel de la nécropole thébaine sous le Nouvel Empire." *Acta Orientalia Belgica* 31 (1963), 185–200.

2279. —. "La répudiation de la femme en Egypte dans les droits orientaux anciens." *BSFE* 47 (1966), 6–19.

2280. —. "Le droit matrimonial dans l'Egypte pharaonique."
       RIDA 3ᵉ série, 23 (1976), 15–55.

2281. Troy, Lana. "Ahotep—A Source Evaluation." *GM* 3 5
       (1979), 81–91.

2282. —. "Good and Bad Women." *GM* 80 (1984), 77–82.

2283. Valloggia, M. "Remarques sur les noms de la reine Sébek-
       Ka-Rê Néferou-Sébek." *RdE* 16 (1964), 45–53.

2284. Vandier, J. "Iousâas et (Hathor)-Nébet-Hétépet." *RdE* 16
       (1964), 55–146; 17 (1965), 89–176; 18 (1966), 67–142.

2285. Velde, H. te, "Egyptian Triads Structured as One God with
       Two Goddesses." *Studies in the History of Religions* 3 1
       (1975), 42.

2286. Verner, Miroslav. "Statue of Twēret (Cairo Museum no.
       39145) Dedicated by Pabēsi and Several Remarks on the
       Role of the Hippopotamus Goddess." *ZÄS* 96 (1970), 52–
       63.

2287. Vittmann, G. "Zwei Königinnen der Spätzeit namens Che-
       debnitjerbōne." *CdE* 49 (1974), 43–51.

2288. Walle, B. van de. "La princesse Isis, fille et épouse d'Améno-
       phis III." *CdE* 43 (1968), 36–54.

2289. Ward, William A. "Some Personal Names of the Hyksos
       Period Rulers and Notes on the Epigraphy of their
       Scarabs." *UF* 8 (1976), 353–369.

2290. —. "Reflections on Some Egyptian Terms Presumed to
       Mean 'harem, harem-woman, concubine.'" *Berytus* 3 1
       (1983), 67–74.

2291. —. "The Case of Mrs. Tchat and Her Sons at Beni Hassan."
       GM 71 (1984), 51–59.

2292. —. "The Supposed *s.t. nt ḳnb.t* 'Female member of a Judicial
       Council' of Pap. Boulaq 18." *GM* 100 (1987), 81–84.

2293. Westendorf, Wolfhart. "Maat, die Führerin des Sonnen-
       lichtes, in der Architektur." *ZÄS* 97 (1971), 143–146.

2294.   Winlock, H. E. "On Queen Tetisheri, Grandmother of Ahmose I." *Ancient Egypt*, 1921, pp. 14–16.

2295.   Yoyotte, Jean. "Les vierges consacrées d'Amon théban." *CRAIBL,* 1961, 43–52.

2296.   —. "La date supposée du couronnement d'Hatshepsout." *Kêmi* 18 (1968), 85–91.

2297.   Zabkar, L. V. "Six Hymns to Isis in the Sanctuary of Her Temple at Philae and Their Theological Significance." *JEA* 69 (1983), 115–137.

2298.   Ziegler, Christiane. "Une famille de grands des Djebels de l'or d'Amon." *RdE* 30 (1981), 125–132.

9. WOMEN AND WOMANHOOD IN ELEPHANTINE

2299. Ahyoueny, M. "The Religion of the Elephantine Jews." *BM* 26 (1981), 217–230 (in Hebrew).

2300. Grelot, P. "Elephantine Araméens et Juifs en Egypte." *MDB* 45 (Aug.-Sept.-Oct. 1986), 32–35.

2301. Porten, B. *Archives from Elephantine.* Berkeley & Los Angeles: University of California Press, 1968.

2302. —. "The Restoration of Fragmentary Aramaic Marriage Contracts." In *Graetz College Anniversary Volume,* pp. 243–261. Philadelphia: Graetz College Press, 1971.

2303. —. "Five Fragmentary Aramaic Marriage Documents: New Collations and Restorations." *Abr-Nahrain* 27 (1989), 80–105.

2304. Porten, B., and Greenfield, J. C. *Jews of Elephantine and Arameans of Syene.* Jerusalem: Akademon, 1974.

2305. Porten, B., and Szubin, H. Z. "Abandoned Property in Elephantine: A New Interpretation of Kraeling 3." *JNES* 41 (1982), 123–131.

2306. —. "A Dowry Addendum (Kraeling 10)." *JAOS* 107 (1987), 231–238.

2307. Rabinowitz, Jacob J. "Marriage Contracts in Ancient Egypt in the Light of Jewish Sources." *HTR* 46 (1953), 91–97.

2308. Türck, U. "Die Stellung der Frau in Elephantine als Ergebnis persisch-babylonische Rechsteinfluses." *ZAW* 46 (1928), 166–169.

2309. Valbelle, D. "Maintien et Transformation de la Societe." *MDB* 45 (Aug.-Sept.-Oct. 1986), 9–12.

2310. Voterra, E. "Osservazioni sul divorzio nei documenti aramaici." In *Studia orientalistici in onore di G. Levi della Vida II,* pp. 586–600. Rome: Instituto per l'Oriente, 1956.

10. WOMEN AND WOMANHOOD IN ANCIENT MESOPOTAMIA: BOOKS AND DISSERTATIONS

2311. Aro, J. and Farber, W. *Beschworungsrituele an Ištar und Dumuzi.* Wiesbaden: Franz Steiner Vorlag, 1977.

2312. Asher-Greve, J. M. *Frauen in altsumerischer Zeit.* Bibliotheca Mesopotamia, vol. 18. Malibu: Undena Publications, 1985.

2313. Bayliss, D. "Ancestry and Descent in Mesopotamia from the Old Babylonian to the Neo-Assyrian Period." Ph.D. diss., School of Oriental and African Studies, London, 1971.

2314. Blocher, F. *Untersuchungen zum Motiv der nackten Frau in der altbabylonistichen Zeit.* Munich: Profil, 1987.

2315. Bridges, Susan Jane. "The Mesaq Archive. A Study of Sargonic (2334–2279) Society and Economy." Ph.D. diss., Yale University, 1981.

2316. Cardascia, G. *Les Lois assyriens.* Paris: Cerf, 1969.

2317. Cassin, E. *La semblable et le different: symbolismes du pouvoir dans le proché-orient ancient.* Paris: La Decouverte, 1987.

2318. Charpin, D. *Archives Familiales et propriété privée en Babylonie ancienne. Etude des documents de "Tell Sifr."* Geneva: Droz/Paris: Champion, 1980.

2319. Dalley, Stephanie. *Myths from Mesopotamia: Creation, The Flood, Gilgamesh and Others.* Translated with an Introduction and Notes. Oxford: Oxford University Press, 1989.

2320. —., and Postgate, J. N. *The Tablets from Fort Shalmaneser.* Oxford: British School of Archaeology in Iraq, 1984.

2321. Dandamaev, Muhammad A. *Slavery in Babylonia from Nabopolassar to Alexander the Great (626–331 BC).* Rev. ed. Translated by M. A. Powell. Edited by Victoria A. Powell and D. B. Weisberg. DeKalb, Ill.: Northern Illinois University Press, 1984.

2322.   Driver, G. R., and Miles, John C. *The Babylonian Laws*. 2 vols. Oxford: Clarendon Press, 1952–1955.

2323.   —. *The Assyrian Laws*. Oxford: Clarendon Press, 1935.

2324.   Eilers, Wilhelm. *Semiramis. Entstehung und Nachhall einer altorientalischen Sage*. Vienna: H. Böhlhaus Nachf., 1971.

2325.   Falkenstein, A. *The Sumerian Temple City*. Introduction and translation by Marie deJ. Ellis. Los Angeles: Undena Publications, 1974.

2326.   Farber, W. T. *Beschwörungsrituale an Ištar und Dumuzi*. Wiesbaden: Steiner, 1977.

2327.   Farber-Flügge, Gertrud. *Der Mythos "Inanna und Enki" unter besonderer Berücksichtigung der Liste M E*. Studia Pohl, no. 10. Rome: Biblical Institute Press, 1973.

2328.   Ferrara, A. J. *Nanna-Suen's Journey to Nippur*. Studia Pohl, Series Maior, no. 2. Rome: Biblical Institute Press, 1973.

2329.   Figulla, H. H. *Old Babylonian nadītu Records*. CT 47. London: Trustees of the British Museum, 1967.

2330.   Gwaltney, William Cary, Jr. "The Qadištum and Ištaritum in Mesopotamian Society." Ph.D. diss., Hebrew Union College, Cincinnati, Ohio, 1964.

2331.   Hallo, W. W., and Van Dijk, J. J. *The Exaltation of Inanna*. New Haven: Yale University Press, 1968.

2332.   Harris, R. *Ancient Sippar. A Demographic Study of an Old Babylonian City (1894–1595 B.C.)*. Istanbul: Nederlands Historisch-Archaeologisch Instituut te Istanbul, 1975.

2333.   Hirsch, Hans. *Untersuchungen zur altassyrischen Religion. AfO Beiheft* 13/14. 2d ed. Osnabrück: Biblio Verlag, 1972.

2334.   Hutter, Manfred. "Nergal und Ereškigal; ein babylonsichen Mythos vom Abstieg in die Unterwelt neu übersetzt und erklärt." Ph.D. diss., Graz, 1984.

2335. Jacobsen, Thorkild. *The Treasures of Darkness: A History of Mesopotamian Religion.* New Haven: Yale University Press, 1976. Contains important material on goddesses.

2336. —. *The Harab Myth.* Sources and Monographs from the Ancient Near East, vol. 2, fascicle 3. Malibu: Undena Publications, 1984.

2337. Joannes, F. *Textes économiques de la Babylonie récente.* Etudies Assyriologiques, Cahier 6. Paris: Editions Recherche sur les Civilisations, 1982.

2338. Klíma, J. *Gesellschaft und Kultur des alten Mesopotamien.* Prague: Verlag der Tschechoslowakischen Akademie der Wissenschaften und Artia, 1964.

2339. Kramer, S. N. *Enki and Ninḫursag: A Sumerian "Paradise" Myth.* BASOR Supplementary Studies 1. New Haven: American Schools of Oriental Research, 1945.

2340. —. *The Sacred Marriage Rite.* Bloomington: University of Indiana Press, 1969.

2341. Kümmel, H. M. *Familie, Beruf und Amt in spätbabylonischen Uruk.* ADOG, 20. Berlin: Mann, 1979.

2342. Landsberger, B. *Die Serie ana ittišu.* MSL, no. 1. Rome: Pontifical Biblical Institute, 1937.

2343. Lerner, Gerda. *The Creation of Patriarchy.* New York: Oxford, 1986.

2344. Lieberman, A. I. "Studies in the Trial by River Ordeal in the Ancient Near East During the 2nd Millenium B.C.E." Ph.D. diss., Brandeis University, 1969.

2345. Lipínski, Edward, ed. *State and Temple Economy in the Ancient Near East.* Orientalia Lovaniensia Analecta, 5–6. 2 vols. Leuven: Departement Orientalistiek Leuven, 1979.

2346. Livingstone, A. *Court Poetry and Literary Miscellanea.* State Archives of Assyria, vol. 3. Helsinki: Helsinki University Press, 1989.

2347. Menzel, Brigitte. *Assyrische Tempel.* 2 vols. Studia Pohl Series

Maior, no. 10. Rome: Biblical Institute Press, 1981.

2348.   Mishali, Ajalah. "A Study of Women's Status According to the Laws of the Royal Assyrian Edicts as Compared to Her Status in the O.T." M.A. thesis, Bar-Ilan University, 1983 (in Hebrew with English summary).

2349.   Perera, S. B. *Descent to the Goddess: A Way of Initiation for Women.* Studies in Jungian Psychology, no. 6 Toronto: Inner City Books, 1981. Ishtar

2350.   Pettinato, G. *Semiramide.* Milano: Rusconi, 1985.

2351.   Praag, A. van. *Droit matrimonial assyro-babylonien.* Amsterdam: Noord-Hollandsche Uitgevers, 1945.

2352.   Roberts, J. J. M. *The Earliest Semitic Pantheon. A Study of the Semitic Deities Attested in Mesopotamia Before Ur III.* Baltimore & London: Johns Hopkins University Press, 1972.

2353.   Roth, Martha T. *Babylonian Marriage Agreements, 7th–3rd Centuries B.C.* AOAT, 222. Kevelaer: Butzon und Bercker, 1989.

2354.   Saggs, H. W. F. *Everyday Life in Babylonia and Assyria.* London: B.T. Batsford, 1965.

2355.   —. *The Might That Was Assyria.* London: Sidgwick & Jackson, 1984.

2356.   —. *Civilizations Before Greece and Rome.* London: B.T. Batsford, 1989.

2357.   Saporetti, Claudio. *Assur 14446 La Famiglia A Ascesca e declino di persone e famiglie all'inizio del medio-regno assiro, I.* Cybernetica Mesopotamia. Malibu: Undena Publications, 1979.

2358.   —. *The Status of Women in the Middle Assyrian Period.* Monographs on the Ancient Near East, vol. 2, fascicle 1. Malibu: Undena Publications, 1979.

2359.   Scheil, J. V. *Une saison de fouilles à Sippar.* Paris: Institut d'archéologie orientale, 1902.

2360. Schmandt-Besserat, Denise, ed. *The Legacy of Sumer*. Bibliotheca Mesopotamica, 4. Malibu: Undena Publications, 1976.

2361. Schorr, M. *Urkunden der altbabylonischen Zivil-und Prozessrechts*. Vorderasiatische Bibliothek, vol. 5. Leipzig: J.C. Hinrich, 1913.

2362. Sephati, Y. "Songs of Love in Sumerian Literature. A Critical Edition of the Songs of Dumuzi-Inanna." Ph.D. diss., Bar-Ilan University, 1985.

2363. Siegel, Bernard J. *Slavery During the Third Dynasty of Ur*. Menasha, Wisconsin: American Anthropological Association, 1947.

2364. Sigrist, Marcel. *Les sattukku dans l'Ešumeša durant la période d'Isin et Larsa*. Bibliotheca Mesopotamica, no. 7. Malibu: Udena, 1984.

2365. Skaist, A. "Studies in Ancient Mesopotamian Law Pertaining to Marriage and Divorce." Ph.D. diss., University of Pennsylvania, 1963.

2366. Sladek, W. R. "Inanna's Descent to the Netherworld." Ph.D. diss., Johns Hopkins University, 1974.

2367. Soleil, Brigitte. "La Statuaire féminine en pierre aus pays de Sumer de l'époque de la IIe dynastie de Lagaš à cella d'Isin/Larsa." Ph.D. diss., Leuven, 1982.

2368. Stol, Martin. *Zwanger schap en gebourte bij de Babyloniers en in de Bijbel*. Leiden: E. J. Brill, 1983.

2369. Tallqvist, Knut. *Akkadische Götterepitheta*. Helsinki: Societas Orientalis Fennica, 1938.

2370. Thompson, W. I. *The Time Falling Bodies Take to Light: Mythology, Sexuality and the Origins of Culture*. New York: St. Martin's Press, 1981. Inanna, pp. 172–181

2371. Weiher, E. von. *Spätbabylonische Texte aus Uruk. Teil III*. Ausgrabungen der deutschen Forschungsgemeinschaft in Uruk-Warka, 12. Berlin: Mann, 1988.

2372. Westbrook, R. *Old Babylonian Marriage Law.* AfO Beiheft 23. Horn, Austria: Ferdinand Berger und Söhne, 1988.

2373. Wolkstein, Diane, and Kramer, Samuel Noah. *Inanna Queen of Heaven and Earth: Her Stories and Hymns from Sumer.* New York: Harper & Row, 1983.

2374. Yaron, Reuven. *The Laws of Eshnunna.* 2d ed. Leiden: E. J. Brill, 1988.

2375. Zadok, Ran. *On West Semites in Babylonia during the Chaldean and Achaemenian Periods: An Onomastic Study.* Jerusalem: Wanaarta & Tel Aviv University Press, 1977.

11. WOMEN AND WOMANHOOD IN ANCIENT MESOPOTAMIA: ARTICLES

2376. Abusch, Tzvi. "Ishtar's Proposal and Gilgamesh's Refusal: An Interpretation of The Gilgamesh Epic, Tablet 6, Lines 1–79." *History of Religions* 26 (1986/87), 143–187.

2377. Al-A'dami, K. A. "A New LU·SHA Text in the Iraq Museum, Including Women's Professions." *Sumer* 25 (1969), 97–98 + 2 pl.

2378. Al-Fouadi, Abdul-Hadi. "Inanna's Journey to Eridu." *Sumer* 27 (1971), 53–62 (in Arabic).

2379. Alster, B. "Sumerian Proverbs Collection 24." *Assyriological Miscellanies I* (1980), 43ff. Refers to "The Fowler and His Wife."

2380. —. "On the Interpretation of the Sumerian Myth 'Inanna and Enki'." *ZA* 64 (1975), 20–34.

2381. —. "Paradoxical Proverbs and Satire in Mesopotamian Literature." *JCS* 27 (1975), 201–230. Refers to "The Fowler and His Wife."

2382. —. "Enki and Ninhursag. The Creation of the First Woman." *UF* 10 (1978), 15–27.

2383. —. "Geštinanna as Singer and the Chorus of Uruk and Zabalam: UET 6/1, 22." *JCS* 37 (1985), 219–228.

2384. —. "Sumerian Love Songs." *RA* 79 (1985), 127–159.

2385. Anbar, M. "Textes de l'époque babylonienne ancienne." *RA* 69 (1975), 109–136.

2386. Arnaud, Daniel. "La prostitution sacrée en Mésopotamie, un mythe historiographique?" *RHR* 183 (1973), 111–115.

2387. Azarpay, G. "Nanâ, the Sumerian-Akkadian Goddess of Transoxiana." *JAOS* 96 (1976), 536–542.

2388. Bailey, J. A. "Male, Female, and the Pursuit of Immortality in the Gilgamesh Epic." *Parola del Passato* 171 (1976), 433–457.

2389. Barré, Michael L. "The First Pair of Deities in the Sefîre I God-List." *JNES* 44 (1985), 205–210.

2390. Benedetti, B. "Nota sulla ^{sal} šu.gi. ittita." *Mesopotamia* 15 (1980) 93–108.

2391. Böhl, Franz M. Th. "The Position of Women in Ancient Babylonia and Israel." *Bibliotheca Sacra* 77 (1920), 4–13; 186–197.

2392. Bottero, J. "La femme, l'amour et la guerre en Mésopotamie ancienne." *Poikilia: Études offertes à Jean-Pierre Vernant*, pp. 165–183. Paris: Éditions d'École des Hautes Études en Sciences sociales, 1987.

2393. —. "L'amour librè et ses desavantages." *Mesopotamie: l'écriture, la raison et les dieux.* Paris: Gallimard, 1987.

2394. Briend, J. "La Création d'après l'épopée d'Atra-hasis, La Création de l'Homme dans les Textes Egyptiens." *MDB*, no. 9 (May-June-July 1979), 25–29.

2395. Brinkmann, J. A. "Sex, Age, and Physical Condition Designations for Servile Laborers in the Middle Babylonian Period: A Preliminary Survey." In *Zikir šumim*, pp. 1–8. Edited by G. van Driel. Leiden: E. J. Brill, 1982.

2396. Brooks, Beatrice Allard. "Some Observations Concerning Ancient Mesopotamian Women." *AJSL* 39 (1922–23), 187–194.

2397. Buccellati, Giorgio. "The Descent of Inanna as a Ritual Journey to Kutha?" *Syro-Mesopotamian Studies* 4, no. 3 (1982), 53–57.

2398. Buchanan, Briggs. "A Snake Goddess and Her Companions." *Iraq* 33 (1971) 1–18.

2399. Cardascia, G. "L'adoption matrimoniale à Babylone et à Nuzi." *RHD* 37 (1959), 1–16.

2400.   Cassin, E. "Pouvoir de la femme et structures familiales." *RA* 63 (1969), 121- 148.

2401.   Civil, M. "The 'Message of LÚ·DINGIR·RA to his mother' and a group of Akkado-Hittite Proverbs." *JNES* 23 (1964), 1–11.

2402.   —. "Enlil and Ninlil: The Marriage of Sud." *JAOS* 103 (1983), 43–66.

2403.   Cooper, J. S. "New Cuneiform Parallels to the Song of Songs." *JBL* 90 (1971), 157–162.

2404.   Dalley, Stephanie. "Old Babylonian Doweries." *Iraq* 42 (1980), 53–74.

2405.   Diakonoff, I. M. "The Structure of Near Eastern society before the middle of the 2nd millenium B.C." *Oikumene* 3 (1982), 7–100.

2406.   —. "Extended Families in Old Babylonian Ur." *ZA* 75 (1985), 47–65.

2407.   —. "Women in Old Babylonia not under patriarchal authority." *JESHO* 29 (1986), 225–238.

2408.   Dijk, J. van. "Note sur l'interpretation d'IM 28051." *Orientalia,* n.s., 39 (1970), 99–102.

2409.   —. "Une variante du thème de 'l'Esclave de la Lune.'" *Orientalia,* n.s., 41 (1972), 339–348.

2410.   Dossin, G. "L'article 142/143 du Code de Hammurabi." *RA* 42 (1948), 113–124.

2411.   —. "Aya, parèdre de Šamaš." *OrAnt.* 18 (1979), 241–243.

2412.   Doty, L. Timothy. "The Archive of the Nanâ-Iddin Family from Uruk." *JCS* 30 (1978), 65–90. Deals with women as sellers of slaves in the Seleucid period.

2413.   Ebeling, Erich. "Kultische Texte aus Assur." *Orientalia,* n.s., 22 (1953), 25–46; 24 (1955), 1–15.

2414.   Edzard, D. O. "Mesopotamien: Die Mythologie der Sumer-er und Akkader." In *Wörterbuch der Mythologie*. Edited by H. W. Haussig. Stuttgart: Klett, 1962. Deals with goddesses.

2415. Ellis, Maria De J. "The Division of Property at Tell Harmal." *JCS* 26 (1974), 133–153. division of the property of Zibbatum the naditu

2416. —. "An Old Babylonian Adoption Contract from Tell Harmal." *JCS* 27 (1975), 130–151. Couple adopts female child.

2417. Fadhil, A. "Die in Numrud/Kalḫu aufgefundene Grabinschrift der Jabâ." *Baghdader Mitteilungen* 21 (1990), 461–470.

2418. —. "Die Grabinschrift der Mullissu-Mukannišat-Ninua aus Nimrud/Kalḫu und andere in ihrem Grab gefundene Schrifftträger." *Baghdader Mitteilungen* 21 (1990), 471–482.

2419. Fales, F. M. "A List of Assyrian and West Semitic Women's Names." *Iraq* 41 (1979), 55–73.

2420. Falkenstein, A. "Der sumerische und der akkadische Mythos von Inannas, Gang zur Unterwelt." In *Festschrift für W. Caskeltt*. pp. 97-110. Edited by E. Gräf. Leiden: E. J. Brill, 1968.

2421. Falkowitz, R. "Paragraph 59 of the Laws of Ešnunna." *RA* 72 (1978), 79–80.

2422. Farber, Gertrud. "Another Old Babylonian Childbirth Incantation." *JNES* 43 (1984), 311–316.

2423. Fawzi, Rashid. "Burying Daughters Alive and the Polygamy Tradition in Ancient Times." *Sumer* 36 (1980), 53–62 (in Arabic).

2424. Feigin, Samuel I. "The Captives in Cuneiform Inscriptions." *AJSL* 50 (1933–34), 217–245.

2425. Filippi, W. de. "New Evidence for the Separate Identity of dŠarrat-Kidmuri and dŠarrat-nipḫi." *RA* 70 (1976), 181–182.

2426. Finet, A. "Hammu-rapi et l'epouse vertueuse. A propos des # 133 et 142–143 du Code." In *Symbolae F. M. Th. Liagre Böhl,* pp. 137–143. Edited by M. A. Beck et al. Leiden: E. J. Brill, 1973.

2427. Finkel, Irving L. "An Early Old Babylonian Legal Document." *RA* 70 (1976), 45–54.

2428. —. "The Crescent Fertile." *AfO* 27 (1980), 37–52.

2429. —. "A Fragmentary Catalogue of Love Songs." *Acta Sumerologica* 10 (1988), 17–18.

2430. Finkelstein, J. J. "Assyrian Contracts from Sultantepe." *Anatolian Studies* 7 (1957), 137–145. Sale of a female slave

2431. —. "Sex Offenses in Sumerian Laws." *JAOS* 86 (1966), 355–372.

2432. —. "Ana bīt emim šasû." *RA* 61 (1967), 127–136.

2433. —. "On some recent Studies in Cuneiform Law. A review article." *JAOS* 90 (1970), 243–256.

2434. —. "Cutting the sissiktu in Divorce Proceedings." *WO* 8 (1975/76), 236–240.

2435. —. "šilip rēmim and Related Matters." In *Kramer Anniversary Volume,* pp. 187–194. Edited by Barry L. Eichler. AOAT 25. Neukirchen-Vluyn: Neukirchener Verlag, 1976.

2436. Foster, B. "A New Look at the Sumerian Temple State." *JESHO* 24 (1981), 225–241.

2437. —. "Gilgamesh: Sex, Love and the Ascent of Knowledge." In *Love and Death in the Ancient Near East. Essays in Honor of M. H. Pope,* pp. 21–42. Edited by J. H. Marks and R. M. Good. Guilford, Ct.: Four Quarters Publishing Co.,1987.

2438. Frankfort, Henri. "A Note on the Lady of Birth." *JNES* 3 (1944), 198–200. Ninhursanga, Ninurta.

2439. Frymer-Kensky, Tikva. "The Atrahasis Epic and Its Significance for our Understanding of Genesis 1–9." *BA* 40 (1977), 147–155.

2440. —. "The Nungal-Hymn and the Ekur-Prison." *JESHO* 20 (1977), 78–89.

2441. —. "Inanna—The Quintessential Femme Fatale." *BAR* 10, no. 5 (1984), 62–64.

2442. Gallery, Maureen. "Service Obligations of the *kezertu*-Women." *Orientalia,* n.s., 49 (1980), 333–338.

2443. Garelli, P. "Femmes d'affaires en Assyrie." *ArOr* 47 (1979), 42–48.

2444. Gelb, I. J. "The Name of the Goddess Innin." *JNES* 19 (1960), 72–79.

2445. —. "From Freedom to Slavery." In *Gesellschaftsklassen in alten Zweistromland und in den angrenzenden Gebieten. XVIII Rencontre assyriologique internationale, München, 29 Juni bis 3 Juli 1970,* pp. 81–92. Edited by D.O. Edzard. Munich: Bayerischen Akademie der Wissenschaften, 1972.

2446. —. "Household and Family in Early Mesopotamia." In *State and Temple Economy in the Ancient Near East,* pp. 1–98. Edited by E. Lipínski. Orientalia Lovaniensa Analecta 5. Leuven: 1978.

2447. Glassner, J. J. "La famille Mesopotamienne." In *Histoire de la Familie,* Edited by A. Colin. Paris: Armand Colin, 1986.

2448. Goetze, A. "Thirty Tablets from the reigns of Abī-Ešuḫ and Ammī-ditānā." *JCS* 2 (1948), 73–112.

2449. —. "The Roster of Women AT 298." *JCS* 13 (1959), 98–103.

2450. Gomi, T. "Shulgi-simti and Her Libation Place." *Orient (Tokyo)* 12 (1976), 1–14.

2451. Görg, Manfred. "Ein weiterer Tonnagel Gudeas für die Göttin Baba." *BN* 38/39 (1987), 30–32.

2452. Grafman, R. "Bringing Tiamat to Earth." *IEJ* 22 (1972), 47–49.

2453. Grayson, A. K., and Van Seters, J. "The Childless Wife in

Assyria and the Stories of Genesis." *Orientalia*, n.s., 44 (1975), 485–486.

2454. Greengus, S. "Old Babylonian Marriage Ceremonies and Rites." *JCS* 20 (1966), 55–72.

2455. —. "The Old Babylonian Marriage Contract." *JAOS* 89 (1969), 505–532.

2456. —. "A Textbook Case of Adultery in Ancient Mesopotamia." *HUCA* 40–41 ((1969–1970), 33–44.

2457. —. "Bridewealth in Sumerian Sources." *HUCA* 61 (1990), 25–88.

2458. Gurney, O. R. "A Case of Conjugal Desertion." In *Zikir šumim*, pp. 91-94. Edited by G. van Driel et al. Leiden: E. J. Brill, 1982.

2459. Hallo, W. W. "The Slandered Bride." In *Studies Presented to A. Leo Oppenheim*, p. 95–105. Edited by R. D. Biggs and J. A. Brinkman. Chicago: University of Chicago Press, 1964.

2460. —. "Women of Sumer." In *The Legacy of Sumer,* pp. 23–40. Bibliotheca Mesopotamica, vol. 4. Malibu: Undena Publications, 1976.

2461. Hansen, Donald P., and Dales, George F. "The Temple of Inanna, Queen of Heaven, at Nippur." *Archaeology* 15 (1962), 75–78.

2462. Harris, R. "Old Babylonian Temple Loans." *JCS* 14 (1960), 126–137.

2463. —. "On the Process of Secularization under Hammurapi." *JCS* 15 (1961), 117–120.

2464. —. "The Naditu laws of the Code of Hammurapi in Praxis." *Orientalia*, n.s., 30 (1961), 164–169.

2465. —. "Biographical Notes on the nadītu women of Sippar." *JCS* 16 (1962), 1–12.

2466. —. "The Organization and Administration of the Cloister in Ancient Babylonia." *JESHO* 6 (1963), 121–157.

2467.   —. "The Naditu woman." In *Studies Presented to A. Leo Oppenheim,* pp. 100–135. Edited by Erica Reiner. Chicago: University of Chicago Press, 1964.

2468.   —. "Some Aspects of the Centralization of the Realm Under Hammurapi and His Successors." *JAOS* 88 (1968), 727–732.

2469.   —. "Notes on the Babylonian Cloister and Hearth: A Review Article." *Orientalia,* n.s., 38 (1969), 133–145.

2470.   —. "Notes on the Nomenclature of Old Babylonian Sippar." *JCS* 24 (1972), 102–104.

2471.   —. "The Case of Three Babylonian Marriage Contracts." *JNES* 33 (1974), 363–369.

2472.   —. "On kinship and inheritance in Old Babylonian Sippar." *Iraq* 38 (1976), 129–132.

2473.   —. "On Foreigners in Old Babylonian Sippar." *RA* 70 (1976), 145–152.

2474.   —. "Notes on the Slave Names of Old Babylonian Sippar." *JCS* 29 (1977), 46–51.

2475.   —. "Images of Women in the Gilgamesh Epic." In *Lingering Over Words: Studies in Ancient Near Eastern Literature in Honor of William L. Moran,* pp. 219–230. Edited by Tzvi Abusch, John Huehnergard, Piotr Steinkeller. Atlanta: Scholars Press, 1990.

2476.   —. "The Female 'Sage' in Mesopotamia (with an appendix on Egypt). In *The Sage in Israel and the Ancient Near East,* pp. 3–17. Edited by J. G. Gammie and L. G. Perdue. Winona Lake: Eisenbrauns, 1990.

2477.   —. "Inanna-Ishtar As Paradox and A Coincidence of Opposites." *History of Religions* 30 (1991), 261–278.

2478.   Hartland, Sidney E. "At the Temple of Mylitta." In *Anthropological Essays Presented to E. B. Tylor,* pp. 190–200. Oxford: Clarendon, 1907.

2479.   Haupt, Paul. "Das fünfte sumerische Familiengesetze." *ZA* 30 (1915/16), 93- 95.

2480. Heimpel, W. "Der Tod der Göttin Baba von Lagaš." In *Festschrift für H. H. Heimpel*, pp. 661–667. 3 vols. Göttingen: Vandenhoeck & Ruprecht, 1972.

2481. ——. "A Catalogue of Near Eastern Venus Deities." *Syro-Mesopotamian Studies* 4 (1982), 59–72.

2482. Held, Moshe. "A Faithful Lover in an Old Babylonian Dialogue." *JCS* 15 (1961), 1–26; Addenda et Corigenda, *JCS* 16 (1962), 37–39.

2483. Hruška, B. "Das spätbabylonische Lehrgedicht 'Innanas Erhölung'." *ArOr* 37 (1969), 497–522.

2484. Ichisar, M. "Un contrat de mariage et la question du lévirat à lépoque cappadocienne." *RA* 76 (1982), 168–173.

2485. Jacobsen, Thorkild. "Notes on Nintur." *Orientalia*, n.s., 42 (1973), 274–298.

2486. ——. "The Gilgamesh Epic: Romantic and Tragic Vision." In *Lingering Over Words: Studies in Ancient Near Eastern Literature in Honor of William L. Moran*, pp. 231–249. Edited by Tzvi Abusch, John Huehnergard, and Piotr Steinkeller. Atlanta: Scholars Press, 1990.

2487. Jakobson, V. A. "The title *šakintu* in Neo-Assyrian Texts." *Peredneaziatskij* 3 (1979), 243–245 (in Russian).

2488. Jastrow, Morris, Jr. "Adam and Eve in Babylonian Literature." *AJSL* 15 (1898–1899), 193–214.

2489. Joannès, F. "Contrats de Mariage d'Epoque Récente." *RA* 78 (1984), 71–81.

2490. Kang, S. T. "The Role of Women in the Drehem Texts." In *Sumerian Economic Texts from the Drehem Archive*, vol. 1, pp. 257–70. Urbana: University of Illinois Press, 1972.

2491. Kilmer, Anne Draffkorn. "How Was Queen Ereshkigal Tricked? A New Interpretation of the Descent of Ishtar." *UF* 3 (1971), 299–309. Contains extensive bibliography concerning the narrative poem "The Descent of Ishtar."

2492. ——. "The Mesopotamian Concept of Overpopulation and

Its Solution as Reflected in the Mythology." *Orientalia,* n.s., 41 (1972), 160–177.

2493. Klein, Harald. "Tudittum." *ZA* 73 (1983), 255–284. Information concerning women's dress

2494. Klein, Jacob. Šeleppūtum: A Hithertho Unknown Ur III Princess." *ZA* 80 (1990), 20–39.

2495. Klengel-Brandt, E. Review of F. Blocher, *Untersuchungen zum Motiv der nackten Frau in der altbabylonischen Zeit.* OLZ 84 (1989), 547–549.

2496. Kornfeld, W. "L'adultère dans l'orient antique." *RB* 57 (1950), 92- 109.

2497. Koschaker, P. "Fratriarchat, Hausgemeinschaft und Mutterrecht in Keilschriften." *ZA* 41 (1933), 1–89.

2498. —. "Zur Interpretation des Art. 59 des Codex Bilalama." *JCS* 5 (1951), 104–122.

2499. Kramer, S. N. "'Inanna's Descent to the Netherworld': Continued & Revised." *JCS* 4 (1950), 199–214.

2500. —. "Cuneiform Studies and the History of Literature: The Sumerian Sacred Marriage Text." *Proceedings of the American Philosophical Society* 107 (1963), 485–527.

2501. —. "Dumuzi's Annual Resurrection: An Important Correction to 'Innana's Descent'." *BASOR,* no. 185 (1966), 31.

2502. —. "Inanna and Šeulgi: A Sumerian Fertility Song." *Iraq* 31 (1969), 18–23.

2503. —. "Sexual Symbolism in Ancient Sumer: The Cult of the 'Sacred Marriage'." *Molad* 5 (1973), 563–577 (in Hebrew).

2504. —. "The Sacred Marriage." *Ariel* 22 (1975), 62–86 + 5 figs. (in Hebrew).

2505. —. "Poets and Psalmists: Goddesses and Theologians. Literary, Religious and Anthropological Aspects of the Legacy of Sumer." In *The Legacy of Sumer,* pp. 3–31. Bibliotheca

Mesopotamica, vol. 4. Malibu: Undena Publications, 1976.

2506.   —. "Inanna and the *Numun*-Plant: A New Sumerian Myth." In *The Bible World: Essays in Honor of Cyrus Gordon,* pp. 87–97. Edited by Gary Rendsburg et al. New York: Ktav Publishing Co., and New York University Institute for Hebrew Culture, 1980.

2507.   —. "BM 98396: A Sumerian Prototype of the *Mater Dolorosa.*" *EI* 16 (1982), 141–146.

2508.   —. "The Weeping Goddess: Sumerian Prototypes of the *Mater Dolorosa.*" *BA* 46 (1983), 69–80.

2509.   —. "BM 23631: Bread for Enlil, Sex for Inanna (Tab. II-IV)." *Orientalia,* n.s., 54 (1985), 117–132.

2510.   —. "Altbabylonische Heiratsprobleme." *RA* 68 (1974), 111–120.

2511.   Kutscher, Raphael. "From the Royal Court to Slavery in the Ur III Period." *Tel Aviv* 11 (1984), 183–188.

2512.   Lackenbacher, S. "Note sur l'ardat-lılı." *RA* 65 (1971), 119–154.

2513.   —. "Un nouveau fragment de la 'Fête D'Ištar'." *RA* 71 (1977), 39–50.

2514.   Lambert, W. G. "Morals in Ancient Mesopotamia." *JEOL* 14–15 (1955–1958), 184–196.

2515.   —. "The Gula Hymn of Bulluṭsa-rabi." *Orientalia,* n.s., 36 (1967), 105–132.

2516.   —. "An Eye-Stone of Esarhaddon's Queen and Other Similar Gems." *RA* 63 (1969), 65–71.

2517.   —. "A Middle Assyrian Medical Text." *Iraq* 31 (1969), 28–39.

2518.   —. "The Problem of Love Lyrics." In *Unity and Diversity: Essays in the History, Literature and Religion of the Ancient Neear East,* pp. 98–135. Edited by Hans. Goedicke and

J. J. M. Roberts. Baltimore & London: Johns Hopkins University Press, 1975.

2519.   —. "The Pair Laḫmu-Laḫamu in Cosmology." *Orientalia,* n.s., 54 (1985), 189–202.

2520.   —. "A Babylonian Prayer to Anū-na." In *DUMU-E₂-DUB-BA-A: Studies in Honor of Åke W. Sjöberg,* pp. 321–336. Edited by Hermann Behrens, Darlene Loding, and Marth T. Roth. Philadelphia: Occasional Publications of the Samuel Noah Kramer Fund, 1989.

2521.   —. "A New Babylonian Descent to the Netherworld." In *Lingering Over Words: Studies in Ancient Near Eastern Literature in Honor of William L. Moran,* pp. 289–300. Edited by Tzvi Abusch, John Huehnergard, Piotr Steinkeller. Atlanta: Scholars Press, 1990.

2522.   Landsberger, B. "Jungfraulichkeit: Ein Beitrag zum Thema "Beilager und Eheschliessung'." In *Symbolae iuridicae et historicae Martino David dedicatae,* vol. 2, pp. 41–105. Edited by J. A. Ankum et al. Leiden: E. J. Brill, 1968.

2523.   Langdon, Stephen. "Hymn in Paragraphs to Ishtar as Belit of Nippur." *AfO* 1 (1923), 12–18.

2524.   Leemans, W. F. "The Family in the Economic Life of the Old Babylonian Period." *Oikumene* 5 (1986), 15–22.

2525.   Leichty, Erle. "Bel-Epuš and Tammaritu." *Anatolian Studies* 33 (1983), 153–155.

2526.   Lerberghe, K. van. "New Data from the Archives Found in the House of Ur-Utu at Tell ed-Dēr." In *28. Rencontre Assyriologique Internationale in Wien 6.–10. Juli 1981,* pp. 280-283. Afo Beinhaft 19. Horn, Austria: Ferdinand Berger & Söhne, 1982.

2527.   Lerner, Gerda. "The Origin of Prostitution in Ancient Mesopotamia." *SIGNS: Journal of Women in Culture and Society* 11 (1986), 236–254.

2528.   Lewy, Hildergard. "Ištar-Sâd and the Bow Star." In *Studies in Honor of Benno Landsberger in Honor of His Sixty-Fifth Birthday April 21, 1965,* pp. 273–281. Edited by Hans G.

Güterbock and Thorkild Jacobsen. Assyriological Studies, no. 16. Chicago: University of Chicago Press, 1965.

2529. Lipinski, Edward, "The Wife's Right to Divorce in the Light of an Ancient Near Eastern Tradition." *JLA* 4 (1981), 9–27.

2530. —. "Le culte d'Ištar en Mésopotamie du Nord à l'époque parthe." *Orientalia Lovaniensia Periodica* 13 (1982), 117–124.

2531. Loretz, O. "Eine sumerische Parallele zu Ez 23, 20 ('Eine dreijährige Frau heiratet man nicht wie Esel (es tun)." *BZ* 14 (1970), 126.

2532. Loucas, Ioannis. "La désse de la prosperité dans les mythes mésopotamiens et égéens de la 'descente aux enfers'." *RHR* 205 (1988), 224–227.

2533. Luckenbill, Daniel David. "The Temple Women of the Code of Hammurabi." *AJSL* 34 (1917), 1–12.

2534. Luke, K. "Iddin-Dagan and Inanna: A Hieros Gamos Text from the 20th Century B.C." *Living Word* 82 (1976), 79–101.

2535. Lyon, David Gordon. "The Consecrated Women of the Hammurabi Code." In *Studies in the History of Religions Presented to Crawford Howell Toy*, pp. 341–360. Edited by David Gordon Lyon and George Foote Moore. New York: Macmillan, 1912.

2536. McEwan, G. J. P. "A Fragment of an Inanna Hymn from Susa." *JCS* 76 (1982), 187–188.

2537. —. "^{d}Ištar $^{(giš)}$tuk." *RA* 77 (1983), 188–189.

2538. Mackawa, K. "Female Weavers and their children in Lagash-Presargonic and Ur III." *Acta Sumerologica* 2 (1980), 81–125.

2539. Marx, Viktor. "Die Stellung der Frauen in Babylonien gemässen den Kontrakten aus der Zeit von Nebuchadnezar bis Darius (604- 485)." *Beiträge zur Assyriologie* 4 (1902), 1–77.

2540. Matouš, L. "Beiträge zum Eherecht der anatolischen Bevölkerung im 2. Jahrtausend v. u. Z." *ArOr* 41 (1973), 309–318 + 4 fig.

2541. —. "Zur Korrespondence des Imdi–ilum mit Tarēm-Kubi." In *Zikir šumim: Assyriological Studies Presented to F. R. Kraus on the Occasion of His Seventieth Birthday,* pp. 268–270. Leiden: E. J. Brill, 1982.

2542. Matoušouá-Rajmova, Marie. "Illustration de la danse sur les sceaux de l'epoque babylonienne ancienne." *ArOr* 46 (1978), 152–163.

2543. —. "Der Tanz bei magisch-medizinischer Behandlung eines Kranken." *ArOr* 55 (1987), 396–398. Discussion of an 8th century (?) B.C.E. Neo-Assyrian cylinder seal impression depicting a female dancer performing a ritual dance during treatment of a sick person.

2544. Matsushima, Eiko. "Le Rituel Hiérogamique de Nabû." *Acta Sumerologica* 9 (1987), 131–175.

2545. —. Les rituels du mariage divin dans les documents accadiens. *Acta Sumerologica* 10 (1980), 95–128.

2546. Mele, Mirella. "Il simbolo del 'Femminile' nell'epopea di Gilgamesh." *OrAnt* 22 (1983), 291–303.

2547. Mendelsohn, I. "Free Artisans and Slaves in Mesopotamia." *BASOR,* no. 89 (1943), 25–29.

2548. Michalowski, P. "The Bride of Simanum." *JAOS* 95 (1975), 716–719.

2549. —. "Royal Women of the Ur III Period, part I: The Wife of Šulgi." *JCS* 28 (1976), 169–172.

2550. —. "Royal Women of the Ur III Period, part II: Geme Ninlila." *JCS* 31 (1979), 171–176.

2551. —. "Tudanapšum, Naram-Sin and Nippur." *RA* 75 (1981), 173–176. Concerns an *entu*-priestess of the god Enlil in Nippur.

2552. —. "Royal Women of the Ur III Period, Part III." *Acta Sumerologica* 4 (1982), 129–142.

2553. Miller, D. Gary, and Wheeler, P. "Mother Goddess and Consort as Literary Motif Sequence in the Gilgamesh Epic." *Acta Antiqua Academia Scientiarum Hungaricae* 29 (1981), 81–108.

2554. Moorey, P. R. S. "What do we know about the people buried in the Royal Cemetary?" *Expedition* 20, no. 1 (1977), 24–40.

2555. Moran, William L. "The Repose of Rahab's Israelite Guests." In *Studi sull' Oriente e la Bibbia offerti al P. G. Rinaldi,* pp. 273–284. Genoa: Edito Stuio e Vita, 1967.

2556. Nashef, K. "Zur Frage der Schutzbottes der Frau." *WZKM* 67 (1975), 29–30.

2557. Nörr, D. "Die Auflösung der Ehe durch die Frau nach altbabylonischen Recht." In *Studi in onore di Emillo Betti III*, pp. 505–526. Milano: Giuffrè, 1962.

2558. Oberhuber, Karl. "Sind wir berechtigt, von Muttergott-heiten in den Frükulturen des Alten Orients zu sprechen?" *Forschungen und Forstchritte* 38 (1964), 52–56.

2559. Oelsner, J., and Westenholz, A. "Weihplatten fragmente der Hilprecht-Sammlung," *AoF* 10 (1983), 212–216.

2560. Oppenheim, A. L. "A Caesarian Section in the Second Millenium B.C." *Journal of the History of Medicine and Allied Sciences* 15 (1960), 292–294.

2561. Owen, D. I. "A Sumerian Letter from an Angry Housewife (?)." In *The Bible World: Essays in Honor of Cyrus H. Gordon,* pp. 189- 202. Ed. G. Rendsburg et al. New York: Ktav, 1980.

2562. —. "Widows' Rights in Ur III Sumer." *ZA* 70 (1980), 170–184.

2563. Parpola, S. "The Neo-Assyrian Word for 'Queen'." *State Archives of Assyria Bulletin* 2/2 (1988), 73–76.

2564. Parr, P. A. "Ninḫilia, Wife of Ayakala, Governor of Umma." *JCS* 26 (1974), 90–111.

2565.   Pinches, Theophilus G. "Sumerian Women for Field Work." *JRAS*, 1915, pp. 457–463.

2566.   Pollock, S. "Women in a Men's World: Images of Sumerian Women." In *Engendering Archaeology: Women and Prehistory*, pp. 366-387. Edited by Joan M. G. Conkey and M. W. Conkey. Oxford: Blackwell, 1991.

2567.   Pompanio, F. "geme·kar·kid, The Sumerian Word for Prostitute." *Oikumene* 5 (1986), 63–66.

2568.   Postgate, J. "On Some Assyrian Ladies." *Iraq* 41 (1979), 89–103.

2569.   Reiner, Erica. "A Sumero-Akkadian Hymn of Nanâ." *JNES* 33 (1974), 221–236.

2570.   —. "Babylonian Birth Prognoses." *ZA* 72 (1982), 124–138.

2571.   —. "Nocturnal Talk." In *Lingering Over Words: Studies in Ancient Near Eastern Literature in Honor of William L. Moran*, pp. 421–424. Edited by Tzvi Abusch, John Huehnergard, Piotr Steinkeller. Atlanta: Scholars Press, 1990.

2572.   Reiner, Erica, and Güterbock, H. G. "The Great Prayer to Ishtar and Its Two Versions from Boghazköy." *JCS* 21 (1967), 255–266.

2573.   Reisman, Daniel. "Iddin-Dagan's Sacred Marriage Hymn." *JCS* 25 (1973), 185–202.

2574.   Renger, J. "Untersuchungen zum Priestertum in der altbabylonische Zeit." *ZA* 58 (1967), 110–188.

2575.   —. *"mārat ilim:* Exogamie bei den semitischen Nomaden des 2. Jahrtausends." *AfO* 24 (1973), 103–107.

2576.   —. "Who Are all Those People?" *Orientalia*, n.s., 42 (1973), 259–273.

2577.   —. "Wrongdoing and Its Sanctions: On 'Criminal' and 'Civil' Law in the Old Babylonian Period." *JESHO* 20 (1977), 65–77.

2578.   Rénie, J. "Une prétendu parallèle sumérien de la création d'Eve." *Mélanges de Science Religieuse* 10 (1953), 9–12.

2579. Rohrlich, R. "State Formation in Sumer and the Subjugation of Women." *Feminist Studies* 6 (1980), 76–102

2580. Röllig, W. "Politische Heiraten im Alten Orient." *Saeculum* 25 (1974), 11–23.

2581. Römer, W. H. Ph. "Eine sumerische Hymne mit Selbstlob Inannas." *Orientalia*, n.s., 38 (1969), 97–114.

2582. —. "Einige Beobachtungen zur Göttin Nini(n)sina auf Grund von Quellen der Ur III-Zeit und der altbabylonischen Periode." In *Lisān mitḫurti: Festschrift Wolfram Freiherr von Soden zum 19.VI.1968 gewidmet*, pp. 279–305. Edited by W. Röllig. AOAT 1. Kevelaer: Butzon & Bercker/Neukirchen-Vluyn: Neukirchener Verlag, 1969.

2583. Roth, Martha T. "Age at Marriage and the Household: A Study of Neo-Babylonian and Neo-Assyrian Forms." *Comparative Studies in Society and History* 29 (1987), 715–717.

2584. —. "'She will die by the Iron Dagger,' Adultery and Neo-Babylonian Marriage." *JESHO* 31 (1988), 186–206.

2585. —. "Women in Transition and the bīt-mār banî." *RA* 82 (1988), 131–138. The technical term in question designates socially sanctioned protection for orphaned, divorced or widowed [i.e., adult single] women in the Neo-Babylonian period.

2586. —. "The Dowries of the Women of the Itti-Marduk-Balāṭu Family." *JAOS* 111 (1991), 19–37.

2587. —. "The Material Composition of the Dowry." *AfO* 36 (1989), 1–55.

2588. Sack, Ronald H. "Some Remarks on Jewelry Inventories from Sixth Century B.C. Erech." *ZA* 69 (1979), 41–46.

2589. San Nicolò, M. "Due atti matrioniali neobabilonesi." *Aegyptus* 27 (1947), 118–143.

2590. Sasson, J. M. Review of Jean-Marie Durand, ed., *La Femme dans le Proche-Orient Antique*. *AfO* 35 (1988), 187–190.

2591. Sauren, H. "ás-áš, áš, aš, 'concubine'." *RA* 84 (1990), 41–43.

2592. Sayce, A. H. "Miscellaneous Notes." *ZA* 4 (1889), 382–393.

2593. Scheil, J. V. "La Déesse Nisaba." *OLZ* 7 (1904), 253–255.

2594. Schroeder, Otto. "ᵈšarrat-nipḫi." *AfO* 1 (1923), 25–26.

2595. Sephati, Y. "The Oath of Chastity in a Sumerian Love Song (SRT 31)?" In *Bar-Ilan Studies in Assyriology Dedicated to Pinhas Artzi*, pp. 45–63. Edited by Jacob Klein and Aaron Skaist. Ramat-Gan: Bar-Ilan University Press, 1990.

2596. Sjöberg, Åke W. "A Hymn to the Goddess Sadarnuna." *JAOS* 93 (1973), 352- 353.

2597. —. "in-nin šà-gur₄-ra. A Hymn to the Goddess Inanna by the en-Priestess Enḫeduanna." *ZA* 65 (1975), 161–253.

2598. Soden, W. von. "Die Hebamme in Babylonien und Assyrien." *AfO* 18 (1957–58), 119–121.

2599. Spycket, A. "La coiffure féminine en Mésopotamie des Origines à la 1ʳᵉ Dynastie de Babylon." *RA* 48/49 (1954/55), 169–177.

2600. —. "La déesse Lama." *RA* 54 (1960), 73–84.

2601. Steinkeller, P. "More on the Ur III Royal Wives." *Acta Sumerologica* 3 (1981), 77–92; 4 (1982), 129–139; 140–142.

2602. —. "Two Sargonic Sale Documents Concerning Women." *Orientalia*, n.s., 51 (1982), 355–368.

2603. Stol, Marten. *Zwangerschap en geboorte bij de babyloniërs en in de Bijbel.* Leiden: E. J. Brill, 1983.

2604. Stone, E. C. "The Social Role of the *nadītu* Women in Old Babylonian Nippur." *JESHO* 25 (1982), 50–70.

2605. Szlechter, E. "Délits mettant en cause les liens conjugaux et familiaux en Droits sumérien et babylonien." *RIDA* 32 (1985), 69–95.

2606. Thorbjørnsrud, Berit. "What Can the Gilgamesh Myth Tell Us About Religion and the View of Humanity in Mesopotamia?" *Temenos* 19 (1983), 112–137.

2607. Van Buren, E. Douglas. "The Sacred Marriage in Early Times in Mesopotamia." *Orientalia*, n.s., 13 (1944), 1–72.

2608. —. "The Rain Goddess as Represented in Early Mesopotamia." *Analecta Biblica* 12 (1959), 343–355.

2609. Vanstiphout, H. I. J. "Inanna/Ishtar as a Figure of Controversy." In *Struggles of the Gods: Papers of the Groningen Work Group for the Study of the History of Religions*, pp. 225–237. Edited by H. G. Kippenberg. Berlin: de Gruyter, 1984.

2610. Veenhof, K. R. "The Dissolution of an Old Babylonian Marriage According to CT 45, 86." *RA* 70 (1976), 153–164.

2611. Veldhuis, Niek. "The New Assyrian Compendium for a Woman in Childbirth." *Acta Sumerologica* 11 (1989), 239–260.

2612. Wakeman, Mary K. "Sacred Marriage." *JSOT* 22 (1982), 21–31.

2613. —. "Ancient Sumer and the Women's Movement: The Process of Reaching, Behind, Encompassing and Going Beyond." *JFSR* 1 (1985), 7–27.

2614. Walters, Stanley D. "The Sorceress and Her Apprentice." *JCS* 23 (1970–71), 27–38.

2615. Weidner, Ernst F. "Altbabylonische Götterlisten." *AfO* 2 (1924–25), 2–18.

2616. —. "Hof- und Harems Erlasse assyrischer Könige aus dem 2. Jahrtausend v Chr." *AfO* 17 (1954–56), 257–309.

2617. Weigle, M. "Women as Verbal Artists: Reclaiming the Daughters of Enheduana." *Frontiers* 3 (1978), 1–9.

2618. Weinfeld, Moshe. "Semiramis: Her Name and Her Origin." *Scripta Hieroslymitana* 33 (1991), 99–103.

2619. Weisberg, David. B. "Royal Women of the Neo-Babylonian Period." In *Le Palais et la Royauté*, pp. 447–454. Edited by P. Garelli. Rencontre Assyriologique Internationale, Paris 29 juin–2 juillet 1971. Paris: Geuthner, 1972.

2620. —. "Kinship and Social Organization in Chaldaean Uruk." Review of H. M. Kümmel, *Familie, Beruf, und Amt. JAOS* 104 (1984), 739–743.

2621. Westbrook, R. "The Enforcement of Morals in Mesopotamian Law." *JAOS* 104 (1984), 753–756.

2622. Westenholz, Joan Goodnick. "Towards a New Conceptualization of the Female Role in Mesopotamian Society." *JAOS* 110 (1990), 510–521.

2623. —., and Westenholz, A. "Die Prinzessin Tutanapsum." *AoF* 10 (1983), 387–388.

2624. Wilcke, Claus. "CT 45, 119: Ein Fall legaler Bigamie mit *nadītum* und *šugītum.*" *ZA* 74 (1984), 170–180.

2625. —. "Familiengründung im alten Babylonien." In *Geschlechtsreife und Legitimation zur Zeugung*, p. 213–317. Edited by E. W. Müller. Freiburg and Munich: Karl Alber Verlag, 1985.

2626. Willemaers, N. "Une identification contesté d'Ištar-Saušga." *Muséon* 86 (1973), 467–473.

2627. Yaron, Reuven. "Matrimonial Mishaps at Eshnunna." *JSS* 8 (1963), 1–16.

2628. —. "The Rejected Bridegroom (LE 25)." *Orientalia*, n.s. 34 (1965), 23–29.

2629. —. "The Middle Assyrian Laws and the Bible." *Biblica* 51 (1970), 549–557.

2630. Zagarell, A. "Trade, Women, Class, and Society in Ancient Western Asia." *Current Anthropology* 27 (Dec. 1986), 415–430.

2631. Zimmern, H. "Die babylonische Göttin im Fenster." *OL* 31 (1928), 1–3.

12. WOMEN AND WOMANHOOD AT MARI

2632. Al-Khalesi, Yasin M. *The Court of the Palms: A Functional Interpretation of the Mari Palace.* Bibliotheca Mesopotamica, 8. Malibu: Undena Publications, 1978.

2633. Anbar (Bernstein), Moshé. *Les tribus amurrites de Mari.* Freiburg: Universitätsverlag, 1991.

2634. Artzi, P., and Malamat, A. "The Correspondence of Shibtu, Queen of Mari in *ARM* X." *Orientalia,* n.s., 40 (1971), 75–89.

2635. —. "Shibtu, Queen of Mari." In *Bible and Jewish History,* pp. 169–183. Edited by Benjamin Uffenheimer. Tel Aviv: Tel Aviv University, Faculty of Humanities, 1971 (in Hebrew).

2636. Batto, B. F. *Studies on Women at Mari.* Baltimore & London: Johns Hopkins University Press, 1974.

2637. —. "Land Tenure and Women at Mari." *JESHO* 23 (1980), 209–239.

2638. Birot, Maurice. "Une recensement de femmes au royaume de Mari." *Syria* 35 (1958), 9–26.

2639. Dossin, G. "Un rituel du culte d'Ištar provenant de Mari." *RA* 35 (1938), 1–13.

2640. —. "Tablettes de Mari." *RA* 69 (1975), 23–30.

2641. Dossin, G., and Finet, A., *Le Correspondence féminine.* ARM X. Paris: Geuthner, 1978.

2642. Durand, Jean-Marie. "Les dames du palais de Mari à l'époque du royaume de Haute-Mesopotamie." *MARI* 4 (1985), 385–436.

2643. Durand, Jean-Marie, and Margueron, Jean. "La Question du harem royal dans le palais de Mari." *Journal des Savants,* 1980, pp. 253–280.

2644. Gawlikowski, K. "Eštar et Ištar au Mari au IIIe millénaire." *Rocznik Orientalistyczny* 41 (1980), 25–28.

2645. Huffmon, Herbert B. *Amorite Personal Names in the Mari Texts.* Baltimore: Johns Hopkins University Press, 1965.

2646. —."Prophecy in the Mari Letters." *BA* 31 (1968), 101–124. Discusses prophetesses.

2647. Lambert, W. G. "The Pantheon of Mari." *MARI* 4 (1985), 525–539.

2648. Muntingh, L. M. "Amorite Married and Family Life According to the Mari Texts." *JNWSL* 3 (1974), 50–70.

2649. Nakata, I. "Deities in the Mari Texts." Ph.D. diss., Columbia University, 1974.

2650. —. "Annu in Mari Texts: A God or Goddess?" *JANES* 5 (1973), 299–307.

2651. Parrot, A. *Les temples d'Ishtarat et de Ninni-Zaza.* Mission Archeologique de Mari, vol. 3. Paris: Geuthner, 1967.

2652. Römer, W. H. Ph. *Frauenbriefe über Religion, Politik und Privatleben in Mari.* AOAT 12. Kevelaer: Butzon & Bercker/Neukirchen-Vluyn: Neukirchener Verlag, 1971.

2653. Sasson, Jack M. "Biographical Notices on Some Royal Ladies from Mari." *JCS* 25 (1973), 59–78.

13. WOMEN AND WOMANHOOD AMONG THE HITTITES

2654. Archi, A. "Il sistema KIN della diviniazione ittita." *OrAnt* 13 (1974), 113–144.

2655. Barnett, R. D. "A Winged Goddess of Wine on an Electrum Plaque." *Anatolian Studies* 30 (1980), 169–178.

2656. Beckman, Gary. *Hittite Birth Rituals: An Introduction.* Sources from the Ancient Near East, vol. 1, fascicle 4. Malibu: Undena Publications, 1978.

2657. —. *Hittite Birth Rituals.* Studien zu den Boğazköy-Texten, vol. 29. Wiesbaden: Harrassowitz, 1983.

2658. Biagov, L. N. "Über die Natur des Gottes Ḫaldi und der Göttin Arubani-Bagbartu." *Oikumene* 2 (1978), 149–152.

2659. Bilgiç, E. "Die originellen Seiten im Eherecht der vorhethitischen Bevölkerung Anatoliens." *Ankara Universitesi Dil ve Tarih Coğrafya Fakültesi Dergisi* 9 (1951), 239–250.

2660. Bin-Nun, S. R. *The Tawananna in the Hittite Kingdom.* Heidelberg: Carl Winter, 1975. queen mother

2661. Carruba, O. *Das Beschwörungsritual für die Göttin Wišurijanza.* Wiesbaden: Harrassowitz, 1966.

2662. Darga, M. "Hititlerin kült törenlerinde kadinlarin yevi ve göreuleri. Stellung und Funkton der Frauen bei hethitischen Kultzeremonien." *Tarih Enstitüsü Dergisi* 5 (1974), 231–245.

2663. Dijkstra, M. "On the Identity of the Hittite Princess Mentioned in Label KTU 6.24 (RS 17.72)." *UF* 22 (1990), 97–101.

2664. Fontaine, Carol R. "Queenly Proverb Performance: The Prayer of Puduḫepa (KUB XXI, 27)." In *The Listening Heart. Essays in Wisdom and the Psalms in Honor of Roland E. Murphy, O. Carm.*, pp. 96–126. Edited by Kenneth G.

Hoglund, et al. JSOT Supplementary Series, no. 58. Sheffield: JSOT Press, 1987.

2665. Friedrich, J. "Churritische Märchen und Sagen im hethitischer Sprache." *ZA*, n.f., 15 (1950), 213–255.

2666. Goetze, A. "The Linguistic Continuity of Anatolia as Shown by Its Proper Names." *JCS* 8 (1954), 74–81. Re: the element *wiya* "woman."

2667. Gurney, O. R. *Some Aspects of Hittite Religion.* The Schweich Lectures for 1976. Oxford: Clarendon Press, 1977.

2668. Güterbock, Hans. G. "An Addition to the Prayer of Muršili to the Sungoddess and its Implications." *Anatolian Studies* 30 (1980), 41–50.

2669. Haas, V. "Ein hethitisches Beschwörungsmotiv aus Kizzuwatna; seine Herkunft und Wanderung." *Orientalia*, n.s., 40 (1971), 410–430.

2670. —. "Leopard und Biene im Kult 'hethitischer' Göttinnen. Betrachtungen zu Kontinuität und Verbreitung altkleinasiatischer und nordsyrischer religiöser Vorstellungen." *UF* 13 (1981), 101–116.

2671. Haas, V., and Gernot, M. *Hurritische und luwische Riten aus Kizzuwatna.* AOAT 3. Kevelaer: Butzon & Bercker, 1974.

2672. Haas, V., and Wäfler, M. "Bemerkungen zu Éḫeštī/ā (2. Teil)." *UF* 9 (1977), 87–122.

2673. Hanfmann, George M. A., and Waldbaum, Jane C. "Kybebe and Artemis: Two Anatolian Goddesses at Sardis." *Archaeology* 22 (1969), 264–269.

2674. Hawkins, J. D. "Kuba at Karkamiš and Elsewhere." *Anatolian Studies* 31 (1981), 147–175.

2675. Hoffner, H. A. "Birth and Name-Giving in Hittite Texts." *JNES* 27 (1968), 198–203.

2676. Hutter, Manfred. "Behexung, Enstühung und Heilung: Das Ritual der Tunnawiya für Königspaar aus mittelhethitischer Zeit." *OBO* 82 (1988), 1–180.

2677.   Imparati, F. "Une reine de Hatti vénère la déesse Ningal."
        In *Florilegium Anatolicum: Mélanges offerts a Emmanuel
        Laroche*, pp. 169–176. Paris: E. De Boccard, 1979.

2678.   Kammenhuber, A. "Die hethitische Göttin Inar." *ZA* 66
        (1976), 68–88.

2679.   Kampman, A. A. "Tawannamans, der Titel der hethitischen
        Königin." *JEOL* 2/6–7 (1939–1942), 432–442.

2680.   Kronasser, H. "Fünf hethitische Rituale." *Die Sprache* 7
        (1961), 140–167.

2681.   Laroche, E. "Le Voeu du Puduhepa." *RA* 43 (1949), 55–78.

2682.   ——. Review of H. Otten, *Keilschrifturkunden aus Boghazköi,
        Heft 36*. *OLZ* 51 (1956), column 421.

2683.   ——. "Koubaba, diesse anatolienne, et le problème des
        origines de Cybèle." In *Eléments orientaux dans la religion
        grecque ancienne*, pp. 113–128. Paris: P.U.F. 1960.

2684.   Lebrun, R. "Considerations sur la femme dans la societé
        hittite." In *Hethitica* III, pp. 109–125. Leuven: Peeters,
        1979.

2685.   Mellaart, James; Hirsch, Udo; and Balpinar, Belkis. *The God-
        dess from Anatolia*. 4 vols. Milan: Eskenazi, 1989.

2686.   Moyer, J. C. "The Concept of Ritual Purity Among the
        Hittites." Ph.D. diss. Brandeis University, 1969.

2687.   Oettinger, N. *Militärische Eide der Hethiter*. Studien zum
        Boğazköy Texten 22. Wiesbaden: Harrassowitz, 1976.
        Sex roles.

2688.   Oezgüç, N. *The Anatolian Group of Cylinder Seal Impressions
        from Kültepe*. Ankara: Türk Tarih Kurumu Basimeri, 1965.

2689.   Orthmann, W. "Die sägende Göttin. Zu einem Relief aus
        Karatepe." *Istanbuler Mitteilungen* 19 (1969), 137–143 +
        Taf. 25–26.

2690.   Otten, H. "Pirwa—Der Gott auf dem Pferd." *Jahrbuch für
        kleinasiatische Forschung* 2 (1953), 62–73.

2691. —. *Puduhepa: eine hethitische Königin in ihren Textzeugnissen.*
       Mainz: Akademie der Wissenschaft und Literatur/Wies-
       baden: Steiner, 1975.

2692. Singer, Ithamar. "The AGRIG in the Hittite Texts." *Anato-
       lian Studies* 34 (1984), 98–127.

2693. Starke, F. "Das luwische Wort für Frau." *Zeitschrift für
       vergleichende Sprachforschung* 94 (1980), 74–86.

2694. Tsevat, M. "The Husband Veils a Wife (Hittite Laws # 197–
       198)." *JCS* 27 (1975), 235–240.

2695. Walker, Christopher. "The Myth of Girra and Elamatum."
       Anatolian Studies 33 (1983), 145–152.

2696. Wegner, I. *Gestalt und Kult der* Ištartar/Šawuška *in Kleinasien*
       AOAT 36. *Hurritologische Studien,* no. 3. Kevelaer: Butzon
       & Bercker, 1981.

14. WOMEN AND WOMANHOOD AMONG THE HURRIANS

2697. Archi, Alfonso. "I poteria della dea Ištar Ḫurrita-Ittita." *OrAnt* 16 (1977), 297–311.

2698. —. "Associations de divinités hourrites." *UF* 11 (1979), 7–12.

2699. Breneman, J. M. *Nuzi Marriage Tablets.* Ph.D. diss., Brandeis University, 1971.

2700. Cardascia, G. "L'adoption matrimoniale à Babylone et à Nuzi." *RHD*, ser. 4/37 (1959), 1–16.

2701. Cassin, E. M. *L'adoption à Nuzi.* Paris: Adrien-Maisonneuve, 1938.

2702. —. "Nouvelles données sur les relations familiales à Nuzi." *RA* 57 (1963), 113–119.

2703. Chamberlayne, J. H. "Kinship Relationships Among the Early Hebrews." *Numen* 10 (1963), 153–164.

2704. Chow, W. W. K. "Kings and Queens at Nuzi." Ph.D. diss., Brandeis University, 1973.

2705. Deller, K., and Abdulillah, F. "NIN·DINGIR·RA/ēntu in Texten aus Nuzi und Kurruḫani." *Mesopotamia* 7 (1972), 193–213.

2706. Eichler, Barry L. "Another Look at Nuzi Sistership Contracts." In *Essays on the Ancient Near East in Memory of Jacob Joel Finkelstein*, pp. 45–59. Edited by M. de J. Ellis. Memoirs of the Connecticut Academy of Arts and Sciences, vol. 19. Hamden, Connecticut: Archon Books, 1977.

2707. —. "Nuzi and the Bible: A Retrospective." In *DUMU-E_2-DUB-BA-A: Studies in Honor of Åke. W. Sjöberg*, pp. 107–119. Edited by Hermann Behrens, Darlene Loding, and Martha T. Roth. Philadelphia: Occasional Publications of the Samuel Noah Kramer Fund, 1989.

2708. Freedman, David. "A New Approach to the Nuzi Sistership Contract." *JANES* 2 (1969/70), 77–85.

2709. Gernot, Wilhelm. *Grundzüge der Geschichte und Kultur der Hurrites.* Grundzüge 45. Darmstadt: Wissenschaftliche Buchgesellschaft, 1983.

2710. Gordon, C. H. "The Status of Women Reflected in the Nuzi Tablets." *ZA* 43 (1936), 146–169.

2711. —. "*Erēbu* Marriage." In *Studies on the Civilization and Culture of Nuzi and the Hurrians in Honor of E. R. Lachemann,* vol. 1, pp. 155–160. Edited by M. A. Morrison and D. I. Owen. Winon Lake, Indiana: Eisenbrauns, 1981.

2712. —. "Marriage in the Guise of Siblingship." *UF* 20 (1988), 53–56.

2713. Greengus, S. I. "Sisterhod Adoption at Nuzi and the 'Wife-Sister' in Genesis." *HUCA* 46 (1975), 5–31.

2714. Grondahl, Frauke. *Die Personennamen der Texte aus Ugarit. II. Die hurritischen Namen.* Rome: Biblical Institute Press, 1967.

2715. Grosz, Katarzyna. "Dowry and Brideprice in Nuzi." In *Studies on the Civilization and Culture of Nuzi and the Hurrians in Honor of E. R. Lachemann,* pp. 161–183. Edited by M. A. Morrison and D. I. Owen. Winona Lake, Indiana: Eisenbrauns, 1981.

2716. —. "On Some Aspects of the Adoption of Women at Nuzi." In *Studies on the Civilization and Culture of Nuzi and the Hurrians,* vol. 2, pp. 131–152. Edited by D. I. Owen and M. A. Morrison. Winona Lake: Eisenbrauns, 1987.

2717. Haas, Volkert, and Thiel, Hans Jochem. *Die Beschwörungrituale der Allaituraḫ(ḫi) und verwandte Texte.* Hurritologische Studien 2. AOAT 31. Kevelaer: Butzon & Bercker/Neukirchen-Vluyn: Neukirchener Verlag, 1978. the Shugi priestess; the goddess Shawushka

2718. Koschaker, P. *Neue keilschriftliche Rechsturkunden aus der El-Amarna Zeit.* ASAW 39/V. Leipzig: Hirzel, 1928.

2719. Lacheman, E. R. "Nuzi Personal Names." *JNES* 8 (1949), 48–55.

2720. —. *Economic and Social Documents.* HSS, vol. 16. Cambridge: Harvard University Press, 1958.

2721. —. *Family Law Documents.* HSS, vol. 19. Cambridge: Harvard University Press, 1962.

2722. —. "Real Estate Adoption by Women in the Tablets from Nuzi." AOAT 22. In *Orient and Occident: Essays Presented to Cyrus H. Gordon on the Occasion of His Sixty-Fifth Birthday,* pp. 99–100. Edited by Harry A. Hoffner, Jr. AOAT 22. Kevelaer: Butzon & Berckner/Neukirchen-Vluyn: Neukirchener Verlag, 1973.

2723. Maidman, Maynard Paul. "A Socio-Economic Analysis of Nuzi Family Archives." Ph.D. diss., University of Pennsylvania, 1976.

2724. —. "The Teḫip-Tilla Family of Nuzi: A Genealogical Reconstruction." *JCS* 28 (1976), 127–155.

2725. Mayer, Walter. *Nuzi-Studien I.* AOAT 205/1. Kevelaer: Butzon & Bercker/Neukirchen-Vluyn: Neukirchener Verlag, 1978.

2726. Morrison, Martha A. "The Family of Shilwa-Teshub mar sharri." *JCS* 31 (1979), 3–29.

2727. Paradise, J. S. "Nuzi Inheritance Practices." Ph.D. diss., University of Pennsylvania, 1972.

2728. —. "A Daughter and Her Father's Property at Nuzi." *JCS* 32 (1980), 189–207. Tells how a daughter can be given the legal status of son.

2729. —. "Marriage Contracts of Free Persons at Nuzi." *JCS* 39 (1987), 1–36.

2730. —. "Daughters as 'Sons' at Nuzi." In *Studies on the Civilization and Culture of Nuzi and the Hurrians,* vol. 2, pp. 203–213. Edited by D. I. Owen and M. A. Morrison. Winona Lake: Eisenbrauns, 1987.

2731. Pfeiffer, R. H., and Speiser, E. A. *One Hundred New Selected Nuzi Texts*. Annual of the American Schools of Oriental Research, vol. 16. New Haven: American Schools of Oriental Research, 1936.

2732. Porada, Edith. "The Origin of Winnirke's Cylinder Seal." *JNES* 5 (1946), 257–259.

2733. Skaist, Aaron. "The Authority of the Brother at Arrapha and Nuz (Nuzi)." *JAOS* 89 (1969), 10–17.

2734. Speiser, E. A. *New Kirkuk Documents Relating to Family Laws*. Annual of the American Schools of Oriental Research, vol. 10. New Haven: American Schools of Oriental Research, 1930.

2735. —. "A Significant New Will from Nuzi." *JCS* 17 (1963), 65–71. Tells how Ukkie the daughter was appointed co-parent of the sons of Arippabni

2736. Stohlman, St. C. "Real Adoption at Nuzi." Ph.D. diss., Brandeis University, 1972.

2737. Yankovskaya, N. B. "The Decline of the Extended Family Community in the Near East of the 2nd Millenium B.C." Ph.D. diss., Leningrad, 1959 (in Russian).

2738. —. "The Landownership of Extended Family House Communities in the Cuneiform Sources." *Vestnik Drevney Istorii* 7, no. 1 (1959), 35–71 (in Russian).

15. WOMEN AND WOMANHOOD AT UGARIT

2739. Ahl, Sally W. "Epistolary Texts from Ugarit." Ph.D. diss., Brandeis, 1973. Includes letters to and from women.

2740. Amiet, P. "Déesses d'Ugarit au XIVe siècle." *AAAS* 29–30 (1979–80), 163–166.

2741. Astour, Michael C. "Some New Divine Names from Ugarit." *JAOS* 86 (1966), 277–284.

2742. —. "La triade de déesses de fertilité à Ugarit et en Grèce." In *Ugaritica* 6, pp. 9–23. Paris: Geuthner, 1969.

2743. —. "King Ammurapi and the Hittite Princess." *UF* 12 (1980), 103–108. Eḫli-Nikkalu daughter of the Hittite king and wife of King Ammurapi of Ugarit.

2744. Barrelet, M.-T. "Les déesses armées et ailées." *Syria* 32 (1955), 222–260.

2745. Beyer, Dominique. "Ougarit. Les sceaux-cylinders." *MDB*, no. 48 (March-April 1987), 31–32.

2746. Brooke, George J. "The Textual, Formal and Historical Significance of Ugarit Letter RS 34.124 (= *KTU* 2.72)." *UF* 11 (1979), 69–87.

2747. Cardascia, G. "Adoption matrimoniale et lévirat dans le droit d'Ugarit." *RA* 64 (1970), 119–126.

2748. Cassuto, U. "The Seven Wives of King Keret." *BASOR*, no. 119 (1950), 18–20.

2749. —. *The Goddess Anath.* Translated by Israel Abrahams. Jerusalem: Magnes, 1971.

2750. Caubet, Annie. "Chante en l'honneur de Baal." *MDB*, no. 48 (March-April 1987), 33. horns decorated with a naked goddess.

2751. Cazelles, H. "L'Hymne Ugaritique à 'Anat." *Syria* 33 (1956), 237.

2752. —. "Quelle vie la déesse Anat proposait-elle au jeune chasseur Aqht?" *AAAS* 29–30 (1979–80), 181–183.

2753. Clifford, Richard. "Proverbs 9: A Suggested Ugaritic Parallel." *VT* 25(1975), 298–306.

2754. Clines, D. J. A. "KRT 111–114 (I iii 7–10): Gatherers of Wood and Drawers of Water." *UF* 8 (1976), 23–26.

2755. Coogan, M. D. *Stories from Ancient Canaan.* Philadelphia: Westminster, 1978.

2756. Coote, R. B. "The Serpent and Sacred Marriage in Northwest Semitic Tradition." Ph.D. diss., Harvard, 1972.

2757. Cunchillos, J.L. "KTU 2.21—Lettre addressée à la Reine. IBRKD̲ a trasmis le message de la Reine." *UF* 13 (1981), 45–48.

2758. —. "Ougarit. Les dieux." *MDB,* no. 48 (March-April 1987), 38–39.

2759. —. "Que mère se réjouisse de père. Traduction et commentaire de KTU 2.16." In *Ascribe to the LORD,* pp. 3–10. Edited by Lyle Eslinger and Glen Taylor. JSOT Supplement Series, no. 67. Sheffield: JSOT Press, 1988.

2760. —. *Estudios de epistologarfia ugaritica.* Fuentes de la Ciencia biblica 3. Valencia: Institùción San Jerónimo, 1989.

2761. Del Olmo Lette, G. "Notes on Ugaritic Semantics IV." *UF* 10 (1978), 37–46.

2762. —. "Le mythe de la Vierge-Mère 'Anatu. Une nouvelle interprétation de CTA/KTU 13." *UF* 13 (1981), 49–62.

2763. Dietrich, M., and Loretz, O. "Anš(t) und (M)inš(t) im Ugaritischen." *UF* 9 (1977), 47–50.

2764. —. "Das Porträt einer Königin in KTU 1.14 I 12–15. Zur ugaritischen Lexikographie (XVIII)." *UF* 12 (1980), 199–204.

2765. —. "Ugaritisch 't r,   aṯ r,   aṯryt   und
       aṯrt." *UF* 16 (1984), 57–62.

2766. Dietrich, M.; Loretz, O.; and Sanmartín, J. "Ein Brief des
       Königs an die Königin-Mutter (RS 11.872 = CTA 50).
       Zur Frage ug. iṯt = hebr.'šh?" *UF* 6 (1974), 460–462.

2767. Eaton, A. W. "The Goddess Anat: The History of Her Cult,
       Her Mythology, and Her Iconography." Ph.D. diss., Yale
       University, 1964.

2768. Fensham, F. C. "Winged Gods and Goddesses in the Uga-
       ritic Tablets." *OrAnt* 5 (1966), 157–164.

2769. Garr, W. Randall. "Population in Ancient Ugarit." *BASOR,*
       no. 266 (1987), 31–43.

2770. Gibson, John C. L. *Canaanite Myths and Legends.* Edinburgh:
       T. & T. Clark, 1978.

2771. Ginsberg, H. L. "Women Singers and Wailers Among the
       Northern Canaanites." *BASOR,* no. 72 (1938), 13–15.

2772. —. "The North-Canaanite Myth of Anath and Aqhat."
       BASOR, no. 97 (1945), 3–10; no. 98 (1945), 15–23.

2773. Gordon, Cyrus H. "Ugaritic Rbt/Rabītu." In *Ascribe to the
       Lord,* pp. 127–132. Edited by Lyle Eslinger and Glen
       Taylor. JSOT Supplement Series, no. 67. Sheffield: JSOT
       Press, 1988.

2774. Gray, John. "Social Aspects of Canaanite Religion." In
       Volume de Congrès Genève,1965, pp. 170–192. VTS, vol.
       15. Leiden: E. J. Brill, 1966.

2775. —. "The Blood Bath of the Goddess Anat in the Ras Shamra
       Texts." *UF* 11 (1979/80), 315–324.

2776. Handy, Lowell. "Dissenting Deities or Obedient Angels: Di-
       vine Hierarchies in Ugarit and the Bible." *Biblical Research*
       35 (1990), 18–35. Anat.

2777. Healey, J. F. "The *Pietas* of an Ideal Son in Ugarit." *UF* 11
       (1979), 353–356.

2778. —. "The Sun Deity and the Underworld: Mesopotamia and Ugarit." In *Death in Mesopotamia: Papers Read at the XXVIe Rencontre Assyriologique,* pp. 239–242. Edited by Bendt Alster. Copenhagen: Akademisk Forlag, 1980.

2779. —. "The Akkadian 'Pantheon' List from Ugarit." *SEL* 2 (1985), 115–125.

2780. Hermann, H. "Aštart." *MIO* 15 (1969), 6–55.

2781. Hermann, W. *Yariḫ und Nikkal und der Preis der Kuṯārat-Göttinnen.* BZAW 106. Berlin: Töpelmann, 1968.

2782. Hillers, Delbert R. "Analyzing the Abominable: Our Understanding of Canaanite Religion." *JQR* 75 (1985), 253–269.

2783. Huehnergard, John. "RS 15.86 (PRU 3, 51f.)." *UF* 18 (1986), 169–171.

2784. Jirku, A. "Neue Götter und Dämonen aus Ugarit." *ArOr* 41 (1973), 97–100.

2785. Kapelrud, Arvid S. *The Violent Goddess.* Oslo: Universitets Forlaget, 1969.

2786. Klíma, J. "Untersuchungen zum ugaritischen Erbrecht." *ArOr* 24 (1956), 356–374.

2787. —. "Die Stellung der ugaritischen Frau." *ArOr* 25 (1957), 313–333.

2788. —. "Le statut de la femme à Ugarit d'après les textes accadiens de Ras-Shamra." *Receuils de la Société Jean Bodin* 11 (1959), 95–105.

2789. Kristensen, A. "Ugaritic Epistolary Formulas." *UF* 9 (1977), 143–158.

2790. Kritikos, Madeleine. "Le Culte à Ougarit." *MDB,* no. 48 (March–April 1987), 36–37.

2791. Kühne, C. "Ammistamru und die Tochter der 'Grossen Dame'." *UF* 5(1973), 175–184.

2792. Lackenbacker, Sylvie. "Trois lettres d'Ugarit." In *DUDMU-E₂-DUB-BA-A: Studies in Honor of Åke W. Sjöberg*, pp. 317–320. Edited by Herman Behrens, Darlene Loding, and Martha T. Roth. Philadelphia: Occasional Publications of the Samuel Noah Kramer Fund, 1989. Letters from three persons, two of them women, and one addressed to the queen of Ugarit.

2793. Levine, Baruch A. "Mulūgu/Melug: The Origins of a Talmudic Legal Institution." *JAOS* 88 (1968), 271–285.

2794. Lipínski, Edward. "Aḫat-Milki, reine d'Ugarit, et la guerre de Mukiš." *Orientalia Lovaniensia Periodica* 12 (1981), 79–115.

2795. —. "Les conceptions et couches mervéilleuses de 'Anath." *Syria* 42 (1965), 45–73.

2796. Loewenstamm, S. E. "Did the Goddess Anat Wear Side-Whiskers and a Beard?" *UF* 14 (1982), 119–123.

2797. —. "Zur Lexikographie des Texts der Einladung Anats durch Baal." *UF* 14 (1982), 125–128.

2798. Loretz, Oswald. "Ugaritisch skn-śknt und hebräisch skn-sknt." *ZAW* 94 (1982), 123–127.

2799. —. "Zur Parallelität Zwischen KTU 1.6 II 28–30 und Ps 131, 2b." *UF* 17 (1986), 183–187.

2800. MacDonald, J. "The Unique Ugaritic Personnel Text KTU 4.102." *UF* 10 (1978), 161–173. Female personnel attached to labor force of the temple

2801. Marcus, I. David, and Loewenstamm, S. E. "Did the Goddess Anath Wear a Beard and Sidewhiskers?" *Israel Oriental Studies* 4 (1974), 1–3.

2802. Margalit, B. "The Kôšārôt/ktrt Patroness-saints of Women." *JANES* 4 (1972), 52–61.

2803. —. "The Ugaritic Tale of the Drunken Gods: Another Look at RS 24.258(*KTU* 1.114)." *Maarav* 2 (1979), 65–120.

2804. —. *A Matter of "Life" and "Death": A Study of the Baal-Mot*

Epic (CTA 4-5-6). AOAT 206. Kevelaer: Butzon & Bercker/Neukirchen-Vluyn: Neukirchener Verlag, 1980.

2805. —. *The Ugaritic Poem of AQHT: Text-Translation-Commentary.* BZAW 182. Berlin & New York: Walter de Gruyter, 1989.

2806. Mettinger, T. N. D. *The Dethronement of Sabaoth—Studies in the Shem and Kabod Theologies.* Coniectanea Biblica, OT Series 18. Lund: CWK Gleerup, 1982. Ashtart Shem-Baal

2807. Metzger, M. "Gottheit, Berg, und Vegetation in vorderorientalischer Bildtradition." *ZDPV* 99 (1983), 54–94.

2808. Miller, G. I. "Studies in the Juridical Texts from Ugarit." Ph.D. diss., Johns Hopkins University, 1980.

2809. Miller, Patrick D., Jr. "Ugarit and the History of Religions." *JNSL* 9 (1981), c. 119–128.

2810. Moor, Johannes C. de. "The Semitic Pantheon of Ugarit." *UF* 2 (1970), 187–228.

2811. —. "An Incantation Against Infertility (KTU 1.13)." *UF* 12 (1980), 305–310.

2812. —. "Athtartu the Huntress." (KTU 1.92) *UF* 17 (1986), 225–230.

2813. —. "The Crisis of Polytheism in Late Bronze Age Ugarit." *OTS* 24 (1986), 1–20.

2814. —. "East of Eden." *ZAW* 100 (1988), 105–111. KTU 1.100; 1.107; Gen. 2–3

2815. Moran, W. L. "The Scandal of the 'Great Sin' at Ugarit." *JNES* 18 (1959), 280–281.

2816. Muntingh, L. M. "The Social and Legal Status of a Free Ugaritic Female." *JNES* 26 (1967), 102–112.

2817. Pardee, D. "A New Ugaritic Letter." *BO* 34 (1977), 3–20. Pente-Shenna the daughter of the King of Amurru and wife of Ammishtamru III of Ugarit; adultery; RS 34.124.

2818.   —. "A Philological and Prosodic Analysis of the Ugaritic
        Serpent Incantation *UT* 607." *JANES* 10 (1988), 73–108.
        mare goddess.

2819.   —. "Ougarit. La vie quotidienne sur des tablettes." *MDB*, no.
        48 (March-April 1987), 29–31.

2820.   Parker, S. B. "The Marriage Blessing in Israelite and Ugaritic
        Literature." *JBL* 95 (1976), 23–30.

2821.   —. *The Pre-Biblical Narrative Tradition: Essays on the Ugaritic
        Poems Keret and Aqhat.* SBL Sources for Biblical Study, 24.
        Atlanta: Scholars Press, 1989.

2822.   Parnas, Moshe. "Epic and Realia in Family Life at Ugarit."
        BM 32 (1986/87), 187–196 (in Hebrew).

2823.   Pope, Marvin H. "Ups and Downs in El's Amours." *UF* 11
        (1979), 701–708.

2824.   Rainey, Anson F. "Organized Religion at Ugarit." *Christian
        News from Israel* 15 (1964), 16–21. klt bt špš; bn ndr

2825.   —. "Family Relationships in Ugarit." *Orientalia,* n.s., 34
        (1965), 10–22.

2826.   —. Review of Wolfram Herrmann, *Yariḫ und Nikkal und der
        Preis der Kuṯarāt-Göttinnen. JAOS* 90 (1970), 532–536.

2827.   Richardson, H. Neil. "A Ugaritic Letter of a King to His
        Mother." *JBL* 66 (1947), 321–324.

2828.   Rummel, T. S. "The 'NT Text: A Critical Translation."
        Ph.D. diss., Claremont Graduate School, 1978.

2829.   Selms, A. van. *Marriage and Family Life in Ugaritic Literature.*
        Pretoria Oriental Series, no. 1. London: Luzac, 1954.

2830.   —. "The Root *k-ṯ-r* and Its Derivatives in Ugaritic Litera-
        ture." *UF* 11 (1979), 739–744.

2831.   Soldt, W. H. van. "Tbṣr, Queen of Ugarit." *UF* 21 (1989),
        389–392.

2832.   Tsevat, M. "Marriage and Monarchical Legitimacy in Ugarit
        and Israel." *JCS* 3 (1958), 237–243.

2833. —. "Comments on the Ugaritic Text UT 52." *EI* 14 (1978), 24–27.

2834. Vawter, Bruce. "Yahweh: Lord of the Heavens and the Earth." *CBQ* 48(1986), 461–467. qnyt ilm 'ṯrt.

2835. Ward, W. "La déesse nourricière d'Ugarit." *Syria* 46 (1969), 225–239.

2836. Watson, W. G. E. "Ugaritic and Mesopotamian Literary Texts." *UF* 9 (1977), 273–284.

2837. —. "Gender-Matched Synonymous Parallelism in Ugaritic Poetry." *UF* 13 (1981), 181–187.

2838. Wyatt, N. "The Identity of Mt w Šr." *UF* 9 (1977), 379–381. CTA 23; sacred marriage rite.

2839. —. "The 'Anat Stela from Ugarit and its Ramifications." *UF* 16 (1984), 327–337.

2840. Yaron, Reuven. "A Royal Divorce at Ugarit." *Orientalia*, n.s. 32 (1967), 21–39.

2841. Young, Dwight W. "With Snakes and Dates: A Sacred Marriage Drama at Ugarit." *UF* 9 (1977), 291–314.

2842. Xella, P. "Tu sei mio fratello ed io sonon tua sorella (KTU 1.18.I.24)." *Aula Orientalis* 2 (1984), 151–153.

16. WOMEN AND WOMANHOOD IN ELAM AND PERSIA

2843. Benveniste, E. "Les classes sociales dans la tradition avestique." *Journal Asiatique,* 1932, pp. 116–134.

2844. Cameron, George C. *Early History of Iran.* Chicago: University of Chicago Press, 1936.

2845. —. "Darius's Daughter and the Persepolis Inscriptions." *JNES* 1 (1942), 214–218.

2846. Cook, J. M. *The Persian Empire.* London: J. M. Dent, 1983.

2847. Dandamaev, M. A., and Lukonin, V. *The Culture and Social Institutions of Ancient Iran.* English edition edited by Philip L. Kohl with the assistance of D. J. Dodson. Cambridge: Cambridge University Press, 1989.

2848. Erdmann, Kurt. *Die Kunst Irans Zur Zeit der Sasaniden,* Berlin: F. Kupferberg, 1943.

2849. Frye, Richard N. *The Heritage of Persia.* Oxford: Clarendon Press, 1966.

2850. Herzfeld, Ernst F. *Iran in the Ancient Near East.* New York: Oxford University Press, 1941.

2851. Hirsch, H. "Zum Fluss-Ordal in Elam." *RA* 67 (1973), 75–77.

2852. Klíma, J. "Zur Problematik der Ehe-Institution im alten Iran." *ArOr* 34 (1966), 554–569.

2853. —. "Das Wasserordal in Elam." *ArOr* 39 (1971), 401–424.

2854. Kramer, Carol. *Village Ethnoarchaeology: Rural Iran in Archaeological Perspective.* New York: Academic Press, 1982.

2855. Mazahéri, A. A. *La famille iranienne aux temps anté-islamiques.* Ph.D. diss., Paris, 1938.

2856. Pomeroy, Sarah B. "The Persian King and the Queen Bee." *American Journal of Ancient History* 9 (1984), 98–108.

17. WOMEN AND WOMANHOOD AMONG THE PHOENICIANS

2857. Barrelet, Marie-Thérèse. "Deux déesses syro-phéniciennes sur un bronze du Louvre." *Syria* 35 (1958), 27–44.

2858. Benigni, G. "Il 'segno di Tanit' in Oriente." *RSF* 3 (1975), 17–18.

2859. Bonnet, C., Lipínski, E., and Marchetti, P., eds. *Studia Phoenicia IV: Religio Phoenicia.* Nanur: Societé des Etudes classiques, 1986.

2860. Branden, Albert van den. "La triade phénicienne." *Bibbia e Oriente* 23 (1981), 35–63. Athtart at Sidon, Baalat-Milk at Byblos, Shtart at Tyre; goddess(es)

2861. Contenau, G. *La civilisation Phénicienne.* rev. Paris: Payot, 1949.

2862. Dall'olmo, M. O. "A Phoenician Goddess in the Papyrus Anastasi IV." *RSF* 9 (1981), 1–4.

2863. Del Olmo Lete, Gregorio. "Atiratu's Entreaty and the Order of the Ugaritic Tablets KTU 1.3/4." *Aula Orientalis* 1 (1983), 67–71.

2864. Delcor, M. "L'inscription phénicienne de la statuette d'Astarté conservée à Séville." *Mélanges de l'Université Saint Joseph* 45 (1969), 319–341.

2865. —. "Le hieros gamos d'Astarté." *RSF* 2 (1974), 63–76.

2866. du Buisson, Du Mensil. "Origine et évolution du panthéon de Tyre." *RHR* 164 (1963), 133–163.

2867. Falsone, G. "Il simbolo di Tanit a Mozia e nella Sicilia punica." *RSF* 6 (1978), 137–151.

2868. Fantar, M. H. "A propos d'Ashtart en Méditerranée occidentale." *RSF* 1 (1973), 19–29.

2869.   Görg, Manfred. "Zur Namen der punischen Göttin Tinnit."
        UF 11 (1979), 303–306. Includes extensive bibliography.

2870.   Gubel, E. "An Essay on the Axe-Bearing Astarte and Her
        Role in a Phoenician 'Triad'." *RSF* 8 (1980), 2–17.

2871.   Guzzo Amadasi, M. G. *'Intervento,' La religione fenicia.* Studi
        Semitici 53. Rome: Consiglio Nazionale delle Richerche,
        1981.

2872.   Harden, Donald. *The Phoenicians.* Ancient Peoples and
        Places, vol. 26. London: Thames & Hudson, 1962.

2873.   Hvidberg-Hansen, F. O. *La déesse Tanit: une étude sur la reli-
        gion canaanéo-punique.* 2 vols. Copenhagen: G. C. E. Gad,
        1982.

2874.   Karageorghis, V. "A Gold Ornament with a Representation
        of an 'Astarte'." *RSF* 3 (1975), 31–35.

2875.   Løkkegaard, F. "Some Reflexions on Reading F. O. Hvid-
        berg-Hansen's Book *La déesse TNT: Une étude sur la re-
        ligion canaanéo-punique* I–II." *UF* 14 (1982), 129–140.

2876.   Moscati, S. *The World of the Phoenicians.* London: Weiden-
        feld & Nicolson/New York: Praeger, 1968.

2877.   —. "Tanit in Fenicia." *RSF* 7 (1979), 143–144.

2878.   —. "Un 'segno di Tanit' presso Olbia." *RSF* 7 (1979), 41–
        43.

2879.   Puech, E. "L'inscription phénicienne du trône d'Aštart à
        Séville." *RSF* 5 (1977), 85–92.

2880.   Sperling, D. S. "An Arslan Tash Incantation: Interpretations
        and Implications." *HUCA* 53 (1982), 1–10.

2881.   Swiggers, P. "Le trône d'Astarté: une inscription tyrienne du
        second siècle av. J.-C." In *Studia Phoenicia,* vol. 1–2, pp.
        125–132. Edited by E. Gubel, E. Lipínski, B. Servais-Soyez.
        Leuven: Peeters, 1983.

2882.   Vadé, Y. "Sur la maternité du chêne et de la pierre." *RHR*
        191 (1977), 3–41.

18. ASHERAH: BOOKS, ARTICLES, AND DISSERTATIONS

2883. Ahlström, G. W. *Aspects of Syncretism in Israelite Religion.* Translated by Eric J. Sharpe. Lund: C. W. K. Gleerup, 1963.

2884. Albright, W. F. "Anath and the Dragon." *BASOR,* no. 84 (1941), 14–17.

2885. —. "The Evolution of the West-Semitic Divinity 'An- 'Anat-'Attâ." *AJSL* 41 (1925), 73–101; critical notes 283–285.

2886. —. "The Goddess of Life and Wisdom." *AJSL* 36 (1920), 273.

2887. —. "A Vow to Asherah in the Keret Epic." *BASOR,* no. 94 (1944), 30–31.

2888. Angerstorfer, Andreas. "'Ašerah als 'Consort of Jahwe' oder Aširtah?" *BN* 17 (1982), 7–16.

2889. Auld, A. Graeme. "A Judean Sanctuary of 'Anat (Josh. 15: 59)?" *Tel Aviv* 4 (1977), 85–86.

2890. Barnett, R. D. " 'Anath, Ba'al and Pasargadae." *Mélanges de l'Universite St. Joseph* (Beyrouth) 45 (1969), 405–22.

2891. Beck, Pirhiya. "The Drawings from Ḥorvat Teiman (Kuntillet 'Ajrud)." *Tel Aviv* 9 (1982), 3–68.

2892. Bernhardt, Karl-Heinz. "Aschera in Ugarit und im Alten Testament." *MIO* 13 (1967), 163–174.

2893. Betlyon, John Wilson. "The Cult of 'Ašērah/'Ēlat at Sidon." *JNES* 44 (1985), 53–56.

2894. Brink, Marthinus Beyers. "A Philological Study of Texts in Connection with Aṭtart and Aṭirat in the Ugaritic Language." D.Litt. diss., University of Stellenbosch, 1979.

2895. Butterworth, E. A. S. *The Tree at the Navel of the Earth.* Berlin: Walter de Gruyter & Co., 1970.

2896. Carter, Jane Burr. "The Masks of Ortheia." *AJA* 91 (1987), 355–386.

2897. Cassuto, U. "Journey of Asherah in II AB, IV, 1–18 from Ugarit." *Tarbiz* 20 (1949), 354 (in Hebrew).

2898. Cooper, Alan. "A Note on the Vocalization of 'aštoret." *ZAW* 102 (1990), 98–100.

2899. Cross, Frank Moore Jr. "The Old Phoenician Inscription from Spain Dedicated to Hurrian Astarte." *HTR* 64 (1971), 189–195.

2900. Day, John. "Asherah in the Hebrew Bible and Northwest Semitic Literature." *JBL* 105 (1986), 385–408.

2901. Dever, William G. "Asherah, Consort of Yahweh? New Evidence from Kuntillet 'Ajrûd." *BASOR,* no. 255 (1984), 21–37.

2902. —. "Recent Archaeological Confirmation of the Cult of Asherah in Ancient Israel." *Hebrew Studies* 23 (1982), 37–43.

2903. Dexter, Miriam Robbins. *Whence the Goddesses: A Source Book.* New York: Pergamon Press, 1990.

2904. Dietrich, M., and Loretz, O. *"Jahwe und seine Aschera": Anthropomorphes Kultbild in Mesopotamien, Ugarit und Israel: des biblische Bildverbot.* Münster: UGARIT-Verlag, 1992.

2905. Dothan, M. "Ten Seasons of Excavation at Ancient Acco." *Qadmoniyot* 18 (1985), 2–14 (in Hebrew).

2906. Dussaud, R. "Astarte, Pontos et Baal." *CRAIBL,* 1947, pp. 201–204.

2907. Emerton, J. A. "New Light on Israelite Religion: The Implications of the Inscriptions from Kuntillet 'Ajrûd." *ZAW* 94 (1982), 2–20.

2908. Engle, James Robert. "Pillar Figurines of Iron Age Israel and Asherah/Asherim." Ph.D. diss., University of Pittsburgh, 1979.

2909. Fensham, F. C. "The Numeral Seventy in the Old Testament and the Family of Jerubbaal, Ahab, Panammuwa and Athirat." *PEQ* 109 (1977), 113–115.

2910. Freedman, David Noel. "Yahweh of Samaria and His Asherah." *BA* 50 (1987), 51–59.

2911. Garner, Gordon G. "Kuntillet 'Ajrud: An Intriguing Site in Sinai." *Buried History* 14, no. 2 (1978), 1–16.

2912. Gaster, Theodor H. "A King without a Castle—Baal's Appeal to Asherat." *BASOR* 101 (1946), 21–30.

2913. Gilula, Mordechai. "To Yahweh Shomron and His Asherah." *SHNATON* 3 (1978–79), 129–137 (in Hebrew); English summary xv–xvi.

2914. Ginsberg, H. L. "Did Anath Fight the Dragon?" *BASOR,* no. 84 (1941), 12–14.

2915. Hadley, Judith M. "The Khirbet el-Qom Inscription." *VT* 37 (1987), 50–62.

2916. — "Some Drawings and Inscriptions on Two Pithoi from Kuntillet 'Ajrud." *VT* 37 (1987), 180–213.

2917. —. "Yahweh's Asherah in the Light of Recent Discovery." Ph.D. diss., St. John's College, Cambridge University, 1989.

2918. Herrmann, Wolfram. "Aštart." *MIO* 15 (1969), 6–55.

2919. Hestrin, Ruth. "The Cult Stand from Taanach and Its Religious Background." In *Studia Phoenicia 5,* pp. 61–77. Leuven: Peeters, 1987.

2920. —. "The Lachish Ewer and the 'Asherah." *IEJ* 37 (1987), 212–223.

2921. Hommel, Fritz. "Asherah among the Ancient Minaeans." *Expository Times* 11 (1899–1900), 190.

2922. Hörig, Monika. *Dea Syria: Studien zur religiösen Tradition der Fruchtbarkeitsgöttin in Vorderasien.* AOAT 208. Kevelaer: Butzon & Bercker/Neukirchen-Vluyn: Neukirchener Verlag, 1979.

2923. Jaroš, Karl. "Zur Inschrift Nr. 3 von Ḫirbet el-Qōm." *BN* 19 (1982), 31–40.

2924. Jensen, P. "Die Götter Amurru(ū) und Ašratu." *ZA* 11 (1896–97), 302–305.

2925. Jeppesen, Knut. "Micah V 13 in the Light of a Recent Archaeological Discovery." *VT* 34 (1984), 462–466.

2926. Keel, Othmer, und Uehlinger, Christoph. *Göttinnen, Götter und Gottessymbole*. Freiburg: Herder, 1992.

2927. Koch, K. "Aschera als Himmelskönigin in Jerusalem." *UF* 20 (1988), 97–120.

2928. Leibovitch, J. "Kent et Qadech." *Syria* 38 (1961), 23–34.

2929. Lemaire, André. "Date et origine des Inscriptions hebraiques et pheniciennes de Kuntillet 'Ajrud." *SEL* 1 (1984), 133–143.

2930. —. "Les Inscriptions de Khirbet el-Qôm et l'ashérah de Yhwh." *RB* 84 (1977), 595–608.

2931. —. "Who or What was Yahweh's Asherah?" *BAR* 10, no. 6 (1984), 42–51.

2932. Lipínski, Edward. "The Goddess Aṯirat in Ancient Arabia, in Babylon, and in Ugarit." *Orientalia Lovaniensia Periodica* 3 (1972), 101–119.

2933. —. "The Syro-Palestinian Iconography of Woman and Goddess (Review Article)." *IEJ* 36 (1986), 87–96.

2934. Løkkegaard, Frede. "The Canaanite Divine Wetnurses." *StTh* 10 (1956): 53–64.

2935. Loretz, O. " 'Anat-Aschera (Hos 14,9) und die Inschriften von Kuntillet 'Ajrud." *SEL* 6 (1989), 57–65.

2936. Louie, Wallace. "The Meaning, Characteristics and Role of Asherah in Old Testament Idolatry in Light of Extra-Biblical Evidence." Th.D. diss., Grace Theological Seminary, 1988.

2937. McKay, J. W. "Helel and the Dawn-Goddess, a Re-examination of the Myth in Isaiah XIV 12–15." *VT* 20 (1970), 451–464.

2938. MacLauren, Edward. "The Canaanite Background to the Doctrine of the Virgin Mary." *Religious Traditions* 3 (1980), 1–11.

2939. Maier, Walter A. III. *'Ašerah: Extrabiblical Evidence.* HSM, no. 37. Atlanta: Scholars Press, 1986.

2940. Margalit, Baruch. "The Meaning and Significance of Asherah." *VT* 40 (1990), 264–297.

2941. —. "Some Observations on the Inscription and Drawing from Khirbet el-Qôm." *VT* 39 (1989), 371–378.

2942. Merhav, Rivka. "The Stele of the 'Serpent Goddess' from Tell Beit Mirsim and the Plaque from Shechem Reconsidered." *IMJ* 4 (1985), 27–42.

2943. Meshel, Ze'ev. *Kuntillet 'Ajrud: A Religious Center from the Time of the Judaean Monarchy on the Border of Sinai.* Israel Museum Catalogue, no. 175. Jerusalem: Israel Museum, 1978.

2944. —. "Did Yahweh have a Consort? New Religious Inscriptions from the Sinai." *BAR* 5, no. 2 (1979), 24–35.

2945. —. "The Israelite Religious Centre of Kuntillet 'Ajrud." *Bulletin of the Anglo-Israel Archaeological Society,* 1982–1983, pp. 52–55.

2946. Miller, Patrick D. Jr. "The Absence of the Goddess in Israelite Religion." *HAR* 10 (1986), 239–248.

2947. Naveh, Joseph. "Graffiti and Dedications." *BASOR,* no. 235 (1979), 27–30.

2948. Oden, R. A., Jr. "The Persistence of Canaanite Religion." *BA* 39 (1979), 31–36.

2949. Offord, Joseph. "The Deity of the Crescent Venus in Ancient Western Asia." *JRAS,* 1915, pp. 197–203.

2950. Olyan, Saul M. "Some Observations Concerning the Identity of the Queen of Heaven." *UF* 19 (1987), 161–174.

2951. —. *Asherah and the Cult of Yahweh in Israel.* SBL Monograph Series, no. 34. Atlanta: Scholars Press, 1988.

2952. Patai, Raphael. "The Goddess Asherah." *JNES* 24 (1965), 37–52.

2953. Perlman, Alice. "Asherah and Astarte in the Old Testament." Ph.D. diss., Graduate Theological Union, 1978.

2954. Pettey, Richard J. *Asherah Goddess of Israel.* American University Studies Series VII, Theology and Religion, vol. 74. New York: Peter Lang, 1990.

2955. Piper, Vera Lydia. "Uprooting Traditional Interpretation: A Consideration of Tree Worship in the Migration of Abraham." Ph.D. diss., University of New York at Buffalo, 1989.

2956. Reed, William L. *The Asherah in the Old Testament.* Fort Worth: Texas Christian University Press, 1949.

2957. Smith, Mark S. "God Male and Female in the Old Testament: Yahweh and His 'Asherah'." *TS* 48 (1987), 333–340.

2958. Tigay, Jeffrey H. *You Shall Have No Other Gods: Israelite Religion in the Light of Hebrew Inscriptions.* HSM, no. 31. Atlanta: Scholars Press, 1986.

2959. Wallace, Howard N. *The Eden Narrative.* HSM, no. 32. Atlanta: Scholars Press, 1985.

2960. Weinfeld, Moshe. "Kuntillet 'Ajrud Inscriptions and their Significance." *SEL* 1 (1984), 121–130.

2961. Whit, William D. "The Divorce of Yahweh and Asherah in Hos 2.4–7. 12ff." *Scandinavian Journal of the Old Testament* 6 (1992), 31–67.

2962. Wiggins, Steve A. *A Reassessment of "Asherah."* AOAT 235. Kevelaer: Butzon & Bercker/Neukirchen-Vluyn: Neukirchener Verlag, 1993.

2963. Yamashita, Tadanori. "The Goddess Asherah." Ph.D. diss., Yale University, 1964.

2964. Zevit, Ziony. "The Khirbet el-Qôm Inscription Mentioning a Goddess." *BASOR,* no. 255 (1984), 39–47.

AUTHOR INDEX

'Amr, Abdel-Jalil 127–129
Abdulillah, F. 2705
Abel, F.M. 626
Abramowitz, Chaim 627–628
Abrams, Judith Z. 629
Abramsky, S. 630
Abschlag, W. 631
Abusch, Tzvi 2376
Achetemeier, Elizabeth 209
Achtemeier, Paul J. 210
Ackerman, James S. 632–633
Ackroyd, Peter A. 634–635
Adams, Charles 211
Adams, Queenie M. 212
Adelman, Joseph 1
Adinolfi, M. 213–214, 636–637
Adler, Elaine June 1972
Aguilar, Grace 215
Aharoni, R. 638
Aharoni, Y. 639
Ahl, Sally W. 2739
Ahlström, G. W. 640, 2883
Ahuvyah, A. 641–643
Ahyoueny, M 2299
Aitken, Kenneth T. 644
Al-A'dami, K. A. 2377
Al-Fouadi, Abdul-Hadi 2378
Al-Gailani-Shakir, Burhan 123
Al-Gailani-Werr, Lamia 122–123
al-Jadir, Walid 122
Al-Khalesi, Yasin M. 2632
Albenda, Pauline 124
Albertz, Rainer 645
Albright, W. F. 2884–2887
Aldred, Cyril 1998, 2072–2073
Aletti, Jean-Noël 646–647
Alexander, George M. 216
Alexander, T. D. 648
Alexander, William 2
Allam, Schafik 2074–2086
Allen, C. G. 649
Allen, T. G. 2087
Alster, B. 2379–2384
Altenmüller, H. 2088–2090
Alter, Robert 217, 650
Altpeter, Gerda 651

Alvarez, Oses, J. A. 652
Amar, A. L. 2166
Amiet, P. 2740
Amiran, Ruth 125–126
Amit, Yairah 653–655
Amram, D. W. 218
Amsler, S. 656
Anbar (Bernstein), Moshé 657–
 658, 2385, 2633
Anderlini, Giampaoh 659
Anderson, A. A. 660
Anderson, Berhard W. 661
Anderson, F. 662
Anderson, Gary 663
Anderson, I. David 664
Andreason, Niels-Erik 665
Andriolo, K. R. 666
Angerstorfer, Andreas 2888
Apostolos-Cappadona, Diane 667–
 668
Aptowitzer, V. 669
Ararat, Nissan 670–672
Arbeli, Shoshana 1973
Archi, Alfonso 2654, 2697–2698
Arensburger, B. 130
Armstrong, A. H. 1999
Arnaud, Daniel 2386
Arnold, Patrick M. 219, 673
Aro, J 2311
Arom, N. 674
Arpali, Boaz 675
Artzi, P. 2634–2635
Aschkenasy, Nehama 220, 676
Aschliman, Sylvia A. 677
Asensio, F. 678
Asher-Greve, J. M. 2312
Asmussen, Jes Peter 679
Assman, Jan 2091
Aston, Sophia 221
Astour, Michael C. 680, 2741–
 2743
Attridge, Harold A. 53
Auffret, Pierre 222
Augustin, Matthias 681
Augustinovich, Agustin 223
Auld, A. Graeme 2889

Aviezer, Nathan 682
Avigad, Nahman 131–135, 683
Azarpay, G. 2387

Bach, Alice 224, 684
Bachofen, Johann Jacob 3
Backer, Louis de 4
Baer, Klaus 2000
Bailey, J. A. 685, 2388
Bailey, R. C. 225
Baines, John 2001, 2002
Bakan, David 226
Bakir, Abd el-Mohsen 2003
Bakon, Shimon 686–687
Bakry, Hassan S. K. 2092
Bal, Mieke 227–232, 688–689,
    1254
Baldensperger, Ph. J. 690
Baldwin, George Colfax 233
Ball, C. J. 691
Ballow, Patricia K. 5
Balmuth, M. S. 169
Balpinar, Belkis 268
Baltzer, Klaus 692
Balz-Cochois, Helgard 234, 693,
    1974
Bar-Asher, Mordechai 694
Bar-Efrat. S. 235
Bardèche, Maurice 6
Bardis, P. D. 2093
Barilqo, H. 695
Barnard, David 236
Barnett, R. D. 136–138, 2655,
    2890
Barré, Michael L. 2389
Barrelet, Marie-Thérèse 139, 2744,
    2857
Barron, Mary Catherine 696
Barstad, Hans M. 697
Barta, Winfried 2094
Bartimus, Rüdiger 698
Bartolomei, M. C. 601
Barton, George A. 699
Baskin, Judith R. 700
Bass, Dorothy C. 701
Basserman, Lujo 7
Batten, J. Rowena 237
Batten, L.W. 702
Batto, B. F. 2636–2637
Baudissin, Wolf Wilhelm Friedrich
    238
Bauer-Kayatz, Christa 239
Bayliss, D. 2313

Beard, Mary R. 8–9
Beattie, D. R.G. 703–707
Beauvoir, Simone de 10
Beck, P. 140, 2891
Becker, Joachim 708
Beckman, Gary 54, 2656–2657
Bedell, Ellen 2004
Beek, M. A. 709
Beer, Georg 240
Beeston, A. F. L. 710
Begrich, J. 711
Bekkenkamp, Jonneke 712
Belkin, S. 713
Bellefontaine, Elizabeth 714–715
Ben-Abu, David 1975
Ben-Arie, Sarah 141–142
Ben-Baraq, Zafrira 55, 716–722
Ben-Reuven, S. 723–724
Ben-Tor, A. 143
Ben-Yasher, M. 725
Benedetti, B. 2390
Bénédite, G. 2005
Benigni, G. 2858
Benjamin, Don C. 726–727
Bennett, Anne McGrew 728–730
Benveniste, E. 2843
Berg, Sandra Beth 242
Berg, Werner 731–732
Bergant, Dianne 733–735
Bergerk, P. R. 736
Bergin, Helen 737
Bergman, J. 2095
Berlandini-Grenier, J. 2096
Berlin, Adele 243, 738–740
Bernard-Delapierre, G. 2097
Bernhardt, Karl-Heinz 2892
Bernstein, Moshe J. 741
Bertman, Stephen 144, 742
Betlyon, John Wilson 2893
Betty, R. 11
Beuken, W. A. M. 743–744
Beyer, Dominique 2745
Beyer, Johanna 12
Beyerle, Stefan 745
Beylin, Z. 746
Biagov, L. N. 2658
Biale, David 747
Biddle, Mark E. 748
Bierbrier, Morris 2006–2007,
    2098
Bigger, Stephen F. 749, 1976
Bilezikian, Gilbert 245

Bilgiç, E. 2659
Bin-Nun, S. R. 2660
Bird, Phyllis 750–756
Birot, Maurice 2638
Birt, Theodor 13
Bitter, S. 246
Black, Edith 757
Blackman, A. M. 2099
Blakely, J. A. 145
Blankenberg-van Delden, C. 2100–2103
Bledstein, Adrien Janis 758–761
Bleeker, C. J. 2104
Blenkinsopp, J. 762
Blocher, F. 2314, 2595
Bloesch, Donald G. 247
Blondheim, Menahem 763
Blondheim, S. H. 763
Bloom, Harold 248, 760–761, 888, 1052, 1463
Bockel, P. 764–765, 2105
Boecker, Hans Jochen 249
Boer, C. Den 250
Boer, P. A. H. 251
Böhl, Franz M. Th. 2391
Bohlen, Reinhold 252, 766
Bonnet, C. 2859
Bonora, Antonio 767–768
Booij, Th. 769
Borbone, Pier Giorgio 770
Bordreuil, Pierre 166
Borghauts, J. F. 2106
Boss, J. 771, 327
Bosse-Griffiths, K. 2107
Bossman, David 772–773
Boström, Gustav 253
Bottero, J. 2392–2393
Bottini, G. Claudio 774
Bowman, C. H. 56
Branden, Albert van den 2860
Braslavi, Y. 775–776
Bratcher, R. G. 777
Bravmann, M. M. 778
Breneman, J. M. 2699
Brennen, J. P. 779
Brenner, A. B. 780
Brenner, Athalya 254–255, 781–791
Bressan, G. 792
Breyfogle, C. 793–794
Brichto, Herbert Chanan 795
Bridenthal, Renata 14

Bridges, Susan Jane 2315
Briend, J. 796, 2394
Briffault, Robert 15
Briggs, Belinda M. 797
Brim, Charles 256
Brin, G. 57, 798
Brink, Marthinus Beyers 2894
Brinkmann, J. A. 2395
Briscoe, Jill. 257
Broadrib, D. 799
Broch, Yitzhak, I. 258
Brock, Sebastian 800
Brodie, Louis 801
Bronner, Leila Leah 802
Bronznick, Norman M. 803
Brooke, George J. 2746
Brooks, B. S. 804
Brooks, Beatrice Allard 2396
Brown, John Pairman 805–806
Brownmiller, Susan 259
Brueggemann, W. 807–809
Bruin, Elizabeth 810
Brun, François 145
Brunet, Gilbert 811
Brunner-Traut, Emma 147–148, 2008
Bruns, J. Edgar 260
Bruppacher, Hans 812
Bryan, B. M. 2108–2110
Bryce, Mary Charles 813
Buccellati, Giorgio 2397
Buchanan, Briggs 2398
Buchanan, Isabelia Reid 261
Bull, G. T. 262
Bullough, Bonnie 17
Bullough, Vern L. 16–7
Burchard, Samuel 263
Burden, J. J. 814
Burgess, E. T. 264
Burke, J. Ashleigh 265
Burns, Camilla 1977
Burns, Dan E. 815
Burns, Rita J. 266
Burrows, Millar 267, 816–819
Burton, Juliette T. 268
Busch, E. 269
Bushnell, Katherine C. 270
Butterworth, E. A. S. 2895
Buttles, Janet R. 2009
Buxenbaum, Yaakov 820

Cades, J. 821
Cady, D. R. 822

Caird, G. B. 271
Callaway, Mary 272
Callaway, Phillip R. 823
Calvocoressi, Peter 273
Cameron, A. 58
Cameron, George C. 2844–2845
Caminos, R. 2111
Camp, Claudia V. 274, 824–828
Campbell, Antony 829
Campbell, E. F., Jr. 830
Campbell, K. M. 831
Campbell, T. 832
Cañellas, Gabriel 833–834
Capart, J. 2112
Caquot, André 59
Cardascia, G. 2316, 2399, 2700, 2747
Carmichael, Calum M. 275–277, 835–838
Carmo, José Manuel Sanchez 839
Carmody, Dennis Lardner 278
Carmody, J. 840
Carr, G. Lloyd 841
Carroll, Michael P. 84242
Carruba, O. 2661
Carter, H. 2113
Carter, Jane Burr 2896
Cartledge, Tony W. 843
Caspi, Mishael. 844–846
Cassin, E. 2317, 2400, 2701–2702
Cassuto, U. 279, 2748–2749, 2897
Castelnuovo, A. 847
Caubet, Annie 2750
Cavalcanti, Tereza 848
Cazelles, H. 60, 849–850, 2751–2752
Černý, J. 2010–2011, 2114–2117
Chamberlayne, J. H. 851, 2703
Chappell, Clovis Gilham 280
Charbel. Antonio 852
Charpin, D. 2318
Chesire, J. Blunt, Jr. 853
Chotzner, J. 854
Chow, W. W. K. 2704
Christ, Carol P. 855
Christenson, Duane L. 856
Civil, M. 2401–2402
Clamer, Christa 149
Clapp, Marie W. 281
Clark, David J. 857–858
Clarkson, Shannon 859
Clifford, Richard 2753

Clines, David J. A. 282–283, 860–862, 2754
Coats, G. W. 863–867
Coche, Christiane 2118
Cody, A. I. 284
Cogan, Mordechai 868–869
Coggins, Richard 870
Cohen, Chayim 871–873
Cohen, D. 874
Cohen, G. H. 875
Cohen, H. H. 876
Cohen, M. 877
Cohen, Shaye J. D. 878–879
Cohn, Robert L. 880
Cole, Dorothea 2119–2120
Cole, William Graham 285
Collins, Adela Yarboro 286, 881
Collins, Oral Edmond 1978
Collins, Raymond F. 882
Collins, Stanley 287
Collun, D. 150
Condon, Virginia 2121
Conroy, Charles 288
Contenau, G. 151, 2861
Conzelmann, Hans 883
Coogan, M. D. 884, 2755
Cook, J. M. 2846
Cook, Johann 885
Cooper, Alan 886–888, 2898
Cooper, J. S. 2403
Coote, R. B. 289, 2756
Copher, C.B. 889
Coppens, J. 890–893
Cortese, Enzo 894
Cosby, Michael R. 290
Costas, Orlando E. 895
Couroyer, Bernard 896
Couturier, Guy 897
Cowan, Margaret P. 1979
Cowling, G. 898
Cox, Francis August 291
Coxon, Peter W. 899–900, 1022
Craghan, John F. 901–902
Craigie, Peter C. 903–904
Crane, T. 905
Craven, Toni 906
Crawley, Joann 907
Crenshaw, James L. 292, 908–909
Criado, R. 910
Croce, Lucia 911
Crocker, P. T. 152, 912
Croix-Rosse, Andre de la 913

Crook, Margaret B. 914
Cropp, Johannes 915
Cross, Earle Bennett 293, 916
Cross, Frank Moore Jr. 294, 917, 2899
Cross, Nancy 918
Crotwell, Helen 295
Crüsemann, F. 153, 296
Cruveilhier, P. 919–920
Cruze-Uribe, Eugene 2122
Culley, Robert C. 297
Cullican, W. 154
Cunchillos, J.L. 921, 2757–2760
Curtis, A. H. 922

Dacquino, Pretro 61
Dales, George F. 2461
Dall'olmo, M. O. 2862
Dalley, Stephanie 2319–2320, 2404
Daly, Mary 298
Dandamaev, Muhammad A. 2321, 2847
Danelius, Eva 923
Daniélou, J. 924–925
Danker, Albert 299
Danmanville, J. 155
Daressy, G. 2123–2128
Darga, M. 2662
Darr, Kathryn Pfisterer 300, 926
d'Auria, S. 2129
David, A. R. 2130
Davidson, Richard M. 927–929
Davies, Eryl N. 930–931
Davis, D. 156
Davis, Elizabeth Gould 18, 301
Davis, M. Stephen 932
Davis, Steve 933
Day, John 2900
Day, Peggy L. 302
Deem, Ariella 935–937
Deen, Elizabeth 303–306
Deger-Halkotzy, S. 62
Deines, H. von 2131
de Koven, Anna 19
Del Olmo Lete, Gregorio 938, 2863, 2761–2762
Delcor, M. 939–942, 2864–2865
Deller, K. 2705
Demers, Patricia 307
DeMerv, I. 943
Dempster, Stephen G. 944
De Pury, A. 934

Deroche, Michael 945–946
Derousseaux, Louis 63
Derret, J. D. M. 947
Descamps, P. 64
Desroches-Noblecourt, Christiane 2012–2013, 2132
Dessel, J. P. 157
Detrick, R. Blaine 308
Deurloo, K. A. 948–951
Dever, William G. 162, 2901–2902
Dexter, Miriam Robbins 2903
Diakonoff, I. M 2405–2407
Diamond, J. A. 952
Diebner, B. J. 953–955,956
Diesel, P. M. L. 309
Diest, Ferdinand 957
Dietrich, M. 2904, 2763–2766
Dijk, J. van 2408–2409
Dijk-Hemmes, Fokkelien Van 958–959
Dijkstra, M. 2663
Dillow, J. 310
Dion, Paul, E. 960
Dodson, A. M. 2133
Dohmen, Christoph 961
Döller, Johannes 311–312
Domeris, W. R. 962
Donadoni Roveriv,Anna Maria 2014
Donaldson, Mara E. 963
Dondelinger, E. 2015
Donner, H. 964
D'Oriega, Guy 20
Dossin, G. 2639–2641, 2410–2411
Dothan, M. 2905
Dothan, Trude 158–159
Doty, L. Timothy 2412
Dresner, Samuel 965
Drimmer, Frederick 312
Driver, G. R. 966, 2322–2323
Dryburgh, B. 314
Dubarle, A.-M. 967–970
du Buisson, Du Mensil 2866
Duché, Jean 21
Duman, Marcel 971
Dumas, A. 972
Dumbrell, W. J. 973
Dunham, Dows 2058, 2016
Dupouy, Edmond 22
Durand, Jean-Marie 65, 2590, 2642–2643

Dus, Jan 974
Dussaud, R. 2906
Duvshani, M. 975–976

Eakins, J. Kenneth 977
Eaton, A. W. 2767
Ebeling, Erich 2413
Eberharter, A. 316
Edwards, I. E. S. 2134
Edzard, D. O. 2414
Egender, D. 66
Eggebrecht, Arne 2056
Ehrlich, Z. H. 978
Eichler, Barry L. 2706–2707
Eider, Dorothy 316
Eilers, Wilhelm 2324
El-Amir, Mustafa 2135
el-Dwakhly, Zenab 2185
El-Sayed, R. 2136
Eller, Vernard 317
Ellermeier, F. 67
Ellington, John 979–980
Ellis, Bob R. 981
Ellis, Maria De J. 2415–2416
Ellison, H. L. 982
Emanueli, Moshe 983–986
Emerton, J. A. 987–989, 2907
Emmerson, G. I. 990
Emswiler, Sharon Neufer 318
Engar, Ann W. 991
Engelbach, R. 2137
Engelken, Karen 319
Engelsman, Joan Chamberlain 320
Engert, Thadaeus 321
Engle, James Robert 2908
Epstein, L. M. 322–333
Epting, Ruth 241, 324
Erdmann, Kurt 2848
Erman, Adolf 2017
Escudero, M. 992
Eskenazi, Tamara C. 283
Eslinger, Lyle 993–995
Evans, Mary T. 325
Exum, J. Cheryl 326–327, 996–1001, 1224
Eybers, I. I. 1002–1003
Eynde, Pierre van den 1004
Eyre, C. J. 2138

Fabretti, N. 1005
Fadhil, A. 2417–2418
Falasca, M. 1006
Fales, F. M. 2419

Falk, Marcia 328
Falk, Z. W. 329, 1007–1010
Falkenstein, A. 2420, 2325
Falkowitz, R. 2421
Falsone, G. 2867
Fantar, M. H. 2868
Farber, Gertrud 2422
Farber, W. T. 2311, 2326
Farber-Flügge, Gertrud 2327
Farnell, Lewis R. 68
Faulhaber, Michael von 330
Faulkner, James 331
Fawzi, Rashid 2423
Fazzini, R. 2139
Federn, Walter 2140
Feigin, Samuel I. 2424
Feilschuss-Abir, A. S. 1011–1012
Feinberg, Charles L. 1013
Feinstein, B. 69
Fensham, F. C. 70, 1014–1017, 2768, 2909,
Ferrara, A. J. 2328
Festorazzi, Franco 1018
Feuillet, André 1019–1020
Fewell, Danna Nolan 1021–1024
Figulla, H. H. 2329
Fildes, Valerie A. 71
Filippi, W. de 2425
Finet, A. 2426, 2641
Finkel, D. J. 160
Finkel, Irving I. 2427–2429
Finkelstein, J. J. 2430–2435
Fiorenza, Elizabeth Schüssler 332–333
Firestone-Seghi, Laya 1025
Fisch, A. H. 1026
Fisch, Harold 334, 1027
Fischer, Alexander 1028
Fischer, Clare Benedicks 335
Fischer, Georg 1029
Fischer, Henry George 2141–2157, 2018–2019
Fishbane, M. 1030
Fisher, Eugene 1031
Fitzgerald, Aloysius 1032
Fleishman, Joseph. 72
Florentin-Smyth, Françoise 1033
Flügge, P. 1034
Flusser, D. 1035
Foh, Susan T. 336, 1036
Fohrer, G. 337
Fokkelman, J. P. 338

Follis, Elaine R. 1037
Fontaine, C. R. 73, 1038, 2664
Forgeau, A. 2158
Foster, B. 2436–2437
Foucault, M 23
Fox, Everett 339
Fox, Michael V. 340–341, 1039–
　1040, 1710
Fraine, Jean de 342
Frankfort, Henri 2438
Frankiel, Tamar 343
Franklin, Cecil L. 1041
Franklin, Paul 1042
Fransen, P.-I. 1043
Franson, Frederik 1044
Frazer, Sir James George 344
Freedman, David Noel 345, 917,
　1045, 2708,2910
Freedman, R. David 1046
Frick, F. 346
Frieden, Abtei Maria 1047
Friedman, Joni 1048
Friedman, Mordechai A. 1049
Friedman, Norman 1050
Friedman, Richard Elliot 1051–
　1052
Friedman, Theodore 1053
Friedmann, Meir 1054
Friedrich, J. 2665
Frost, Francis 1055
Frost, Stanley B. 1056
Frotstig-Adler, N. H. 1057
Frye, Richard N. 2849
Frye, Roland M. 1058
Frymer-Kensky, Tikva 74, 347,
　1059–1064, 2439–2441
Fubini, Guido 1065
Fuchs, Esther 1066–1070
Fuchs-Kreimer, Nancy 1071
Fuhr, I. 161
Furman, Nelly 1072

Gabel, J. B. 1073
Gablenz, Clara von 1074
Gadala, Marie-Thérèse 348
Gallery, Maureen 2442
Galvin, Marianne 2020, 2159
Gammie, John G. 349
Garbini, Giovanni 350, 1073–1078
Gardiner, Alan H. 2160–2161
Gardiner, Anne 1079
Garelli, P. 2443
Garner, Gordon G. 2911

Garnot, Moshe 1080
Garr, W. Randall 2769
Garrett, Duane A. 1081
Garsiel, Moshe 351–352, 1082–
　1083
Gaspari,Christof 353
Gaster, Theodor H. 75, 354–355,
　2162, 2912
Gaugel, K. H. 1084
Gauthier, H. 2163
Gauthier-Laurent, M. 2164
Gawlikowski, K. 2644
Gehrke, R. 1085
Gelander, S. 1086
Gelb, I. J. 2444–2446
Gelin, A. 1087
Geller, Stephen A. 1088
Gendler, Mary 1089
Geraci, P. 214
Gerber, Aaron H. 356
Gerl, Hanna-Barbara 1090
Gerleman, G. 1091
Gernot, M. 2671
Gernot, Wilhelm 2709
Gerstenberger, Erhard S. 357,
　1092–1093
Gevirtz, S. 1094
Geyer, Marcia L. 1095
Ghalioungui, P. 2165–2166
Gibert, P. 358
Gibson, John C. L. 2770
Gilbert, Maurice 359, 1096
Gilliland, Dolores Scott 360
Gilner, David Jonathan 1980–1981
Gilula, Mordechai 2913
Giménez, Clementina M. 1097
Ginsberg, H. L. 361, 1098–1099,
　2771–2772, 2914
Girardet, Giorgio M. 1100
Gitay, Zefira 1101
Gitin, S. 162
Gitton, M. 2021–2022, 2167–
　2169
Giveon, Raphael 163, 2170
Glassner, J. 2447
Glazier-McDonald, Beth 1102–
　1103
Glickman, S. Craig 362
Glück, J. J. 1104–1105
Godron, G. 2171
Goedicke, H. 2060, 2172–2174
Goetze, A. 2448–2449, 2666

Goitein, S. D. 1114
Goldfarb, S. D. 1115–1116
Goldingay, John. 363, 1117
Goldstein, Bernard R. 888
Gomi, T. 2451
Good, Edwin M. 1118
Gordis, Robert 1119–1123
Gordon, Cynthia 1124
Gordon, Cyrus H. 1125, 1126, 2710–2712, 2773
Görg, Manfred 164–165, 1106–1113, 2175, 2451, 2869
Gorgulho, L-B. 1127
Goto, K. 1128
Gottlieb, Freema 1129
Gottlieb, I. B. 1130
Gottwald, Norman 364–365
Goulder, Michael D. 366
Gow, Murray D. 1131
Graefe, E. 2023
Graetz, Naomi. 1132–1133
Graff, D. F. 345
Grafman, R. 2452
Granot, Alison M. 1134–1135
Granqvist, Hilma 367
Grapow, H. 2176
Graupner, Axel 1136
Graves, Robert 368
Gray, Elmer L. 76
Gray, John 2774–2775
Grayson, A. K. 2453
Green, Alberto R. 1137–1138
Green, Barbara 1139
Green, L. 2024
Greenberg, Moshe 1040–1142
Greenfield, J. C. 2304
Greengus, S. 2454–2457, 2713
Greenspahn, Frederick E. 1143
Greenstein, Edward L 1144–1145
Grelot, P. 369–370, 1146, 2300
Grey, Mary C. 1147
Griffith, J. G. 2177
Griffith, K. A. 371
Grimal, Peter 77, 1183
Grimm, Alfred 2178
Grober, S. F. 1148
Grondahl, Frauke 2714
Gross, R. M. 372
Gross, Walter 1149
Grossberg, Daniel 1150–1151
Grosz, Katarzyna 2715–2716
Grottanelli, Cristiano 1152

Gruber, Mayer I. 1153–1163
Gubel, E. 166, 2870
Guentch-Ogloueff, M. 2179
Guest, Edith M. 2180
Gunn, David M. 373–374, 1022–1024, 1164–1165
Gunnel, André 1166
Gurney, O. R. 2458, 2667
Güterbock, H. G. 2572, 2668
Guzzo Amadasi, M. G. 2871
Gwaltney, William Cary, Jr 2330

Haag, Herbert 1167
Haas, V. 2669–2672, 2717
Habachi, L. 2181–2182
Hacket, Jo Ann 78, 1168
Hadas, Pamela White 375
Hadley, Judith M. 2915–2917
Hagan, Harry 1169
Haines, Richard C. 167
Hale, Sara Josepha 24
Halevy, B. 1170–1171
Halivni, David Weiss 1172
Hall, Gary 1173, 1982
Hallet, Mary Thomas 376
Hallo, W. W. 1174–1175, 2331, 2459–2460
Halpern, Baruch 1176, 1351
Hambrick-Stowe, Charles E. 1177
Hamiel, H. Y. 1178
Hamill, Thomas 1179
Hančar, Franz 168
Handy, Lowell 2776
Hanfmann, G. M. A. 169, 2673
Hansen, Donald P. 2461
Hansen, Tracy 1180
Hanson, P. 1181
Harari, I. 2183–2184
Harden, Donald 2872
Hardesty, Nancy 1182
Harer, W. Benson, Jr. 2185
Hari, R. 2025
Harris, J. R. 2186–2189
Harris, R. 1183, 2332, 2462–2477
Harrison, Eveleen 377
Hart, George 2026
Harter, L. Blagg 1184
Hartland, Sidney E. 2478
Hartmann, Anton T. 378
Hartmann, K. C. 1185
Hartsoe, Colleen Ivey 379
Hassenfuss, J. 2190
Haupt, Paul 2479

Hauser, Alan J. 1186–1187
Hawkins, J. D. 2674
Hayes, William C. 2027
Haytes, M. 380
Headley, Phineas Camp 381
Healey, J. F. 2777–2779
Heidt, William G. 382
Heiler, Friedrich 25
Heim, Suzanne 205
Heimpel, W. 79, 2480–2481
Heindl, Edith 1188
Heister, Maria-Sybilla 383
Heitzmann, Alfonso Alegre 1189
Helck, Wolfgang 2191
Held, Moshe 1190, 2482
Heller, Jan 1191
Heltzer, Michael 1192
Hendel, Ronald S. 1193–1194
Henry, A.-M. 1195–1196
Henry, Sondra 26
Hentschel, Georg 384
Hermann, H. 2780
Hermann, W. 2781, 2826
Herr, Ethel L. 385
Herrmann, Wolfram 1197, 2918
Herzfeld, Ernst F. 2850
Herzog, Kristin 1198
Hess, Margaret 386
Hess, R. S. 1199
Hestrin, Ruth 2919–2920
Heywood, Thomas 27
Hickmann, Hans 2192
Higgins, Jean M. 1200–1201
Hillers, Delbert R. 170, 2782
Hindson, E. E. 1202
Hirsch, Hans 2333, 2851
Hirsch, Udo 268
Hirschberger, R. 1203
Hoch-Smith, Judith 28
Hoek, J. 387
Höffken, Peter 1204
Hoffman, I. 2193
Hoffner, Harry 80–81, 1205, 2675
Hoftijzer, J. 1206–1207
Hohenwart-Gerlachstein, Anna 2194
Holladay, William L. 1208–1209
Hollis, Susan T. 2195
Holzinger, H. 1210
Hommel, Fritz 2921
Honeywell, Betty 388
Hongisto, Leif 1211

Hoogewoud, F. J. 1212
Hooks, Stephen M. 1983
Hopkins, D. 389
Hopkins, Ian W. J. 1213
Hoppe, Leslie J. 1214
Hörig, Monika 2922
Horner, Thomas M. 390
Horowitz, Maryanne C. 1215
Horton, F. L. 1216
Hoshino, Mitsuo 1217
House, H. Wayne 1218
Houtman, C. 1219
Hruška, B. 2483
Huber, Elaine C. 1220
Huehnergard, John 82, 1221, 2783
Huey, F. B., Jr. 1222
Huffmon, Herbert B. 2645–2646
Hull, William E. 1223
Humphrey, W. L. 1224
Hunhold, Gerfried 1149
Hurley, James B. 391
Hurton, F. L. 145
Hurvitz, Avi 1225
Hutter, Manfred 1226, 2334, 2676
Hvidberg-Hansen, F. O. 2873, 2875
Hyers, C. 392
Hyman, Frieda C. 1227–1228
Hyman, Ronald T. 1229–1230

Ichisar, M. 2484
Ide, Arthur Frederick 83, 393–394
Ihromi 1231
Imparati, F. 2677
Ireland, Norma 29
Iriarte, María Eugenia 1232
Isser, Stanley 1233
Istavrides, Vasil T. 1234

Jack, J. W. 171
Jackson, B. S. 1235
Jacob, Edmond 1236–1237
Jacob, Paul F. 1238
Jacobsen, Dan 395
Jacobsen, Thorkild 2335–2336, 2485–2486
Jacobson, Anita 30
Jacobson, Diane 1239
Jacobson, H. 1240
Jacquet-Gordon, H. 2196
Jagendorf, Zvi 1242
Jakobson, V. A. 2487

James, E. O. 172
James, T. G. H. 2028
Janssen, J. J. 2197–2201, 2245
Janzen, J. Gerald 1243
Janzen, Waldemar 396
Japhet, Sara 1241
Jaroš, Karl 2923
Jasper, G. 1244
Jastrow, Morris, Jr. 2488
Jay, Nancy 1245–1246
Jay, William 397
Jeansonne, Sharon Pace 398, 1247
Jenny, H. 1248
Jensen, Jans Jørgen Lundager 1249–1250
Jensen, Mary E. 399
Jensen, P. 2924
Jentgens, Gerhard 1251
Jeppesen, Knut 2925
Jepsen, Alfred 1252–1253
Jéquier, J. 2029
Jirku, A. 2784
Joannès, F. 2337, 2489
Jobling, David 400, 1254
Johanan, J. D. 401
Johnson, Buffie 84
Johnson, Elizabeth A. 1255–1256
Johnson, Sally Barber 2030
Jonckheere, Frans 2202
Jones, B. W. 1257–1258
Jones, David Clyde 1259–1260
Jones, G. H. 402
Jongeling, B. 1261
Jongeling, K. 1262
Jost, Renate 542
Joüon, P. 1263
Julian, A. K. 1264
Jüngling, H.-W. 403
Junker, H. 1265
Junsson, Gunnlauger A. 404

Kaiser, Barber Bakke 1266
Kaiser, Walter C. 1267
Kaithathara, J. 1984
Kamesar, Adam 1268
Kammenhuber, A. 2678
Kampman, A. A. 2679
Kang, S. T. 2490
Kapelrud, Arvid S. 2785
Kaplan, H. R. 2203
Kaplan, J. 174
Kaplan, Lawrence 1269
Kaplony, P. 2204

Karageorghis, V. 2874
Karssen, G. 405
Katan, Norma Jean 2031
Katzenstein, H. J. 1270
Katzoff, Louis 1271–1273
Kearney, Peter J. 1274
Keay, Kathy 406,
Keel, Othmar 175, 1275, 2926
Kees, H. 2205
Keimer, L. 2032, 2206
Kellenbach, Katharine von 1276, 1985
Keller, Carl A. 1277
Kellerman, D. 407
Kelly, William 1278
Kemp, Barry J. 2207–2208
Kennet, R. H. 408
Kessler, Martin 1279–1280
Kessler, Rainer 1281–1282
Keukens, Karlheinz H. 1283
Kevers, Paul 1284–1285
Khalil, S. 2166
Kieffer, René 1286
Kiev, Ari 322
Kikawada, I. 1287
Kilian, R. 409, 1288
Kilmer, Anne Draffkorn 2491–2492
Kimball, Gayle 1289
Kinal, F. 85
King, Philip J. 1290
King, William C. 31
Kipper, J. Balduino 1291–1292
Kirk, Martha Ann 410
Kitchen, K. A. 1293, 2033
Klaus, Natan 1294
Klein, Hans 1295
Klein, Harald 2493
Klein, Jacob 2494
Klein, L. R 411
Klein, Ralph W. 1296
Kleinig, John W. 1297
Klengel-Brandt, E 2495
Klíma, J. 2338, 2786–2788, 2852–2853
Kloner, A. 156
Knapp, A. B. 86
Knierim, Rolf 1298
Knight, Douglas A. 1299
Knox, W. L. 1301
Koch, K. 2927
Kogut, S. 1300

König, Eduard 1302–1303
Koonz, Claudia 14
Korenhof, Mieke 542
Kornarakis, John 1304
Kornfeld, W. 87, 2496
Korr, Craig S. 2209
Koschaker, P. 2497–2498, 2718
Kosmala, H. 1305
Kottackal, Joseph 1306
Kraeling, Emil G. 1307
Kramer, Carol 2854
Kramer, S. N. 1308, 2339–2340, 2373, 2499–2510
Kraus, H. J. 412
Krause, Martin 1309
Krebs, Walter 1310
Kreuzer, Siegfried 1311
Krinetzki, Leo 1312
Kristensen, A. 2789
Kritikos, Madeleine 2790
Kroeze, J. H. 413
Kronasser, H. 2680
Kronholm, Tryggve 1313
Kruger, P. A. 1314–1316
Kruse, H. 1317
Kruse, Ingeborg 414
Kubler, Franz 415
Kuchman (-Sabhaly), L. 2034, 2210–2211
Kuentz, C. 2013
Kugel, James L. 416
Kuhlmann, K. P. 2212
Kühne, C. 2791
Kühne, H. 176
Kuhrt, A. 58
Kulow, Nelle Wahler 417
Kümmel, H. M. 2341, 2620
Kutler, Laurence 1318
Kutscher, Raphael 2511
Kuyperk, Abraham 418

Labuschagne, C. J. 1319
Lacheman, E. R. 1320, 2719–2722
Lachs, Rosalyn 419
Lachs, Samuel T. 1321
Lackenbacher, S. 88, 2512–2513, 2792
Lacocque, André 420
Lacroix, Paul 32
Laffey, Alice L. 421
Lambert, G., S. J. 1322
Lambert, J. 1323
Lambert, W. G. 2514–2521, 2647

Lamphere, L. 44
Landau, Lazare 1324
Landsberger, B. 2342, 2522
Landy, Francis 422, 1325–1326
Lang, Bernhard 423–425, 1327
Langdon, Stephen 2523
Langdon-Davies, John 33
Langemeyer, Bernhard 1328
Langer, Heidemarie 426
Langlamet, F. 1329–1330
Lanser, Susan S. 1331
Laroche, E. 2681–2683
Lasine, Stuart 1332–1333
Lattey, Cuthbert 1334–1335
Lawler, G. L. 427
Lawlor, John I. 1336
Lawton, Robert B. 177, 1337–1338
Lebrun, R. 2684
Leca, L. 2035
Leclant, M. J. 2213–2215
Le Déaut, R. 1339
Ledrus, M. 1340
Lee, G. M. 1341
Leemans, W. F. 2524
Leggett, D. A. 428
Legrand, L. 429, 1342–1343
Lehmann, M. R. 1344
Lehming, S. 1345
Leibovitch, Joseph 2216, 2928
Leibowitz, Eliyahu 1346
Leibowitz, Gilah 1346
Leichty, Erle 2525
Leipoldt, Johannes 34
Lemaire, André 2929–2931
Lemche, N. P. 1347
Leonard, Jeanne M. 1348
Lerberghe, K. van 2526
Lerner, Gerda 2343, 2527
Lesko, B. S. 89, 2036, 2217–2219
Lesko, L. H. 2220–2221
Letourneau, Charles 35
Lettinga, J. P. 1349
Levenson, Jon D. 1350–1351
Levenson, Paul H. 1352
Leviant, Curt 1353
Levin, Christoph 430
Levinas, E. 1354
Levine, Baruch A. 1355, 2793
Levine, M. H. 1356–1359
Levoratti, Armondo J. 1360
Lévy, Edmond 36

Levy, Ludwig 1361
Levy-Bruhl, H. 1362
Lewis, Ethel Clark 431
Lewy, Hildergard 2528
Licht, Jacob 432
Lichtenstein, Murray H. 1363
Lieberman, A. I. 90, 2344
Lieberman, S. R. 91
Limburg, James 433
Lindars, Barnabas 1364–1365
Linder, Helgo 1366
Lipínski, E. 92–93, 178, 1367,
   2345, 2529–2530, 2794–2795,
   2859, 2932–2933
Liptzin, Sol 1368–1372
Lissner, Anneliese 37
Livingston, Dennis H. 1373
Livingstone, A. 2346
Livio, Jean-Bernard 1374
Ljung, Inger 1375
Loader, J. A. 1376
Loades, Ann 434
Locher, Clemens 435, 1721, 1829
Lockerbie, J. 436
Lockyer, Herbert B. 437
Loewenstamm, Samuel E. 1377–
   1379, 2796–2797, 2801
Lofts, N. 438
Lohfink, Norbert 1380–1381
Löhr, Max 439
Løkkegaard, F. 2875, 2934
Long, Burke O. 440, 1382
López, Félix Garcia 1383
Loretz, O. 1384–1386, 2531,
   2763–2766, 2798–2799, 2904,
   2935
Lorton, David 2222
Loucas, Ioannis 2532
Louie, Wallace 2936
Lucas, Fr. Maria, O.F.M. 1388
Luckenbill, Daniel David 2533
Lüddeckens, Erich 2037
Luke, A. B. 1389
Luke, K. 1390–1396, 2534
Lukonin, V. 2847
Lundholm, Algot Theodore 441
Luria, Y. 1397
Lurie, B-Z. 1398
Lyon, David Gordon 2535
Lyons, Ellen Louise 1399
Lys, Daniel 1400

Maccoby, Hyam 1418

MacDonald, Elizabeth Mary 94
MacDonald, J. 2800
MacDonald, J. R. B. 1405
MacDonald, John 1406
Mace, David R. 444
MacHaffie, Barbara J. 445
Macht, David I. 1419
Mackawa, K. 2538
MacLauren, Edward 2938
Maertens, Thierry 446
Magonet, J. 1420
Maidman, Maynard Paul 2723–
   2724
Maier, Walter A. III 2939
Maigret, J. 1421
Maillot, A. 447, 1422–1423
Mair, Lucy Philip 38
Malamat, A. 2634–2635
Málek, J. 2002, 2223–2224
Malkiel, Sh. 1424
Mannheimer, Louise 1425
Manniche, Lise 2038
Manor, Dale W. 1426
Marble, Annie Russell 448
Marchetti, P. 2859
Marcus, David 449, 1427, 2801
Margalit, Baruch 2802–2805,
   2940–2941
Margalith, Othniel 1428–1431
Margueron, Jean 2643
Margulies, H. 1432
Marocco, Giuseppe 1433
Marrs, Rick 1434
Marshall, J. 1435
Marshall, Zona Bays 450
Martin, D. C. 1436
Martines, Lauro 40
Martyn, Sarah Towne 451
Marx, Viktor 2539
Marzel, Y. 1437
Mason, Maggie 452
Matheson, George 453
Mathon, G. 1438
Matouš, L. 2540–2541
Matoušouá-Rajmova, Marie 179,
   2542–2543
Matsushima, Eiko 2544–2545
Matthews, Edwin LeBron 1986
Matthews, Victor H. 454
Matthiae, M. Paolo 180
Mauldin, F. Louis 1439
May, H. G. 1440–1441

Mayer, Walter 2725
Mayes, A. D. H. 455
Mazahéri, A. A. 2855
Mazar, A. 181–182
Màlek, J. 2003
McAllister, Grace Edna 442–443
McBride, Mary 1401
McCarter, P. Kyle, Jr. 1402
McCarthy, Carmel 1403
McComiskey, Thomas E. 95
McConville, J. G. 1905
McCreesh, T. 1404
McEvenue, Sean S. 1407
McEwan, G. J. P 2536–2537
McGee, Daniel B. 1408
McGrath, B. 1409
McHatten, Mary T. 1410–1411
McKane, W. 1412–1413
McKay, J. W. 1414, 2937
McKeating, Henry 1415
McKenzie, J. L. 1416
McKinley, Judith 737
McPheeters, W. M. 1417
Meek, James 1442
Meer, W. van der 1443
Meier, Samuel A. 96, 1444
Meijer, Alexander 1445
Meijer, Amos 1445
Meilvitz, A. 1446
Meinhold, Arndt 1447–1448
Melamed, Evelyn B. 1479
Mele, Mirella 2546
Mellaart, James 183, 2685
Meller, Vilma 1449
Meltzer, Edmund S. 2225
Mendelsohn, I. 97–100, 1450, 2547
Mendenhall, George E. 456, 1451–1453
Menu, Bernadette 2039–2040, 2226–2228
Menzel, Brigitte 2347
Merhav, Rivka 2942
Merli, Dino 1454
Merodie, Marie de 1455
Mertz, B. 2041
Meshel, Ze'ev 2943–2945
Mesters, Carlos 457
Mettinger, Tryggve N. D. 1456–1457, 2806
Metzger, M. 2807
Meyers, Carol L. 458, 1458–1464

Michaelson, W. 1465
Michalowski, P. 2548–2552
Michel, Walter L. 1467–1468
Midant-Reynes, B 2229
Middlekoop, P. 1469
Miles, John C. 2322–2323
Milgrom, Jacob 1470
Millard, A. 2042
Miller, Clyde M. 1471
Miller, D. Gary 2553
Miller, G. I. 2808
Miller, John W. 1472
Miller, Patrick D., Jr. 2809, 2946
Millet, Nicholas B. 2230
Mills, Watson E. 1473
Milne, Pamela J. 1474–1475
Minc, Rachel 1476–1477
Mink, Hans-Aage 1478
Minkoff, Harvey 1479
Miquell, Violetta 39
Miscall, Peter D. 1480
Mishali, Ajalah 2348
Mitchell, Mike 1481
Mitchell, Sarah 737
Mittwoch, H. 1482
Möbius, H. 101
Molin, G. 1483
Mollenkott, Virginia R. 459–460,1484
Moltmann, Jürgen 1485
Moncure, John 1486
Mondersohn, Ernst 461
Monlobou, Louis 1487
Moor, Johannes C. de 2810–2814
Moore, Carey A. 462, 1488–1490
Moorey, P. R. S. 2554
Morag, S. 1491
Moran, William L. 2555, 2815
Moreno, Antonio C. 1492–1493
Morey, Ann-Janine 1494
Morgenstern, Julian 1495–1496
Morlan, Gail 1497
Morrison, Martha A. 1498, 2726
Morton, Henry Cnova Vollam 463
Mosca, Paul G. 1499
Moscati, S. 102, 184, 2876–2878
Motyer, J. A. 1500
Moyer, J. C. 2686
Mulder, Martin Jay 1503
Mulier, Stockton 1504
Müller, Hans Wolfgang 2043
Müller, Hans-Peter 464, 1501

Müller, Iris 1502
Mulliken, Frances Hartman 465
Mullo-Weir, C. J. 1505
Münster, Maria 2044
Muntingh, L. H. 1506
Muntingh, L. M. 2816, 2648
Murnion, P. J. 1507
Murphy, Roland E. 1508–1513
Murray, D. F. 1514
Murray, Margaret Alice 2045
Musgrave, Peggy 466
Mussell, Mary-Louis 1515
Myśliwiec, Leslaw 2231
Myers, A. E. 1516

Naaman, N. 103
Naar, Karl J. 185
Nadel, M. 1517
Nagy, Antal 1518
Nakata, I. 2649–2650
Naor, M. 1519
Nashef, K. 2556
Naveh, Joseph 2947
Neal, Hazel G. 467
Neef, Heinz-Dieter 1520
Neff, R. W. 1521, 1987
Neher, A. 1522
Nel, Philip 1523
Nestle, Eb 1524
Neu, Rainer 1525
Neufeld, Ephraim 468
Neveu, Louis 469, 1526
Newberry, P. E. 2232
Newman, Murray L. 1527
Newsom, Carol A. 470
Nichol, Charles Ready 471
Nickels, Peter 1528
Nicol, George G. 1529–1530
Niditch, Susan 472, 1531–1534
Nielsen, Eduard 1535–1537
Nims, C. 2233–2234
Niwinski, Andrzey 2235
Nord, D. 2236
Nörr, D 2557
Nowell, Irene 1538–1539
Nunnally-Cox, Janice 474
Nur el-Din, M. A. 1540, 2237

O'Callaghan, Martin 1541
O'Connell, Robert H. 1542
O'Connor, Kathleen M. 1543
O'Connor, M. 1544
O'Day, Gail 1545

O'Faolain, Julian 40
O'Reilly, Bernard 475
O'Rourke, John J. 1546
O'Shea, W. J. 1547
Oberhuber, Karl 2558
Ochshorn, Judith 41, 476
Ockenga, Harold J. 477–478
Oded, B. 2238
Oden, R. A., Jr. 53, 2948
Oduyoye, Modupe 479
Oelsner, J 2559
Oettinger, N. 2687
Oezgüç, N. 2688
Offord, Joseph 2949
Ogden, Graham S. 1548
Ogdon, J. R. 2239–2240
Ohler, A. 480
Okure, Teresa 1549
Oliver, Dennis 1550
Olyan, Saul 1551–1552, 1988,
    2950–2951
Oppenheim, A. L. 2560
Ord, D. R. 289
Oren, Elyashiv 1553–1554
Orthmann, W. 2689
Osiek, Carolyn 1555–1558
Otten, H. 2690–2691
Otto, E. 1559
Ottosson, Magnus 1560
Otwell, John H. 481
Ouellette, L. 1561
Owen, D. I. 2561–2562

Pagels, Elaine 482
Palmer, B. 483
Palmer, M. S. 2046
Papayiannopoulos, Ioannis 1562
Paradise, J. S. 2727–2730
Pardee, D. 1563, 2817–2819
Pardes, Ilana 484
Parijs, Paul van 1564
Parker, Margaret 1565
Parker, S. B. 1566–1569, 2820–
    2821
Parnas, Moshe 1570, 2822
Parpola, S. 2563
Parr, P. A. 2564
Parrot, A. 2651
Patai, Raphael 368, 485–486, 2952
Paterson, J. 1571
Paton, Lewis Bayles 1572
Patrich, Yosef 2241
Patte, Daniel 487

Patterson, Richard D. 1573
Paul, Shalom M. 488, 1574–1576
Payne, J. Barton 1577
Pease, Alice Campbell 489
Pedersen, Johannes 490
Peet, T. E. 2117, 2242
Peifer, Claude J. 1578
Peirce, F. X. 1579
Peradotto, John 42
Perdu, Olivier 2243
Perdue, Leo G. 349
Perera, S. B. 2349
Peritz, I. J. 1580
Perkins, Pheme 1581
Perlman, Alice 2953
Perrot, Jean 186
Perugni, Cesare 1582
Pestman, P. W. 2047, 2201, 2244–2245
Petermann, Ina 1583
Peters, Norbert 491
Petersen, David L. 1584–1585
Petrozzi, M. 1586
Pettey, Richard J. 2954
Pettinato, G. 2350
Pfeiffer, R. H. 2731
Pfister, Herta 492
Pfluger, K. 2246
Phillips, Anthony 493, 1587–1591
Phillips, John A. 494
Philotea, M. 1592
Phipps, William E. 495, 1593–1596
Pillet, Marice 2247
Pinch, G. 2048, 2248
Pinches, Theophilus G 2565
Pintore, Franco 2049
Piper, Otto A. 496
Piper, Vera Lydia 2955
Pirenne, J. 1597, 2249
Pitt-Rivers, Julian 497
Plaskow, Judith 498, 1598
Platt, Elizabeth Ellen 1599
Plaut, W. G. 499, 1600
Plautz, W. 1601–1603, 1989
Plum, Karin Friis 1604–1605
Pobee, John S. 500
Podella, Thomas 187
Poethig, E. B 1990
Pogrebin, Letty Cottin 1606
Pollock, S. 2566
Polzin, Robert 501–502, 1607

Pomeroy, Sarah B. 2856
Pompanio, F. 2567
Pope, Marvin H. 1608, 1707, 2823
Porada, Edith 2732
Porten, B. 1609, 2301–2306
Porter, J. R. 1610
Porter, Joshua 503
Posner-Krieger, P. 2250
Postgate, J. N. 2320, 2568
Poulssen, N. 1611–1612
Powell, Marvin A. 105
Power, E. 1613
Praag, A. van 2351
Press, R. 1614
Preston, James J. 504
Previn, Dory 1615
Price, Eugenia 505
Priest, John 1616
Prince, J. Dyneley 1617
Pritchard, J. B. 188–189
Pritchard, Linda 1618
Puech, E. 1619, 2879

Qimron, Elisha 1620
Quitslund, S. 1621

Rabinowitz, Isaac 1622
Rabinowitz, J. J. 106, 2251, 2307
Radday, Y. T. 1623
Radwan, A. 2252
Rae, Hugh Rose 1624
Rainey, Anson F. 2824–2826
Rak, Y. 130
Rallis, Irene Kerasote 1625
Ramingo, Ida 1502
Rammant-Peeters, Agnes 2253
Ramras-Rauch, Gila 1626
Ramsey, George W. 1627
Rand, Herbert 1628
Ranke, Hermann 2017
Rapaport, D. I. 1629
Rashid, Fawzi 190
Rast, Walter E. 1630
Ratié, A. 2050
Ratner, Robert 1631
Rattray, Susan 1632
Rauh, S. 1991
Raurell, Frederic 506–507, 1633–1635
Ravenna, A. 1636
Read, D. 1638
Rebera, Basil 1637

Redford, D. R. 508, 2051, 2254
Reed, William L. 2956
Rehm, Martin 1639
Reid, S. B. 1640
Reif, S. C. 1641
Reik, Theodor 509
Reiner, Erica 2569–2572
Reines, H. S. 1642
Reiser, Elfriede 2052
Reiser, W. 510
Reisman, Daniel 2573
Rembold, Annette 1643
Remy, Nahida 511
Rémy, P. 107
Renaud, Bernard 1644–1645
Rendsburg, Gary A. 1646–1647
Renger, J. 108, 2574–2577
Rénie, J. 2578
Reviv, Hanoch 513
Reymond, Robert L. 1648
Rice, Gene 1649
Richards, Alberta Rae 514
Richardson, H. Neil 2827
Richter, Hans-Friedemann 1650
Ridout, G. 1651
Riefstahl, Elizabeth 2255–2256
Rigaux, B. 1652–1654
Ringe, Sharon H. 470
Ringgren, Helmer 109, 1655–1656
Ritchie, Maureen 43
Ritterspach, A. D. 1657
Robbins, Gregory Allen 515
Roberts, J. J. M. 2352
Robertson, Noel 1658
Robins, Gay 2053, 2257–2259
Robinson, Bernhard P. 1659
Robinson, Ira 1660–1661
Roccati, A. 2260
Rodd, Cyril S. 1662
Roddy, Lee 516
Roellenbleck, E. 517
Rofé, Alexander 518, 1664–1668
Rogerson, J. W. 519
Rohrlich, R. 2579
Röllig, W. 2580
Rolston, H. 520
Romaniuk, Kazimierz 521
Römer, W. H. Ph 110, 1663,
    2581–2582, 2652
Romero, Joan A. 498
Rosaldo, M. Z. 44
Rosenberg, David 522

Rosenberg, Joel W. 1669–1670
Rosenberg, Z. 523
Rosenzweig, Michael L. 1671
Rost, L. 524
Roth, Martha T. 2353, 2583–2587
Roth, Wolfgang W. 1672
Rothe, Rosa M. 1673
Rothschild, Max M. 1674
Rottenberg, Meir 1675–1676
Rouillard, H. 1677
Rowley, H. H. 1678–1679
Rozner, Fred 1680
Rudolph, W. 1681–1682
Ruether, Rosemary 1683–1685
Rummel, T. S. 2828
Ruppert, Lothar 1686
Rusche, Helga 525
Russell, Letty M. 526–529, 1687
Rylaarsdam, J. Coert 1688

Sack, Ronald H. 2588
Sacon, Kiyoshi K. 1689
Sadakata, H. 1690
Sadgrove, M. 1691
Sagan, Carl 1692
Saggs, H. W. F. 2354–2356
Sakenfeld, Katherine Doob 530,
    1693–1698
Salkin, Jeffrey K. 1699
Salts, Margaret 465
Salvoni, F. 531, 1700–1701, 2261–
    2263,
Samson, J. 2054
San Nicolò, M. 2589
Sander-Hansen, C. E. 2055
Sangster, Margaret Elizabeth 532
Sanmartín, J. 2766
Saporetti, Claudio 2357–2358
Sapp, S. 533, 1702
Sarna, Nahum M. 1703–1705
Sasson, Jack M. 534, 1608, 1706–
    1711, 2590, 2653
Sasson, Victor 1712
Satzinger, Helmut 2264
Saucy, R. L. 1713
Sauge, Kirsten 1714
Sauren, H. 2591
Saussy, Carroll 535
Saviv, S. 1715
Sawyer, John F. A. 1716
Sayce, Archibald Henry 111, 2592
Scanzoni, Letha 536, 1717–1718
Schäfer, P. W. 537

Scharbert, J. 1719
Schechter, Solomon 1720
Scheil, J. V. 2359, 2593
Schelkle, Karl Hermann 538
Schenker, Adrian 1721
Scheppes, David 539
Schierling, Marla J. 1722
Schildenberger, J. 1723–1726
Schilling, Othmar 540
Schipflinger, Th. 112
Schley, D. C. 541
Schlossman, Betty L. 191
Schmandt-Besserat, Denise 2360
Schmid, Herbert 1727
Schmidt, Anne 1728
Schmidt, Eva Renate 542
Schmidt, Klaus 1729
Schmitt, John J. 1729–1735
Schmitz, Bettina 192
Schneeman, Gisela 1992
Schorr, M. 2361
Schoske, Sylvia 2056
Schott, S. 2265
Schottroff, Luise 543, 552, 1736–
 1737
Schottroff, Willy 543
Schrage, Wolfgang 357
Schretter, Manfred K. 113
Schroeder, Otto 2594
Schroer, Silvia 544
Schulman, A. R. 2266
Schult, H. 957
Schulze, Peter H. 2057
Schunck, Klaus-Dietrich 1746
Schüngel-Straumann, Helen 545,
 1738–1741
Schüssler Fiorenza, Elisabeth 546,
 1742–1745
Schwartz, B. J. 1747
Seebass, H. 1748–1754
Segal, J. B. 1755
Segal, M. H. 1756
Seger, Joe D. 193
Segert, Stanislav 1757–1758
Seibert, Ilse 114
Sell, Henry Thorne 547
Selman, M. J. 1759
Selms, A. van 1760, 2829–2830
Seltman, Charles 45
Sephati, Y. 2362, 2595
Serra, Aristide 1761
Shanks, Hershel 194

Shapira, D. S. 1762
Sharp, D. B. 1763, 1993
Shashar, M. 1764
Sheres, Ita 548
Sherlock, P. 1765
Shideler, M. M. 1766
Shout, W. R. 1994
Shrager, Miriam Y. 1767
Siebert-Hommes, J. C. 1768
Siegel, Bernard J. 2363
Sigrist, Marcel 2364
Silver, Morris 115
Silverman, D. P. 2267
Simms, Tom 1769
Simon, Uriel 1770–1771
Simpson, W.K. 2016, 2058, 2268–
 2269
Singer, Ithamar 2692
Sjöberg, Åke W. 1772, 2596–2597
Ska, Jean-Louis 1773–1775
Skaist, A. 2365, 2733
Sladek, W. R. 2366
Smelik, K. A. D. 1776
Smith, H. S 2270–2271
Smith, Joyce Marie 549
Smith, Judith Florence 550
Smith, Mark S. 551, 2957
Snaith, N. H. 1777–1778
Soden, W. von 1779–1780, 2598
Soggin, J. A. 1780–1783
Soldt, W. H. van 2831
Sole, Francesco 1784
Soleh, A. 1785
Soleil, Brigitte 2367
Sölle, Dorothee 552
Song, Theo 553
Souza, Luís de 1786
Spalinger, A. 2272
Speiser, E. A. 1787–1788, 2731,
 2734–2735
Sperling, D. S. 2880
Spiegelberg, W. 2273
Sprague, William Buell 554
Spreafico, Ambrogio 1789
Spring, Anita 28
Spycket, A. 116, 195, 2599–2600
Stager, L. 196
Stamm, J. J. 1790
Stanton, Elizabeth Cady 555
Starke, F. 2693
Starr, Lee Anna 556
Staton, Julia 557

Stavnik, É. 2274
Stecher, Reinhold 1791
Steck, O. H. 558
Stedman, R. C. 559
Steele, Eliza R. 560
Steffgen, U. 192
Steinberg, Naomi 1792
Steiner, F. 1793
Steinkeller, P. 2601–2602
Steinmueller, John C. 1794
Stendahl, Krister 561
Stern, Ephraim 197
Sternberg, Meir 562, 1024
Stevens, John M. 2275
Steyn, J. 1795
Stinespring, W. F. 1796
Stitzinger, Michael F. 1797
Stockton, E. D. 1798
Stohlman, St. C. 2736
Stol, M. 2368, 2603
Stolz, Fritz 1799
Stone, E. C. 2604
Stone, Merlin 46, 563
Stowe, Harriet E. Beecher 564
Stradling, F. S. 1995
Strauss, Joseph 1800
Streefkerk, Nic 1801
Strenge, John H. 117
Strika, F. I. 118
Strus, Andrzej 565
Stuart, Susan M. 14
Stuhlmueller, Carroll 1802
Stulman, Louis 1803–1804
Sudlow, Elizabeth W. 566
Sullivan, J. P. 42
Surberg, Raymond F. 1805
Swanston, H. F. G. 1806
Swartley, Willard M. 567
Swidler, Leonard J. 568–569, 1807
Swiggers, P. 2851
Szlechter, E. 2605
Szubin, H. Z 2305–2306

Tadmor, Miriam 126, 198–199
Taha, Munir Yousif 200
Taitz, Emily 26
Tallqvist, Knut 2369
Tamez, Elsa 1808
Tångberg, K. Arvid 1809–1810
Tanner, R. 2276–2277
Taylor, A. B. 1811
Taylor, J. Glen 201, 1812
Teachout, R. P. 1996

Tefnin, R. 2059
Terrien, Samuel 570, 1813–1814
Teubal, Savina J. 571–572
Thausing, G. 2060
Théoridès, A. 2278–2280
Thiel, Hans Jochem 2727
Thomas, Edward 119
Thomas, Metta Newman 573
Thompson, D. 1818
Thompson, Henry Adams 574
Thompson, J. A. 1815–1816
Thompson, Lucy Gertsch 575
Thompson, Michael E. W. 1817
Thompson, Th. 1818
Thompson, W. I. 2370
Thompson, Yaakov 1819
Thorbjørnsrud, Berit 2606
Thyen, H. 296
Tigay, Jeffrey H. 2958
Tijn, M. van 1820
Tillion, Germaine 576
Tinney, Ethel 577
Tischler, Nancy Marie Patterson 578
Toeg, A. 1821
Tolbert, Mary 579, 1822–1823
Toorn, Karel van der 1824–1826
Tosato, Angelo 580, 1827–1829
Toueir, Kassem 202
Tournay, Raymond Jacques 581, 1830
Trible, Phyllis 582–584, 1472, 1831–1847
Trigger, Bruce 2061
Tropper, J. 1677
Troy, Lana 2062, 2281–2282
Tsevat, M. 1848, 1849, 2694, 2832–2833
Tsimariyon, Tsemah 1850
Tsmudi, Yosef 1851
Tucker, Gene M. 1852
Tucker, N. 1853
Türck, U. 2308
Turner, Mary Donovan 1854
Turnham, Timothy J. 1855–1856
Tuya, Manuel de 1857

Ubell, Lori 1858
Uehlinger, Christoph 2926
Ullendorff, Edward 1859
Utzschneider, Helmut 585, 1860
Uys, P. H. de V. 1861

Vadé, Y. 2882
Valbelle, D. 2309, 2063
Valloggia, M 2283
Van Buren, E. Douglas 2607–2608
Van Dijk, J. J. 2331
van Dijk-Hemmes, Fokkelien 232
Van Gemeren, Willem A. 1862
van Ginneken, Grietje 232
Van Selms, A. 1863
Van Seters, John 1864–1865, 2453
Van Wolde, E. J. 587
Vande, S. J. 1881
Vander Velde, Frances 588
Vandier, J. 203, 2284
Vanel, Jean 589
Vanstiphout, H. I. J. 2609
Vasholz, P. Ivan 1866
Vaux, Roland de 120, 590
Vawter, Bruce 2834
Veenhof, K. R. 2610
Veijola, T. 1867
Velde, H. te 2285
Veldhuis, Niek 2611
Vellanickal, Matthew 1868
Vendrame, C. 1869
Verkhovskoy, Serge 1870
Verner, Miroslav 2286
Viberg, Åke 591
Vickrey, J. F. 1871
Villiers, D. W. de 1872
Visser 't Hooft, Willem Adolph 592
Vittmann, G. 2287
Vogels, Walter 1873–1875
Vonier, Anscar 593
Vos, Clarence J. 594
Voterra, E. 2310

Wacker, Marie-Therese 595–596
Wadsworth, Tom 1876
Wäfler, M. 2672
Wagner, W. H. 1877
Wahrmund, Ludwig 47
Wakeman, Mary K. 48, 1878, 2612–2613
Waldbaum, Jane 2673
Waldman, Nahum M. 1879
Walker, Barbara G. 597
Walker, Christopher 2695
Walker, Norman 1880
Wallace, Howard N. 598, 2959
Walle, B. van de 2288
Walle, R. 1881

Walsh, Jerome T. 1882
Walter, K. 601
Walter, Karin 599–600
Walters, Stanley D. 1883, 2614
Waltke, B. K. 1884
Wander, Nathaniel 1885
Ward, William A. 2064–2065, 2289–2292, 2835
Wartenberg-Potter, Barbel von 500
Watson, W. G. E. 1886, 2836–2837
Webb, B.-G. 602
Weber, S. C. 1887
Webster, Edwin C. 1888
Weder, H. 1889
Weeks, Noel 1890
Weems, Renita J. 603, 1891
Wegner, I. 2696
Weidner, Ernst F. 2615–2616
Weigle, M. 2617
Weiher, E. von 2371
Weiler, Gerda 604–605, 1892
Weinfeld, M. 606, 1893–1895, 2618, 2960
Weingreen, J. 1896
Weisberg, David. B. 2619–2620
Weiser, Asher 1897
Weisman, Ze'ev 1898–1899
Weiss, Harvey 204
Weitenmeyer, M. 1900
Welch, G. W. 1623
Weld, Horatio H 607
Wenham, G. J. 608, 1901–1905
Wenig, Stephen 2066
Wente, Edward F. 2067
Werbrouck, Marcelle 2068
Werner, Hazen G. 609
Wesselius, J. W. 1906–1907
West, Angela 1908
West, Stuart A. 1909–1910
Westbrook, R. 610–611, 1911–1913, 2372, 2621
Westendorf, Wolfhart 2293
Westenholz, A. 2559, 2623
Westenholz, Joan Goodnick 1914, 2622–2623
Westermann, Claus 612
Westermarck, E. 49
Wharton, James A. 1915
Whatham, Arthur E. 1916
Whedbee, J. William 1001
Wheeler, C. B. 1073

Wheeler, P. 2553
Whit, William D. 2961
White, Ernest 1917
White, Hugh C. 1918
White, J. B. 613, 1997
Whitelan, Keith W. 1919
Whybray, R. N. 614
Wickham, L. R. 1920
Wieth-Knudsen, K. A. 50
Wifall, Walter 1921
Wiggins, Steve A. 2962
Wijk-Bos, Johanna van 615
Wijngaarden, W. D. van 616
Wilcke, Claus 2624–2625
Wildeboer, G. 1922
Wildung, Dietrich 2056
Willemaers, N. 2626
Willi-Plein, I. 1923
Williams, Ellen Reeder 205
Williams, James G. 617, 1924–1925
Willis, J. T. 1926–1928
Wilson, Elizabeth 618
Winlock, H. E. 2069–2071, 2294
Winter, Alice Ames 51
Winter, Irene J. 206
Winter, Urs 619
Wiseman, D. J. 1929
Wolff, Hans Walter 620–621
Wolkstein, Diane 2373
Wöller, Ulrich 1930
Wolmarans, H. P. 1931
Wolters, Al 1932–1933
Woodrow, Ralph 622
Worden, T. 1934–1935
Wormser-Migot, Olga 52
Wright, C. J. H. 1936
Wright, David P. 623
Wright, G. E. 1937

Wright, G. R. H. 1938
Wurmnest, Karl F. 624
Wyatt, N. 1939–1941, 2838–2839

Xella, P. 2842

Yakar, Jak 207
Yamashita, Tadanori 2963
Yamauchi, Edwin M. 1942–1943
Yankovskaya, N. B. 2737–2738
Yaron, Reuven 1944–1946, 2374, 2627–2629, 2840
Yee, Gale A. 1947–1950
Yeivin, S. 1951
Yoshikoka, Barbara 1952
Young, Dwight W. 2841
Yoyotte, Jean 2295–2296
Yubero, Galindo D. 1953

Zabkar, L. V. 2297
Zadok, Ran 2375
Zagarell, A. 2630
Zakovitch, Yair 1954–1957
Zalcman, Lawrence 1958
Zalevsky, S. 1959
Zappone, Katherine E. 1960
Zelechow, Bernard 1961
Zevit, Ziony 2964
Ziderman, I. Irving 1962
Ziegenaus, Anton 1963
Ziegler, Christiane 2298
Zimmerman, C. L. 1964
Zimmern, H. 2631
Zingg, E. 1965–1966
Zipor, Moshe 1967–1969
Ziv, Y. 1970
Zivie, Alain-Pierre 208
Zschokke, Hermann 625
Zyl, A. H. van 1971

Aahmès-Henuttamehu 2125
Abiah 1970
Abigail 684, 723, 1294, 1350
Abishag 695, 937, 1503
abortion 1379, 1809, 1810
Achsah 1499
adoption 2076, 2077, 2111, 2160,
    2416, 2701, 2716, 2722, 2736
adoption, matrimonial 2399, 2700
adornment 622
adultery 87, 1035, 1377, 1378,
    1415, 1590, 1803, 2138, 2251,
    2456, 2496, 2584, 2627, 2817
adultery metaphor 1032, 1314
adultery motif 1986
agnate marriage 713
Agur 1042
Ahat-milki 2795
Ahhotep 2100, 2101, 2281
Ahmes Merytamon 2101
Ahmes-Néfertary 2168, 2227,
    2228, 2168
Ahmes Satamon 2103
Akkadian 1824
Alalakh 100, 103
alien wives 1192
Amorites 2633, 2645
Anat(h) 56, 136, 137, 923, 935,
    1328, 1467, 1812, 2134, 2260,
    2762, 2767, 2772, 2775, 2776,
    2785, 2796, 2797, 2839, 2884,
    2885, 2989, 2890, 2935
Anat Epic (Ugarit) 2749, 2828
Anatolia 168, 169, 183, 185, 2530,
    2540; see also Hittites
ancestress in danger see wife-sister
    motif
Ancient Near East 53–208, 1451,
    1498, 1759, 1865
angry housewife 2561
Annu (deity) 2650
annunciation 650; see also birth
    announcement
anti-feminism 50
anti-Semitism 1606; see also
    feminist hermeneutics and

Judaism
Anūna 2520
Aqhat 2805, 2821
art, Egyptian 1091
Asenath 508, 1368
Asherah 2763, 2834, 2883–2964
Ashtoreth 699, 1812, 2780, 2812,
    2860
Assyria 1677, 2653, 2568, 2611
Assyrian contracts 2430
Astarte 197, 693, 939, 2134, 2162,
    2179, 2864, 2865, 2868, 2870,
    2874, 2879, 2881, 2899, 2906,
    2918, 1953
Athaliah 430, 711, 1270, 1619,
    1728
Athtart see Ashtoreth
Atiratu 2863, 2909, 2932
Atrahasis 2394, 2439, 2492
Aya (goddess) 2411

Baal-Mot Epic 2804
Baalat-Milk 2860
Baba (goddess) 2458, 2480
Babylonia 111, 2932; see also
    Mesopotamia; Neo-Babylonia
Baketamnum (princess) 2129
barren 820, 1004, 1924
barren wife 272, 700, 963, 1184,
    1439, 2453
Bat (Egyptian goddess) 2145
Bathsheba 520, 684, 695, 723,
    877, 899, 1028, 1082, 1083,
    1350, 1356, 1382, 1530, 1770,
    1915, 1919
Beena marriage 1495
Beersheva 186
betrothal 1067,1924
biblical narrative 217, 227–229,
    235, 243, 254, 297, 334, 338,
    339, 398, 400, 410, 432, 433,
    440, 617, 675, 688, 740, 741,
    742, 766, 861, 862, 988, 996,
    999, 1026, 1066, 1067–1070,
    1086, 1164, 1165, 1211, 1254,
    1294, 1353, 1407, 1514, 1551,
    1689, 1725, 1770, 1771, 1785,

1954, 1956, 1957
bibliography 5, 43, 89, 244, 549,
    2869
bigamy 2624
Bilhah 1271, 1345, 1529
birth 2603, 2611, 2675
birth announcement 1569, 1987
birth ceremonies 2158
birth control 1884, 2492
birth promises 2570
birth rituals 2656, 2657
birth scenes 2247
breast feeding 71, 148, 1161
brideprice 2715
bridewealth 2457

caesarian section 2560
Cain's wife 1916, 1940
capital punishment 7
career woman 566, 590, 825
celibacy 833
Chentkaue 2088
childbirth 771, 1473; see also
    obstetrics
Cleopatra 2054
cobra goddess 2030
coiffure 2072, 2164, 2599,
communication 96
conception 1309
concubine 1108, 2132, 2591
concubine at Gibeah 219, 403,
    583, 673
consanguineous
    marriage 2115, 2135
consecration of women 60
copulation, terms for 1575
covenant 1017, 1451
covenant as marriage metaphor
    1972
covenant code 1014
creation and cosmology 63, 69,
    257, 358, 509, 540, 545, 558,
    598, 627, 1509, 1723, 1870,
    2319, 2394
creation of woman 943, 1012,
    1444, 1546, 1934, 2382
cultic organization 2183
cultic roles of women 25, 28, 68,
    412, 438, 594, 754, 793, 805,
    806, 1054, 1417, 1580, 1417,
    1580, 1720, 1926, 1988, 2533,
    2535, 2663, 2800
cuneiform evidence 1825

Cushite woman 889, 954, 955,
    1750
Cyprus 1658

Dahanunzu 2140
Dame Wisdom see Lady Wisdom
dance 2008, 2542
dancing girl 1359
dancing women 667, 2542, 2543
Darius's daughter 2845
daughter as metaphor 1548
daughter of Cheops 2127
daughter of goddess 108, 112
daughter of Shua 1647
daughter (of) Zion 849, 1037,
    1127, 1266, 1796
daughters as sons 2728, 2750
daughters of Job 719, 722
daughters of Judah 1213
daughters of Zelophehad 718–720,
    1597, 1696, 1698, 1778, 1896
David's concubines 1330
David's wives 739, 1278, 1351
dawn goddess 141
Dea Syria see goddess, Syrian
Deborah I 953, 1646
Deborah II 230, 632, 897, 903,
    1080, 1129, 1302, 1410, 1432,
    1673, 1729; see also Judg. 5
deception 1169, 1592
Delilah 292, 1430, 1431, 1711,
    1757
desertion 1571, 2458
Dinah 497, 548, 670, 845, 934,
    983, 1024, 1088, 1153, 1271,
    1279, 1284, 1285, 1345, 1391,
    1640, 1699, 1703, 1909, 1941
diplomatic marriage 2266, 2579
divorce 93, 218, 608, 1065, 1103,
    1217, 1222, 1226, 1267, 1547,
    1571, 1603, 1682, 1719, 1821,
    1902, 1944, 2310, 2365, 2434,
    2529, 2557, 2610, 2840,
dowry 1866, 2306, 2404, 2586,
    2587, 2715
Drehem 2490
Dumuzu 2326, 2362; see also
    Tammuz
dying god 1657

Ebla 180, 204, 205
economy 92, 105, 115
Eden 1322, 1325, 1331, 1670,

2959
education 908
Egypt 3, 33, 34, 89, 106, 111, 765,
    1039, 1112, 1998–2298, 2476
Egyptian wife of Solomon 1137,
    1138, 1397, 1769
Ehli-Nikkalu 2743
El-'Uzza (Egyptian goddess) 2241
Elam 106, 116, 2853
Elam and Persia 2843–2856
Elephantine 2299–2310
Emar 54, 82, 1221
enchantress 2108
endogamy/exogamy 772, 786,
    2135, 2575
Enheduanna 347, 2597, 2617
Enki 1456
Enkidu 1388
entu-priestess 2551, 2705
erēbu marriage 2711
Ereshkigal 2334, 2491
eros 1385
Esarhaddon's queen 2516
Eshnunna Code 2374, 2627
Eshnunna Code #25 2628
Eshnunna Code #59 2420, 2498
Esther 420, 832, 901, 902, 1050,
    1177, 1228, 1321, 1410, 1420,
    1881
Esther, fast of 1446
Eve 91, 220, 257, 282, 309, 413,
    494, 509, 515, 540, 545, 558,
    598, 652, 668, 832, 969, 1196,
    1201, 1242, 1287, 174, 1526,
    1546, 1596, 1761, 1772, 1820,
    1871, 1880, 1953, 2488, 2578
exclusion of women 1375
Ezra 839
Ezra's marriage reform 772; see
    also alien wives

fall of humankind 933
family 98, 196, 293, 303, 315,
    485, 503, 553, 609, 611, 624,
    1084, 1100, 1662, 1870, 1897,
    2078, 2116, 2357, 2446, 2447,
    2524, 2620, 2625, 2648, 2737,
    2738, 2777, 2810, 2822, 2825,
    2829, 2855
family archives 2318, 2412, 2723,
    2724, 2726
family law 611, 1014, 1059, 1587,
    1589, 1667, 1936, 1965, 1966,

1991, 2479, 2606, 2621, 2721,
    2734
family life 1968
family structures 1632
father's brother's daughter marriage
    1885
fecundity figures 2001
female correspondence (letters)
    2634, 2641, 2652, 2739, 2746,
    2757, 2759, 2760, 2766, 2789,
    2792, 2817, 2827
female cult figurines 199
female literacy 2109
female metaphor 1605
female roles 396
female weavers 2538
feminine geographical names 1758
feminine takes precedence syntagm
    1631
feminine titles (Egyptian) 2000,
    2064, 2065, 2110, 2148, 2159,
    2163, 2180, 2210, 235
feminist biblical scholarship, history
    of 701, 1479, 1717, 1718; see
    also Woman's Bible
feminist hermeneutics 210, 212,
    213, 244, 286, 298, 302, 307,
    317, 327, 333, 336, 343, 348,
    372, 380, 420, 421, 434, 445,
    470, 458, 472, 474, 476, 484,
    500, 512, 526–530, 535, 536,
    542, 552, 555, 568–572, 579,
    582–584, 603, 654, 676, 745,
    870, 881, 905, 998, 1021,
    1072, 1093, 1147, 1168, 1181,
    1182, 1200, 1256, 1286, 1323,
    1331, 1375, 1398, 1465, 1474,
    1484, 1485, 1556, 1557, 1558,
    1643, 1684, 1693, 1694, 1696,
    1717, 1718, 1742–1745, 1813,
    1814, 1822, 1823, 1831–1847,
    1908, 1960
feminist hermeneutics and Judaism
    1071, 1266, 1606, 1892, 1985;
    see also anti-Semitism
feminist hermeneutics, critique of
    1468, 1472
fertility 968
fertility cult 804, 1273, 1328,
    1440, 1938, 1994
fertility goddess 2921
forbidden mixtures 838

foreign woman (Prov. 1–9) 1949
foreign women 361, 1375, 1661, 1674
Fowler and His Wife 2379, 2381
free Ugaritic female 2816
freeborn daughters, sale of 1450

gender 1041, 1063, 1085, 1092, 1460, 1461, 1605, 1792
gender, grammatical 694, 738
gender-matched parallelism 738, 1886, 2837
gender of ancient Israel 1730, 1733
gender roles 1792
Genesis Apocryphon 1894, 1895
genitals, terms for 1422; see also vagina
Geshtinanna 2383
gestation 2202, 2226
Gilgamesh 685, 1388, 2376, 2388, 2475, 2486, 2553, 2606
God as Woman 260, 298, 320, 380, 460, 535, 563, 592, 619, 726, 802, 808, 1090, 1264, 1311, 1740, 1741
goddess(es) 41, 73, 78, 84, 101, 102, 116, 118, 138, 140, 142, 151, 154, 157, 163, 169, 170, 172, 174, 188, 203, 207, 347, 486, 595, 941, 2096, 2158, 2193, 2196, 2216, 2225, 2231, 2239, 2285, 2335, 2349, 2369, 2389, 2414, 2553, 2615, 2647, 2649, 2655, 2658, 2661, 2667, 2670, 2673, 2678, 2683, 2685, 2689, 2740–2742, 2779, 2784, 2810, 2857, 2862, 2867, 2946
goddess in the window 2631
goddess Segal 59
goddess, Syrian 53, 2921
goddesses of love 79
goddesses of music 2192
"the great sin" 2251, 2815
Gomer 234, 246, 620, 693, 702, 1133, 1874, 1891
gynecology 214, 1309, 2275

Hadassah 1321
Hagar 583, 648, 732, 864, 869, 985, 1043, 1101, 1124, 1170, 1272, 1370, 1407, 1439, 1751, 1808, 1843, 1855, 1918

hairdressers 2256
Hamurappi, Code of 2322, 2533, 2535, 2574
Hamurappi Code #142/143 2410, 2426
handmaid 872, 1015
Hannah 640, 641, 650, 654, 698, 885, 1004, 1045, 1296, 1302, 1349, 1545, 1883, 1913, 1958, 1971
Harab 2336
harem 2052, 2207, 2236, 2290, 2616
harem conspiracy 2174
harem investigation 2172
harlot see prostitution
Hathor 2091, 2159
Hatshepsut 2050, 2059, 2113, 2178, 2233, 2296
helpmeet 1282, 1455, 1873
hem of the garment 1315
Henut 2256
hieros gamos see sacred marriage
hippopotamus goddess 2286
Hittite(s) 75, 940, 1849, , 2654–2696, 2743
Hittite Laws #197–198, 2694
Hnwt 2211
Hoglah 978
Huldah 511, 856, 1188, 1380, 1425, 1597, 1616, 1807, 1842
Hurrian(s) 1505, 2665, 2672, 2697–2738; see also Nuzi

image of God 387, 404, 752, 948, 1055, 1215, 1457, 1621
image of woman in the Bible 1135
impurity of women 879, 2686
Inanna 2327, 2331, 2362, 2366, 2373, 2378, 2421, 2441, 2461, 2477, 2483, 2499, 2506, 2509, 2536, 2580, 2597, 2609
Inanna and Enki 2327, 2380
Inanna and the Numun Plant 2506
Inanna's Descent 2366, 2421, 2483, 2499, 2532
incest 81, 749, 2094
inclusive language 1694
industry in Israel 1815
infertility 2811; see also barren wife
inheritance 57, 611, 717, 719, 720, 722, 836, 930, 2727,

2728, 2786
inheritance by daughters 55, 717–
720; see also daughters as sons
Innin 2444
Inti (Egyptian princess) 2224
intermarriage 878, 879, 1103,
1222
Inu 2256
Ishmael 1855
Ishtar 88, 103, 155, 1128, 2311,
2326, 2349, 2376, 2477, 2491,
2523, 2530, 2537, 2572, 2609,
2639, 2644, 2697
Ishtar, Descent of 2491, 2521,
2532
Ishtar-Sad 2528
Ishtar-Shaushga 155, 2626
Ishtarat 2651
Isis (goddess) 2043, 2044, 2177,
2297
Isis (princess) 2288

J 248, 760, 761, 888, 1052, 1388,
1463, 1723
Jabâ 2417
Jael 230, 639, 853, 1129, 1673,
1714
Jephthah's daughter 449, 583, 767,
1000, 1057, 1070, 1224, 1283,
1839, 1841
Jeremiah 1592
jewelry 1600, 2588
Jezebel 252, 384, 774, 784, 1056,
1551, 1567, 1570, 1668, 1726,
1783, 1785, 1900
Jezebel's seal 131
Job 735
Job's wife 1477, 1676
Jochebed 1690

Katimala (Egyptian princess) 2176
Keret 2748, 2754 2821
Khenemet-Nefer-Hedjet 2243
Kheñsa (queen) 2167
Khirbet el-Qom 2915, 2923, 2930,
2941, 2944, 2958, 2964
kinship 963, 1632
kotharot goddesses 2826, 2830
Kiya 2188
Kuntillet 'Ajrud 2891, 2901, 2902,
2907, 2911, 2916, 2929, 2943,
2944, 2945, 2958, 2960

labor 105
Lachish ewer 2920
Lady Wisdom 423, 424, 1327,
1509, 1511, 1543, 1791, 1979
Lahmu-Lahamu 2519
Lama 2600
language, feminist 1058
law and law codes 4, 93, 95, 106,
107, 275–277, 315, 329, 408,
468, 488, 493, 591, 610, 611,
919, 920, 1010, 1014, 1059,
1064, 1216, 1235, 1355, 1377,
1378, 1450, 1451, 1667, 1905,
1936, 1980, 2322, 2323, 2361,
2365, 2372, 2374, 2427, 2479,
2540, 2557, 2577, 2584, 2694
law, Egyptian 2004
law in historical books 715, 716
law in Ruth 704
Leah 574, 952, 965, 1051, 1242,
1271, 1324, 1345, 1347, 1498,
1529, 1964
levirate marriage 428, 660, 713,
919, 930, 1221, 1362, 1426,
1650,
levirate marriage in Assyira 919,
2484
Lilith 1310
Lot's daughters 1018, 1130, 1242,
1395, 1610, 1954
Lot's wife 1304, 1387
love 285, 531, 768, 967, 968,
1020, 1039, 1115, 1120, 1385,
1392, 1538
love goddesses 2481
love poetry 340, 1039, 1582, 1997,
2250, 2362, 2384, 2403, 2429,
2482, 2518, 2595
Luwians 2671, 2693

Ma'adonah 133, 164
Maat 2293
Mafdat 2097
Manoah's wife 292, 644, 1429
manumission see slavery
Marah 1318
mare goddess 2818
Mari 1016, 2632–2653
marriage 30, 38, 47, 49, 61, 100,
209, 267, 315, 322, 369, 370,
444, 468, 486, 496, 553, 580,
608, 624, 819, 922, 992, 1003,

1006–1009, 1084, 1087, 1120,
1146, 1172, 1210, 1248, 1274,
1315, 1366, 1388, 1506, 1547,
1564, 1632, 1642, 1719, 1784,
1827, 1848, 1865, 1917, 1966,
1976, 1984, 1989, 2037, 2047,
2079, 2081, 2083, 2118, 2365,
2583, 2584, 2589, 2648, 2829,
2832, 2852
marriage blessing 1566, 2820
marriage ceremonies (Babylonian)
2454, 2545; see also wedding
ceremonies
marriage contracts 2302, 2303,
2307, 2353, 2455, 2471, 2484,
2729
marriage fidelity 1316
marriage imagery 1982
marriage metaphor 1017, 1173,
1522, 1974
marriage motif 1656
marriage, restoration of 1902,
1912, 1945
marriage to a daughter 2191
matriarch 571, 572, 1277, 1468,
1515
matriarchy 3, 48, 604, 605, 679
matrimonial influence 1445
matrimonial law 468, 2279, 2280,
2351, 2372, 2659
matrimonial property 2047
matrimonial squabbles 2107
matronymic family 916
medicine 256, 483, 2517, 2543,
2560; see also gynecology
medicine, Egyptian 2035, 2119,
2165, 2185, 2275
menstruation 911, 1594, 1629
Merab 165, 1105, 1338
Meresankh III (queen) 2058
Meribaal 717, 720, 1867
Meritamum 2258
Meritamun 2258
Meryet-Amun 2070
Meryet-Nit 2203
Merysankh (queen) 2016
Mesopotamia 1161, 1377, 1378,
1824, 2311–2631
Michal 283, 684, 716, 1105, 1338,
1352, 1371, 1466, 1611, 1806,
1825
Middle Assyrian Laws 1576, 2323,

2629
Law #8 1767
Law #22 1894, 1896
midwife 726
Milkah 1486
Miriam 1048, 1107, 1132, 1318,
1339, 1545, 1572, 1643, 1659,
1690, 1750, 1779, 1844, 1847
Miriam, Song of 917
misogyny 1381, 1423, 1556, 1755
Molech 1777, 1893
monogamy 1313, 1602, 1654,
1682, 2135
Moses's adoptive mother 1690
Moses's wives 1002, 1624
mother 1601, 1729, 1803
mother bereft of children 1266
mother earth 1727
mother goddess 168, 172, 202,
517, 634, 2553, 2558
mother of Apis 2270
mother of Chefren 2129
mother of God 66
mother of Lemuel 957
mother of Rameses II 2252
mother worship 504
motherhood 15, 112, 221, 151,
1069
motherhood of God 726, 802,
1731
mother's first born 798
mother's house 1464
mourning women 158, 159, 187
Mutnodjme 2073
Mwt rmt 2131
Mylitta 1157, 1159, 2478, 2527

Naamah 691, 1034
naked woman motif 2314, 2495
naming of children 1281, 1995,
2675
Nanâ 2387, 2569
Nanna-Suen 2328
Naomi 785, 875, 900, 1123, 1261,
1939
Naunakhte 2114
nazirite 843
Nbt (queen) 2211
Nebt (princess) 2182
necromancer see witch of Endor
necropolis workmen 2199, 2200,
2201, 2245, 2278
Nedebiah 171

Neo-Babylonian 2583–2585, 2589, 2619, 2620
Nefertari 2197
Nefertiti 1998, 2054, 2187, 2253, 2261, 2262
Neferure (princess) 2204
Nehemiah 839
Neit (queen) 2029, 2136
Ningal 2678
Ninhilia 2564
Ninhursag 1456, 2382, 2438
Ninni-zaza 2651
Nintur 2485
Ninurta 2438
Nisaba 2593
Nitocris 2232
Nofretari 2015, 2056, 2060
Noub-ounet (queen) 2215
nursing 2158; see also breast feeding
nursing goddess 2835
Nut (goddess) 2095, 2195, 2265
Nuzi 1272, 1450, 1505, 1677, 1890, 2399, 2699–2738

oaths, biblical 1344
obscenity in the Bible 265
obstetrics 763, 2560
Onan 780
ordeal 74, 90, 1413, 1614, 1680, 2344, 2851, 2853
Orpah 875, 1123, 1555
Ouadjit wp t3wy 2118
ovulation 1309

P 1388, 1727
patriarchal narratives 998, 1751
patriarchal period 1126
patriarchal stamp of Scripture 1475
patriarchs 1245, 1890
patriarchy 232, 1908
patrilinearity 1525, 1860
patrilocality 1525
Pente-Shenna 2817
perfumes 783, 912
Persia 2530, 2539
personal names 177, 2375, 2419, 2645, 2719
personification as women 1960
Peseshet 2185
Pharaoh's daughter 1397
Phoenicians 1076, 2857–2882

Pilgrim Bible 1846
pollutant female 1266; see also impurity of women in index of biblical texts
polygamy 190, 932, 1244, 1313, 1602, 1636
Potiphar's wife 401, 416, 500, 508, 1240
priestesses 2045, 2169, 2551, 2574, 2717
priestesses of Hathor 2020, 2267
priesthood 238, 284
princess, Hittite 2663
princesses, Egyptian 2024, 2071, 2124, 2212
promiscuity 1316
property 611
prophecy addressed (through men) to women 1411
prophesying daughters 1044
prophetess 848, 1048, 1253, 1572, 1643, 2646
prostitution 7, 16, 22, 23, 32, 756, 814, 1157, 1159 1179, 1803, 1826, 1978, 2527, 2567
prostitution, sacred 347, 686, 804, 960, 1031, 1081, 1914, 1943, 1983, 2386, 2478
Puah 1705
Puduhepa 2665, 2682, 2692
purification 153, 312, 623, 1060
purity 312
PY An. 607 62

Qaus (Edomite deity) 2238
queen(s) 2563, 2680, 2704, 2764 see also royal women
queen mother 665, 721, 850, 964, 1231, 1483, 1540, 2156, 2660
queen of heaven 942, 1552, 1893, 2827, 2950
queens of Egypt 2009, 2024, 2034, 2042, 2062, 2104, 2133, 2137, 2149, 2225, 2272
Qudshu 2134

Rachel 629, 674, 907, 952, 965, 1115, 1140, 1242, 1271, 1324, 1345, 1347, 1410, 1498, 1529, 1825
Rachel weeping for her children 1364
Rahab 626, 657, 697, 709, 831,

924, 1191, 1329, 1527, 1560,
  1661, 1852, 1929, 2555
rain goddess 2608
rape 259, 395, 1250, 1357, 1562,
  1651
Rebekah 644, 649, 832, 907,
  1247, 1272, 1340, 1382, 1410,
  1646, 1664, 1665, 1672, 1763,
  1792, 1853, 1854, 1923, 1962,
  1993
request of a wife to her husband
  2153, 2154
Reuben 1094
Rizpah 1867
royal cemetary 2554
royal women 2549, 2550, 2552,
  2601, 2619, 2653
Ruth 420, 812, 819, 832, 875,
  901, 1123, 1127, 1177, 1374,
  1412, 1661, 1938

sacred marriage 110, 233, 841,
  1582, 2340, 2500, 2503, 2504,
  2534, 2544, 2545, 2574, 2607,
  2612, 2838, 2841, 2865
sacrifice 1245, 1246
sage, female 2476
Sadarnuna 2596
Samson 1001, 1361, 1554, 1795,
  1879
sandal, removing of 835
Sarah 232, 457, 589, 732, 759,
  764, 800, 907, 985, 1170,
  1272, 1390, 1410, 1622, 1774,
  1855, 1858, 1918, 1951, 1993
Sarai 1439
Sarrat-Kidmuri 2425
Sarrat-Niphi 2425, 2594
Sat-Hathor-Ycount 2274
seal 122, 123, 157, 1174, 2542,
  2543, 2688, 2732
seals of women 131, 133–135,
  164, 165, 683
secondary wife 94
Sédjémet-Nébet 2171
Sefadi 194
Semiramis 3, 2324, 2350, 2618
Senenmout 2096
Senmut 2087
serving women see Ex. 38:8 in
  index of biblical texts
sex and sexuality 23, 265, 285,
  290, 310, 314, 323, 356, 390,

396, 485, 495, 496, 531, 533,
  678, 689, 753, 803, 820, 857,
  882, 927–929, 972, 1041,
  1064, 1116, 1117, 1151, 1171,
  1303, 1316, 1361, 1400, 1418,
  1422, 1436, 1438, 1492, 1507,
  1632, 1633, 1638, 1701, 1702,
  1804, 1859, 1872, 1903, 1917,
  2038, 2428, 2431, 2437
sex roles 2687; see also gender
sexist language 755, 971, 1181,
  1937
sexual politics 1069
Shaddai 424, 747
Shahar and Shalim 2833
Shawushka 2696, 2717
Sheba, Queen of 1369, 1396, 1615
Shelepputum (princess of Ur III)
  2494
Sheulgi 2502
Shibtu 2634, 2635
Shiloh 541
Shiphrah 1705
Shtart 2860
Shugi 2717
Shulgi-simti 2451
Shunem see Abishag
Sinuhe's foreign wife 2085
Sippar 122, 2332, 2359, 2465,
  2472, 2473
Sisera's mother 230, 1129
sistership adoption 2842
sistership contract 2706, 2708,
  2712, 2713
slandered bride 2459
slavery 97, 99, 567, 1241, 1280,
  1450, 1856, 2003, 2321, 2363,
  2395, 2412, 2430, 2445, 2474,
  2511, 2547
snake goddess 2398
sodomy 81
son of a handmaid 1015
sorceress 2614
Sotah see Num. 5
spouses, divine 2021, 2022, 2055
ST-Imm 2229
succession narrative 524, 633, 635,
  865, 1075, 1164, 1169, 1299,
  1382, 1402, 1689, 1906, 1915
Sumerian love songs 1308, 1583
Sumerians 1456, 1582, 1760,
  2312, 2325, 2331, 2360, 2362,

2367, 2373, 2377, 2378, 2382,
2383, 2387, 2414, 2436, 2457,
2460, 2479, 2499–2509, 2531,
2534, 2538, 2549–2552, 2555,
2561, 2562, 2564–2567, 2578,
2580–2582, 2591, 2595, 2597,
2601, 2605, 2613
sun goddess (Ugarit) 2668, 2778

Taanach cult stand 2919
Tamar I (Gen. 38) 671, 680, 1210,
1242, 1389, 1531, 1541, 1647,
1775, 1914, 1979
Tamar II (2 Sam. 13) 395, 520,
583, 653, 936, 984, 989, 1180,
1206, 1278, 1382, 1524, 1651,
1910, 1915
Tammuz 1128, 1942, 2311, 2327
Tammaritu 2525
Tanit 2209, 2873, 2875, 2877
Tanit, sign of 2209, 2858, 2867,
2878
Tany 2268
Tausret (queen) 2089, 2090
Tbṣr (queen) 2831
Tchat 2291
Tefnout 2213
Tekoite woman 1207, 1262, 1348
teraphim 634, 1140, 1221, 1677
Teta-Chera 2128
Teticheri 2294
Thenti-Hapi 2113
Thermouthis (goddess) 2264
Thihi 2005
Ti-mienêse (queen) 2204
Tiamat 2452
Tinnit 2869
Touy 2181
trickster 472, 827, 991
Tseneh ure'enah 1479
Tutanapsum 2623
Twosre (queen) 2093, 2161
typology of women 924

Ugarit 75, 294, 1566, 1568, 1570,
1848, 2162, 2739–2842, 2867,
2897, 2932
Ugaritic fertility myth 1935
Ugaritic juridical texts 2808
Ukkie the daughter (Nuzi) 2735

vagina 1316
Vashti 1617

Venus deities 2381, 2949
victory song 1990
virgin 1467, 1876; see also 'almah;
betulah in index of Hebrew
terms
virgin birth 1013
Virgin (of) Israel 1735
virginity 429, 435, 631, 1047,
1283, 1343, 1471, 2524
virgins, consecrated 2295
virgins, disposal of 947
vows 843, 1568, 2824

wedding ceremony, Egyptian 2077,
2198
weeping goddess 2508
well as symbol for wife 945
wet-nursing 1704
wetnurses, divine 1934
widow 871
widow's rights 863, 2562
wife 312, 624, 625
wife as metaphor 1548
wife of God 1732
wife of Merneptah 2123
wife-sister motif 638, 681, 748,
866, 906, 950, 1390, 1505,
1585, 1600, 1607, 1787, 1924,
2713
wine 1996
winged goddesses (Ugarit) 2768
Winnirke 2732
wisdom 222, 305, 327, 349, 359,
425, 823, 826–828, 883, 1038,
1113, 1121, 1239, 1293, 1327,
1509, 1691
wisdom, divine 1301
wisdom, Egyptian 1293
wisdom of women 656
wise woman 743, 824, 826–828,
1907
witch of En-Dor 686, 743, 806,
1421, 1428, 1587, 1776, 1786
woman as child 2121
Woman as God 260
Woman Wisdom see Lady Wisdom
womanhood, in biblical perspective
1497
Woman's Bible 555, 729, 730,
1220, 1289, 1618, 1952
women, adult single 2585
women, Egyptian contribution of
2219

women, role in Hebrew Scripture
1298, 1401, 1435, 1458, 1539,
1805, 1922
women, role in Sumer 2490
women, role in Mesopotamia 2622
women, skeletal remains 130, 156,
160
women, statues of 126, 127, 158,
159, 194, 195, 199, 200, 2367
women, status of 31, 34–36, 42,
44, 45, 64, 65, 85, 94, 104,
107, 114, 119–121, 240, 245,
254, 269, 270, 296, 319, 325,
364, 408, 420, 556, 557, 600,
616, 728, 788, 793, 794, 797,
821, 822, 854, 898, 910, 962,
973, 990, 1012, 1053, 1066,
1074, 1224, 1275, 1435, 1454,
1487, 1518, 1559, 1800, 1975,
1980, 1981, 2041, 2046, 2074,
2086, 2099, 2120, 2184, 2194,
2248, 2249, 2259, 2276, 2277,
2308, 2348, 2358, 2391, 2539,
2582, 2585, 2684, 2710, 2787,
2788, 2816
women, subjugation of 2582
women in business 2443
women in David's life 723
women in early Israel 1458, 1559
women in period of the Judges 913
women in pictorial art 122, 124,
129, 191, 192, 198, 206, 206
women in Samson's life 292, 1795

women in positions of power 1973
women physicians 2120, 2165
women power 19, 825, 855, 1046,
1811, 2400, 2407
women sailors 2151
women singers 1054, 1462, 2771
women's dress 2493
women's history 1, 2, 6, 8, 14, 27,
31, 33, 34, 50, 51, 52, 58, 77,
86, 458, 1458
women's occupations 2377, 2412,
2565
women's performance 1462
women's personal names (Hebrew)
1790
women writers 347 , 1114, 2597,
2617, 2664
women's liberation 1683, 1685
women's rites 46, 1265
women's work 1824
writing 1816

Yahweh depicted 201, 551
Yahwist (ic) 248, 289, 760, 861; see
also J

Zelophehad 978; see also
daughters of Zelophehad
Zibbatum 2415
Zilpah 1271, 1345, 1964
Zion as mother 1731, 1733
Zipporah 773, 1219, 1269, 1305,
1661

Pentateuch 499

Gen. 276, 375, 398, 612, 1802,
 1870, 1908
Gen. 1:26–28 404
Gen. 1:27 380, 752, 1089, 1457,
 1502, 1766
Gen. 1:1–2:3 1468
Gen. 1:26–31 1456
Gen. 1:27 948, 1215, 1517, 1635,
 1671, 1963
Gen. 1:1–11:9 1722
Gen. 1–2 927, 1237
Gen. 1–3 296, 509, 515, 753,
 1535, 1797
Gen. 1–4 371, 1199, 1410
Gen. 1–5 979
Gen. 1–9 2439
Gen. 1–11 469, 479
Gen. 1–18 873
Gen. 1 1360, 1781
Gen. 2:7–22 1517
Gen. 2:18 1773
Gen. 2:18–20 852, 1282
Gen. 2:18–24 1455. 1671
Gen. 2:20–23 1820
Gen. 2:21 540
Gen. 2:23 405, 1301, 1627, 1921
Gen. 2:23–24 1444
Gen. 2:24 710, 778, 1096, 1337,
 1366
Gen. 2:25 1709
Gen. 2:25–3:7 1113
Gen. 2–3 222, 257, 282, 400,
 487, 545, 558, 587, 598, 627,
 652, 663, 678, 685, 758, 807,
 815, 933, 943, 1012, 1079,
 1167, 1187, 1242, 1274, 1275,
 1295, 1322, 1325, 1331, 1456,
 1475, 1493, 1526, 1638, 1670,
 1723, 1724, 1832, 1882, 2864
Gen. 2–4 1474, 1536
Gen. 3 928, 1925
Gen. 3:1–6 1200
Gen. 3:5 1011
Gen. 3:14 1110
Gen. 3:15 1579

Gen. 3:14–15 1652, 1653
Gen. 3:16 890, 1036, 1461, 1561,
 1692, 1734
Gen. 4:1 846
Gen. 4:1–6 1187
Gen. 4:7 949, 1036
Gen. 4:22 691
Gen. 5:2–3 948
Gen. 6:1–4 921, 986, 993, 1193–
 1194, 1197, 1263, 1307, 1386,
 1434, 1437, 1519, 1585
Gen. 6:2 1920
Gen. 6:4 1394
Gen. 11:30 809
Gen. 12–50 998
Gen. 12:10–13 1480
Gen. 12:10–20 638, 748, 866,
 1272, 1390, 1584, 1787, 1924
Gen. 14:24 2834
Gen. 16:1 1946
Gen. 16:1–16 583, 648, 732, 864,
 869, 1043, 1101, 1272, 1407,
 1808, 1855,1918
Gen. 16:4–14 1217
Gen. 16:6 1170
Gen. 16:11–12 1521
Gen. 16:13 769
Gen. 16:13b 1738,1748
Gen. 18:1–15 1774
Gen. 18:10 873, 1163
Gen. 18:14 873
Gen. 18–19 1130
Gen. 19 1332
Gen. 19:12–28 1304
Gen. 19:30–38 1018, 1395, 1954
Gen. 20 638, 748, 866, 951,
 1272, 1480, 1584, 1787, 1894,
 1895, 1924
Gen. 20:12 1951
Gen. 21:6–7 1622
Gen. 21:8ff 1521
Gen. 21:9–21 583, 648, 864, 869,
 1043, 1101, 1407, 1808, 1855,
 1918
Gen. 21:10, 12 1575
Gen. 22 800

Gen. 23–29 649
Gen. 24 644, 1383, 1664, 1665,
  1672, 1853, 1854, 1924
Gen. 24:11 1962
Gen. 24:59 1646
Gen. 25:19–26 1393
Gen. 25:22 1675
Gen. 26:1–11 1480, 1924
Gen. 26:1–16 638, 748, 866,
  1272, 1584, 1787
Gen. 27 1923
Gen. 29 1501, 1924
Gen. 29:18–25 674, 952, 1051
Gen. 29:25 1242
Gen. 29:31–30:24 1345, 1995
Gen. 29:32 1529
Gen. 30:3 1946
Gen. 30:9 1946
Gen. 30:14ff. 776
Gen. 31:19 1140, 1825
Gen. 31:35 1086
Gen. 34 497, 643, 670, 845, 934,
  983, 1016, 1024, 1088, 1153,
  1279, 1284, 1285, 1295, 1391,
  1640, 1699, 1703, 1909,
  1956
Gen. 35 1646
Gen. 35:8 953
Gen. 35:18 874
Gen. 35:22 1529
Gen. 37–50 508, 796
Gen. 37–Ex. 765
Gen. 38 671, 680, 780, 814, 863,
  984, 987, 988, 989, 1242,
  1295, 1389, 1426, 1531,
  1541, 1647, 1775, 1914, 1979
Gen. 38:14 1660
Gen. 38:27–30 1393
Gen. 39 401
Gen. 39:10–18 1240
Gen. 47 1930
Gen. 47:29–31 1793
Gen. 48:1–16 1793
Gen. 49:3–4 1094
Gen. 49:6 643

Ex. 1–2 1768
Ex. 1:7 1160
Ex. 1:8–2:10 997
Ex. 1:19 966
Ex. 2:5–21 1924
Ex. 4:24 1269
Ex. 4:24–26 1219, 1305, 1469,

  1496, 1661, 1992
Ex. 4:26 775
Ex. 15 917
Ex. 15:20 1643
Ex. 15:21 1545
Ex. 18:2 938
Ex. 20:12 708, 1936
Ex. 20:13 1936
Ex. 20:14 1559, 1746, 1936
Ex. 20:15 1035
Ex. 20:17 1136, 1866
Ex. 21:1–6 1241
Ex. 21–24 488
Ex. 21:7–11 1450
Ex. 21:10 776, 1153, 1780
Ex. 21:22–23 1233, 1809, 1810
Ex. 21:22–25 980, 1218, 1379
Ex. 21–22 1667
Ex. 21–24 488
Ex. 22:15f. 1559
Ex. 38:8 238, 1112

Lev. 12:1–5 1419
Lev. 15:19–23 1629
Lev. 15:19–25 911
Lev. 15:19–28 1309
Lev. 18 749, 893, 894
Lev. 18:6–18 1216
Lev. 18:18 1828
Lev. 18–19 1325
Lev. 19:20–22 1747, 1788
Lev. 19:29 1967
Lev. 20 893, 894
Lev. 21:7 1967, 1968
Lev. 21:9 1967
Lev. 21:13 1968
Lev. 21:14 1967, 1968
Lev. 24:10–16 1073
Lev. 24:10–23 1482, 1576
Lev. 24:11 1373
Lev. 25:39–46 1241

Num. 5:11–31 74, 407, 795,
  1030, 1061–1062, 1470, 1680
Num. 6:1–21 843
Num. 11–12 1750
Num. 12 1659
Num. 12:1 889
Num. 12:12 886
Num. 25:8 1641
Num. 27 1694, 1696f
Num. 27:1–11 1778
Num. 30:2–17 643

Num. 36 1694, 1696
Num. 36:1–9 1778

Deut. 241, 275–277, 501, 513,
    518, 606, 1803, 1804
Deut. 5:16 708, 1936
Deut. 5:17 1035, 1136, 1936
Deut. 5:18 1746, 1936
Deut. 5:21 1866
Deut. 7:13 939
Deut. 15:12–18 1241
Deut. 21 836, 1803
Deut. 21–25 1667
Deut. 21:10–14 915
Deut. 21:18–21 714, 823
Deut. 22 1803
Deut. 22:5 1663
Deut. 22:13–29 1905
Deut. 22:13–19, 28 1217
Deut. 22:13–21 435, 1416, 1721,
    1829
Deut. 23:19 811
Deut. 24:1–4 1217, 1502, 1682,
    1821, 1902, 1912, 1955
Deut. 25:4–12 995
Deut. 25:5–10 428, 660, 713,
    1362, 1426
Deut. 25:9 591
Deut. 25:10 1650
Deut. 25:9–10 835
Deut. 25:11–12 994, 1576, 1767
Deut. 32:18 1635

Josh. 501
Josh. 2:9–21 831, 1329
Josh. 15:18 1499
Josh. 17:1–16 1778

Judg. 411, 455, 501, 602, 1449
Judg. 1:14 1499
Judg. 2:10 1616
Judg. 4:4–22 1514
Judg. 4–5 230, 632, 639, 655,
    1023, 1714
Judg. 5 884, 944, 1176, 1186,
    1357, 1358, 1365, 1782, 1812
Judg. 5:25 1613
Judg. 5:29 1898
Judg. 6:27 1357, 1358
Judg. 9 1243
Judg. 11 449, 583, 1224, 1283
Judg. 13 996
Judg. 13–15 292, 1001

Judg. 13–16 1757
Judg. 14 1144, 1501, 1523
Judg. 14–15 1760, 1819
Judg. 16 1501, 1711, 1795
Judg. 16:21 1824
Judg. 19 219, 4032, 583, 1332
Judg. 19:3 1955
Judg. 19–20 1532
Judg. 21 541, 1295
Judg., women in 1544

1–2 Sam. 373, 520, 1278
1 Sam. 351, 502
1 Sam. 1 974, 976, 1771, 1883,
    1959
1 Sam. 1–2 1926, 1971
1 Sam. 1:8 1913
1 Sam. 1:15 640
1 Sam. 2:1–10 698, 834, 1045,
    1296d, 1349, 1443, 1545,
    1657, 1927
1 Sam. 2:11 885
1 Sam. 2:22 1112
1 Sam. 6–9 976
1 Sam. 8:3 820
1 Sam. 12:17a 867
1 Sam. 18 1338
1 Sam. 19 1501
1 Sam. 19:11–17 1677, 1825
1 Sam. 25 283, 684, 1350, 1480
1 Sam. 28 686, 743, 806, 1586,
    1776, 1786, 1801
2 Sam. 824
2 Sam. 3:14–16 1217
2 Sam. 3:12–16 716
2 Sam. 6:16, 20–23, 1611
2 Sam. 9–20; 1 Kgs.
    1–2 633, 635, 1075, 1169,
    1906, 1915
    (see also "succession narrative")
2 Sam. 10–12 225, 1336
2 Sam. 11 1028, 1082, 1083,
    1480, 1948
2 Sam. 11–12 1038
2 Sam. 11:4 1309
2 Sam. 12 1749
2 Sam. 12:1–15 651
2 Sam. 13 222, 395, 583, 653,
    936, 1180, 1956
2 Sam. 13–20 288
2 Sam. 14 1907
2 Sam. 14:1–20 1348
2 Sam. 14:1–24 1207

2 Sam. 14:4–21 715
2 Sam. 16:21–22 1330
2 Sam. 20 1907
2 Sam. 20:13–22 1095
2 Sam. 21:10 1612

1 Kgs. 1:2, 4 1503
1 Kgs. 1:3, 15 937
1 Kgs. 2:19 1540
1 Kgs. 3 1038
1 Kgs. 3:16–28 744, 951, 970,
   1333, 1346, 1628
1 Kgs. 9:16 658
1 Kgs. 10 1113
1 Kgs. 10:1–13 1396
1 Kgs. 11:8b 877
1 Kgs. 21:1–16 1900
1 Kgs. 21:1–20 1668
1 Kgs. 21:8 1570
2 Kgs. 4:17 1163
2 Kgs. 5 880
2 Kgs. 6:24–33 1333
2 Kgs. 9 1551, 1567, 1658
2 Kgs. 9–10 1785
2 Kgs. 22:14–20 16165
2 Kgs. 23:7 1273

Isa. 975
Isa. 1:16–21 1736
Isa. 3:16–4:1 1411
Isa. 3:18–23 1600
Isa. 6–12 801
Isa. 7:14–17 409, 427, 631, 724,
   731, 777, 779, 891, 892, 961,
   1013, 1110, 1125, 1185, 1202,
   1204, 1268, 1288, 1291, 1320,
   1334, 1335, 1500, 1577, 1639,
   1648, 1649, 1700, 1817, 1857,
   1928
Isa. 7–8 820
Isa. 8:3 1253
Isa. 14:12–15 2937
Isa. 32:9–14 1411
Isa. 40:2 1029
Isa. 40–55 977
Isa. 40–66 802, 1155, 1156, 1574
Isa. 42:1–9 1737
Isa. 42:10–17 926, 1155, 1156
Isa. 47:1–4 1576
Isa. 49:14–26 1264
Isa. 49:15 1122, 1154
Isa. 54:1–13 809
Isa. 62 664

Jer. 945, 975, 1007
Jer. 2:2–13 1520
Jer. 2:13 945
Jer. 2:32 1574
Jer. 2–3 1982
Jer. 3:1 1955
Jer. 4 1266
Jer. 7:17–18 1552
Jer. 7:18 942, 1630
Jer. 31:15 809
Jer. 31:15–22 661, 1364, 1837
Jer. 31:22 1208, 1209, 1235
Jer. 34 1280
Jer. 44:15–30 1411, 1552
Jer. 44:17–19, 25 942
Jer. 44:19 1630

Ezek. 8:14 1128, 1141, 1658
Ezek. 13:17–23 1411
Ezek. 16 1142, 1950
Ezek. 16:7 1969
Ezek. 16:8 591
Ezek. 23:20 2531
Ezek. 23:24–25 1576

Hos. 361, 424, 585, 736, 746,
   982, 1009, 1171, 1273, 1319,
   1408, 1440, 1491, 1506
Hos. 1 1681
Hos. 1–2 1290, 1625
Hos. 1–3 246, 620, 628, 687,
   701, 733, 841, 1003, 1098,
   1405, 1579, 1644, 1645,
   1679, 1686, 1762, 1874, 1875
Hos. 1–4 1295
Hos. 1–5 1974
Hos. 1:2 659
Hos. 1:2–9 1017
Hos. 2 860, 958, 959, 1732
Hos. 2:4 1424
Hos. 2:4–5 1221
Hos. 2:4–9 1314
Hos. 2:4–7:12 2961
Hos. 2:17b 1049
Hos. 3:1 770
Hos. 4 1099
Hos. 4:4–10 946
Hos. 10:9 673
Hos. 11 1311, 1740, 1741
Hos. 11:1–4 1635
Hos. 14:9 2935

Am. 1994

Am. 1:13 868
Am. 2:7 1575
Am. 4:1 1238

Mic. 1994
Mic. 4:9 1158
Mic. 5:13 2925

Nah. 2:8 941

Zeph. 2:4 1958

Zech. 5:5–11 940
Zech. 5:7 858

Mal. 773, 981, 1009
Mal. 2:10–16 1103, 1222, 1259,
    1266,1548, 1682
Mal. 2:12 1102
Mal. 2:14–16 636
Mal. 2:16 1260, 1931

Ps. 45 1409, 1550, 1573, 1726
Ps. 48:11 1213
Ps. 97:8 1213
Ps. 113 904, 1045, 1927
Ps. 113:9 844, 1427
Ps. 123 222
Ps. 128 222
Ps. 131 222
Ps. 139 1810

Prov. 274, 425, 826–828, 945,
    1511
Prov. 1–9 239, 253, 647, 762,
    1448, 1949
Prov. 1–24 1293
Prov. 1:20–33 1512, 1836
Prov. 5:15–18 1316
Prov. 6:26 736
Prov. 7 630
Prov. 8 1791
Prov. 8:22–31 646, 1509, 1947
Prov. 9 1543
Prov. 9:1 1327
Prov. 9:1–12 1297, 1528
Prov. 21:9, 19 1556
Prov. 25–29 1293
Prov. 27:15 1556
Prov. 30 1042, 1293
Prov. 30:15a 1104
Prov. 30:18–20 768
Prov. 31 1293, 1363
Prov. 31:1 957

Prov. 31:1–9 909
Prov. 31:27 1933
Prov. 31:10–31 914, 1399, 1404,
    1932

Job. 2:9 1676
Job. 10 1810
Job. 17:14 1119
Job. 19:15 1631
Job. 31:1 1467

Cant. 245, 310, 314, 328, 340,
    362, 366, 382, 422, 464, 581,
    637, 712, 782, 799, 841, 929,
    945, 959, 967, 1020, 1039,
    1040, 1077, 1078, 1091, 148,
    1189, 1274, 1303, 1308, 1312,
    1325, 1326, 1385, 1400, 1418,
    1434, 1442, 1460, 1508, 1582,
    1593, 1608, 1633, 1634, 1678,
    1691, 1707, 1708, 1710, 1712,
    1715, 1752–1754, 1756, 1764,
    1830, 1888, 1997, 2403
Cant. 1:5 1111
Cant. 2:8–17 1510
Cant. 3:8 1295
Cant. 3:9f 1109
Cant. 3:10 1150
Cant. 5:10–11 782
Cant. 5:16 1341
Cant. 7:1 937, 1513
Cant. 8:6 1174, 1513

Ruth 258, 262, 287, 420, 428,
    510, 513, 523, 537, 534, 660,
    704, 741, 742, 812, 813, 837,
    875, 1022, 1025–1027, 1086,
    1139, 1152, 1229–1230, 1355,
    1362, 1384, 1426, 1476, 1481,
    1537, 1583, 1591, 1609, 1623,
    1706, 1725, 1838, 1850, 1851,
    1887, 1938
Ruth 1:10 1318
Ruth 1:19 1261
Ruth 2:7 705, 707, 1225
Ruth 3 706, 1441, 1954
Ruth 3:9 591, 1315
Ruth 3:16 1637
Ruth 4:5 703, 1131
Ruth 4:8 591
Ruth 4:14–15 1650
Ruth 4:16 591, 1162
Ruth 4:18–22 1403

Lam. 2 1266

Eccles. 341
Eccles. 7:23–8:1 692, 1381

Esth. 242, 287, 420, 462, 559,

671, 681, 781, 842, 847, 862,
895, 1050, 1121, 1145, 1175,
1257, 1258, 1353, 1376,
1447, 1488, 1489, 1490

Neh. 361

INDEX OF HEBREW AND AKKADIAN TERMS

HEBREW

ādām 979, 1134, 1199
'amâ 872, 1252
ʾîš 1134
ʾiššâ zārâ 1949
ʾešet zĕnûnîm 659
b' 'el 803
bepetaḥ 'ênayim 1660
betulah 1467, 1876, 1901
betulim 1283
gebirah 1483, 1861; see also queen
  mother in subject index
go'el 428, 931, 1481, 1706
dibber 'al leb 1029
hlk 'el 803, 1575
znh 1978
ḥălālâ 1359, 1967
ka 'et ḥayah 1163
MAR 1318
melug 2793
mārîm 1563
mrḥm 1122, 1154, 1620
na 'arah 1405
nebi'ah 1253
nebalah 1588
sokenet 1503, 2798
'ezer kĕnegdô 1671, 1773
'almah 724, 427, 731, 777, 779,
1125, 1291, 1334, 1406, 1516,
1639, 1648, 1649, 1794, 1817,
1857
'alah 1575
'anah 935
'ônâ 1780
pilegeš 1108
ṣôpiyyâ 1933
qĕdēšāh 1157, 1159, 1914
qnh 1172
rḥm 1122, 1154, 1620
šilluḥîm 1397
šipĕḥāh 872, 1252
šārôtêāh 1898
tšwqh 949, 1036

AKKADIAN

ištarītum 22330, 2533, 2535, 2574
kezertum 2442
mulugu 2793
nadītum 2329, 2415, 2464–2467,
2469, 2533, 2535, 2574, 2604,
2624
qadištum 1157, 1159, 1914, 2330,
2533, 2535, 2574
šakintu 2487
šugītum 2624

ABOUT THE AUTHOR

MAYER I. GRUBER is a graduate of Duke University. He earned his Master of Hebrew Literature Degree and Rabbinic Ordination from the Jewish Theological Seminary of America and his M.A., M.Phil., and Ph.D. in Ancient Semitic Languages and Literatures from Columbia University. From 1970 to 1980 he served on the faculty of Spertus College of Judaica in Chicago. Dr. Gruber was rabbi of Mikdosh El-Hagro Hebrew Center in Evanston, Illinois from 1976 to 1980. Since 1980 he has taught in the Department of Bible and Ancient Near East at Ben-Gurion University of the Negev in Beersheva, Israel. Gruber's honors include a Grant-in-Aid from the American Council of Learned Societies in 1979, and a bibliographic award from the American Theological Library Association in 1990. Gruber's previous publications include *Aspects of Nonverbal Communication in the Ancient Near East* (2 vols.; Rome: Biblical Institute Press, 1980) and *The Motherhood of God and Other Studies* (South Florida Studies in the History of Judaism, no. 57; Atlanta: Scholars Press, 1992).